A YOUNG GIRL READING
Jean-Honoré Fragonard
National Gallery of Art, Washington, D.C.
Gift of Mrs. Mellon Bruce
in memory of her father, Andrew W. Mellon

WALTER O'DONNELL
MEMORIAL

The Organizational Life Cycle

Issues in the Creation,
Transformation, and Decline
of Organizations

John R. Kimberly

Robert H. Miles

and Associates

The Organizational Life Cycle

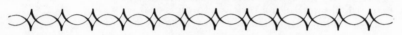

*Issues in the Creation,
Transformation, and Decline
of Organizations*

Jossey-Bass Publishers

San Francisco • Washington • London • 1980

THE ORGANIZATIONAL LIFE CYCLE
Issues in the Creation, Transformation,
and Decline of Organizations
        by John R. Kimberly, Robert H. Miles, and Associates

Copyright © 1980 by: Jossey-Bass Inc., Publishers
                      433 California Street
                      San Francisco, California 94104
                      &
                      Jossey-Bass Limited
                      28 Banner Street
                      London EC1Y 8QE

Library of Congress Cataloging in Publication Data
Main entry under title:

The Organizational life cycle.
   Includes bibliographies and index.
   1. Organizational change—Addresses, essays, lec-
tures. 2. Organization—Addresses, essays, lectures.
I. Kimberly, John R. II. Miles, Robert H.
HD58.8.O74   658.4′06   79-92466
ISBN 0-87589-459-3

Manufactured in the United States of America

JACKET DESIGN BY WILLI BAUM

FIRST EDITION

Code 8019

To J. Stacy Adams and William Foote Whyte,
who piqued our curiosity, encouraged
our searching, and tolerated our intolerance

Preface

A recent newspaper story on business and finance described the activities of an entrepreneur who is characterized as a "corporate mortician." According to the story, this person, who likes to "buy, get in and out, and on to the next deal," has accumulated millions of dollars over the past few years by dismantling companies and selling off the rest of their merchandise or inventory. As a corporate mortician, he has developed a thriving practice by disposing of the remaining assets of bankrupt enterprises.

A strange story to cite, perhaps, but one that illustrates two points we are trying to make with this book. First is the cyclical quality of organizational existence. Organizations are born, grow, and decline. Sometimes they reawaken, and sometimes they disappear. The second point involves the consequences of this cyclic pattern. Organizational morticians, for example, would not have a trade to ply were it not for the facts of organizational birth and death. Neither point is reflected well in most current organization theory and research. Our motivation in putting this book together is to increase the visibility of what are currently somewhat scattered efforts among a few researchers to explore patterns of organizational growth, evolution, change, and decline.

The Organizational Life Cycle is a joint venture in every sense of those words. It was born out of a variety of discussions in which we began to examine our previous involvements with the creation of organizations and their implications for theory and research. Kimberly had been involved for four years in a study of the birth and early development of a new medical school, and Miles had participated in the creation of an institute for public welfare management funded by the Department of Health, Education, and Welfare. Miles was also in the process of developing an organizational simulation that focused on problems of organizational formation and development. Both of us participated in the creation of Yale's new School of Organization and Management, a process that was unfolding while we were gingerly exploring our other experiences. These discussions led us to put together a doctoral seminar at Yale called "The Organization Life Cycle." The students in that seminar—Timber Dick, Michael Gerlach, Gary Jusela, Mary Dean Lee, Jeffrey McNally, Helen Mitchell, Judith Neal, Harold Oppenheimer, Michael Rion, and Susan Sturm—helped us begin to structure an area of inquiry that we had found to be without much structure or content. Our experience in that course, greatly enhanced by the work of our colleague Seymour Sarason and discussions with him, as well as by conversations with many researchers all over the country, made us think that interest in what we were doing extended substantially beyond the borders of New Haven. Miles' move to Harvard in the fall of 1978 ensured that it did.

At the meeting of the Operations Research Society of America/The Institute of Management Sciences in New Orleans in April 1979, Miles chaired a session that provided a formal opportunity to test the level of interest. A number of colleagues wrote papers for the session, apparently agreeing with our sense that we were developing a theme of potential significance. In New Orleans we played to a packed house and have since been deluged with reprint requests. The original material has been revised for this book and four additional chapters have been prepared.

One of the important features of the book is the quality of the contributors. John Freeman, Thomas Lodahl, William Ouchi, Johannes Pennings, Noel Tichy, Andrew Van de Ven, Richard Walton, and David Whetten are all individuals whose work is already well known or is becoming well known. They are part of a third generation of organizational scholars, and their work and thought will undoubtedly have a strong influence on the field. That they all should be enthusiastic contributors to this volume is an important indicator of some of the directions in which this influence is likely to move. The participation of Jack Brittain, Stephen Mitchell, W. Alan Randolph, and Amittai Niv, newcomers to the field, ensures at least some intergenerational transfer of the themes.

Anyone interested in the general issues of organizational creation, transformation, or demise will find relevant material in the book. Potential readers include not only sociologists, political scientists, economists, and psychologists interested in various aspects of organizational theory but also scholars interested in managerial or administrative theory and behavior. Because the issues addressed are not limited to specific types of organizations, the book should interest those in the public, private, and nonprofit sectors, as well as those in education, health, manufacturing, and social services.

The approaches to understanding and the foci of attention in the following chapters collectively represent an important statement about the directions in which organizational theory and research are likely to head. It was exciting for us to find so many leading scholars—much of whose earlier research could be characterized as "mainline" social science—asking different questions about organizations and pursuing different approaches to answering them, all at the same time. Common to all the chapters they have written is an emphasis on strong conceptual development. Readers, we hope, will find no dearth of new ideas with supporting conceptual frameworks and operational definitions and new approaches to old subjects that have remained frontiers for organizational research. This boldness is complemented by the high degree of personal involvement by the researcher in most of the settings.

Kimberly, Lodahl, Tichy, Van de Ven, and Walton all had action-research ties to the organizations on which their chapters focus. Niv used his dissertation at the Harvard Business School to explore the causes and consequences of the social disintegration that he had experienced earlier as a member of a kibbutz. And Miles and Randolph created the simulation that provided the basis for their study of organizational learning.

All of the chapters in this volume also recognize explicitly the roles of history and maturation in understanding organizational behavior. All of the empirical chapters employed a longitudinal design. As a result, they were able to provide substantial insight to the origins and destinies of organizational cultures, structures, behaviors, and outcomes. There are, of course, serious obstacles to the conduct of longitudinal field research. Among those that must be overcome are the natural reluctance of hosts to have their activities scrutinized over time, especially during the more dynamic periods of organizational life; the energy and time commitment imposed on the researcher to bring his or her understanding to market by the reward system that governs academic careers; and the thorny methodological issues embedded in longitudinal data collection and analysis. To some extent longitudinal archival investigations and simulation studies can be used to complement the needed fieldwork, but further development of the issues and questions raised by developmental perspectives on organizations will be accomplished under those who do their work up close in the field.

The chapters are grouped into three parts—organizational creation, organizational transformation, and organizational decline. As the reader will see, there is some arbitrariness involved in the grouping—a fact that signals imperfections in the life cycle metaphor. It is also true that organizational termination, like graduation, is sometimes a form of commencement, not an ending but a beginning. But in a general way, the three parts of the book do correspond to the three major clusters of events, activities, and outcomes in an organization's life.

Each part also has its own internal structure. There is at least one chapter in each section that focuses on the organizational level of analysis, one that concentrates on the ecological level of analysis, and one empirical study in a particular organizational setting designed to illustrate the kinds of understandings about organizational phenomena that can emerge from a view derived explicitly or implicitly from a life cycle perspective. Each part is preceded by an introduction summarizing and synthesizing the issues posed by subsequent chapters. The final chapter of the book reviews the themes, the approaches, and the areas of convergence and divergence contained in the various chapters and sketches the implications of the life cycle metaphor for research and theory. In this sense, we hope, the end of the book represents a beginning.

The creation of this volume owes much to many. Miles wishes to acknowledge the support of the Division of Research at the Harvard Business School that provided release time from other duties during the formative stage of this project. Finally, we want particularly to thank Karen Lupoli, Carolee Weber, and our families; in their own ways they contributed to the process by which many late-night conversations and weekend retreats ultimately became a book.

February 1980　　　　　　　　　　　　JOHN R. KIMBERLY
　　　　　　　　　　　　　　　　　New Haven, Connecticut

　　　　　　　　　　　　　　　　　ROBERT H. MILES
　　　　　　　　　　　　　　　　　Boston, Massachusetts

Contents

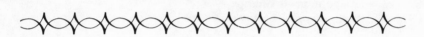

xv

Contents

The Authors

JOHN R. KIMBERLY is associate professor of administrative science in the School of Organization and Management at Yale University. Prior to joining the faculty at Yale in 1976, he taught at the University of Illinois in Urbana and, in 1975–76, was a visiting fellow in the Centre de Recherche en Gestion at the Ecole Polytechnique, Paris. He was awarded the B.A. degree in sociology from Yale University (1964) and the M.S. and Ph.D. degrees in organizational behavior from Cornell University (1967 and 1970, respectively).

Kimberly's research has focused on problems of organizational and managerial innovation and change, organizational structure and performance, organizational design, and organization-environment relations, particularly in the context of human service organizations such as hospitals, educational institutions, and rehabilitation agencies. A central concern of this research was to identify the forces that propel and retard change within organizations. His research results have been published in such journals as *Administrative Science Quarterly, Journal of Health and Social Behavior, Sociological Methods & Research, Academy of Management Journal,* and *Revue Française de Sociologie,* as well as in numerous chapters in books on organizational theory and behavior. Kimberly is on the editorial boards of *Administrative Science Quarterly* and *Academy of Management Journal.* He is currently completing a research monograph based on a comparative study of hospital innovation in the United States and France and is conducting research on the creation of a variety of institutions, from academic health centers to educational service centers.

ROBERT H. MILES is associate professor of organizational behavior at the Harvard Business School where he teaches and conducts research in the areas of organizational design, adaptation and change. He was awarded a B.S. degree in economics from the University of Virginia (1967), the M.B.A. degree from Old Dominion University (1969), and the Ph.D. degree in organizational behavior from the University of North Carolina at Chapel Hill (1974).

Miles has been involved in both the creation of new organizations and in the management of temporary research and development projects. He was a charter faculty member of the Yale School of Organization and Management and a cofounder of a public welfare management institute sponsored by the U.S. Department of Health, Education, and Welfare. He has also served as project manager for the Office of the Secretary of Defense and general manager of a small aerospace contracting firm. His current consulting focuses on the processes of organizational adaptation and the management of both corporate-division and business-government relations.

Miles is the author of *Macro Organizational Behavior* (1980) and, with W. A. Randolph, *The Organization Game* (1979), a behaviorally played simulation of the creation and early development of organizations. His research has been reported in such journals as *Academy of Management Journal, Behavioral Science, Journal of Applied Psychology, Organizational Behavior and Human Performance, Personnel Psychology,* and *Sociometry.* He is an associate editor of *Management*

Science and a member of the editorial board of *Administrative Science Quarterly.* Miles is completing two books; one, with K. S. Cameron, is a study of organizational adaptation in the U.S. tobacco industry to the smoking-and-health controversy. His other book concerns the internal politics of organizational adaptation.

JACK W. BRITTAIN is a doctoral candidate in the School of Business Administration, University of California, Berkeley.

JOHN H. FREEMAN is associate professor, School of Business Administration, University of California, Berkeley.

THOMAS M. LODAHL is professor, Graduate School of Business and Public Administration, Cornell University.

STEPHEN M. MITCHELL is research associate, New York State School of Industrial and Labor Relations, Cornell University.

AMITTAI NIV is assistant professor, the Jerusalem Institute for Management.

WILLIAM G. OUCHI is professor, Graduate School of Management, University of California at Los Angeles.

JOHANNES M. PENNINGS is associate professor, Graduate School of Business, Columbia University.

W. ALAN RANDOLPH is assistant professor, College of Business Administration, University of South Carolina.

NOEL M. TICHY is associate professor, School of Business Administration, University of Michigan, Ann Arbor.

ANDREW H. VAN DE VEN is associate professor, the Wharton School, University of Pennsylvania.

RICHARD E. WALTON is professor, Graduate School of Business Administration, Harvard University.

DAVID A. WHETTEN is associate professor, Department of Business Administration, University of Illinois.

The
Organizational
Life Cycle

*Issues in the Creation,
Transformation, and Decline
of Organizations*

1

The Life Cycle Analogy and the Study of Organizations: Introduction

John R. Kimberly

This introductory chapter points out some deficiencies in contemporary organizational theory and research, many of which are addressed by the content of later chapters. It argues that much of this theory is static, ahistorical, and arid and that redirection of the paradigms used by researchers may be helped along by thinking about organizations in life cycle terms. There is a growing restiveness in the field with current theory, and researchers are beginning to look for alternative theories, models, and metaphors. This book is designed to help crystallize that search by providing some concrete examples of alternative perspectives. The chapters it contains represent, in many cases, work in progress, embryonic theories,

1

nascent perspectives. Although the chapters are divergent in focus and content, there is a common theme that runs through them all. Change is a fact of organizational life. Organizational researchers and theorists should be better able to capture this characteristic than they do at present.

I would not argue that there is *a* life cycle perspective that is theoretically robust enough to end the search for alternatives. One message this book is intended to spread is that, just as change characterizes the organizations we study, so it characterizes the perspectives we use in our work. The chapters in this volume illustrate both an increasing awareness of the cyclical character of organizational life and the dialectical nature of social theory. They also illustrate that a field at an early stage of theoretical development can benefit by exploring analogies and metaphors from other fields.

Organizations are social inventions. They exist, at least in part, because of the benefits of coordination that they provide. In the absence of organizations, individuals would not have the means at their disposal to create the interdependencies necessary for the accomplishment of numerous sets of tasks. Organizations provide the social mechanism necessary to realize the benefits that can be gained by coordinating the activities of a large number of people toward some common end. Organizations, however, are hardly mechanical devices. They are owned, designed, and managed by people. As such, they possess most of the limitations and potentials that people have. Organizations are fluid and dynamic: they move in time and in space; they act and react.

New organizations are continuously being created in both the public and the private sectors. New business firms, new public agencies, new consumer advocate groups—the list is nearly endless—are formed with great frequency. The daily newspaper is just one source of data on the frequency of organizational birth. But just as the rates of formation are high, so, apparently, are the rates of demise. The rates of failure of small businesses are legendary. Although no comparative data exist, one has the impression that organizations in the public sector disappear as well (see Kaufman, 1976). The point is that when one views the population of organizations, one sees demographic changes. These demographic changes reflect, in the aggregate, the fact of birth, life, and death among organizations.

Organizational Research

This dynamic quality of organizational life, however, is curiously absent from most research and writing in the area. Most organizational analysts seem to take the existence of organizations as a given and to assume survival as their fundamental "goal." There are, of course, exceptions. The "institutional school," best represented by the work of Selznick and his students, has developed in-depth case analyses of internal and external influences on some aspects of organizational activity. The population ecology approach, as represented by the work of Hannan and Freeman (1978a) and Aldrich (1979), explicitly inquires into the expansion and contraction of populations of organizations. In general, however, the arrangement of the internal structural characteristics of organizations and the way in which environmental factors at a particular point in time impinge on these characteristics and affect organizational performance are the major focuses of research. Whether the writers are sociologists concerned primarily with the macro level of analysis, or social psychologists and psychologists concerned with the micro level of analysis, the end result is generally the same in one important sense: their research assumes the existence of a relatively fixed organizational structure and does not inquire into its etiology or focus too much on the question of organizational survival. There is, in other words, a decidedly static orientation in much of the literature.

Why does this static orientation exist? There are at least five reasons. First, in most cases researchers are involved with a subject organization or set of organizations only at a particular point in time. The research that gets carried out is thus inevitably cross-sectional. This fact limits the kinds of understandings of organizational life that are possible, and organizational snapshots become the rule, not the exception. A related point is that researchers generally do their work in already existing organizational systems.

These systems have gone through the processes of role negotiation, value formation, and structural development. In every organization, there is a rich fabric of norms, values, and myths that help to shape and determine behavior in the organization. However, because researchers tend to come into organizations with already defined normative structures, there is a tendency not to focus on the questions of where these structures came from, how they developed, and what implications etiology and development may have for present and future structure, process, and performance. The organizational context is taken as a given. But organizations do have memories, they do learn and, occasionally, they unlearn. Snapshots tend to underestimate seriously the significance of organizational memories and learning abilities.

A second reason for the static quality of much research on organizations is that organizations, almost by definition, tend to outlive individual members. This means that research that relies on data collection from organizational participants runs the risk of personalization. A single time slice is being examined, and the fact that the informants themselves have only a relatively temporary affiliation with the organization limits, in some ways, the kinds of responses that are likely to be given. People are bound to see and interpret organizational life and events in a truncated fashion. Thus, data from organizational members, as well as the perspectives of organizational researchers, tend to have a somewhat static quality to them.

A third reason for the lack of dynamic perspectives on organizations is a function of the tension in organizational research between science and history. Organizational researchers, most of whom have been trained in the disciplines of psychology or sociology, are usually socialized in the values of traditional science, which emphasizes the importance of objectivity and empirical evidence. It also emphasizes the central role of verifiability and reproducibility and, hence, leads researchers not to trust their own intuitions and judgments but instead to rely on the tools of science for explanation of the phenomena of interest. This often results in ahistorical perspectives on organizations and places a generally negative value on historical analysis and in-depth descriptive case studies. The effects of the widespread acceptance of traditional scientific values have been a positivistic bias in organizational research and, more subtly, limitations on both the kinds of problems organizational researchers define as legitimate and on the accompanying research strategies.

A fourth reason for the prevalence of static research is that much, if not most, organizational research is sponsored by clients whose objective is to improve organizational performance. Whether the client is a government agency, a giant corporation, or a small, nonprofit social service unit, its concern over performance generally constrains the kinds of questions asked by researchers and the kind of time frame within which they seek answers. Finally, as many people have pointed out, the reward structure for academic researchers and the demands of longitudinal research are generally incompatible. Young scholars are implicitly encouraged to tackle research that holds the promise of relatively rapid and prolific publication. Cross-sectional research holds just such promise, but longitudinal research usually does not. Add these forces together and the result is a powerful set of inducements for static research.

I believe strongly that more dynamic perspectives on organizations are badly needed. On the theoretical side, there are now diminishing returns from cross-sectional comparative and quantitative research. This is not to say that nothing is to be learned from this kind of research, only that there are very apparent limitations to what can be learned. In my view, the comparative, quantitative paradigm assumes implicitly that organizational developmental processes are either irrelevant or that their effects are randomized out in a sample of organizations. I simply do not believe that this assumption is appropriate. I have noted elsewhere (Kimberly, 1976) that a given sample of organizations is likely to include some very young ones, some middle-aged ones, some senior-citizen ones, and some very elderly ones. To include them all in the same sample of organizations implicitly assumes that those differences are unimportant. Although the theory spelling out how those differences are important awaits development, the assumption that they are unimportant does not seem tenable.

Some researchers, it is true, have used organizational age as a variable in their analyses, but this procedure, while to be applauded because of its recognition of the possible effects of time, does not seem to be wholly satisfactory. Chronological age may have very little to do with where an organization is going or where it has been. Calendar time and organizational time are not necessarily identical. Organizations often have rhythms and cycles that are quite independent of their chronological age (Kimberly, 1980b). Greater sensitivity to and understanding of organizational cycles should greatly enrich the content of organization theory. It may have important practical payoffs as well. It may be, for example, that the kinds of intervention strategies appropriate for organizational change vary depending upon an organization's stage of development. Strategies that are effective for the brand-new organization may be relatively ineffective in a steady-state or declining organization. At the very least, if the effectiveness of intervention strategies is to be maximized, they need to take into account the historical context of organizations. This context includes both the variety of external forces that shape organizations and set them on particular courses and the internal culture that constrains their decision-making and strategic choice processes.

Biological Metaphors

But where and how do we begin in trying to capture the dynamic quality of organizational life? It is obvious that populations of organizations ebb and flow and that individual organizations are created, grow, sometimes become stagnant, sometimes revitalize, and sometimes pass from the scene. Although my own concern at present is with understanding the influences on the life course of particular organizations, there are quite obvious interconnections between the fates of particular organizations and the fates of populations of organizations. Thus, it is often difficult, in fact undesirable, to try to disentangle the fates of populations of organizations from those of particular organizations.

Biology provides certain concepts and models that, at first glance, appear to have some relevance for understanding organizational cycles. After all, one can speak of organizational birth, life, and death, and terms such as *conception, gestation, birth trauma,* and even *miscarriage* and *abortion* are useful for describing some important events in organizational life. For organizations, as for people, conditions of birth and early infancy may shape later development in significant ways. Again, the behavior of both organizations and people is shaped by a combination of environmental and internal factors, whose relative importance is controversial.

Yet when one goes beyond these intriguing surface similarities, questions begin to arise. Two questions, in particular, are generally raised by critics. First, biological organisms begin to die the minute they are born. Death is an inevitable feature of biological life. The same cannot be said of organizations. There is nothing about organizational life in itself that, of necessity, implies organizational death. Death is not an inevitable feature of organizational life. Second, whereas biological organisms seem to go through relatively clear and predictable stages in development from simple to more complex, the same is not necessarily true of organizations. There is no inevitable linear sequence of stages in organizational life, although there may be remarkable similarities among the developmental patterns of certain clusters of organizations. If there are laws that govern the development of organizations, analogous to those that apparently govern the development of organisms, they are yet to be discovered.

Social scientists, however, have been intrigued with the biological analogy for years. Debates about the appropriateness of applying theories of evolution adapted from biology to social aggregates have raged, died down, and raged again. No social science discipline has been immune to seduction by this analogy or to the controversies it has created.

The content of the debate is illustrated vividly in economics, where scholars pursuing the development of theories of the business firm have flirted with biological analogies for nearly three quarters of a century. In a paper published in 1914, Chapman and Ashton asserted that "the growth of a business and the volume and form which it ultimately assumes are apparently determined in somewhat the same fashion as the development of an organism in the animal or vegetable world. As there is a normal size and form for a man, so, but less markedly, are there normal sizes and forms for business" (p. 512). Somewhat more recently Boulding (1950) wrote that: "we must go on further to discuss the problem of what

determines the 'optimum' or equilibrium balance sheet itself, as this
is to some extent under the control of the firm. This should bring
us directly into 'life-cycle' theory, and indeed one would have expected Marshall's famous analogy of the trees of the forest again to
have led economists to a discussion of the forces which determine
the birth, growth, decline, and death of a firm. . . . [There is an]
inexorable and irreversible movement toward the equilibrium of
death. Individual, family, firm, nation, and civilization all follow
the same grim law, and the history of any organism is strikingly
reminiscent of the rise and fall of populations on the road to extinction" (p. 38).

Enthusiasm for a life cycle theory of the business firm has
hardly been universal, however. A particularly forceful critique was
made more than twenty-five years ago by Penrose (1952), who contended that:

> The purposes a life cycle theory of the firm would
> serve are obvious, yet the theory as a base undeveloped
> hypothesis has existed for a long time and nothing has been
> done to construct from it a consistent theoretical system
> with sufficient content to enable it to be used for any pur-
> pose whatsoever. . . . Although we have a respectable collec-
> tion of information about firms, it has not stimulated
> economists even to suggest the further hypotheses neces-
> sary to the development of a life cycle theory of the firm.
> This, I think, is primarily because the available evidence
> does not support the theory that firms have a life cycle
> characterized by a consistent transition through recogniza-
> ble stages of development similar to those of living or-
> ganisms. Indeed, just the opposite conclusion must be
> drawn: the development of firms does not proceed accord-
> ing to the same "grim" laws as does that of living organisms
> [p. 806].

Similar debates have taken place in sociology, where the concern has generally been with understanding and perhaps occasionally with predicting the rate and direction of change within
societies. A recent exchange in the *Administrative Science Quarterly*
captures some of the controversy quite well. In a review of Aldrich's book (1979) on organizations and their environments—a

book based on a population ecology approach to organizational analysis—Van de Ven (1979) wonders "whether analogies to the biological evolution are needed for explaining organizational change. I do not believe they are" (p. 325). He essentially argues that Aldrich does not need biology to do what he has done theoretically and that there are analogies in social science that might provide the theoretically necessary meat without creating controversy over the bones. In a response to Van de Ven's review, McKelvey (1979) stridently leaps to Aldrich's defense by proclaiming that "Van de Ven is a well-entrenched reductionist who could not escape from that principle of enquiry to see the world in light of the rational principle, which of course is the one the population ecology or natural selection approach is rooted in" (p. 490).

The specifics of the debate need not be rehearsed here. What is noteworthy is the fascination among social scientists with the potential gains from using biological analogies, on the one hand, and the withering criticism of most efforts to do so, on the other. Also interesting is the somewhat cyclical character of these efforts. They seem to roll in and out of fashion. My chief reason for noting these debates, however, is to suggest that there is an either/or quality to the dialogue that may lead us ultimately to miss the mark. For in the rush either to advocate or excoriate the use of biological analogies in the study of nonbiological phenomena, we tend to lose sight of the fact that significant insights may emerge through the use of imperfect metaphors. Detractors tend to get so caught up in demonstrating deficiencies in the biological analogy that they seem incapable of recognizing the potential benefits of a less strict view of it. By contrast, its advocates become perhaps too concerned with demonstrating the universal applicability of the analogy to be able to understand and acknowledge its limitations.

My belief is that biological metaphors, imperfect though they most certainly are, can serve a very useful purpose in the study of organizations. By forcing theorists to think through carefully where the metaphors are appropriate and inappropriate, their use can lead to the raising of important new questions and perhaps to the recasting of old ones. This should not be construed as a request to reinvent the wheel. Rather it is a challenge that at worst may represent a form of intellectual pragmatism but that viewed more positively represents an effort to freshen and reanimate organizational theory and research.

Although it is not possible within the confines of a single chapter to explore the full range of questions in organizational theory and research that the use of metaphors from biology might stimulate, a few examples will help illustrate some of the possibilities. As the usefulness of these examples is pondered, we might do well to reflect on developments in the field of biology. It is my strong impression that biological models appear much less controversial to those outside the field than to those within it. Social scientists working with biological models and analogies tend to impute a certainty to their content that may well be unjustified. In our efforts to borrow, we tend to accept uncritically what we borrow. We are apparently willing to believe, in other words, that biologists really *know* and *agree upon* what they are talking about.

How sensible is this belief? It does, of course, remove an area of potential equivocality for us. After all, we have enough trouble with our own theories and models. We are certainly not anxious to create more trouble by exploring *their* controversies and theoretical problems. Ignoring controversy in their work makes our job in one sense easier. But the uncritical acceptance of biological models ultimately makes our job more difficult. As sociologists and philosophers of science are wont to point out, any field of scientific inquiry is subject to internal issues, debates, and controversies, and biology is certainly not immune to these. To cite but one relatively superficial example, Penrose (1952) noted that "it is not an easy task even for the biologist to state unambiguously what is meant by an organism or what distinguishes the biological organism from nonliving matter" (p. 807). If we assume that biological theories and models are noncontroversial, if we insist that there be an isomorphic relationship between biological and social or organizational phenomena as a test of the utility of the comparison, and if we reject entirely the utility of the comparison when that test is not met, we are putting ourselves in a rather difficult position to say the least.

If, however, we recognize that theories and models in biology, as in social science, may change as new knowledge is generated and new perspectives develop, we can perhaps feel less inhibited about using metaphors that we know in advance are imperfect. Take the issue of predetermination as one example of the kind of question about organizations that use of metaphors from biology might help illuminate. There appears to be an inevitable, genetically predetermined sequence to biological life. Organisms are born, develop, age, and die. Some may live longer than others; but, depending upon the type of organism in question, it is possible to make reasonably accurate predictions about both stages and life expectancy. As was noted earlier in this chapter, however, there does not appear to be similar predictability with organizations. Thus, Penrose (1952) has argued that "we have no reason whatsoever for thinking that the growth pattern of a biological organism is *willed* by the organism itself. On the other hand, we have every reason for thinking that the growth of a firm is willed by those who make the decisions of the firm and are themselves part of the firm. . . . We know of no general 'laws' predetermining men's choices, nor have we as yet any established basis for suspecting the existence of such laws. By contrast, . . . we have every reason for thinking that these matters are predetermined by the nature of the living organisms" (pp. 808–809).

For Penrose, organizations, in contrast to biological organisms, have "wills," or the capacity for self-determination. The issue, then, is settled. Or is it? Kaufman (1975), writing about organizational evolution, argues that "probably the chief reason for the demise of organizations is change in their internal or external environments that renders ineffective their established processes of self-maintenance. Most organizations, to be sure, are capable of modifying those processes to some extent and are thus able to survive changes of modest proportions. But this capability is always circumscribed; organizational flexibility is sharply limited. . . . Organizations often persist in courses of action that were previously beneficial even when new conditions necessitate new patterns of behavior. . . the norm is inflexibility of behavior" (pp. 139–140).

Who is right, Penrose or Kaufman? This, in my view, is not a very interesting question. The more interesting question is what issues about organizations the two apparently different perspectives raise. To what extent do organizations develop mechanisms that set them on particular life courses from which deviation is difficult? What are these mechanisms? How can we account for exceptions? Stinchcombe's (1965) hypothesis about structural stability over time would tend to support Kaufman's view, whereas Sills' classic study (1957) of goal succession in the March of Dimes campaign tends to support Penrose. But if we go beyond these arguments there is no doubt a perspective—as yet undeveloped—that could reconcile these apparent differences. Such a perspective would help us understand the empirical and theoretical basis for the flexibility attributed to organizations by an economist using a biological comparison and the inflexibility attributed to them by a political scientist also using a biological comparison. Differences resulting from the use of biological comparisons themselves, then, can stimulate creative tension and can suggest new possibilities for theoretical synthesis.

A second example of the usefulness of the biological metaphor arises from reflection on the process of birth. In the case of human beings, there are no particular mysteries about when a child is born. There is a visible event—the emergence of the child from the birth canal—that most of us would agree constitutes "birth." There are a number of questions, however, that might be raised about birth in human beings. First, much that precedes the birth event conditions how well the child will do once born. Second, with new developments in knowledge and technology, it is conceivable that fetuses will someday be nurtured *ex utero* and that the actual process of birth will not necessarily involve passage through the birth canal.

For the birth of organizations, there is no event directly comparable to emergence from the birth canal. In fact, it is often exceedingly difficult to specify exactly when an organization was born—so difficult that one wonders whether it is even worth the effort conceptually. And yet there is much in the natural histories of organizations to lead one to believe that the processes of conception and gestation are not at all irrelevant as descriptors of early organizational activity. Furthermore, one might be led to speculate about comparative rates of birth and death of organizations in the public and private sectors. The impression that failure rates are lower in the public sector is widespread. If this is in fact the case, how might it be accounted for? One possibility is that public-sector organizations may not be "born," that is, their existence may not be made publicly visible, until there is some reasonable certainty about the adequacy of their resource base. Comparative analysis of the birth process of organizations in the public and private sectors, stimulated by the biological metaphor, might well reveal similarities and differences that would explain later patterns of behavior and development.

The Life Cycle Concept

I am convinced that the generally moribund state of much current organizational theory and research is owing to the lack of appreciation for the role of history in, and the effects of context on, organizational life. And I believe that there is a tight coupling in science between content of understanding and method for understanding. Furthermore, I have been intimately involved in the process of creation and early development of two organizations of reasonable social significance in the past eight years, and I think that I have learned something about this process along the way.

There is a sense in which use of the life cycle metaphor is misguided. It certainly has limitations, many of which have already been discussed in this chapter, some of which will be discussed in coming chapters, and others of which, though not discussed explicitly, will become obvious to the reader of this volume. If used improperly, and by that I mean if tested strictly, the life cycle metaphor will be found wanting. It is the strict test that in my view is misguided at this stage of development in the field. There is a more compelling sense, however, in which the life cycle concept is constructive. It does push us to ask new questions about organizations, it does lead us to take seriously the proposition that history and, as Sarason (1972) suggests, prehistory powerfully shape the organizational here and now, and it does force us to think deeply about the influence of context on organizational life. It also causes us to rethink the relation between theory and methods and thus to reflect on what techniques for understanding are compatible with our newly defined needs for understanding.

The more conservative side of me called for a different title for the book, one that might be less patently controversial or at least less open to uninformed dismissal. After all, why risk alienating potential readers on the basis of the title alone? The less conservative side, in an all-too-rare victory, argued for the present title. The life cycle notion does capture some important themes in organizational life and does so in interesting ways. Being a firm believer in the dialectical nature of social theory, I am under no illusions about the infinite utility of the promise that the book's title offers. But behind and beyond the title lie some intriguing pathways to explore.

PART I

Creation of Organizations

The four chapters in this section each deal with quite different settings, yet they are addressed to a common conceptual problem: What kinds of factors shape the process of organizational creation? Either implicitly or explicitly, each chapter also explores the extent to which the creation process affects organizational futures.

Kimberly bases Chapter Two on a longitudinal study of the creation of an innovative medical school. He argues that creation is a time when individual personalities may have an unusually strong influence on organizational outcomes. As organizations mature, however, they develop mechanisms designed to limit this influence. Only under unusual circumstances, such as severe performance declines, are individuals likely to have the pervasive influence they seem to enjoy during the process of creation. Kimberly also points to the paradoxical nature of success in innovative organizations. Over time, those things that made the medical school initially successful as an innovation became increasingly incompatible with those things that appeared to be requirements for long-run success. Kimberly argues that the process of institutionalization generates a set of demands on an innovative organizational system that make it difficult to sustain the quality of innovation for very long.

In Chapter Three Miles and Randolph explore the role of learning in the creation and early life of organizations. They distinguish two archetypical approaches to organizational learning—the enactive and proactive approaches—and argue that the enactive approach, which relies less on the content of previous experiences as a guide for present strategy, is more appropriate than the proactive for the creation of new and different organizational settings. Data from a study of two simulated organizations reveal that although the two faced nearly identical initial conditions, they developed very differently. Miles and Randolph attribute the differential patterns of development to differences in organizational learning styles, concluding that "there appear to be circumstances of organizational creation and transformation, so far only crudely charted, that require more emphasis on one learning approach than on the other. An overdetermined innovative organization is no better off than an underdetermined conventional creation. The first runs the risk of innovation shortfall; the second is threatened by the prospect of operational inefficiency under conditions of minimum organizational slack. In either case, a mismatch during creation among setting, learning mix, management style, and member orientations increases the probability of premature organizational termination."

Chapter Four by Van de Ven reports on a comparative analysis of the creation of fourteen childcare agencies. It attempts to identify forces that impinged on the development and success of these agencies, thus extending the work of Kimberly, Miles, and Randolph. To a greater extent than Kimberly or Miles and Randolph, Van de Ven examines the role of planning in the creation process and attempts to link outcomes with the presence or absence of earlier planning efforts. He also identifies the kinds of obstacles to success that organizations are likely to encounter as they move from planning to implementation: efforts to grow too quickly; lack of formalization of rules, policies, and procedures from the outset; lack of qualified personnel; early overemphasis on efficiency; and financial dilemmas. Van de Ven argues that behavorial approaches provide a richer understanding of the creation process than do structural perspectives, although he warns of the danger of focusing too extensively on the role of entrepreneurs. An important link among the first three chapters in this section is established when Van de Ven asserts that the methods used in planning the childcare organizations were clearly related to the implementation success they achieved during their first two years of operation. Moreover, the early chapters of an organization's biography are strongly influenced by prehistory and powerfully condition the shape and content of later chapters.

An important shift in the level of analysis from individual organizations to populations of organizations occurs in Chapter Five by Pennings. In contrast to the first three chapters in this section, Pennings' chapter addresses the urban-contextual factors that promote or inhibit organizational birth, and it attempts to answer the question of why new organizations are created more frequently in some urban environments than in others. In the course of his analysis, Pennings notes that there is an extensive amount of interorganizational structural variation within an organizational population. This variation, he argues, suggests a limitation on the biological analogy and is something that earlier proponents of the population ecology approach to organizations may have overlooked. It is extremely difficult, argues Pennings, to classify organizations into complementary and competing populations. Rather, we should focus on size, differentiation, and change in urban contexts as correlates of organizational birth.

Pennings' arguments also point out the importance of exploring the links between product life cycles and organizational life cycles. Although there is currently some debate about how much can or should be made of this link, it is clearly an area that warrants further exploration. It also forces us, in the context of the Kimberly and Van de Ven chapters, to think more deeply about the kinds of external forces that account for the creation of particular kinds of organizations at particular points in history.

2

Initiation, Innovation, and Institutionalization in the Creation Process

John R. Kimberly

What makes some organizations more successful than others? This question is either implicitly or explicitly part of most research on organizations and management. There are obviously both practical and theoretical reasons for the salience of the issue. On the one hand, managers are concerned with increasing the success of their organizations—and hence of their own careers. To the extent that research can contribute to that end, it is welcomed and supported

Note: This chapter was originally published as "Issues in the Creation of Organizations: Initiation, Innovation and Institutionalization" in *Academy of Management Journal*, 1979, 22, 437–457. It is reprinted here in slightly modified form with permission.

by them. The early history of organizational research, in fact, suggests that its origins were stimulated as much by the needs and concerns of industry as by those of researchers. Researchers, on the other hand, have recognized the importance of differing levels of success as dependent variables in the study of organizational behavior and have devoted much time and energy to attempting to understand both their correlates and determinants.

The measurement of success—or of effectiveness—has of course been problematic. (The terms *success* and *effectiveness* will be used interchangeably here, although I recognize that there are theoretical debates about the appropriateness of doing so.) Although it is generally agreed that success is multidimensional, there has been little consensus about what its components are (Steers, 1975; Goodman, Pennings, and Associates, 1977). Survival is one criterion that most researchers agree is a necessary—albeit not sufficient—condition for success, although truly effective organizations may put themselves out of business. There is less agreement about other dimensions, however, and many managers are themselves hard pressed to justify traditional measures and to suggest viable alternatives. And when the focus shifts from industrial to nonindustrial or "people-processing" organizations, the problem of determining what success or effectiveness is becomes exacerbated (Kimberly, 1980a). What distinguishes a successful prison, mental hospital, or educational institution from a less successful one? Debates over appropriate criteria are intense, and few widely accepted ones have been developed.

One very real problem in research on organizations, then, has been determining what success is, although the problem does not appear to be insoluble. Various researchers have made progress in answering this question (Mahoney and Weitzel, 1969; Price, 1968; Yuchtman and Seashore, 1967), but the most comprehensive account of current attempts to conceptualize and measure effectiveness is found in the collection of papers edited by Goodman, Pennings, and Associates (1977).

This chapter is framed around a sampling and research strategy issue in the analysis of effectiveness. It is an issue that has received little attention, but it has important implications. Very simply, most research on the question of effectiveness has been carried out in mature organizations that have existing structures, domains, control systems, and normative codes, and it has been based on cross-sectional designs. This means that the perspective is usually static and that the possible relevance of what stage an organization has entered in its life cycle (Kimberly, 1976a) is overlooked.

Most researchers are involved with an organization for only a brief period at some (usually unspecified) point during its life. As a result, the question of what implications the conditions surrounding its birth and early development may have for levels of success or effectiveness later on is not considered. There is at least the possibility that, just as for a child, the conditions under which an organization is born and the course of its development in infancy have crucial consequences for its later life. Just as one might be interested in similarities and differences in the backgrounds of executives as one important element in an explanation of their personal success, so might one be interested in the backgrounds of organizations. I would not argue that the analogies here are perfect by any means, only that they raise a question about the analysis of organizational effectiveness that has not been pursued to any great extent in the literature. Pursuing it might lead to some new insights.

This chapter analyzes the question of effectiveness in the context of the birth and early development of an innovative organization. In so doing, it directly confronts the issue of sampling and research design noted above. The organization studied is not "mature," and the analysis is not cross-sectional. It is a case study, and thus the usual cautions are in order. As Cummings (1977) has argued, however, intensive longitudinal analysis of individual cases is likely to enrich our perspectives on organizations and lead to theoretically interesting conceptualizations of effectiveness and its etiology.

Three separate but related bodies of literature—apart from that on effectiveness—have influenced the development of this chapter. First is the literature on organizational innovation, much of which has been summarized in Rogers and Shoemaker (1971), Zaltman, Duncan, and Holbek (1973), and Kimberly (1980a). This work highlights the effects of both internal and external factors on the fate of innovation. Second is the literature on organizational environments. The importance of this research, the leading edge of which is contained in the volumes by Meyer and Associates (1978), by Pfeffer and Salancik (1978), and by Aldrich (1979), is to demonstrate that both organizational process and outcomes are strongly influenced by environmental factors that may be only partially within the control of any single organization. Finally, research on organizational growth and development, summarized and extended by Starbuck (1965, 1971), suggests that growth and development are not linear processes and may be influenced by a variety of political, economic, and social factors. The analysis presented in the following pages owes much to these literatures even as it attempts to move in some new directions.

Setting and Research Design

New organizations are being created continuously in both the private and public sectors. Very little data exists on the rates of foundation of new organizations, but they would appear to be high. It also appears that the rates are higher in the private sector than in the public sector, although the rate of growth of government as an employer in recent years has risen rapidly, while that for industry has leveled off considerably. Whether this is indicative of a shift in rates of foundation of new organizations is unknown. All that can be said with certainty is that rates of organizational birth are nontrivial in both sectors.

The organizational subject of this chapter is a new school of medical education that opened its doors to its first class of students in September 1971. At the time it was started, there were eighty-six other medical schools in the United States. The majority of these schools were very similar in terms of both their organizational structure and the content of their curriculums. They all had four-year programs in which the first two years consisted of basic science training (biochemistry, physiology, and so forth), while the final two were spent in clinical training (direct contact with patients in the hospital setting). With very few exceptions, the basic science curriculums were composed of discipline-oriented, lecture-laboratory courses taught by Ph.D.'s in their particular disciplines.

The students had no contact with patients during this time. This contact came during clinical training.

Whether the remarkable similarity among the schools of medicine can be accounted for by the Stinchcombe (1965) hypothesis about structural stability and date of founding and/or by the widespread impact of the Flexner Report on the state of medical education in the United States at the beginning of this century is debatable. What was interesting about the new school, however, was that its structure and curriculum departed significantly from the norm, and it thus faced not only those problems that any new organization might be likely to confront—what Stinchcombe (1965) has called the "liability of newness"—but also the problems that result from being different. Being both new and different proved to be both an advantage and a disadvantage.

The observations that form the basis for the present paper were made during the application of a "process research" design for evaluating the birth, development, and impact of the new school. This approach, which has been described in detail elsewhere (Kimberly, Counte, and Dickinson, 1972), was based on the belief that significant insights into organizational phenomena can result from intensive longitudinal analysis of organizational processes.

At the time, I was a faculty member in a social science department on the campus where the medical school was started. The dean of the new school contacted me during the spring of the year prior to its formal opening. He was interested in a social science appraisal of his program by an outsider and was willing to provide a modest amount of seed money to help launch such an effort. In turn, I was pleased by the opportunity to get in on the ground floor of the birth of an organization, to develop a longitudinal study, and to conduct research on organizational behavior in a nonindustrial setting. An understanding was reached whereby the dean agreed to provide access to those data sources that I defined as relevant, and I agreed to share observations and findings with the dean on a regular basis.

The research effort extended over a four-year period, and funding was obtained from a number of federal and state sources. The strategy for collecting data involved a variety of survey, interview, observational, and archival research techniques. Data collected systematically from community physicians, students, faculty, and administrators at multiple points in time were combined with data from conversations, observations made both formally and informally in and around the school, minutes from a variety of different kinds of meetings, and memoranda of all sorts to form a rich store of information. In addition to learning a great deal about organizational behavior, the researcher gained insight into the problems and opportunities associated with the process research approach to the assessment of organizations (Kimberly and Nielsen, 1977).

The observations and interpretations presented here represent an effort to stand back from the specifics of the data that were collected and to piece together a more general mosaic based on, but not directly tied to, those data. It is an effort to understand some important things about the context in which the questions of birth and effectiveness were explored and to tease out their implications for organizational theory and research.

Any new organization faces two general problems, and this analysis of the birth and early development of the medical school deals with both. First is the problem of getting off the ground. Thus, the origins of the school will be considered and the conditions of its birth described. Second is the problem of institutionalization. Once off the ground, organizations must develop strategies for survival and growth—strategies that basically involve, according to Thompson (1967), sealing off their core technologies from the effects of environmental uncertainty. Here problems that the school faced as it grew will be discussed, and what I have chosen to call the "paradoxical nature of success" will be described.

Creating a New Medical School

While the birth of any organization is affected by a complex set of political, economic, social, and psychological factors, it is beyond the scope of this paper to deal systematically with all these. Instead, the analysis will take into account what are felt on the basis of careful observation to be the two most important sets of factors involved in the birth of the new medical school: (1) the circumstances favoring its emergence at a particular point in history, and (2) the ambition and vision of its first dean, who was largely responsible for defining the particular shape the school took and the directions it followed.

Situational Factors

There was a particular mix of social, economic, and political factors existing in the late 1960s and early 1970s that together created a favorable climate for the founding of a new medical school. For purposes of analysis, it is convenient to adopt Hall's (1972) distinction between general and specific environmental conditions and to distinguish between concerns at the national level—general environmental conditions—and those at the state and local level—specific environmental conditions.

On the national level in the middle and late sixties there was an increasing concern with the adequacy of existing supplies of physicians. Although there was much debate about whether a shortage of doctors did, in fact, exist, the federal government was persuaded that it did and developed a number of policies designed to increase the production of new doctors. Particularly influential was its decision to make federal monies available to medical schools on a per capita basis, thus encouraging the schools themselves to admit and graduate increasing numbers of students. Money also became available from the federal government and a number of private foundations to help finance the establishment of new schools. Thus, the national mood favored the establishment of new medical schools at this time, and this mood was reinforced by the availability of resources.

During this period there was also a national debate within the community of medical educators about the viability of traditional structures of medical education. This debate was influenced, of course, by the debates of that era over education in general and higher education in particular. Traditional values and structures were being called into question, and cries for reform came from many sources. Students were demanding more "relevance" in their education and a greater voice in determining the form and content of the educational process. The utility of grading systems was called into question, and there was much experimentation with pass-fail systems and ungraded courses. Faculties were reexamining the basic assumptions of their own careers, and much of the initiative for reform came from them. Medical education was not immune from these debates, in spite of the generally conservative character of most medical schools. Criticisms of the existing system abounded. It was argued that the traditional structure with its lockstep approach was one in which time (four years) was the constant and learning was the variable. It was also argued that the two years of basic science had negative effects on student motivation because it was simply more of what they had experienced as undergraduates in college. The fact that they could not see patients until their third year of medical school, it was argued, prevented students from understanding the relevance of the basic sciences for the practice of medicine. The strong explicit and implicit emphasis on specialization as opposed to general practice resulted in pressures on most students not to consider general practice seriously as a career alternative. The socialization process in medical school, in other words, was a major contributor to the oft-cited imbalance between specialists and general practitioners on a national basis.

Other things were happening on the state and local levels, that is in the specific environment, to favor the establishment of a new medical school. The university's College of Medicine, headquartered in a major metropolitan area, had long been one of the largest medical schools in the country as measured by the number of doctors it graduated per year. It was the unchallenged leader in medical education in the state. Doctors and politicians in other parts of the state, however, had felt for some time that it cast an uncomfortably long shadow over medicine in their localities, and they looked upon developments nationally as an opportunity to initiate medical education programs outside the metropolis. Accordingly, there was a move to establish a new medical school in the state capital. Not to be outdone, the College of Medicine proposed a substantial growth program of its own that involved establishing semiautonomous branches in three other cities as well as increasing its own capacity at home. The existence of a campus of the state university with a number of distinguished basic science departments, three hospitals, and a sizable medical community in another city made that city a logical site for one of the three branches.

There was also a good deal of concern among policy makers at the state level over the large numbers of state-trained doctors who were leaving the state to practice elsewhere. The major urban area was not affected by this exodus, but the rest of the state was. Some hope was expressed, therefore, that if branches were established outside that area, students would be exposed to the practice of medicine in nonurban settings and would thus be more inclined to locate in those settings once their training had been completed.

For its part, the campus of the university that was the potential site of the new school looked on the possibility of a medical program with mixed emotions. It was clearly attractive in the short run, since a new medical school would undoubtedly help generate other new resources, and by the late sixties it was evident that the days of abundant resources and rapid growth were over. Prospects for the longer run were less clear, however, and there was considerable uncertainty about how the administrative linkages with the College of Medicine could be established on the most favorable of terms. In the end, however, the advocates of growth overcame the proponents of caution, and it was agreed that one of the branches would be established on this campus.

Role of Entrepreneurship

Thus, a number of forces combined at a particular point in time to lead to the decision to establish a new medical school in a particular locale. An understanding of these forces alone, however, is not sufficient for an understanding of the kind of school that was established and the course of its early development. For this it is necessary to look carefully at the ambitions and character of the individual who was hired as the school's first dean.

There is a good deal of controversy among organizational theorists about the advisability of attributing organizational outcomes to the characteristics of particular individuals. Sociologists label such attribution psychological reductionism and argue that organizational analysis is most fruitfully pursued apart from considerations of individual personalities and motivations. This position has been perhaps most forcefully argued by Perrow (1970). In his critique of the "leadership" approach to organizational analysis, he contends that a structural approach is more useful. In reflecting on the development of the medical school, however, I am led to conclude that Perrow's position needs to be emended. In the case examined here, an understanding of the school's first dean and his values and objectives is necessary for an understanding of the school he developed. Purely structural explanations are inadequate. Whether this would be as true in the case of the birth of other organizations, I cannot say, but I suspect that if enough research were available on organizational birth, one would find that the role of the early leaders was critical. Sarason's (1972) work on the creation of new settings tends to substantiate this view. As an organization matures, develops norms, and acquires a history and identity, the importance of the person at the top diminishes in explaining organizational outcomes. Organizational mechanisms are designed to remove the equivocality that attaches to individual personalities. Thus, Perrow's position may apply to mature organizations but not necessarily to brand-new ones.

The new dean, a cardiologist by training, was in full-time private practice at the time of his hiring and was also a clinical assistant professor at a leading medical school that had been one of the first schools to break from the traditional structure of medical education and move in some new directions. He thus came to his job from an environment that encouraged innovation. Although he had served for five years on the board of education in the city where he practiced and had founded and served on the executive committee of a prepaid group practice in the same city, his administrative experience was nevertheless limited. His hiring thus represented a certain amount of risk both for the university and for him.

Five characteristics of the dean help to explain the nature of his influence on the early development of the school. First, he had a deep-rooted dissatisfaction with traditional forms of medical education and a very real commitment to the importance of developing new structures. Second, he was a risk taker, willing to experiment with new ideas in an often uncritical fashion. Third, he was a man of action as opposed to a man of reflection and was given to making very quick decisions. Fourth, he was an idea man as opposed to a detail man, ready to paint scenarios for the future in very broad strokes, leaving his staff—often unprepared—to fill in the blanks. Finally, he was an optimist with very strong instincts for self-preservation and quickly learned the often intricate rules of survival in the highly political and politicized university environment.

He came to the position with a budget and an associate dean. The school he developed was, in a very real sense, his school, and it represented in concrete terms at the outset his vision of what medical education should be. In the beginning he was reacting instinctively and intuitively, and what he did—and what he did not do—had important consequences for the early life of the school. The major constraint imposed from without was the fact that the school was to start out as a one-year basic science program. The intention was then to send students to one of the other three campuses of the College of Medicine for the three years of clinical training that were to follow. Another, initially latent, constraint was the fact that the school served two administrative masters, the College of Medicine located in another city and the university campus. As long as the school was small and neither commanded nor demanded large amounts of resources, it posed little threat, and the dean had a good deal of freedom to design the kind of program he wanted. As soon as it started to increase its visibility, however, administrative constraints were activated and came to play an important role in the school's development.

The dean's first commitment was to generate enthusiasm for the school in the medical community. This commitment was the direct result of his vision of what the program should do—expose new students to patients from the outset. He felt that this would enhance their motivation and would help demonstrate the relevance of the basic sciences to the practice of medicine. To do this, however, it was necessary to find doctors willing to work with the students, and the dean turned to the local medical community for help. His view was that community physicians represented an untapped resource for medical education. If they could be persuaded to participate in his program, they would not only provide important learning experiences for the students but might in turn be motivated by their contact with the students to keep up with current developments in medicine themselves. And if they would be willing to participate on an unsalaried basis, that would result in considerable cost effectiveness for the school. The inducement for participation was the status accompanying the title of clinical asso-

ciate at the medical school. Thus, the dean's major initial investment was in the community—an investment that was to have positive payoffs initially in terms of physician response but that had
certain costs as well because of lack of attention to the importance
of campus-based bridges.

Development of the curriculum was influenced by the dean's
views about medical education. He had strong feelings that (1) students do not all learn at the same rate and (2) that it made more
sense from the perspective of medical practice to take a so-called
disease system approach rather than to set up a discipline-centered
curriculum. He also felt that he could reasonably devise a one-year
basic science program to supplant the usual two-year one.

The program was designed to start small, with 16 students in
the first year. That number was to double each of the next three
years until the class size reached the target figure of 128. Five faculty members, hired on the basis of their interest in the innovative
character of the program, aided in design of the curriculum. The
curriculum was to consist of a number of disease-centered problems, and each student was to be assigned to a community physician
who would act as an adviser, expose the student to patients, and let
the student see individuals afflicted with the particular problem the
student was currently studying. Progress was to be evaluated by
another community physician, who would examine the student or-
ally. The role of the faculty was to provide advice, expertise, and
counseling as the students felt they needed it.

When the school opened its doors, it was modest in size. It
consisted of the dean, an associate dean, an assistant dean, an
executive secretary, two secretaries, five faculty members, sixteen
students, commitments from over 100 physicians in the local community to participate if called upon, a curriculum that was not fully
developed, and a structure that departed substantially from that of
most basic science medical programs. The dean had an enormous
capacity for work and often put in sixteen-to-eighteen-hour days.
The results were impressive. He managed to develop a high degree
of credibility in the local medical community in a very short period
of time. In fact, in a study of factors affecting their willingness to
participate in the new program, the local physicians most frequently cited the influence of the dean as singularly important

(Counte and Kimberly, 1974). He was also able to begin to build a reputation for the innovative nature of the school both in the state (Sorlie and others, 1971) and nationally (Bloomfield and others, 1972).

Rapid growth is often equated with success. Our culture places a strong positive evaluation on evidence of growth and a negative evaluation on steady state and particularly on decline. Although recent stringencies in the general environment have forced many institutions, including institutions of higher education, to reconsider the relevance of this value, in the early days of the medical school it was still occupying center stage. At that point in time, one way members of both the organization and of its external constituencies evaluated performance was on the basis of growth. (Of course, use of growth as a criterion for success has persisted, even in the face of evidence that it may not be *the* or even *a* major factor.)

Defined in terms of growth, the initial success of the school is readily apparent. During the period from 1971–72 to 1975–76, the number of students increased from 16 to 101, faculty from 4 to 18, administrators from 4 to 6, and clerical workers from 1 to 12. At the same time, budget expenditures increased from $240,000 to $1,303,000. In addition, a new building to house the school opened in the spring of 1975.

Available evidence indicated that the innovative curriculum of the school was favorably received by the students and that they performed as well as their peers in other basic science programs in the college on standard year-end exams. Thus it appeared that the school was an institution whose time had come, headed by a man of ambition and vision, and that this combination had spawned an organization that could conceivably serve as a model for others to follow. Circumstances and an entrepreneurial dean had together given birth to an organization that gave every indication of being highly successful.

The Paradox of Success

Does success breed success? This question is often asked, but observation of the new medical school suggests that it may be the wrong one. Success, as noted earlier, is multifaceted, and in the case of the medical school the composition of success changed as the process of institutionalization unfolded. For the variety of reasons described below, the early success of the organization as an innovation was difficult to sustain once the organization began to develop. Paradoxically, those things that accounted for its early success were among those things that had to be changed to ensure its long-run success. The paradox is explained by the nature of the process of institutionalization, and this process indicates why the notion that success breeds success vastly oversimplifies the realities of organizational evolution.

Institutionalization is that process whereby new norms, values, and structures become incorporated within the framework of existing patterns of norms, values, and structures. This process is one that lends stability and predictability to social relationships and enables them to persist. It is especially visible in the context of formal organizations, where a frequent problem is developing mechanisms to sustain planned change efforts (Goodman and Bazerman, 1979).

At the medical school, institutionalization was highly visible. in the way three problems in particular were dealt with. The problems of internal social control, of the structure of work, and of managing relationships with the environment are faced by all organizations (Kimberly, 1976b). As an organization is born and begins to develop, the process of institutionalization is inevitably joined in each of these areas. The organization seeks to increase the predictability of its own outcomes, and, at the same time, organizations and institutions in its environment attempt to increase the predictability of its outcomes for them. Assessments of performance are both internal and external (Pfeffer, 1977a). To trace the process of institutionalization and its effects, therefore, one needs to look both inside the organization and outside. How does it deal with the three problems noted above and with what consequences?

Because a complete description of the process at the new medical school is beyond the scope of this chapter, I will present an example illustrating the nature of the response to each of the three problems. These illustrations can then serve as the basis for some more general observations.

Structural Differentiation

The school's first year of existence was characterized by an atmosphere of experimentation and tolerance of one another's mistakes on the part of all the participants—students, administrators, faculty, and local physicians. The interest of each group in seeing the school get off the ground meant that there were important degrees of freedom for everyone. The dean had been successful, for example, in enlisting the active participation of twenty local physicians on a nonsalaried basis, and they had agreed to spend at least four hours per week with their student advisees. He had been less successful, however, in defining precisely what should happen during the time they spent with their advisees, because he and his staff had not had enough time to work on that problem and because he did not in fact have a very specific vision of what should happen. Although the physicians often felt in the dark about what they should be doing with their advisees, they were willing to continue through the year because it was important to them to have a medical school in the community. And the dean made several efforts to reassure them personally, through phone conversations and meetings, that they were doing well and that a clearer set of guidelines for their role would be provided as experience with the new format was gained.

The first sixteen students also lived in an atmosphere of uncertainty. The curriculum was not fully developed, facilities were crude, there were few guidelines for their behavior, and it was difficult for them to judge how "well" they were doing in the program. But the dean and his staff spent a great deal of time with the students during the year, fostering a sense of comradeship and building up enough social capital to offset concerns about the lack of structure in the program itself. The students, in fact, responded positively to the program during the first year. Internal social control, then, was established and maintained during the early stages of development on a personalized basis. The dean devoted an enormous amount of time to pattern maintenance activities, maintaining an open-door policy and encouraging interaction. This provided greatly needed support and encouragement to both physicians and students.

But the basis of internal social control began to change from a highly personal to a highly impersonal one when the number of students increased and when other administrative demands reduced the amount of time the dean could spend with students and physicians. As the number of students increased over the next years from 16 to 100, the dean hired staff to perform the important linking role between the school and the local physicians and between the school and the students. But whereas in the first year the program had been the dean, over time the program became the school. The atmosphere changed from personal to impersonal, with effects on the reactions of both physicians and students. Both groups were more willing to challenge each other and less willing to tolerate errors. The less time the dean spent with them, the more true this became. Thus, structural differentiation—the hiring of staff to perform tasks formerly performed by the dean—had the effect of producing a more highly bureaucratized system—a system that had a conservative impact on the initially innovative character of the school.

Structural differentiation did not occur solely in response to the increasing numbers of students. It also reflected changing administrative demands on the dean. Whereas in the first year he could focus primarily on problems of internal social control, in ensuing years he had to devote increasing amounts of his time and energy to the structure of work and particularly to managing relations with the environment. These demands were independent of changes in size, and they reflect, perhaps, an important aspect of the process of institutionalization. It is not a linear process or one that involves a particular sequence of problems. The dean could have made different decisions about how to spend his time during the first year and the years following and attended to the various problems raised by institutionalization in any number of sequences and combinations. Ultimately, however, all of them had to be dealt with. One result of structural differentiation as a response to the problem of internal social control was that the dean was able to devote his energies to other areas, and in that sense it represented an effective response. The cost, however, was a diminishing of the initially organic relationship among the dean, the faculty, the students, and the local physicians. There came to be less tolerance for experimentation and error and hence less willingness to accept the uncertainty that inevitably accompanies innovation.

Formalization of the Structure of Work

One of the explicit objectives of the dean was to create a medical school in which the students would be able to pace themselves, to learn at their own rate, and to study independently. There was a deliberate effort to avoid the lockstep rigidity that characterized basic science education in most medical schools. Accordingly, during the first year a disease-centered curriculum was developed that required students to learn those aspects of the basic sciences (for example, biochemistry and physiology) that would apply to the specific diseases that they were studying. After doing an introductory problem together, students were able to do succeeding problems in any order and at any time they chose. Their physician advisers were to help them by showing them patients who had the particular disease they were studying, but the definition of when a student had mastered a given problem came from his physician adviser. The faculty played a consultative role only and were not directly involved in a major way in the learning process.

There was a good deal of anxiety and uncertainty created by the lack of structure of work during the first year. Physician advisers were not sure that they were giving the students what they needed, students were not sure that they were getting what they needed, and the dean and his staff were not sure that the students would perform adequately on the college-wide standard year-end exam or on the National Medical Boards, Part I. As it turned out, the students did very well on the exams, and fifteen out of sixteen passed the boards. This, it must be remembered, after only one year of basic sciences as opposed to the usual two.

Yet in spite of this "success," there were pressures from a number of sources to structure the curriculum more tightly. The uncertainty was not pleasant for anyone, there was some concern that the students' performance was a fluke, and it was felt that ways needed to be found to ensure that performance would be as impressive in the future. Over the next three years, therefore, the physician advisers were given job descriptions, and the curriculum developed to the point where students had to finish a required number of problems in a required sequence in a set amount of time. There was, in other words, a dramatic increase in the extent of formalization of the work. While formalization was undoubtedly required in part by the increase in the number of students, this is not the sole explanation. The level of uncertainty required by the innovative independent study format was simply not felt to be supportable over time. As the program began to attract national attention and as requests for documentation of the curriculum were received, the professional motivations of the staff led to the production of such documentation. Paradoxically, however, this very production process represented a kind of formalization that limited freedom and constrained innovation in the program. And perhaps even more significantly, the demands of accreditation bodies made formalization imperative. Thus, although the disease-centered concept underlying the content of the curriculum did not change, the independent study format changed dramatically. Those characteristics of the original structure of work that contributed to its success as an innovation were incompatible with the need felt in the long run for predictability and stability. Formalization as a response enhanced stability but diminished innovativeness.

Role of the Faculty

Earlier it was noted that there were both specific and general environmental conditions that created a favorable climate for the establishment of a new medical school at a particular site. It was also the case that the school had to manage relationships with both environments. A good example of the process of institutionalization and its effects in the specific environment is provided by the evolving role of the faculty. An important component of this environment was the school's relationship to the basic science departments on campus. During the first year this was not an issue. The faculty of the medical school was small, and all its members were busy trying to define their roles. By the end of the first year, however, faculty members had come to feel that they were not as directly involved in educating the students as they wanted to be and persuaded the dean that they should have a broader and more clearly defined teaching and advising role. It was only natural that this role, over time, should evolve in the direction of the traditional conceptualization of teaching and research. The school's faculty members were part of a large, conventionally organized university where this role was the norm and where their role was clearly a low-status exception. More important still was the fact that all the faculty members from the beginning had joint appointments with the regular departments on campus. Joint appointments enhanced their academic credibility among research colleagues at other universities. The dean, too, realized the importance of the joint appointments as a mechanism for enhancing the legitimacy and reputation of his school both within the university and in the larger arena of academic medicine.

In the short run, the university could welcome the innovative program as a potentially interesting addition. Over time, however, the school would have to prove its merit—on terms comparable to those of other campus units. The first real testing ground was the question of evaluation and promotion of faculty. What criteria should be used and who should be involved in the evaluation process? It was clear that the medical school would not be able to enjoy special privileges and that its faculty would be subject to the general campus-wide criteria of research and publication. This was a way in which the specific environment could remove any equivocality that might surround the medical school. The not-unexpected effect was a conservatizing one on the faculty members. Because they were to be evaluated largely in terms of traditional criteria, there were few incentives for them to engage in nontraditional behavior.

Once again, one can see the paradox of institutionalization and success at work. The school attracted qualified faculty members both because of the personal persuasiveness of the dean and the record of success of the first year. Although perhaps initially attracted by the innovative character of the program, the faculty members nevertheless responded to the traditional nature of the reward structure that emerged. Their attention became focused more on research and publication and less on developing their roles in ways that would help to maintain the innovative character of the program. Early success as an innovation created conditions that made continued success on that basis difficult.

Creation of a Public Face

If building credibility in the specific environment of the university in which the new school was located led to important changes in the role of the faculty, creating a public face for the general environment required certain readjustments for the dean. His interest was not in building an organization of local reputation only. That was important, but he was also interested in national recognition. Such recognition not only would be personally rewarding but would make the job of fund raising less problematic.

The dean had a personal conviction that one of the problems in medical education was an overemphasis on specialization, and he wanted to build a program that did not have such an emphasis. He felt that the best form of medical education would be one that produced good general physicians who could specialize in anything. Utilization of local physicians, many of whom were general practitioners, as participants in the program was designed, in part, to expose students to the physician's role in a broad way from the very beginning of their training. The hope was that they would then be good general physicians once their training had been completed. This was another innovative aspect of the school at the time of its birth.

But the need to create a public face and the desire to have a program that produced good general physicians led to a dilemma for the dean. The public face had to be acceptable first and foremost in the medical profession and particularly in the field of medical education. Yet the dean's concept of a good general physician was somewhat vague and could easily be confused with the concept of the general practitioner. General practice, however, did not rank high in the status hierarchy in the field. If his program was to become publicly identified as a general practice program, the dean realized, it would by definition be a low-status program. Status in the medical profession is highly prized, and for good reason, because resources tend to flow up the status hierarchy. Needing resources and, hence, recognition, the dean could not afford a public face that had too strong an overtone of general practice attached to it. Thus, although the program initially was

developed around the importance of producing good general
physicians, the need to project an acceptable public image gradually led to a diminishing emphasis on this aspect of the school. On
yet another dimension, therefore, the program became less successful as an innovation as it became more successful as a medical
school.

Today's Hopes for Tomorrow

The first four years of the new organization's existence witnessed many interesting and dramatic changes—both quantitative
and qualitative—in its structure and operations. As the school grew,
it became more conservative. The initial period of heady enthusiasm gave way to a period of negotiating the terms for continued existence. Administrators, staff, faculty, community physicians, and students all made extraordinary contributions to the
development of the school, particularly during its first two years of
existence. But the initial enthusiasm proved impossible to sustain
for a variety of reasons, and by the third year life at the school was
characterized by many of the same conflicts, jealousies, and problems that typify life in the school's more "mature" counterparts.
Altruistic orientations were replaced by instrumental orientations
as career imperatives began to intrude. Analytically, one might
argue that the emerging dominance of instrumental orientations at
the level of individual persons involved with the school was not only
inevitable but also a necessary condition for effectiveness. To the
extent that each participant was able to maximize his or her own
personal goals, the organization as a whole would be more effective
(Cummings, 1977). In any case, people began to think more in
terms of their own goals than of the school's future, and this shift
from a collective to an instrumental point of view reinforced many
of the dynamics that accompanied the shift from a personal to an
impersonal atmosphere within the school itself.

Our process research evaluation of the school continued on
a formal basis for four years. Since that time, a new development
has been unfolding in the school's biography that has already further complicated the evaluation of its success. In the back of the
dean's mind from the day he was hired was a vision of a full medical

school. Although he was committed to starting a school of basic sciences, he also hoped that one day he would preside over a full program. His entrepreneurial appetites were not satisfied with the creation of a basic sciences program alone.

It is simply not possible here to deal systematically with the implications of the launching of the clinical component of the school. The promise of such an addition has created a renewed sense of enthusiasm both in the school and in the local medical community. The present enthusiasm, however, is not comparable to that generated by the inauguration of the medical school itself. Although the new component is itself innovative, and although the dean has continued to exercise his considerable entrepreneurial skills in its evolution, the enthusiasm is tempered by a history of uneasy relations between the dean and his faculty, by a decidedly wait-and-see posture on the part of the local medical community, and by apprehension and resistance both in other parts of the university and in the state legislature. This development will add new dimensions to the evaluation of the success of the school—a fact that underlines the often evanescent nature of the evaluation criteria used.

Implications

The birth and early development of a new medical school cannot be considered to be typical or to embody the full range of patterns and possibilities present in the creation of organizations. Yet some of the dynamics are surely not idiosyncratic. The interaction between situational factors and the personal characteristics of the founder as a significant constraint on the shape of the early chapters of an organization's biography, the tension between innovation and institutionalization, and the transition from personal to impersonal and from collective to instrumental points of view— all these are themes that transcend any particular organizational setting.

Identification of general themes, of course, pushes one in the direction of elaborating general frameworks, but I will resist that temptation here. There may be differences in the process of creating nested organizations as opposed to freestanding and fully autonomous entities, public agencies as opposed to private organizations, organizational clones as opposed to innovative organizational forms, corporations as opposed to privately held enterprises. The inventory of possible influences on the process of creation is lengthy, and organizational researchers are only beginning to appreciate their range and complexity. In addition, there is an intricate web of institutional factors that need to be more fully integrated into theoretical perspectives on the creation of organizations. The role of environmental legislation, of tax incentives, of governmental regulation, and of patent law—to name just a few—are significant and should not be treated merely as a residual category of exogenous influences. As the process of creation captures the imagination of more researchers and more data are accumulated, the task of building more general frameworks will be facilitated.

Five more specific conclusions and implications emerge from our analysis of the early history of the new medical school. First, entrepreneurial activity played an important part in shaping its early development. There appeared to be conditions in both the general and specific environments that combined at a particular point in time to favor the birth of a new medical school at a particular site. The decision to establish the school was made by individuals in the specific environment who responded to these conditions, and their decision can be understood in macrostructural terms. The school's early development, however, cannot be understood without some knowledge of the ambitions, visions, strengths, and weaknesses of its first dean. He was able to take advantage of the conditions that gave birth to the school and use them to help create an innovative program of his own design. Whether one chooses to call him an entrepreneur, a leader, or a guru, the fact is that his personality, his dreams, his flaws, and his talents were largely responsible for the school's early structure and results. One reason that organizational sociologists typically play down the influence of particular individuals on organizational outcomes is that they study organizations that have already gone through the process of institutionalization—a process that is designed to remove as much uncertainty as possible from organizational life. Mechanisms have already been developed, in other words, to reduce the amount of influence particular individuals can have on outcomes, and it is not surprising that structural explanations then become more efficacious. But for the early stages of organizational development and perhaps for certain periods of relatively major transformations at other points in an organization's biography, a more catholic approach is necessary than the structuralist one supplies.

Second, the condition of being both new and different creates short-run opportunities and long-run problems for an organization because of the uncertainty that accompanies this combination of newness and differentness. And this uncertainty, which is both internal and external, itself adds another dimension to the problem of evaluating success. Inside the organization, individuals are in the process of negotiating new roles with new people in unfamiliar surroundings where performance criteria are often unclear. Externally, other organizations do not know what to expect from the focal organization and are trying to negotiate relations that will result in greater predictability for them. Where an organization is only new, that is, where it is essentially a replication of an existing organizational form, roles are familiar even if the surroundings and people are not. Performance rules and criteria for evaluation of performance are relatively clear, and the basic transition involves applying rules learned in one setting to another. Outside organizations know what to expect and know how—or believe they know how—to evaluate progress and performance. Thus, at the very least, studies of organizational birth and theories of organizational effectiveness should distinguish between the two kinds of cases.

Third, birth and early development, on the one hand, and institutionalization, on the other, are two relatively distinct chapters in the biography of an organization. When an organization is both new and different, as in the case of the medical school, the transition between the two stages is likely to be problematic, as those factors that lead to an organization's success as an innovation are not the same as those that lead to longer-run success. For the entrepreneur, the transition is likely to be particularly difficult because the institutionalization stage involves removing equivocality and reducing degrees of freedom, both of which are needed in an organization's infancy and both of which appear to be important entrepreneurial hallmarks. Although a public-sector organization has been discussed here, private-sector organizations no doubt go through similar stages. When an initially successful enterprise goes public to generate more funds for expansion, for example, there is bound to be a conservative effect on development because of the addition of investors with their concerns for predictability and stability in the decision-making process.

Fourth, the processes of initiation, innovation, and institutionalization are not the particular province of new organizations. Many organizations go through similar processes at various points in their biographies (Kimberly, 1980a), and thus many of the observations made about the new medical school may be applicable to existing organizations as well. What is different is that change in existing organizations has to come in the context of an established culture and an institutionalized set of norms, values, and procedures, whereas in the creation of new organizations, new cultures develop and new norms, values, and procedures are established. For organizational researchers, the interesting question is why some organizations, once born, are more susceptible to substantial transformations than others and what circumstances create the possibility for transformations to occur. It appears that it is during such transformations that particular individuals can exert unusually large amounts of influence over organizational outcomes; by contrast, in periods of relative stability, highly visible personal contributions are less likely.

Finally, an intensive, longitudinal research design was used to analyze the birth of the new school. The depth of understanding of organizational processes that results from this approach more than offsets costs due to questions about its external validity, and the substantive significance of this study is directly traceable to its longitudinal design. The limitations of cross-sectional research are all too apparent and have been discussed elsewhere (Kimberly, 1976a). But what is really challenging for the field is the observation that organizational birth—a phenomenon about which relatively little is known—may be an important constraint on later development and that birth, although important, is only one chapter in an organization's biography. These observations suggest an exciting new agenda of research and theory building. Systematic, in-depth, comparative analysis of the birth, life, and death of organizations should lead both to a clearer understanding of the complex nature of organizational success and to more dynamic perspectives on organizations than are currently available. Both would certainly be welcome.

3

Influence of Organizational Learning Styles on Early Development

Robert H. Miles
W. Alan Randolph

Although the creation and early development of organizations and of units within organizations involve complex, often nonroutine processes about which very little systematic evidence has been gathered, the failure rate of new settings is alarmingly high. It is difficult to accept, therefore, that we know practically nothing about the process of organizational learning in new settings, since it is reasonable to assume that this process is an important, if not the most important, link between organizational creation and maturity or failure. This chapter's purpose is to begin to understand how the process of organizational learning influences the creation and early development of organizations.

Creation and Early Development of Organizations

Recent comprehensive reviews of the literature on organizational design and adaptation (Starbuck, 1976; Miles, 1980) reveal a paucity of longitudinal research on the early development of organizations. To a disturbing extreme, the knowledge set forth in this literature was built upon static, cross-sectional research into chronologically mature organizations. Virtually no attempt has been made to examine how these organizations reached maturity or why others did not.

As a consequence, we know almost nothing about either the evolution of structures and processes or the patterns of learning and decision making that occur as organizations attempt to move from creation to maturity. Yet, one has the impression that the termination rate of new organizations is alarmingly high. Indeed, the author of *The Rise and Decline of Small Firms* has observed: "Infant mortality among new businesses is still a subject of almost complete ignorance. Virtually all we know is that most firms that die, die young. For example, in the United States the vast majority of business failures occur before firms are ten years old" (Boswell, 1973, p. 57). Thus, the development of knowledge about the creation and early development of organizations is important because of the substantial costs to society and to individual members and stakeholders that result from both ill-advised organizational creations and premature organizational terminations.

What is known, based on the few preliminary studies of organizational creation, is that choices made early in the development of organizations serve both to shape their enduring character and to constrain the range of options available to them in later stages of organizational life. Stinchcombe (1965), for example, has argued that the character and structure of an organization that are formed during its creation persist even when the context in which they were created has changed; and Kimberly (1975) has demonstrated this phenomenon of organizational "imprinting" in a longitudinal study of sheltered workshops. In addition, the case studies of organizational creation and early development by Simon (1963), Sarason (1972), and Kimberly (1979) have provided evidence of the constraining effect of early decisions on subsequent organizational behaviors and outcomes. Indeed, Kimberly found that initial decisions that led to early success in the founding of an innovative medical school were incompatible with its requirements for survival in the long run. He identified two general problems that new organizations must cope with: first, the problem of "getting off the ground"; and, second, the problem of "institutionalization" of effective organizational structures and processes. These problem situations are roughly analogous to what we will refer to as the stages of organizational infancy and maturation. Each presents the organization and its management with different requirements.

The stage of organizational infancy, particularly for organizations that are both new and different, is characterized by high uncertainty in decision making. The work to be done must be identified and assigned, and new roles and relationships must be negotiated and developed. Fundamental cause-effect relations among organizational structures, processes, behaviors, and outcomes must be discovered. Actual enactment of the new setting creates information that the organization uses to gradually convert nonroutine portions of the setting into routine activities. The organizational structure, as well as the roles and tasks it controls, gradually takes form. Rules and policies are elaborated to cover issues that become better understood. Belief systems emerge to govern decision making and behaviors.

Successful passage through the creation phase is evidenced by the institutionalization of structures and processes that the organization has discovered "work." This does not imply that the chosen structures and processes are the most effective or, indeed, that the organization has consciously explored all the available alternatives. Instead, it is just as likely that in most new and different settings, the structures and processes of the organizations emerge by default, and this condition is even more likely when the enterprises are deprived of definitive (i.e., objective, comparative, and timely) feedback about their performance. Finally, institutionalization does not necessarily imply movement away from an organic form and toward a mechanistic one, though one can imagine that this may be the case in the development of a majority of new organizations. Institutionalization does imply that the organizational form that key decision makers have become comfortable with will probably assume a more consistent and enduring character.

Organizational Learning

Organizational stages of infancy and maturity are joined, if at all, by the process of organizational learning. But very little is known about (1) how new organizations learn to develop and survive and (2) what knowledge they acquire as a result. Definitions of organizational learning and knowledge are as scarce as the studies dealing with them. Therefore, if progress is to be made in addressing the issue of premature organizational termination, preliminary theoretical and empirical work on the subject of learning within new organizations will be required. The purpose of this chapter is to initiate this preliminary work and to stimulate others to pursue this line of inquiry in more depth and with broader scope in their field studies of organizational creation, development, and adaptation.

The few relevant studies that have been reported may be sorted into categories based on the aspect of organizational learning that each investigated, as shown in Figure 1. First, these studies may be categorized in terms of their focus on *whether* learning occurs, *how* learning occurs, or *what* learning occurs. In addition, the evidence used to demonstrate one or more of these aspects of organizational learning may usually be sorted into one of three categories: *outcome* data, *behavioral* data, and *cognitive* data.

Finally, these inquiries into organizational learning may be distinguished on the bases of the *type* of learning that occurs (for example, general or specific) and the organizational *setting* in which learning takes place (for example, chronologically mature organizations versus nascent organizations). Some studies have focused on specific types of organizational learning, as in McKenney's (1978) study of learning associated with the introduction of new technology into the U.S. Forest Service and Duncan's (1974) investigation of the decision-making structures within organizational subunits. In contrast, Simon's (1963) account of the birth and early

Outcome Evidence ←	Behavioral Evidence →	Cognitive Evidence
Aspect of Organizational Learning Investigated		
Whether learning occurs	How learning occurs	What learning occurs

(row labels on left: Type of Organizational Learning Investigated — General learning / Specific learning)

	Whether learning occurs	How learning occurs	What learning occurs
General learning			
Specific learning			

Source: Reprinted by permission from Miles and Randolph (1979a).

Figure 1. A Typology for the Study of Organizational Learning

development of the Economic Cooperation Administration provides some general insight into how one organization worked through the processes of identifying its initial domain and developing its initial strategy.

Few studies have been comprehensive even in the sense of considering aspects of each component found in this rough typology of organizational learning. For example, none of the studies of *organizational* learning has measured *what* learning occurs from a cognitive point of view. Several, it is true, have been able to demonstrate—by pointing to performance mastery or behavioral change—that learning *did* occur, and some have been able to distill from retrospective interviews or process observation certain conditions that related to *how* organizations learned. But no study has tracked all three aspects of learning during the creation and early development of organizations.

Other unanswered questions in the study of organizational learning include: Who does and should do the learning on behalf of the organization? What are the similarities and differences between individual and organizational learning (Duncan, 1974; Cangelosi and Dill, 1965)? What are the consequences of different approaches to organizational learning? And what are the conditions necessary for organizational learning to occur? Although the preliminary studies have touched on some of these issues, only the last question has been systematically investigated.

Conditions for Organizational Learning. The preliminary literature on organizational learning reveals only one consistent finding: the stress produced by negative performance feedback is an important condition for organizational learning. For instance, studies of decision making in governmental administration, international economic development, and research and engineering programs led Hirschman and Lindblom (1962) to conclude that organizational learning occurs in response to immediate problems, imbalances, and difficulties much more than it does in response to deliberate planning. They argue that the intraorganizational conflicts and tensions created by these immediate problems serve a constructive function in stimulating search behaviors that lead to organizational learning.

An early study of a business firm simulation, based on process observation (Cangelosi and Dill, 1965), resulted in similar conclusions. The researchers found that players eschewed prior planning and strategy formulation in favor of immediate task activities. However, early decisions that produced negative firm outcomes, such as a decline in profits or market share or an increase in operating costs, were likely to be abandoned or quickly modified. They concluded: "Failure, we agree, leads to change. The consequences of success, we argue, are less clear" (p. 196). McKenney (1978), however, takes a more catholic view of the sources of organizational learning on the basis of his longitudinal study of the U.S Forest Service. In addition to recognizing what he refers to as "reasonable" stress as a primary stimulus to organizational learning, he lists three other important stimuli: the availability of organizational slack, the ability to reflect upon the ongoing operations of the enterprise, and "a leader's catalytic action that both facilitates and legitimizes change."

Combining the results of these studies, we can identify at least three primary conditions for organizational learning: (1) reasonable stress induced by negative performance feedback, (2) the catalytic leadership of powerful organizational members, and (3) the creation of slack for organizational reflection and problem solving. It seems reasonable to assume that the first two conditions may on occasion operate independently to stimulate organizational learning. However, the creation of slack will be necessary to accomplish the learning stimulated by either or both of the other conditions.

Definitions. After Simon (1963), *organizational learning* may be defined as a *process* in which growing insights and successful restructurings of organizational problems by the individuals dealing with them reflect themselves in the structural elements and outcomes of the organization itself. This definition is consistent with one developed by Argyris and Schön (1978), who assert that organizational learning is the testing and restructuring of organizational theories-in-use.

The *content* produced by this learning process, or *organizational knowledge,* may be defined as the patterns of cognitive association that develop among the context, structures, processes, and outcomes of a membership's organizational experience. These definitions suggest that evidence in the form of changes in organizational structures, processes, and outcomes will be more appropriate for the analysis of whether and how *learning* has occurred, whereas cognitive evidence will be better suited to the task of ascertaining the *content,* or knowledge, that a learning process produces.

Approaches to Organizational Learning: Two Archetypes

Among the various approaches to learning that organizations may choose are two extremes. The first is organizational learning by *enactment,* the other is organizational learning by *proaction.* It would be rare, indeed, to find new organizations relying exclusively on either learning approach. In virtually all conceivable instances of organizational creation and development, some mixture of the two will be found. Nevertheless, it is important, as a preliminary step in understanding the influence of learning on the creation and early development of organizations, to discover what kinds of effects these two archetypical approaches are likely to generate for organizations and their members.

Enactive Approach. Some of the content and process of organizational learning, but certainly not all of it, will be derived from the activity of organizational enactment (Weick, 1969), which asserts that understanding follows behavior. Weick argues that much organizational learning occurs during the creation and early development of the new setting. It is only then that alternative behaviors and structures are tested against the real, as opposed to the hypothetical, contingencies surrounding the new organization.

This learning through enactment at the organizational level is fraught with even more difficulties than learning at the individual level. Learning is more difficult for organizations because it is a function of the learning of a collection of individuals, and the differences that exist among individuals and among their immediate work settings increase the error component in the organizational learning equation. Moreover, what a collectivity learns about making its organization more effective depends not only on the accuracy of reinforcing feedback but also on the repertoire from which operant behaviors are chosen (Skinner, 1953). Most organizations, for example, receive something less than definitive performance feedback, and different organizations and dominant coalitions within them may have different behaviors at their command to cope with, and test against, similar situations. In addition, members may associate organizational behavior with outcomes in erroneous ways, thereby developing inaccurate conceptions of cause-effect relations—what Skinner refers to as "superstitious learning."

Proactive Approach. But organizational learning does not depend solely on the enactment process. Most new organizations are different in only certain respects; therefore, much of the knowledge acquired by the founding members in other organizational settings will be relevant for the new setting. Moreover, few new organizations are afforded the slack to experiment freely with alternative behaviors and forms. They are accountable in varying degrees for the outcomes they are expected to generate. Therefore, some learning always does, indeed should, precede the organizational creation process. Usually this takes the form of advance planning in which individuals attempt to anticipate what form and direction the new organization will take and the problems and opportunities that it will likely encounter. In many instances, this proactive kind of learning is generated from the previous organizational experiences of the planning group, its consultants, and whatever organizational literature the group has at its disposal.

The important question of which approach should, or can, dominate the learning mix in the creation of a particular organization is not a moot one, but it can only be responded to in general terms given our current understanding of organizational creations. One general response is that the proactive approach to initial organizational learning will probably be somewhat less helpful than the enactive approach in the creation of organizational settings that are both new *and different*. In these settings, more of the learning will have to take place through the process of enactment because less of the initial members' previous experience and of the knowledge they can extract from consultants and the body of general knowledge on organizations will be relevant for their experience in creating an innovative setting. We will return to the question of the appropriate mix of learning approaches, but first it is important to understand what effects each has when employed almost exclusively in the creation of organizations. A recent study of organizational learning during the creation and early development of simulated organizations (Miles and Randolph, 1979a) provides some insights into the effects of these archetypical approaches.

Learning in Simulated Organizations

The study of simulated organizations was an attempt to understand how the form and content of organizational learning influence the speed and success of early organizational development. In order to accomplish this research objective, we were required to carefully track the creation and early development of organizations that differed initially only in the organizing choices—and consequently the primary learning approaches—that would govern their behaviors. Simulated organizations were well suited to this requirement.

We expected to find that early organizing choices would result in different learning and development patterns. Put another way, we expected to demonstrate that knowledge of an organization's history or biography, particularly of its approach to learning during and immediately following its creation, would be essential to explain its form, its belief system, and the outcomes it achieved as it attempted to move toward maturity. On a more specific level, we sought to provide some insight into all three aspects of general organizational learning. Organizational learning was therefore operationalized in three ways. The first way was by changes in organizational outcomes toward ideal states—an indicator of *whether* learning had occurred. The second was by the patterns of association comprising the belief system an organizational membership forms among its perceptions of important organizational characteristics and outcomes—a measure of learning *content* or knowledge. The third way involved process observation of organizational behaviors to understand *how* learning occurred.

Research Design and Setting

The initial settings were created through use of *The Organization Game* (Miles and Randolph, 1979b). These initial settings were both new and in some respects different for the public-sector managers and professionals who were assigned randomly to one of two simulated organizations as part of a four-week management development program. The fundamental objective of this game is to allow participants to build their own organization. Organization members, not computers as in other simulations, do the work and build the organization. (See the instructor's manual for *The Organization Game* and refer to Randolph and Miles, 1979a, for more details on the structure and use of this simulated organization.)

The Organization Game creates a minimal organization structure for beginning play. This initial structure assigns participants to one of four physically separated divisions, each having its unique complement of eight operating units. These basic units include three line or service delivery units and five staff units. Thus, the physical separation and structural variety among the four organizational divisions combine to form a highly differentiated beginning organization.

To round out the minimal beginning structure, only the unit heads and a few designated controllers of certain resources are assigned before the simulation begins. Therefore, participants must decide how to staff the organization and what structures and processes to implement in order to achieve an effective system for the division and coordination of work. In addition, they must develop processes for organizational learning and development and be prepared to adapt to internal and external forces for change.

Play unfolded for each of our two simulated organizations as a series of seventy-five-minute sessions that gradually tapered to forty-five-minute sessions; they were run in marathon fashion over a one and one-half day period. Each session was followed by a fifteen-minute break period during which organization members completed survey cards, and simulation coordinators calculated the performance of their organizations. Comparative performance feedback was delivered to both organizations at the beginning of the subsequent session of play. In all, six sessions were run for each organization, followed by a one-hour debriefing within each organization and a two-hour comparative discussion involving members of both organizations.

Both organizations began with the same minimal structure and experienced identical conditions throughout the simulation. Each organization received session-by-session performance feedback about its own effectiveness and that of the other organization. The survey data that were collected after each session of play but before performance feedback for the previous session were not reported until the end of the simulation, when they were given in the form of trends in means on selected member perceptions. (See Miles and Randolph, 1979a for more details on the design of the study and the instruments employed.)

The development of organizational processes and outcomes was tracked by using the self-reports of members who completed surveys during the breaks between playing sessions. Members were asked to describe features of their organization and of their experiences in it through use of seven-point Likert rating scales. The following member perceptions were measured: (1) task uncertainty, (2) organizational differentiation and integration, (3) unit, divisional, and organizational teamwork, (4) organizational conflict, and (5) individual, unit, divisional, and organizational effectiveness. In addition, while the simulation was being conducted, each coordinator was free to roam among the units and divisions of his organization. This made it possible to corroborate the perceptual indicators of structures and processes by means of direct observation.

Evidence of Movement from Organizational Infancy to Maturity.
Evidence of movement in the two organizations from infancy to maturity was demonstrated in two ways. First, both organizations mastered the objective performance situation, though at different rates of progress. Second, the process of institutionalization was evidenced by the patterns of adjacent-session, test-retest reliabilities that emerged in the perceptions of members during the early development sequences. Because of the developing nature of the organizations, few statistically significant test-retest reliabilities between adjacent-waves were expected or found during the early period of development, when both organizations were undergoing substantial change and development. However, as expected, the adjacent-wave reliabilities began to emerge in strength with organizational maturity.* This consistent pattern across virtually all measures of member perceptions reflects a gradual "firming up" of organizational form and processes, indicating that by the last sessions of play the process of institutionalization was well underway in both organizations.

Results

Process observation revealed that each of the two organizations adopted one of the two extreme approaches to organizational learning. These dramatic differences occurred even though both

---

*For instance, of the twenty-two reliability coefficients for all eleven measures from both organizations, calculated for each adjacent-wave pair, only eight were statistically significant between sessions one and two; however, between the last two playing sessions twenty became statistically significant (Miles and Randolph, 1979a).

organizations were virtually identical at creation. They shared the
same minimal structure and set of rules, the same allocation of
resources, and the same performance expectations. They were assigned identical roles and tasks. Their memberships were drawn
randomly from a pool of experienced managers and professionals.
They were subjected to the same conditions, and they received
identical, unequivocal feedback regarding the actual performance
of *both* organizations. One might then ask, Why the large difference
in approaches to organizational learning?

The answer came from both process observation and the
postsimulation debriefing. Although participants were assigned
randomly to the organizations, role assignments were made initially
for the unit heads and certain resource controllers. It was expected
that the initial dominant coalition would be most likely to emerge
from this core group. In one organization, certain individuals who
had prepared diligently for the simulation found themselves in
these initial power positions. Their positional power was bolstered
by the expert influence they brought with them to the organizational setting. We were not surprised, therefore, to observe that
these individuals quickly assumed the status of an organization-
wide management group.

All had carefully studied the underlying structure of the
simulation in preparation for play, and they wasted no time in
convincing others that they understood the basic cause-effect linkages that would guarantee organizational success. This small coalition persuaded other members of the organization that they should
begin by planning and coordinating, not by trying to perform as
yet. As a result of this early decision, resources in the coalition-
driven organization during the first session of play were expended
not for the purchase of raw materials to be used in production, but
for the maintenance of the organization during the first session,
when production (enactment) was subordinated to planning and
organizing (proaction). Thus, the first organization adopted a
proactive approach to organizational learning during its formation,
and this choice eventually led to very different organizational
learning and performance outcomes from those in the comparison
organization.

The other organization pursued an almost exclusively *enactive approach* to organizational learning during much of its early development. No dominant coalition of "experts" emerged during the first few sessions of play to plan and coordinate the overall organizational effort. In contrast, members of this organization plunged directly into the tasks assigned to their immediate work units. The decisions to embark on these tasks were made within each division, without preliminary planning or consultation with the other parts of the organization.

In addition, each "part" of the organization followed the narrow, minimal role assigned to it in the simulation manual. An organization-wide management group did not begin to form until late in the third session. The primary stimulus to this development was the startling difference in the performance of the two organizations—a difference strongly favoring the proactive organization—that members of the enactive organization discovered after the first session of play. Conflict erupted within the low-performing organization and was not brought under control until session four, when a dominant coalition representing all four divisions emerged.

Thus, by researcher luck, our two archetypical approaches to learning occurred within organizations created under identical simulated conditions and running simultaneously. The subsequent differences that emerged in the performances and belief systems of the two organizations demonstrate the strong imprint that key individuals can have on both the creation and early development of organizations—a fact almost completely ignored in the static, structuralist perspective on organizations that enjoys popularity in the current literature.

Organizational Learning and Development: Trend Analyses. Two sets of data provided insight into the influence of learning approaches on the early development of both organizations. The first included data on the actual performance achieved by each organization measured against game criteria—an indicator of mastery of the performance situation or of whether learning occurred. The second consisted of the perceptions of members concerning their organization's processes and outcomes.

Organizational learning was demonstrated by the eventual mastery of the performance situation by the two organizations. As shown in Figure 2, both ended the simulation with positively sloped performance curves and at levels above the base performance level. Moreover, they achieved these performance increases despite the fact that the duration of the playing sessions was reduced by 40 percent during the developmental sequence. More important,

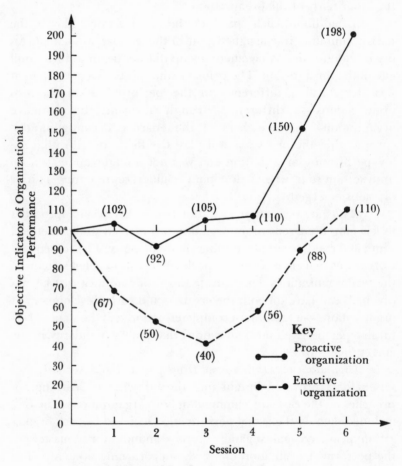

ᵃBase performance level.

Figure 2. Objective Performance Results for the Proactive and Enactive Organizations

however, for our present purposes is that the initial approaches to organizational learning led to different performance returns and different organizational belief systems during the early development of our two settings.

We expected that with identical initial organizations, the one that adopted the proactive approach, emphasizing advance planning and coordination, would achieve a higher initial level of performance, and we were not disappointed by the early performance returns. After all, many of the underlying simulation relationships could be gleaned from the player's manual through diligent preparation. As shown in Figure 2, however, large performance differences, favoring the proactive organization, not only emerged after the initial playing session but persisted throughout the early development sequence.

Because first-session performance results were not announced until the beginning of the subsequent session, the survey results collected during the break between sessions were not contaminated by the effects of comparative performance feedback. The organizational trends and differences that emerged in these means are shown in Table 1 for both the first session and all subsequent sessions.

The most remarkable difference between the infant organizations, and the only difference that reached a statistically significant level in the first session, was in the degree of integration that members perceived their organizations had achieved. Members of the proactive organization perceived greater integration among their divisions than did their counterparts in the enactive organization. Thus, the difference between the initial organizing activities observed by the simulation coordinators during the first session was corroborated by the perceptions of the organizations' members. In the absence of definitive, comparative performance feedback, however, members of both organizations perceived no differences in the effectiveness of their organizations or the units and divisions within them and no differences in the degree of organizational differentiation, teamwork, or conflict. But differences in many of these perceptions emerged in session two after it had become obvious to members that there were large, objective differences in the early performances of their organizations.

Table 1. Differences and Trends in Member Perceptions

Member Perceptions
Task Uncertainty

Organization	Session:	1	2	3	4	5	6	Slope	Trend
Proactive		4.3	3.1	2.2	1.5	1.2	1.0	Decreasing	Quadratic[b]
Enactive		3.5	3.8	2.1	1.2	1.2	1.1	Decreasing	Cubic[b]
Difference		0.8	-0.7	0.1	0.3	0.0	-0.1		

Structural Differentiation

	Session:	1	2	3	4	5	6	Slope	Trend
Proactive		3.5	3.2	2.3	1.8	1.3	1.2	Decreasing	Linear[b]
Enactive		3.6	4.0	3.0	1.6	1.5	1.4	Decreasing	Cubic[b]
Difference		-0.1	-0.8	-0.7	0.2	-0.2	-0.2		

Structural Integration

	Session:	1	2	3	4	5	6	Slope	Trend
Proactive		4.8	4.7	5.0	5.7	5.5	5.7	Increasing	Linear[b]
Enactive		3.8	3.6	4.3	6.1	6.1	5.3	Increasing	Cubic[b]
Difference		1.0[a]	1.1[a]	0.7	-0.4	-0.6	0.4		

Experienced Organizational Conflict

	Session:	1	2	3	4	5	6	Slope	Trend
Proactive		2.6	2.0	1.7	1.7	1.7	1.3	Decreasing	Linear[b]
Enactive		3.0	3.9	3.0	2.2	1.5	1.0	Decreasing	Cubic[b]
Difference		-0.4	-1.9[a]	-1.3[a]	-0.5	0.2	0.3		

Unit Teamwork

	Session: 1	2	3	4	5	6	Slope	Trend
Proactive	5.3	6.3	6.5	6.6	6.8	6.9	Increasing	Quadratic[b]
Enactive	5.8	5.0	6.4	6.8	6.8	7.0	Increasing	Cubic[b]
Difference	−0.5	1.3[a]	0.1	−0.2	0.0	−0.1		

Divisional Teamwork

	Session: 1	2	3	4	5	6	Slope	Trend
Proactive	5.2	5.9	6.2	6.7	6.7	6.8	Increasing	Quadratic[b]
Enactive	5.5	4.7	6.1	6.7	6.9	7.0	Increasing	Cubic[b]
Difference	−0.3	1.2[a]	0.1	0.0	−0.2	−0.2		

Organizational Teamwork

	Session: 1	2	3	4	5	6	Slope	Trend
Proactive	4.5	5.3	5.7	6.5	6.5	6.8	Increasing	Linear[b]
Enactive	4.7	4.3	5.3	6.2	6.7	7.0	Increasing	Cubic[b]
Difference	−0.2	1.0[a]	0.4	0.3	−0.2	−0.2		

Perceived Individual Effectiveness

	Session: 1	2	3	4	5	6	Slope	Trend
Proactive	3.6	5.0	5.5	6.3	6.3	6.8	Increasing	Quadratic[b]
Enactive	4.3	3.7	5.4	6.5	6.6	6.8	Increasing	Cubic[b]
Difference	−0.7	1.3[a]	0.1	−0.2	−0.3	0.0		

Table 1. Differences and Trends in Member Perceptions (Continued)

	Session:	1	2	3	4	5	6	Slope	Trend
				Unit Effectiveness					
Proactive		4.1	5.6	5.9	6.6	6.7	6.9	Increasing	Quadratic[b]
Enactive		4.2	3.9	5.4	6.6	6.7	7.0	Increasing	Cubic[b]
Difference		-0.1	1.7[a]	0.5	0.0	0.0	-0.1		
				Divisional Effectiveness					
	Session:	1	2	3	4	5	6	Slope	Trend
Proactive		3.8	5.5	5.9	6.4	6.7	6.9	Increasing	Quadratic[b]
Enactive		4.1	3.5	5.5	6.5	6.7	6.8	Increasing	Cubic[b]
Difference		-0.3	2.0[a]	0.4	-0.1	0.0	0.1		
				Organizational Effectiveness					
	Session:	1	2	3	4	5	6	Slope	Trend
Proactive		3.6	5.1	5.5	6.5	6.7	6.8	Increasing	Quadratic[b]
Enactive		3.6	2.8	5.0	6.4	6.6	6.8	Increasing	Cubic[b]
Difference		0.0	2.3[a]	0.5	0.1	0.1	0.0		

[a]T-test of differences in means (two-tailed) is significant at p .05 (Enactive organization N = 23; Proactive organization N = 22)
[b]Test of indicated trend is significant at p .05.

In the proactive organization, early performance success led to a confirmation of the dominant coalition. The coalition's strategy had paid off, and its ability to master the performance setting was recognized by the membership. As a consequence, an uninterrupted (linear or quadratic) trend toward favorable end states emerged for all member perceptions over the remainder of the early development sequence. The categories of "task uncertainty," "experienced organizational conflict," and "perceived structural differentiation" (Table 1) all approached the minimum scale limit during the mature end of the developmental episode. Over the same developmental sequence, members of the proactive organization believed their organization had achieved progressively more integration, teamwork, and effectiveness. The progress of early development in the enactive organization, however, was quite different. In terms of the trends for member perceptions (all cubic in form), matters became worse, beginning in session two, before they became better.

Although the only organizational difference separating member perceptions during session one was degree of integration, many differences emerged in session two, all favoring the proactive organization. In the enactive organization, conflict erupted and was not brought under control until late in the developmental sequence, that is, during session four. Many rival theories about how to make the organization more effective emerged, but none of their sponsors had enough strength or evidence to prevail. Thus, the organizational difference in integration persisted and during session two was accompanied by differences in member perceptions of conflict, teamwork, and both organizational and individual effectiveness. In the absence of a dominant coalition, more independent actions and partial solutions were pursued before members of the enactive organization brought actual performance under control.

It was not until session four that a dominant coalition, composed of representatives from each division, emerged in the enactive organization. This session was the first in which no organizational differences existed in member perceptions and in which the performance of the enactive organization took a positive turn. Moreover, from this point on, performance increased steadily for both organizations, and the absence of organizational differences in mean perceptions persisted throughout the early development sequence.

In summary, the comparative trend analyses revealed that learning had occurred within both organizations, but at different rates and by different processes. Moreover, the organization adopting the proactive approach to learning outperformed the one opting for learning by enactment during the early developmental episode. From a developmental perspective, both organizations progressed from uncertainty and disorganization to relative certainty and organization, although the proactive group did so more quickly. These results made it evident that members of the dominant coalition of the high-performing organization had correctly interpreted the high initial uncertainty and had developed the means for assuring organizational coordination and direction as well as for anticipating problems and opportunities. Members of the low-performing organization had, in contrast, embarked on a course that quickly forced them into a reactive mode in which problems and opportunities were discovered not through anticipatory planning but through negative performance feedback and the member disagreements and interunit conflict it generated.

By the last two sessions of performance, both organizations had developed a workable division of labor and a system for control and coordination; both possessed a recognized organization-wide management group; and both had staffed the required roles with individuals capable of performing them. Toward the end of the developmental sequence, uncertainty and conflict were at a minimum in both organizations, which were in fact experiencing increasing success in their overall performance. These trends provided validity for the identification of infant and mature organizational stages of development and indicated that organizational learning had occurred. They did not, however, tell us much about *what* had been learned by members of each organization.

Organizational Knowledge: Patterns of Association

The kind of organizational knowledge gained was inferred from the patterns of association that emerged among members' perceptions of organizational processes and outcomes. These patterns were operationalized by the strength and direction of correlations among member perceptions at different points in the early development of their organizations. An assumption of the measurement approach we chose was that statistical associations approximate the cognitive associations formed by members as their organizational experience increases. Correlational associations do not necessarily correspond to mental associations, but they are likely to give us a first approximation of what the latter will be. From the total set of perceptual measures, we distilled a set of general propositions. We anticipated that those correlational associations generally regarded as axiomatic in chronologically mature organizations that have been the major focus of contemporary organizational research would be nonexistent in infant organizations. These associations would have to be learned as members gained experience with their new setting.

As each setting matured, enactment would lead to the creation of organizational knowledge, that is, to the emergence and strengthening of a belief system within an organizational membership. Based on this belief system, the institutionalization of organizational processes could proceed. What we expected to find, therefore, was a gradual emergence in the direction and strength of the patterns of association among member perceptions as their organization's biography unfolded. Beliefs were examined regarding the relationships among (1) individual and organizational effectiveness, (2) teamwork and organizational effectiveness, and (3) organizational structure and conflict. Changes in these patterns of association between the infant and mature stages of both simulated organizations are summarized in Table 2.

Individual and Organizational Effectiveness. First, we anticipated that members would increasingly identify themselves with the organization as their experience grew. In particular, we expected that members' perceptions of their own effectiveness would become associated with the beliefs they held about the effectiveness of (1) their immediate work unit, (2) the division in which their unit was located, and (3) the organization as a whole. The results, summarized in Table 2 and displayed in Figure 3, were confirming only for members of the low-performing (the enacting) organization. That is, the patterns of Pearson product-moment correlations between these predicted relationships of individual and organiza-

Table 2. The Development of Organizational Knowledge: Patterns of Association in Proactive and Enactive Organizations

Components of Belief System	Proactive Organization			Enactive Organization		
	Infant Stage[a] →	Mature Stage	Significant Change?	Infant Stage →	Mature Stage	Significant Change?
Individual Effectiveness ←+→ Unit Effectiveness	++	None	(Yes)[b]	++	+++	Yes
Individual Effectiveness ←+→ Division Effectiveness	None	None	No	++	+++	Yes
Individual Effectiveness ←+→ Organization Effectiveness	None	None	No	++	+++	Yes
Differentiation ←+→ Conflict	−	None	No	None	+	Yes
Integration ←−→ Conflict	None	None	No	−	− −	No
Unit Teamwork ←+→ Organization Effectiveness	++	None	No	None	+++	Yes
Division Teamwork ←+→ Organization Effectiveness	++	++	No	None	+++	Yes
Organization Teamwork ←+→ Organization Effectiveness	+	++	No	++	+++	Yes

Note: The following symbols summarize the association patterns formed by members between variable pairs at the designated stage of organizational development:

None: No significant correlation
+++: High positive correlation ($r > .75$)
++: Moderate positive correlation ($.50 < r \leq .75$)
+: Weak positive correlation ($.30 < r \leq .50$)
− − −: High negative correlation ($r < -.75$)
− −: Moderate negative correlation ($-.75 \leq r < -.50$)
−: Weak negative correlation ($-.50 \leq r < -.30$)

[a] Stages of organizational development: Infant stage (Session 1); Mature stage (Session 5).

[b] Although this two-tail test of difference in correlation coefficients was significant, the direction of change was opposite that predicted for a maturing organization.

Source: Miles and Randolph (1979a).

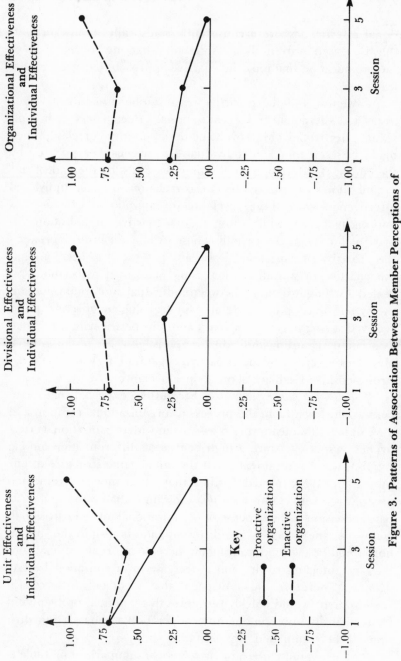

Figure 3. Patterns of Association Between Member Perceptions of
Dimensions of Effectiveness

tional effectiveness were consistently statistically significant, and they increased in strength of association—but only for members of the organization that took the enactive approach to organizational learning.

Members of the proactive organization, in contrast, never associated divisional and organizational effectiveness with individual effectiveness. Moreover, the initial positive correlation they made between unit and individual effectiveness disappeared by the end of the developmental sequence. Thus, by the end of this organization's early development, correlations between individual effectiveness and three levels of organizational effectiveness approached zero, while those in the enactive organization approached unity (1.00) as a limit. These striking differences between the proactive organization (decreasing pattern of association) and the enactive organization (increasing pattern of association) revealed a stronger bonding between individual and organization in the system that opted by default for learning by enactment and received strong negative feedback about its performance. No such association regarding individual responsibility for organizational outcomes emerged in the proactive organization, which received strong positive feedback about its performance.

Teamwork and Effectiveness. Second, we expected that members would learn from the process of organizational creation and development that teamwork is associated with organizational effectiveness, especially since a high degree of differentiation among subunits was a central feature of the initial game structure of our simulation. We expected further that, if members became too preoccupied with teamwork *within* their immediate work unit or its parent division at the expense of organizational (or interdivisional) teamwork, the effects of the differentiation built into the simulation would be elevated, causing an increase in organizational conflict and interunit rivalry and a decrease in organizational effectiveness. Therefore, we anticipated that members of successful organizations would quickly recognize this potential problem and focus their attention on building cooperation among all four divisions of their simulated organization.

The overall pattern of correlations, summarized in Table 2, between member perceptions of unit, divisional, and organizational teamwork, on the one hand, and organizational effectiveness, on the other, again revealed wide differences between the proactive and enactive organizations. For members of the proactive organization, unit teamwork was associated with organizational effectiveness only for session one; thereafter, no association between these two variables occurred. The patterns of association between teamwork at divisional and organizational levels and organizational effectiveness remained relatively constant and moderately positive throughout the developmental sequence. In contrast, all three correlations for teamwork effectiveness increased in strength over time in the enactive organization, and all approached unity (1.00) by the end of session five. No associations between unit or divisional teamwork and organizational effectiveness were made during the first three rounds of play in the enactive organization.

These patterns of association over time once more revealed very strong learning effects in the enactive organization. Indeed, in terms of divisional and organizational teamwork, it took the low-performing enactive organization several sessions to discover what the high-performing proactive organization knew by the end of session one.

Organizational Structure and Conflict. Third, we expected that organizational learning would result in positive associations between structural differentiation and conflict and in negative associations between structural integration and conflict. However, by the end of the developmental sequence, these elements of the belief system were present only within the membership of the enactive organization. Thus, throughout the developmental sequence, members of the proactive organization exhibited no correlation between organizational integration and conflict. In contrast, members of the enactive organization exhibited negative correlations between these variables—correlations that gained strength over the developmental episode.

Members of the enactive organization did not associate differentiation with conflict until the last stage of organizational development. At that point, the two variables became positively correlated. In contrast, a negative correlation between differentiation and conflict occurred after session one in the proactive organization, but this association disappeared by the middle of the organiza-

tional development sequence. Thus, once again members of the
organization receiving negative performance feedback achieved a
pattern of association that one would predict from the literature on
mature organizations, whereas no connection between structural
differentiation or integration and conflict existed in the proactive
organization receiving positive performance feedback.

Organizational Knowledge: How Much and How Well? Organizational knowledge, as operationalized by the emerging patterns of
perceptual associations, was quite different for our two organizations. Moreover, the emergent belief systems appeared to be influenced substantially by very early events in the biography of each
organization. This observation was reinforced by the fact that no
significant organizational differences in the perceptual means
existed during the last half of the developmental sequence — a time
when organizational differences in strength had assumed their
greatest magnitudes and the direction of many patterns of association among member perceptions was most pronounced.

Changes in these patterns of association between infant and
mature stages of organizational development are summarized in
Table 2. The most obvious difference between the two organizations is that the belief system was relatively stable for the proactive
organization over its early development while the belief system
within the enactive organization underwent dramatic change. Only
one of the eight relationships changed significantly in the proactive
organization, and this change was in the opposite direction from
what we would normally expect in an effective, chronologically
mature organization. In contrast, seven of the eight pairwise relationships changed significantly in the enactive organization, and
the one that did not reach this magnitude of change exhibited a
trend toward the expected mature state. Moreover, as demonstrated by the strength of correlations in session five, all eight expected relationships emerged in the mature enactive organization.
Together, these relative changes in the strength and direction of
perceptual patterns of association revealed that a much stronger
bonding between individual and organization, between teamwork
and effectiveness, and between structure and conflict evolved within the belief system of the enactive organization's membership.

Did one organization, therefore, learn "more" or "better"

than the other? A loaded question, but one for which we were able to venture tentative answers:

First, of the eight predicted relationships given in Table 2, only two emerged as statistically significant in the mature, proactive organization. In contrast, all eight assumed a directionality and strength in the enactive organization that are consistent with what we expected from the literature on chronologically mature organizations. Thus, the enactive organization receiving early negative performance feedback appears to have learned "better" than the comparison organization, at least insofar as the belief systems that emerged with their respective memberships are concerned.

Second, we were able to estimate how much learning took place in each organization by examining the amount of cognitive restructuring that took place within their memberships over the early developmental sequence. In general, the enactive organization exhibited the greatest amount of cognitive restructuring during the simulation. For example, as shown in Table 2, none of the pairwise relationships changed in the expected direction as the proactive organization moved from infancy to maturity. During the same interval, however, seven of the eight patterns of association changed significantly within the enactive organization. When both direction and magnitude of change were combined, the average change in all eight correlations toward mature organizational ideal states was +.43 in the enactive organization, indicating strong cognitive restructuring among the members in the direction of the mature ideal. The same net directional change in correlations within the proactive organization was −.23, indicating movement away from the mature ideal. Together, therefore, these results provide some basis, although a very tentative one, for suggesting that the general membership of the enactive organization learned both "more" and "better" than did its counterpart in the proactive organization.

The cognitive data reveal that the belief system in currency among members of the enactive organization during the final sessions of play was characterized by (1) a strong bonding between individual and organization, with very high positive associations between the individual's own effectiveness and that of his unit, division, and organization; (2) a strong positive association between teamwork, particularly at divisional and organizational levels, and organizational success; and (3) a recognition that structural differentiation was associated positively with organizational conflict and that structural integration was associated negatively with organizational conflict.

The belief system produced by the proactive approach to learning differed considerably, however, from the one that emerged from the enactive approach. The members of the proactive organization never associated their own effectiveness with the effectiveness of their division or organization. Moreover, the very early association they made between individual effectiveness and that of their immediate work unit quickly extinguished with organizational experience. In addition, although they did associate structural differentiation with organizational conflict during the infant stage, neither differentiation nor integration was associated with conflict by the time the proactive organization approached its mature stage. Indeed, the only portion of the emergent belief system in this organization that was congruent with the mature organizational ideal was in the associations its members maintained between divisional and organizational teamwork, on the one hand, and organizational effectiveness, on the other.

In summary, more cognitive restructuring, or learning, occurred within the enactive than the proactive organization. But, obviously, the organization pursuing the purely enactive approach had more to learn. More important, therefore, is that the knowledge generated by the enactive approach was more congruent with what one would expect in a successful, mature organization than was the knowledge produced by the other approach. The implications of these differences are not trivial for those seeking to understand and manage not only the creation and early development of organizations but also the subsequent stages of organizational life. It is to these implications that we now turn in closing this chapter.

Effects of Early Choices

The most obvious implication of our simulation study is that organizations cannot be understood apart from their history. The initial organizing choices, along with the ability to amass enough power and trust to carry them out, set into motion processes that lead to different developmental patterns, belief systems, and out-comes even for organizations that began their existence with iden-tical constraints and resources. Moreover, these effects were dem-onstrated without the artifact of growth in organizational size that sometimes, but not always, accompanies the early stage of an or-ganization's life. Without an appreciation for these early choices, it would be very difficult, if not foolhardy, to attempt to interpret the differences in the belief systems that existed in these organizations as they reached maturity. But this is precisely what the static, cross-sectional research into chronologically mature organizations, which typifies much of the organizational research of the past decade and a half, attempts to do.

The longitudinal, multimethod research design permitted an investigation of all three aspects of organizational learning over time. *Whether* learning occurred was demonstrated by evidence based on organizational outcomes (for example, by mastery of the performance situation); *how* learning occurred was revealed by process observation or organizational behaviors and by the self-reports of members during the simulation debriefing; and *what* knowledge was acquired was measured by the patterns of cognitive association that developed within each membership as its organiza-tional experience increased. Although the results of the simulation demonstrated that learning occurred within both settings, it is clear that the primary processes by which each organization learned and the knowledge they gained as a result were markedly different.

Learning Conditions. The influence of all three learning con-ditions (that is, leadership, performance feedback, and organiza-tional slack) was at work in the simulated organizations. (The ef-fects of initial learning approach and early performance feedback, however, are difficult to disentangle because they are so tightly related.) Under most conditions of creation, an organization that opts exclusively for the proactive mode is very likely to discover and put to use more relevant knowledge than a purely enactive organi-zation will. Some knowledge that may be applied to any new setting always exists. Therefore, as long as the focus is on the extreme learning archetypes, it is highly probable that the proactive mode will result in higher initial performance returns than will the enac-tive one. Moreover, the initial proactive choice requires that more energy or resources be spent in organizing *before* start-up, and this allocation problem requires the catalytic action of strong leaders. In the case of our proactive organization, for example, the primary stimulus and agent of learning was the catalytic action taken by the emergent dominant coalition—action that both facilitated and legitimated the initial process of organizing.

In contrast, the enactive approach, when pursued to an extreme, is more likely to be characterized by the absence of strong central direction. As a consequence, this approach requires the stress of negative performance feedback, or what Downs (1967) has referred to as a "performance gap," to energize organizational search and information-processing activities. Again, as in the case of our enactive organization, learning may be explained primarily on the basis of negative performance feedback that creates stress and causes conflict to erupt.

In either case, the creation of slack is a necessary ingredient in learning. For example, our proactive organization bought the slack to enable it to reflect and plan during the initial session of play. But without strong leadership, such as the kind we witnessed in that group, a beginning organization would be hard pressed to accept the price of creating slack. Indeed, the enactive organization created slack grudgingly, and then only after it had received definitive negative performance feedback and experienced an episode of disruptive internal conflict as a consequence. These extreme initial organizing choices, together with their predictable, immediate consequences, are summarized in Figure 4.

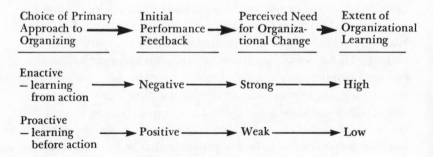

Figure 4. Important Primary Linkages Between the Creation and Learning of Organizations

Initial Learning Approaches and Emergent Belief Systems. In terms of how much cognitive restructuring occurs, our simulated organizations demonstrated that the *membership* of an enactive organization is likely to do the most learning. Because the enactive approach exposes many members and parts of the organization to the performance situation and encourages them to experiment with their own theories of action, learning is likely to be broadly distributed within the membership. Members of an enactive organization, therefore, are likely to internalize their experiences and translate them into theories that eventually become the focus of organizational debate. This high degree of member involvement in the fundamental decision-making activities of the organization is also likely to create a sense of responsibility for organizational performance that is broadly distributed among the organizational membership.

The learning that takes place within a proactive organization, in contrast, is likely to be monopolized by the dominant coalition. Indeed, so accurate was the dominant coalition's understanding of its task and role in our proactive simulated organization that, by the end of the first few sessions, its representatives were able to correct the coordinator's performance calculations! However, not much cognitive restructuring occurred within the organizational membership as a whole, and the general belief system that emerged within that membership bore little resemblance to what we would expect in a mature organization that was doing as well as this simulated one.

Instead of experiencing freedom to experiment with the performance setting, members of the proactive organization were obliged to perform their tasks according to the dominant coalition's plan. Therefore, it was not surprising to discover that no cognitive association emerged between members' perceptions of their effectiveness in their own jobs and the effectiveness achieved by their immediate work units, their divisions, and the organization as a whole. After all, it was the dominant coalition's plan that would succeed or fail, not their own. Much as in the case of a professional baseball team, not only successes but especially problems and difficulties encountered by a proactive organization are likely to be attributed to its manager, regardless of whether the manager is the cause of such problems (Gamson and Scotch, 1964).

Just the opposite belief system emerged within the membership of the enactive organization, with its emphasis on member experimentation and decision making. In this organization the pattern of correlations revealed that members had assumed a highly developed sense of personal responsibility for the performance of the organization as a whole. These differences in the organizational belief systems generated by different learning approaches raise some important questions about where organizational knowledge should reside and suggest some weaknesses to which each learning approach is susceptible.

Threats to Learning Approaches

Because organizational knowledge was operationalized in terms of the belief system that emerged across the entire organizational membership, and not simply among members of the dominant coalition, we could conclude that more cognitive restructuring took place and more appropriate knowledge emerged within the *total membership* of the enactive organization than in that of the proactive one. But this finding raises some important issues that have been skirted in other studies of organizational learning: Who should possess this organizational knowledge? Under what conditions is it sufficient for the dominant coalition to monopolize organizational knowledge? Under what conditions would it be beneficial for this knowledge to be widely distributed within the membership of an organization? Partial answers to these questions can be found by examining the major threats to each archetypical approach to organizational learning.

Threats to the Proactive Approach. The proactive approach, emphasizing management's role in planning and the employees' role in performing the work according to plan, has assumed the status of a management education ideal in the Western world. However, it has several drawbacks. First, when workers recognize and accept this split in organizational roles, they are apt to attribute the responsibility for organizational successes—and failures—not to themselves but to the dominant coalition. The consequences of this displacement of responsibility in terms of worker motivation to perform, especially when the fallibility of management becomes known to them, are obvious. In the same way, if employees are deprived of the ability to experiment with new ideas and behaviors, they are denied important avenues to their own growth and development, and their commitment to the organization will be doubtful.

Furthermore, the proactive organization runs the risk of becoming captive to the dominant coalition's definition of the initial performance situation and to its model for coping with that situation. Not only will its early success tend to suppress the dominant coalition's own active search for new or better ways, but members outside the dominant coalition, who may be in touch with new developments, will be less likely to confront their management group with new information or theories of action than will their counterparts in an organization pursuing a more enactive approach to organizational learning. Thus, the proactive organization runs a higher risk of finding itself confronted by Kimberly's (1979) paradox of early success and of being unable to adapt to the constraints and opportunities presented by later stages of its development. The proactive approach, with its heavy reliance on conventional wisdom developed out of the previous experiences of its key decision makers, may not be appropriate during the creation of especially unique or innovative settings in which much of the required knowledge resides in the process of enactment itself.

Threats to the Enactive Approach. Learning exclusively through organizational enactment, however, is also subject to a number of serious threats. Perhaps the most obvious threat is that the organization will fail or be judged a failure before its members have developed an adequate understanding of the requirements of the performance situation. The amount of slack an organization is given to get off the ground varies from setting to setting. What is clear, however, is that innovative settings tend to have more slack during creation than do conventional settings. The former are inherently nonroutine, their cause-effect relations are uncharted, and there are no immediate standards or comparison organizations that may be used to assess their early effectiveness. A condition often exists for the new *and different* setting that not only affords it considerable slack during start-up but implies an expectation that experimentation will be required as a normal part of that process. The enactive approach, therefore, is more feasible for the creation of an innovative organization than of a conventional one in which cause-effect relations are known and for which both standards of performance and comparison organizations exist to facilitate early assessment and thus to deny start-up slack. By the same token, the threat of premature termination is very real for conventional organizations pursuing a predominately enactive approach to early organizational learning.

In addition, there is no guarantee that the enactive approach will generate *a* theory of organizational action. The real possibility exists that an overreliance on this approach, involving a broad spectrum of the organization's members and interest groups, will generate too many competing models of organizational effectiveness, each having its own constituency but none of them possessing the power or evidence to prevail. Experimental interdependence may border on organizational anarchy and result in an inability to focus resources where they can do the most good. Such a case emerged during the initial sessions of play in the simulated organization that pursued the enactive approach. Thus, just as too little knowledge poses problems for new organizations, so might too much knowledge.

Mixing the Approaches to Organizational Learning

Until now, we have focused on the differences between proactive and enactive approaches to organizational learning, yet it is obvious that they are seldom employed as independently of each other in the creation of organizations as they were in the simulation study. The question is not which one to employ, but rather what *mix* to employ during the process of creating a new organization. The most important determinant, we believe, is the nature of the new setting.

Conventional Organizational Creations. New organizational settings may be distinguished in many ways, but for the present purpose we believe the most important characteristic is whether the setting is new and different (innovative) or just new (that is, conventional). If the setting is only new, a number of factors inherent in that setting and in its context argue for more reliance on the proactive than the enactive approach to learning. There is more extant cause-effect knowledge, and people not only know what to expect of the setting but also have a reasonable understanding of what it takes to achieve those expectations. These people include the manager and his or her core group, rank-and-file members, and representatives of stakeholders and other organizations upon which the new enterprise is dependent for the acquisition of needed resources and the exportation of its products, by-products, and wastes. Because the organization is only new and not innovative, existing comparison organizations will provide performance standards by which its early effectiveness may be judged. Therefore, the new but not different organization will probably not be afforded the start-up slack that is usually accorded the new innovative setting. All these conditions strongly favor an emphasis on the proactive approach to learning in the creation of a new but conventional setting.

Innovative Organizational Creations. The more innovative the new setting, however, the more problematic the proactive approach will be, since it emphasizes centralized development of a theory of action before action occurs. In other words, organizational model building based on the conventional knowledge at hand will be more inappropriate the more unique the performance situation is. Therefore, when an innovative setting is being created, members will have to place greater reliance on learning from the actual process of enactment than from prior planning. Points argue against an either-or choice within a new organization concerning the approach that it will take to learning. Instead, they suggest use of a continuum of learning approach mixes anchored by the nature of the organizational setting at the time of creation (see Figure 5).

Organizational Transformation and Learning

The transition from infant to mature stages of organizational life often presents a need for reassessment and reapportionment of the mix of approaches that an organization takes to learning. For the innovative setting, the process of enactment will lead gradually to greater knowledge of the performance requirements of the situation. This knowledge, when combined with the knowledge gained about the capabilities inherent in organizational

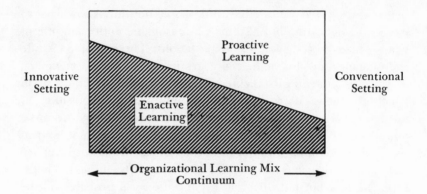

Figure 5. Organizational Learning Mix in the Creation of Innovative and Conventional Settings

arrangements and resources, will lead to the gradual institutionalization of a theory of organizational action. As organizational form and processes take on a more enduring and reliable character, the need for rival theories of action will diminish, and there will be a new emphasis on efficiency. Successful passage from infancy to maturity in the innovative organization, therefore, will require an adjustment in the learning mix toward more, but certainly not exclusive, reliance on the proactive approach.

But this transition may be problematic for both the innovative organization's leadership and the membership, both originally having been attracted to the new setting presumably because of its congruence with their styles and orientations. The shift in learning mix away from the enactive end of the learning continuum may mean that, if the organization is to make the passage successfully, some of its founding members who contributed substantially toward its creation must step aside. To some extent, depending on the degree of innovation desired, entrepreneurs may have to concede to administrators, professionals to technicians, artists to replicators. And yet, if the adjustment becomes an overcorrection, the venture runs the risk of losing its uniqueness and becoming much like the existing organizations it was created to complement or displace.

The passage from infancy to maturity is no less perilous or potentially traumatic for the new but conventional organization.

Trading initially on the strength of conventional knowledge, this type of organization may become so wedded to its initial theory of action that it suppresses the means by which that theory can be questioned when it comes under pressure from a changing context. Thus, there is need for the conventional organization to maintain at least minimal search and information-processing activity, and this need increases with the degree of its initial success. The problem again, however, is that the kinds of individuals who were initially attracted to the conventional setting may have neither the skills nor, more importantly, the interest or motivation to introduce equivocality where order prevails.

In summary, there appear to be circumstances of organizational creation and transformation, so far only crudely charted, that require more emphasis on one learning approach than on the other. An overdetermined innovative organization is no better off than an underdetermined conventional creation. The first runs the risk of innovation shortfall; the second is threatened by the prospect of operational inefficiency under conditions of minimum organizational slack. In either case, a mismatch during creation among setting, learning mix, management style, and member orientations increases the probability of premature organizational termination.

As the biography of either type of new setting unfolds, however, the match that works initially may be expected to evolve with developments both inside and outside the organization. Movement away from the enactive end of the organizational learning mix continuum may be required in the innovative setting as it converts the nonroutine into the routine and becomes concerned with efficiency. In contrast, movement toward the enactive end of the continuum may be required in the conventional organization as it attempts to anticipate changes in the performance context. Moreover, these transformations are likely to be problematic for both organizations because of the kinds of leaders and members they attract at birth and the kinds of early reinforcement they receive for their initial learning approaches. For the present, however, these are hypotheses born of preliminary theoretical development and exploratory research and thus hypotheses that beg for more evidence as to their reliability and generalizability.

Conclusion

We have attempted to begin the process of understanding learning and development as they unfold within new organizations. The evidence generated by the simulation study adds substance to the argument that organizations cannot be understood apart from their histories. Indeed, how could one possibly explain the wide differences in organizational belief systems from one stage to another that we found without knowledge of the events, the key individuals, the decisions, and the reinforcements of each organization during its creation and early development.

It seems clear, therefore, that if we are to begin to understand important organizational processes, we must first develop ways for coping with the obstacles to longitudinal field research (Kimberly, 1976a). Among the more important obstacles are organizational access and commitment to the longitudinal approach by the host organization, the time commitment imposed upon the researcher and its relation to career rewards, and the thorny methodological issues surrounding longitudinal data collection and analysis. Toward this end, we refer the reader to a conclusion reached a decade and a half ago by Cangelosi and Dill (1965) but largely ignored until now. They noted that use of "a complex management game, intermediate in complexity and duration between the laboratory experiment and real-life organizational experience, provides a good environment for such studies" (p. 203).

The results and issues generated in our simulation study will, we hope, encourage others to examine more closely the benefits of organizational simulation for studying not only the organizational learning process but other important features of the creation and early development of organizations as well. Together with longitudinal field studies, simulated organizations can tell us much about how to avoid the high costs to society and to organizational members of ill-advised organizational creations and premature organizational terminations.

4

Early Planning, Implementation, and Performance of New Organizations

$\prec\!\!\prec\!\!\prec\!\!\prec\!\!\prec\!\!\prec\!\!\prec\!\!\prec\!\!\prec\!\!\prec\!\!\prec\!\!\prec\!\!\prec\!\!\succ$

Andrew H. Van de Ven

How are new organizations created? Does it make a difference in implementation success how new organizations are planned and organized? What obstacles are experienced in creating organizations, and how much do these obstacles influence the success of new organizations during their early and later life? To what degree can one predict (and thereby manage) the incidence of these obstacles from the ways in which new organizations are initially conceived and planned?

With a few notable exceptions, these questions on the creation stage of organizations have been ignored in the management and organizational literature. This is unfortunate because about one fourth of all business firms in the United States are one year old or less, and the median age of all firms is only about seven years. Furthermore, the life expectancy of new organizations is very short. In the American business population as a whole, 54 percent of all newly formed or acquired businesses survive one and a half years or less, one quarter survive six years or less, and only 19 percent remain in operation under the same ownership for more than ten years. In the period following the Second World War, the median life expectancy of new business firms has been about one and three-fourths years. (These data are based on estimates provided by the U.S. Department of Commerce, Office of Business Economics. Similar data were not found available on nonprofit public or private organizations.) When viewed as indicators of the age and life expectancy of the population of organizations, these data underscore the need for theorists and researchers to go beyond their fixation on mature organizations and to pay greater attention to the birth, growth, and dissolution stages of organization life.

This chapter focuses on the creation stage of organizational life and will attempt to partially answer the questions asked above on the basis of a longitudinal study of the creation of fourteen early childhood development organizations. Still in progress, this study was begun in December 1972 in an effort to measure and explain the behavior and performance of these childcare organizations from their initial inception, during their planning phases, and throughout their early years of implementation as service-providing organizations to children and families in Texas communities.

After a conceptual overview of the approach taken to study the creation of organizations, this chapter will describe the context in which the childcare organizations were created and will attempt to explain their implementation success in terms of (1) the planning processes employed to create them, (2) the obstacles that the organizations encountered when implementing their plans, and (3) the structural designs of the new organizations during their first two years of operation.

Studying Organizational Creation

Research and theorizing on the creation of organizations can be usefully classified into three approaches: (1) entrepreneurial, (2) ecological, and (3) behavioral. These approaches focus on different aspects of the creation of organizations, work at different levels of analysis, and usually employ different methodologies. Each approach has its own distinct strengths and weaknesses. The few researchers who are presently studying the creation of organizations tend to take one of the three approaches and simply dismiss the other two—and this researcher is no exception. Fortunately, the three approaches are or may become highly complementary, so that a synthesis of future research may come to yield a rich and comprehensive understanding of the creation of organizations.

The *entrepreneurial* approach focuses on the characteristics of the individuals who are the founders and promoters of new organizations. The entrepreneur has been, and continues to be, the prevailing subject in the literature and folklore on organizational creation and innovation. Many writers have described entrepreneurs as forming a heterogeneous collection of individuals that includes the scientific inventor who creates a new technology and peddles it, as well as the self-made man who possesses some resources, some ability, and perhaps some capital to start a new business. The entrepreneur has been characterized as a profit maximizer, as an agent of change, and as a lone wolf who triggers a new wave of innovations. This intriguing individual has been studied from a variety of viewpoints—for example, his or her personality characteristics (McClelland, 1965) and uniqueness in contrast with other managers (Howell, 1972; Litzinger, 1965). The entrepreneur has been characterized as having a high need for achievement, as having difficulty in dealing with authority, and as being able to make effective decisions under conditions of uncertainty (Filley, House, and Kerr, 1976.)

Unfortunately, research on the distinctive traits, biographies, personalities, expertise, and images of entrepreneurs has been inconclusive and has thus far produced little empirical evidence to substantiate their existence as a class of individuals different from other leaders (see review in Filley, House, and Kerr, 1976.) As a consequence, a theory or program of research on the creation of organizations that is based on this quasi-mythical figure would seem to be built on a precarious assumption. Furthermore, if future research does produce consistent evidence on the characteristics of entrepreneurs, it would seem equally dangerous to try to develop a practical concept of organizational creation based on entrepreneurs, inasmuch as they appear to be in short supply at the present time.

Researchers wedded to the concept of entrepreneurship for studying the creation of organizations can learn much from the history of research on leadership. Like the studies of entrepreneurship, this research began by investigating the traits and personality characteristics of leaders. However, no consistent empirical evidence was found to support the expectation that there are a finite number of characteristics or traits of leaders and that these traits differentiate successful from unsuccessful leaders. More recently, research into leadership has apparently made some progress by focusing on the behavior of leaders (that is, on what they do instead of what they are) and by determining what situational factors or conditions moderate the effects of their behavior and performance.

The *ecological approach* is a second and more recent view on the creation of organizations and is linked with the population ecology perspectives on the relation between an organization and its environment (Campbell, 1967; Hannan and Freeman, 1978a; Aldrich, 1979). This approach takes the population of organizations as its unit of analysis and examines the structural, political, and economic conditions in the environment that give rise to the creation and dissolution of various forms of organizations. For example, Aldrich (1979) argues that several historical forces—including the transformation of the world economy from a feudal to a capitalist mode of production, the long-term trend toward increasing urbanization, and the frequent occurrence of political revolutions—lead to the creation of waves of new organizational forms and that some forms, once established, remain viable for a considerable length of time, whereas others change rapidly. Aldrich further argues that the role of the state is a critical factor in accounting for patterns of organization creation, because state support and protection constitute an overwhelming advantage for certain organizations. Chapter Five in this volume also exemplifies the ecological approach by examining how urban-territorial factors explain differences in organizational birthrates in three selected industries.

This ecological research will provide important insights on

the environmental conditions that are conducive to the creation of organizations. It may also prove useful for examining broad macrosocial policy decisions and the consequences of government intervention to promote or inhibit the creation of new organizations. However, the ecological approach will probably not provide useful advice to managers and analysts interested in knowing how to create organizations. Indeed, the ecological perspective emphasizes that it is the environment—and not the motives, decisions, or behavior of individuals—that is the driving force that determines whether organizations will be created and, if so, which ones. Some environmental characteristics do, of course, constrain and facilitate organizational births but so also do human motives, decisions, and behavior. What is needed is a more balanced viewpoint on the relative importance of environmental conditions versus human choices and behavior in shaping the structures and processes of new organizations (Van de Ven, 1979). If such a balanced viewpoint is taken, the ecological approach can then complement the behavioral approach to understanding the creation of organizations.

The *behavioral approach* will be the predominant one used in this chapter to study organizational creation. This approach takes an applied managerial view by arguing that the conditions under which an organization is born and the processes followed in its initial development have important consequences on its structure and performance in later life. The behavioral approach attempts to describe and explain the consequences of the series of events, strategic decisions, and human activities that occur when organizations are created. The behavioral view incorporates the entrepreneurial focus on the individual founders but centers on their behavior rather than on their traits. It also focuses on the behavior of other interest groups and constituencies who come to have a stake in the creation of the organization. The ecological perspective can make significant contributions to the behavioral approach by identifying the environmental conditions that may qualitatively shape and influence the success of alternative events, decisions, and activities in creating new organizations.

Central to behavioral studies of organizational creation are the *time period* used to define the creation stage of organizations and the way one conceptualizes the *processes* that go on during the creation stage. This chapter defines the creation stage of organizations as beginning with their initial inception, moving through their planning and implementation phases, and culminating with their institutionalization—usually two to three years after initial implementation. Although this definition does not pinpoint when creation stops and institutionalization begins, it underscores the fact that organizations are not created in one fell swoop. Organizational birth covers an extended period of time, and the behavioral approach relies heavily on the literature related to organizational change and planning to conceptualize the processes that go on in the birth of organizations.

Planning is here defined as the sequence of events, decisions, and activities undertaken to develop an innovation. An *innovation* is defined as the introduction or implementation of a new organizational design, program, or product. From his pioneer studies of group decision making and social change, Lewin (1947) set forth his well-known three-phase process of group and organizational change: unfreezing (if necessary), moving, and refreezing. Unfreezing requires the entry of new forces, pressures, or tensions to move a social system to change, while refreezing requires establishing a new constant pattern of forces different from the initial pattern. Most organizational planning and change theorists subsequently drew and expanded upon Lewin's early work to suggest what activities are necessary in these three phases to manage an organizational change process. Table 1, for example, illustrates the basic developmental phases that have been proposed by several writers to examine processes of individual decision making, program planning, and organizational change. Although many of these planning models assume the introduction of change within an existing mature organization, they provide a starting point for conceptualizing developmental processes in organizational creation.

The particular process model examined in this study is the Program Planning Model (PPM), which was developed by Delbecq and Van de Ven (1971) and extended by Van de Ven and Koenig (1976). As applied to the creation of new community human service organizations, the PPM divides planning into five phases and

Table 1. Comparison of Developmental Phases in Planning Process Models

Author(s) & Focus of Analysis	Phases of Program Planning, Decision Making, or Change		
Lewin (1947) —Social-psychological description of change process in individuals and small groups	1. Unfreezing —Recognition of a need —Willingness to give up old ways	2. Moving —Activities undertaken to design and implement change	3. Freezing —Institutionalizing new behavior
March and Simon (1958) —Description of administrative problem solving under conditions of bounded rationality	Parenthood of invention is necessity, opportunity, and moderate stress — 1. Intelligence —Problem formulation	2. Design —Search, screen and evaluate alternatives —Factor design elements into substantive programs	3. Choice —Decision to implement satisfactory solution
Mintzberg, Raisinghani, and Theoret (1976) —Field study of 25 strategic, unstructured decision processes	1. Identification Phase —Decision recognition routine —Diagnosis routine	2. Developmental Phase —Search routine —Design routine	3. Selection Phase —Screen routine —Evaluation- Choice routine —Authorization routine

Table 1. Comparison of Developmental Phases in Planning Process Models (Continued)

Utterback (1971) —Summary of research on process of technological innovation within corporations	1. Idea Generation Phase —Recognition of a need —Recognition of technical means to meet need —Synthesis of information to create an idea or proposal for development	2. Problem-Solving Phase —Divide problems into separable subproblems —Assign priorities to goals —Design and evaluate alternative solutions	3. Implementation and Diffusion Phase —Manufacture prototype solution for first use or market introduction
Lippitt, Watson and Westley (1958) —Normative model developed from case studies of change process in groups, organizations, and communities	1. Develop need for change	2. Establish relation with change agent	3. Diagnose problem of client
	4. Examine alternatives and establish goals and action routes	5. Transform intentions into change efforts	6. Generalize and stabilize change
	7. Terminate relation with change agent		

Dalton, Lawrence and Greiner (1970) —Normative model of change process developed from case studies of large-scale organizational changes	1. Pressure on top management	2. Intervention from outside and reorientation	3. Diagnoses and recognition of problems and their determinance by gathering information at all levels of organization	4. Invention of solution and obtain commitment to change through participation	5. Experiment with solution and search for results	6. Reinforce new practices with rewards and feedback
Hage and Aiken (1970) —Description of program change process within medical organizations	1. Evaluation. Organizational elite identify need for change and consider alternative means and ends	2. Initiation. Elite choose solution and search for resources	3. Implementation. Start of new activity	4. Routinization. Stabilize program change		

Table 1. Comparison of Developmental Phases in Planning Process Models (Continued)

	1	2	3	4	5	6
Warren (1971) based on Ross (1955) planning steps — Normative "concrete-processual" model for planning community and societal programs. Developed in reaction to abstract-rational model	1. Define problem by involving all parties affected by problem area	2. Study nature, meaning, and implications of present-state problems	3. Develop tentative solution that responds to technical, social and political realities	4. Activate agreed upon solution on flexible pilot basis	5. Incremental adjustment and continuous evaluation of social program	
Friedmann (1973) — Normative model of innovative planning for "retracking" American institutions and communities	1. Identify and describe problem as collective phenomena	2. Identify and describe patterns of collective behavior	3. Identify and involve institutions responsible for behavior	4. Analyze and relate performance of institutions to the problems	5. Formulate proposal for structural innovation in response to problem	6. Implement strategy and make adjustments on an ongoing basis as necessary in the course of action

	1.	2.	3.	4.	5.	6.
Ackoff (1974), Ozbekan (1971), Trist (1976) —Normative model of "interactive planning" for designing idealized futures of social systems	Ends Planning. Design idealized future goals that are technologically feasible	Means Planning. Invent alternative courses of action	Resource Planning. Determine type, amount, and sources of resources needed	Organizational Planning. Determine and design organizational arrangements needed to implement plan	Implementation and Control Planning. Implement, control, evaluate, and improve plan under changing internal and external conditions	
Delbecq and Van de Ven (1971), Van de Ven and Koenig (1976) —Normative model of program planning and evaluation process for groups, organizations, and communities	Prerequisites. Identify complexity of problem or goal to be dealt with	Problem Exploration. Involve users to identify need priorities	Knowledge Exploration. Involve experts to reconceptualize problems and identify alternative solutions	Program Design. Involve affected parties in developing new program proposal and implementation plan	Program Activation and Evaluation. Trial implementation and formative evaluation of new program	Program Operation/Diffusion. Institutionalize program as ongoing activity and/or transfer program to adopters

suggests that the following activities be performed in each phase:

Phase I: Planning Prerequisites. The formal initiation of a planning effort begins with selection and organization of a planning policy board (representing various constituents of a community) and a planning unit (staff planners reporting to the policy board). Within the broad guidelines of the phases described below, the policy board and the planning unit develop a specific process of tasks and steps that they will perform in planning a new human service organization in their community. The scope of the planning process is expected to reflect the nature, complexity, and uncertainty of local community needs.

Phase II: Problem Exploration. The planning unit attempts to discover the human service needs of the community by asking local citizens and prospective clients what problems they are experiencing in the area being investigated (for example, child care). Data are obtained through a variety of survey techniques, including door-to-door interviews, neighborhood block meetings, and questionnaires. The results of this assessment are summarized in a report, reviewed by the planning policy board, and distributed to participants as well as to other affected interest groups (for example, administrators, politicians, service-providing organizations, and news media in the community).

Phase III: Knowledge Exploration. During this phase the planners reconceptualize problem priorities and identify alternative ways to solve them by surveying the perceptions of experts in the problem area. The experts' diagnoses of problem priorities and their strategies for alternative solutions are summarized in a report by the planners, reviewed by the policy board, and distributed to Phase II and Phase III participants and other interest groups.

Phase IV: Program Design. The purpose of this phase is to develop a specific program proposal that realistically responds to the Phase II problem priorities and incorporates the Phase III recommendations of experts. The planning unit first conducts workshops and problem-solving meetings with representatives from other planning units, service-providing agencies, and interest groups in the community. This information is then summarized in a preliminary program proposal, which the planners then review with the planning policy board and other resource controllers. When possible, modifications are made to satisfy divergent constituents before the proposal is submitted for funding and trial implementation.

Phase V: Program Implementation, Evaluation, and Operation. After the proposed program has been implemented on a pilot demonstration basis, it is evaluated to determine how the program can be made more effective, efficient, and acceptable to clients and affected agencies in the community. After corrective adjustments are made, the program is transferred and/or operated as an ongoing human service organization by implementing procedures to routinize and stabilize it.

Pragmatically, this PPM process provides a broad series of overlapping phases to guide planners in creating new organizations, and this chapter will report the consequences experienced by various Texas communities in using the PPM to plan new childcare organizations. From a research viewpoint, the PPM offers a process framework for examining behavior in key developmental phases in the creation of organizations over time.

Context of the Childcare Organizations

In 1972, the Office of Early Childhood Development in a state government agency in Texas (hereafter, the agency) initiated demonstration projects in fourteen counties and communities to plan and implement services for preschool children and their families. In addition to providing childcare services to citizens in need, the agency's purpose for sponsoring the fourteen demonstration projects was to conduct a public policy experiment to learn how to plan and implement childcare programs at the grass-roots level. The agency awarded two types of contracts to local communities: one that was patterned after the Program Planning Model (PPM) and one that was not contingent upon any particular planning model (non-PPM). In addition to the kind of planning contract, the PPM and non-PPM projects differed in the ways they were selected by the state agency.

PPM Projects

In order to stimulate planning and problem solving in local communities, the agency selected nine of the fourteen communities on the basis of a set of demographic indicators of need for childcare services (for example, infant mortality rate, number of working mothers with children under six years of age, percent of population with children under six years old that receive welfare, and so on). After negotiations with county judges and commissioners' courts (the highest elected body of government in a county), the agency contracted with a planning unit designated by the judge in each selected county.

By terms of the contract, these nine planning units agreed to follow the Program Planning Model in designing their childcare programs as described previously and as summarized in Table 2. The PPM contracts were ratified by the agency during Winter 1972 on the basis of a planning prerequisites report submitted by the nine PPM projects. The PPM projects began the problem exploration (Phase II) in February 1973, and most completed Phase IV (program design) by September 1973. To provide the projects with a realistic opportunity to become established during Phase V, program implementation, the agency funded the projects for three additional years, after which they were expected to obtain financial support elsewhere.

The Non-PPM Projects

A second objective of the agency was to respond to initiatives taken by local communities for obtaining funds to implement already planned childcare programs. Table 2 outlines the criteria used by the agency for responding to community proposals for funding childcare programs. Proposals from five communities that satisfied these criteria were selected by the agency during the spring and summer of 1973, and contracts were made by August 1973. The contract was not contingent on any particular planning process because the programs were already planned. Instead, the "non-PPM" contract required that the selected projects implement their childcare programs, submit quarterly reports on their performance, and cooperate in this evaluation study.

Shortly after the five projects were selected and contracted by the agency, a member of the research team conducted a site visit to each project to obtain a detailed historical account of the steps followed to plan the childcare programs. Although there was considerable variance in the actual planning processes used by these projects, a conventional unstructured approach to planning was common. In contrast to the PPM projects, planning activities for the five non-PPM projects centered on Phase IV program design activities and did not include the problem exploration and knowledge exploration phases.

As part of the contracts to both PPM and non-PPM projects, the agency recruited and assigned to each project a professional consultant who was an expert in early childhood development (most often a university professor). The consultants provided periodic on-site technical assistance (when requested by the projects) during the three-year implementation period, and additionally during the planning phases for the PPM projects. In addition, a professional specialist on the staff of the agency was assigned to each project to provide technical assistance and to coordinate contract-related issues through on-site visits and telephone calls. The university consultants and agency specialists were encouraged to work together as teams in providing technical assistance to their assigned projects.

By September 1973, most planning activities had been completed, and the program proposals submitted to the agency had been reviewed and approved for funding. The planning efforts resulted in a variety of early childhood development programs, each unique and each designed to respond to need priorities in the local communities.

Six of the fourteen projects designed comprehensive daycare programs with social and educational services, health and nutrition components, and parent education components. Four of the projects developed more specialized health care programs. For example, one project designed a program to provide prenatal care and instruction to pregnant women and a health screening and treatment clinic for children up to six years old. The remaining projects developed programs that were even more distinctive. For example, one community proposed to establish a system of family

Table 2. Key Differences Between PPM and Non-PPM Projects

Distinguishing Factors	Nine PPM Projects	Five Non-PPM Projects
Selection Process		
Agency Goals	To initiate planning in local communities.	To respond to local planning initiatives.
Criteria	1. Need as determined by demographic indicators.	1. A program plan that responds to community childcare needs.
	2. Areas with a lack of available services.	2. Indication of local support for program plan.
	3. Areas with high potential for obtaining federal matching funds.	3. Commitment of matching funds.
Notification	Agency approached county officials of selected counties with offer to enter into PPM planning contract.	Local agencies approached the agency for funds to implement already-planned program.
Selection	Responsible agent to perform contract selected by county judge.	Self-selection by local agency sponsoring the program.
Activities		
Planning (Phase I)	Formation of planning policy board; report on plan to implement PPM.	No planning policy board formed. No documented plan to implement planning process existed.
Problem Exploration (Phase II)	Community-wide assessment of parents and citizens to identify needs; findings documented, reviewed by policy board, and disseminated.	No needs assessment was conducted.
Knowledge Exploration (Phase III)	Survey of experts to identify alternative means for dealing with needs; findings documented, reviewed by policy board, and disseminated.	No knowledge exploration was conducted.

Program Design (Phase IV)	Workshops and meetings conducted with community agencies to design a specific program; plan was documented, reviewed by policy board, and disseminated.	The starting point in all five cases. A proposal was initially written and subsequent revisions were negotiated to obtain funding.
Program Implementation (Phase V)	The program proposals were implemented and evaluated during a three-year period of funding and technical assistance from the agency.	The program proposals were implemented and evaluated during a three-year period of funding and technical assistance from the agency.
Contract Administration and Funding	Funding made in increments and contingent upon satisfactory completion of prescribed phases of planning, submission of quarterly financial and performance reports, and cooperation in evaluation study on program planning.	Funding contingent upon implementation of program proposal (not on following any prescribed planning process), submission of quarterly financial and performance reports, and cooperation in evaluation study on program planning.

daycare homes scattered throughout the rural county to provide services to children whose mothers were working and to help operators of daycare homes become licensed for providing childcare. Another community proposed to obtain demographic information on young children and their families in order to (1) improve planning of educational programs in the local school districts and (2) work on the early identification and treatment of children's health and developmental problems.

Funding to the fourteen projects by the agency varied according to the nature of the program and ranged from $50,000 to $95,000 per project per year. Over the entire three-year contract period, the agency allocated about $2.5 million to the fourteen projects.

Organization Design and Early Performance

Table 3 shows the growth in the organizational design and performance of the childcare projects during the first two years of implementation. As the table shows, the size and structure of the childcare organizations expanded considerably. Although there were wide variations among the organizations, on the average their size more than doubled from ten full-time employees in April 1974 to twenty-three employees in July 1975. Corresponding to this growth in size were increases in the number of childcare service centers in the communities and greater formalization of rules, policies, and procedures to guide role behavior of employees in the organizations. During the first two years there were no significant changes in the degree of staff participation in decision making (an indicator of centralization) or in the frequency of communications with other organizations in the community for the average childcare organization. However, as will be explained below, there was a considerable decrease in the average level of education of staff in the organizations from April 1974 to July 1975.

Table 3 shows that there was a significant growth in the quantity of services provided by the childcare organizations during their first two years, as indicated by the total units of services in all functions. Figure 1 illustrates the quarterly growth rate in services provided during the first two years of operation. The figure summarizes the average number of units of services provided each quarter in five functional areas: childcare, health care, parent education, public information and education, and indirect services. In each of these functions, there were significant increases in the quantity of services provided by the childcare organizations from September 1973 to September 1975. The decreasing trend in the units of health care provided from March to September 1975 is explained by the fact that by 1975 many of the childcare organizations had established referral arrangements for health services through the regional offices of the Department of Public Welfare, which administer the federal health-screening program. Despite this explainable decrease and a leveling off in parent education and indirect services in fiscal year 1975, the rate of growth over the two years remained strong for childcare (the primary function of most of the organizations) and for public information and education.

Table 3 shows that there was also a measurable increase in the efficiency of services provided by the average childcare organization in the first two years. Efficiency was computed as the dollar cost per unit of service in each of the five functional areas shown in Figure 1. Overall, there was a 9 percent increase in the efficiency of providing services to children between the first and second year of operation. In 1974, the fourteen organizations together served 2,981 children on a combined operating budget of $1,214,913. In 1975, the organizations served 4,942 children on a combined budget of $1,831,952. Thus, the same services that cost $407.55 in 1974 cost $370.69 in 1975.

It is important to note that the dramatic growth in services and operating budgets of the childcare organizations occurred as a result of the additional funding they were able to obtain from other organizations. While the combined operating budgets of all the childcare organizations increased 50 percent from 1974 to 1975, the state agency's funding to the childcare organizations increased only 22 percent over the period from 1973 to 1975. Indeed, as Table 3 shows, while the average childcare organization was dependent upon the state agency for 68 percent of its total operating budget in the first three quarters of its operation (September 1973 to May 1974), financial dependence on the state agency decreased to 25 percent by November 1975. Thus, although there are considerable variations among the fourteen childcare organizations,

Table 3. Design and Performance of Childcare Organizations in First Two Years

	Average 14 Organizations	Standard Deviation	Range Minimum-Maximum
Design of Childcare Organizations			
1. *Organization Size (No. of employees)*			
—April 1974	9.8	6.18	4 — 21
—December 1974	16.5	10.31	5 — 35
—July 1975	23.1	8.03	4 — 45
2. *Number of Service Sites in Community*			
—April 1974	2.2	1.23	1 — 5
—December 1974	2.6	2.13	1 — 8
—July 1975	2.7	2.18	1 — 10
3. *Formalization of Procedures*			
(1–5 scale: 1 = little, 5 = very much)			
—April 1974	3.5	.54	2.6 — 4.4
—December 1974	3.9	.51	2.8 — 4.6
—July 1975	4.0	.47	3.2 — 4.8
4. *Participation in Decisions by All Employees*			
(1–5 scale: 1 = none, 5 = much)			
—April 1974	2.3	.82	1.3 — 4.0
—December 1974	2.5	.78	1.6 — 4.0
—July 1975	2.4	.57	1.8 — 3.8
5. *Average Education of All Employees*			
(1–5 scale: 1 = no high school, 2 = high school, 3 = 1–3 yrs. college, 4 = bachelor's degree, 5 = master's degree)			
—April 1974	3.2	1.03	2 — 5
—December 1974	2.6	.84	1 — 4
—July 1975	2.5	.85	1 — 4

6. Frequency of Communications with Other Organizations

	Mean	SD	Low		High
—April 1974	3.1	.73	1.7	–	4.8
—December 1974	3.2	.67	1.9	–	4.0
—July 1975	3.1	.96	1.1	–	4.6

Performance of Childcare Organizations

1. Total Units of Services in All Functions (see Figure 1)

	Mean	SD	Low		High
—September 1973 to May 1974	4,388.8	6,149	472	–	21,461
—June 1974 to February 1975	9,462.4	10,970	1,873	–	40,489
—March 1975 to November 1975	10,845.0	13,234	2,035	–	44,034

2. Efficiency of Childcare Services (2 scores)[a]

	Mean	SD	Low		High
—September 1973 to May 1974	.01	.63	-.84	–	+1.18
—June 1974 to February 1975	.08	.41	-.76	–	+.69
—March 1975 to November 1975	.19	.39	-.31	–	+.94

3. Percent Financial Dependence on State Agency

	Mean	SD	Low		High
—September 1973 to May 1974	68%	.41	16%	–	100%
—June 1974 to February 1975	46%	.33	14%	–	100%
—March 1975 to November 1975	25%	.41	9%	–	54%

4. Perceived Effectiveness of Project by Community Organizations
(1–5 scale: 1 = little, 5 = great extent)

	Mean	SD	Low		High
—Summer 1974	3.5	.78	1.80	–	4.40
—Spring 1975	3.9	.53	3.11	–	4.63
—Fall 1975	4.0	1.40	1.00	–	5.00

Note: The data reported here were obtained with three instruments: (1) a standardized questionnaire that was completed by the directors of the childcare organizations in April 1974, December 1974, and July 1975; (2) quarterly reports on financial and performance indicators submitted to the state agency in order to receive funding from the agency; and (3) a questionnaire that was completed by representatives from seven to eleven other organizations in the local community in summer 1974, spring 1975, and fall 1975. Readers are referred to Van de Ven (in press) for a description of the data collection instruments and specific procedures used to measure the dimensions listed here.

[a]To weight equally the efficiency of services in each of the five functions, the data were transformed to a z-score (which produces a mean of zero and a standard deviation of one for each function across all time periods) before averaging to obtain an overall efficiency measure.

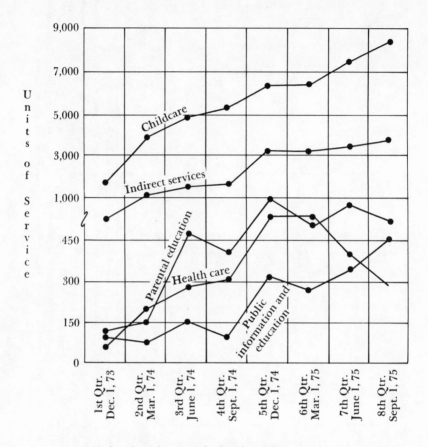

Note: Units of service are calculated as follows:

Childcare
Number of children times
days served
Health Care
Number of health screenings,
referrals, and treatments

Parental Education
Number of individual and group
sessions and mail-outs
Public Information and Education
Number of staff and volunteer
hours devoted to these functions.

Indirect Services
Number of interagency referrals,
contacts, and mechanisms plus hours
in training, planning, and reporting

**Figure 1. Quarterly Profile of Average Number of
Units of Services Provided by All Childcare Organizations**

on the average they demonstrated significant progress in establishing their financial independence from the state agency—a particularly important indicator of the likelihood that the childcare organizations could continue to survive after the state agency terminated its financial support on August 31, 1976.

Finally, a survey of representatives from other childcare-related agencies in the communities where the fourteen organizations were located was conducted in order to obtain their perceptions of the effectiveness and contributions of the new organizations in serving the needs of children and their families in the local communities. In each community, representatives from between seven to eleven agencies were contacted in the summer of 1974 with a mailed questionnaire, and these same people were again contacted in the spring and fall of 1975. Table 3 shows that, on the average, the respondents from other agencies perceived a measurable increase in the effectiveness of the childcare organization in their community during its first two years of operation. However, the table reveals that there was a wide range among the fourteen childcare organizations in their perceived effectiveness (as is true for all other performance indicators).

Interpreting the Outcomes

How and why did the fourteen childcare organizations on the average achieve these impressive outcomes during the first two years of program implementation? What accounts for the wide ranges in performance among the organizations shown in Table 3? Did the low-performing organizations encounter unique obstacles that hampered the implementation of their programs? Or are the variations in implementation success largely predictable from the processes followed in planning and organizing the new childcare organizations? Answers to these questions are important because they have not been addressed in the literature on organizations, most of which has been preoccupied with the design of mature organizations. Further, answers to these questions can provide useful knowledge to practitioners attempting to plan and implement new human service programs to meet the needs of clients in local communities. For these reasons, a major portion of the study of the childcare organizations was devoted to measuring the behavior of project planners and implementers over time. Specifically, the remainder of this report attempts to explain the variations in implementation success on the basis of the following factors.

1. The *planning activities* performed in creating the new childcare organizations.
2. The *obstacles* encountered by the new organizations as they implemented their childcare programs.
3. The *structural designs* of the organizations as they evolved and grew during the first few years of implementation.

Planning Process and Implementation Success

One of the central hypotheses of the research was that success in creating new human service programs is strongly related to planning processes initiated before the programs are implemented. More specifically, it was hypothesized that implementation success is a function of (1) *participation*—the number and kinds of people in the community who are involved in early phases of planning; (2) the *involvement of a planning policy board* (representing constituents of the local community) in making strategic decisions in each phase of planning; (3) *technical assistance*—the number of days of professional consultation obtained by planners to help them work out problems during the planning stage; (4) *planning team effort*—the number of hours worked by planners in each planning phase; and (5) *deviations from the PPM process*—the degree to which planners varied from an initial plan to implement the Program Planning Model in actually planning their programs. There are four major reasons for this hypothesis:

First, the PPM process, which nine of the community projects contracted to follow, provides clear guidelines to planners for dividing a complex effort into workable task phases that are similar to the basic stages of creative problem solving as discussed by Bales and Strodtbeck (1951). Group problem-solving processes that separate ideation or fact finding (Phases II and III in the PPM) from evaluation and choice (Phases IV and V) are generally superior to processes that combine them or that spend proportionately little work effort in fact finding (Maier and Hoffman, 1960; Rotter and

Portugal, 1969). Performance is generally greater in those planning processes that retard speedy decisions and cause one to perceive the task with an initial attitude of "problem-mindedness" as opposed to "solution-mindedness" (Maier and Solem, 1952; Van de Ven, 1974). Hence, the greater the number of hours spent by planners in the ideation and fact-finding stages of planning and the fewer the deviations from the phases and tasks prescribed by the PPM work plan, the more successful the implementation of the childcare program.

Second, most social planning theorists emphasize the importance of taking small, tentative, but consecutive steps in planning, with each step being subject to review and modification by a policy-making body on the basis of experience and knowledge gained during the intervening period (Delbecq and Van de Ven, 1971; Warren, 1971; Friedmann, 1973; Ackoff, 1974). In community planning contexts, the policy-making body generally consists of representatives from the target population who are the recipients of the program being planned and also includes representatives of other service-providing organizations, as well as public officials and influential community leaders. In addition to the institutional legitimation, cooptation, and fund-raising functions of these policy boards (Warren, 1971; Thompson, 1967; Zald, 1967), they tend to be particularly sensitive to the social, political, and economic realities of the program in each phase of its development (Rabinovitz, 1969; Delbecq and Van de Ven, 1971; Clark, 1968; Pressman and Wildavsky, 1973). If this "reality-testing" function is carried out, more tangible and practical objectives may emerge during the planning process than would otherwise be possible. Alternative means to achieve ends and practical ways to implement changes may become apparent. Planning and implementing thereby become fused during the course of the planning activity itself (Warren, 1971; Friedmann, 1973). Thus, the involvement of a policy board that represents the interests of the organization's strategic local constituencies is hypothesized to increase program implementation success.

Third, most planning theorists emphasize the importance of obtaining participation of clients, experts, and influential decision makers in the planning process (see review in Havelock, 1973).

Delbecq and Van de Ven (1971) state that citizen or client participation during Phase I of the PPM is necessary for an understanding of the nature and importance of problems as perceived by the people experiencing them. This increases the probability that solutions will be responses to user needs. During Phase II of the PPM the involvement of experts is needed to obtain a conceptual understanding of the nature and causes of the problems, as well as to identify alternative means for addressing them. Experts bring an awareness of the current state of knowledge and technology with respect to problems, and they can facilitate the selection of technically adequate solutions and provide witness and testimony for whatever solution is chosen. During the program design phase, the participation of resource controllers and other service providers in designing specific components of a program increases the probability that the proposal will be realistic, will be found acceptable to affected interest groups, and will thereby encounter fewer problems during implementation than it otherwise would. Overall, therefore, the participation of citizens, experts, and agency representatives enables planners to become aware of the technical and social complexities of childcare needs in their communities. This is expected to increase the likelihood that planners will develop a program that is technically feasible, responsive to client needs, and supported by those who will be affected by it when implemented.

Finally, most organization development theorists link the success of a planned change effort with the nature and degree of process consultation that is provided to the client system in helping it resolve problems encountered in achieving its objectives (Lippitt, Watson, and Westley, 1958; Bennis, Benne, and Chin, 1961; Shein, 1969; Argyris, 1970). This view assumes that the technical assistance provided by outside consultants not only helps the client system learn how to solve particular sets of problems but also increases the probability that if the problem sets recur they can be solved without the help of an external consultant (Argyris, p. 21). In sponsoring the community projects, the state agency provided three kinds of technical assistance to the projects: (1) training in the theory and practice of the PPM through three statewide workshops for all planners, (2) consultation from agency specialists in conducting the PPM process in the local community and implementing procedural matters of the planning contract, and (3) consultation in the content of early childhood development programs from childcare experts hired by the agency and assigned to each project. It was hypothesized that the more the project planners made use of these forms of consultation, the fewer the problems they would encounter in designing and implementing their childcare programs.

Table 4 shows the means, standard deviations, and ranges on the five process dimensions during each phase of planning for the nine PPM community projects. Within the ranges specified in Table 4, Table 5 shows the simple correlations between the dimensions over all planning phases and the performance of the PPM projects during their first two years of implementation. The reader is referred to Van de Ven (forthcoming) for an examination of how the process dimensions *within* each planning phase are interrelated and affect the performance of the childcare organizations during their first year of program implementation. Correlations on only nine observations will, of course, be highly unstable. This is why the correlations need to be very large (in general, with absolute magnitudes of .50 or larger) to be statistically significant. However, another good indication of the stability of the relationships between planning process and implementation performance is the consistency of the correlations that was found over several time periods, each nine months apart. Therefore, we can make meaningful and prudent interpretations of the relationships between planning process and implementation outcomes in terms of the consistency of the correlations over time, even though they may not be statistically significant.

Overall, the results show substantial support for the hypothesis that the process followed in planning a new community human service program does relate in a predictable way to how successful the program is during its first few years of operation. The PPM projects involved an average of 320 citizens, experts, and community organization representatives (ranging from 193 to 520) in all phases of planning from February to August 1973. Within this range, the number of people involved in planning the childcare programs is consistently and positively correlated with the effectiveness of the childcare organizations as perceived by rep-

Table 4. Basic Statistics for Nine PPM Projects on Process Dimensions During Planning Phases (February to August 1973)

	Mean	Standard Deviation	Range Minimum – Maximum	
1. *Participation in Planning*	320	108	193	520
a. Citizens involved in Phase II	276	91	168	427
b. Experts involved in Phase III	33	15	7	53
c. Organizations involved in Phase IV	11	7	6	24
2. *Policy Board Involvement*	2.45	1.19	1.00	4.00
(1 = none, 5 = very much)				
a. During Phase II, problem exploration	3.8	.5	3.0	4.5
b. During Phase III, knowledge exploration	3.3	.8	2.0	4.5
c. During Phase IV, program design	3.3	.7	2.0	4.5
3. *Planning Team Effort*	592	165	308	832
a. Hours worked during Phase II	244	70	140	350
b. Hours worked during Phase III	187	81	60	248
c. Hours worked during Phase IV	161	71	48	250
4. *Technical Assistance in Planning*	15.1	5.3	9	22
a. Days of consultation in Phase II	7.8	2.5	4	11
b. Days of consultation in Phase III	4.2	2.5	1	8
c. Days of consultation in Phase IV	3.1	3.5	0	8
5. *Deviations from PPM Plan*	2.35	.91	1.17	3.50
(1 = little, 5 = much)				
a. During Phase II, problem exploration	1.9	.9	1.0	3.5
b. During Phase III, knowledge exploration	2.4	.8	1.5	3.5
c. During Phase IV, program design	2.8	1.3	1.0	4.0
6. *Expertise of Planners*	4.1	1.0	3.0	6.0
(Education, years experience, number of planning conferences attended by planning staff)				

Note: Data on these planning process dimensions are available only on the nine PPM projects. It was not possible to obtain these quantitative measures on the five non-PPM projects.

resentatives from other community agencies, and negatively corre-lated with the barriers or obstacles that project directors perceived in implementing their programs during the first two years. How-ever, participation in planning was found not to relate to the quan-tity of services provided or to the financial independence of the childcare organizations, and the correlations are mixed for service efficiency during the initial years of implementation. Thus, the major effects of participation in planning appear to be that of generating community support for a program and of decreasing motivational and organizational problems in implementing the program.

The degree of involvement of the policy board (consisting of representatives of clients, members of other childcare organiza-tions, community leaders, and elected officials) in early phases of planning is most strongly correlated with increases in the efficiency of services and decreases in the financial dependence of the childcare organization on the state agency. These findings, along with qualitative information obtained in phase-end interviews, suggest that policy board involvement in planning community pro-grams serves two basic functions. First, activities and decisions of policy boards in early planning phases appear to direct the efforts of planners to the development of a realistic and economically fea-sible program. Second, as noted above, the involvement of other organizations, community leaders, and public officials serves as an important cooptation strategy for linking the new organization into existing resource allocation channels within the community and thereby enhances its probability of obtaining funding support when the program is implemented.

Planners in the PPM projects worked an average of 592 hours (ranging from 308 to 832 hours) in planning their programs; most of this time was spent in the problem and knowledge explora-tion phases (see Table 4). Table 5 shows that the planning of team efforts is strongly correlated with increases in the quantity and efficiency of services provided, with the perceived effectiveness of the childcare organizations by other community agencies, and with moderate decreases in the implementation obstacles encountered during the first two years of operation. Simply put, these findings suggest that the more front-end work performed in planning a new

Table 5. Correlations Between Planning Process and Implementation Success

	Participation	Policy Board Involvement	Hours Spent In Planning	Days of Consultation	Expertise of Planners	Deviations From PPM Plan
Planning Process of Nine PPM Projects During February 1973 to August 1973						
1. Number of citizens, experts, agencies that participated in planning	—					
2. Degree of policy board involvement	.09	—				
3. Hours spent in all phases of planning by planners	.47	.23	—			
4. Days of consultation obtained during planning	.23	-.33	.18	—		
5. Expertise of planners (education, experience, conferences)	-.05	.52[a]	.42	.52[a]	—	
6. Degree process deviated from PPM plans	-.57[a]	-.02	-.63[a]	-.29	-.24	—
Implementation Performance of PPM Projects from September 1973 to November 1975						
1. Total Units of Services in All Functions						
—September 1973 to May 1974	.08	.02	.56[a]	.36	.66[a]	-.37
—June 1974 to February 1975	.03	.02	.50[a]	.31	.63[a]	-.35
—March 1975 to November 1975	.05	.11	.45	.36	.55[a]	-.37

2. Efficiency of Childcare Services						
—September 1973 to May 1974	.36	.03	.36	.39	.06	-.54[a]
—June 1974 to February 1975	-.28	.68[a]	.31	.17	.74[a]	-.13
—March 1975 to November 1975	.21	.66[a]	.63[a]	.25	.43	-.46
3. Percent Financial Dependence on State Agency						
—September 1973 to May 1974	-.10	-.36	-.19	-.69[a]	.05	.40
—June 1974 to February 1975	.05	-.37	-.04	-.32	-.09	.26
—March 1975 to November 1975	.16	-.59[a]	.11	-.28	.09	.20
4. Perceived Effectiveness of Project by Community Organizations						
—Summer 1974	.39	.02	.64[a]	.24	.29	-.09
—Spring 1975	.49[a]	.31	.48	-.01	-.05	.00
—Fall 1975	.06	.30	.19	-.16	.23	.01
5. Implementation Obstacles Experienced						
—April 1974	-.14	-.28	-.12	.34	-.40	.26
—December 1974	-.55[a]	-.32	-.42	.30	-.45	.36
—July 1975	-.43	-.11	-.41	.22	-.22	.15

[a]Correlations significant beyond .05 level

program, the more effective the program when implemented. Furthermore, the larger the scope and quantity of services to be provided in the initial years of implementing a program, the greater the amount of hours required to plan the program.

The expertise of the planners and the number of days of consultation obtained by the planners in developing their childcare programs are strongly correlated, and they indicate that two types of professional input are of particular value in program planning. Table 5 shows that planners' expertise and amount of consultation in planning are both positively correlated with the quantity and efficiency of services provided by the childcare organizations during their first two years of implementation. In addition, consultation in planning is strongly related to decreased financial dependence on the state agency when an organization's programs are actually implemented. Presumably this is because of the assistance that many consultants gave to planners and policy boards in obtaining financial support from other sources.

Unexpectedly the number of days of consultation obtained during planning is positively correlated with the perceived degree of obstacles encountered in the first two years of implementation. When this result was presented to the childcare directors at a feedback session in 1976, several attributed it to the fact that the consultants tended to suggest higher standards for childcare programs than planners had initially envisioned. From this we can tentatively interpret the positive correlations between consultation and implementation barriers as reflecting an increase in the aspiration levels of project directors. Finally, the levels of education and experience of planners are negatively correlated with implementation barriers. This result is consistent with qualitative impressions obtained in the phase-end interviews with planners. Experienced planners tended to explain their planning behavior more often in terms of previous efforts in planning human service programs than did less trained and experienced planners.

Deviations from PPM work plans refer to the degree to which the project planners and the state agency specialists judged that the processes followed by the projects in each planning phase varied from the detailed work plans for undertaking the Program Planning Model contracts with the state agency. These PPM work plans were developed by the project planners during the prerequisite planning stage, were evaluated and renegotiated where necessary, and were approved by the state agency specialists. Since they provided the terms of the planning contracts between the state agency and the community projects, deviation from PPM work plans is an overall indicator of how closely the projects followed the specific phases and steps of the Program Planning Model.

Table 5 shows that the more planners deviated from the process steps prescribed in their PPM contracts while planning their childcare programs, the lower the quantity and efficiency of services, the more dependent they remained on the state agency for financial assistance, and the greater the implementation obstacles they encountered during the first two years of operation. The findings thus provide good support for the Program Planning Model as developed by Delbecq and Van de Ven (1971) and indicate that the more closely the projects followed the basic phases and steps of the PPM, the more successful they were in implementing their programs.

Program Planners and Implementers

The findings noted above provide evidence for the major hypothesis that a close connection exists between how an organization is planned and how successful it is during its first two years of operation. Another aspect of this connection is commonly known as the relationship between the "planner" and the "doer." Current literature on this subject suggests that the more closely planners and doers are merged, the more likely it is that a program will be implemented successfully (Bass, 1970; Friedmann, 1973; Van de Ven and Koenig, 1976).

In five of the fourteen projects, the planning directors ultimately became the implementation directors of the childcare organizations. In the others, planning was done by another organization, a group of planners, or by individuals who did not become involved in implementing the direct childcare programs. A comparison was made of the service efficiency in the first year of implementation between the organizations whose planners did become the implementation directors and the organizations whose planners did not. In terms of a normalized (z-score) measure, the

average efficiency of services in all functions in the first year for
projects whose planners also became the implementers was +.31,
while it was −.30 for the projects whose planners did not become
the implementers. Although the differences are not statistically
significant, the results show that the childcare programs whose
planners did become the implementation directors were above the
average of the fourteen projects in service efficiency in their first
year of operation, while those projects whose planners did not
become the implementers fell below the average. Furthermore, it
was found that the organizations in which planners ultimately became the implementers were quicker to implement their programs.
Two reasons for these findings are that program continuity was
maintained by having planners become the implementers and that
time was not spent searching for a qualified person and orienting
him or her to the nature of the planned program.

Implementation Obstacles

In varying degrees, all the community projects encountered
obstacles in implementing their programs. Table 6 shows the extent
to which the fourteen project directors encountered six kinds of
implementation problems during the early life of their organizations. A comparison of the responses over the three time periods
shows that there were considerable decreases in the degrees of
implementation obstacles between April 1974 and July 1975. Before it is shown how these implementation obstacles are related to
the organization design and performance during the first two years
of operation, the qualitatively different types of obstacles encountered by the childcare organizations over time must be described.

Staff recruitment was the most frequently mentioned difficulty encountered by the childcare organizations, with at least 70
percent of the directors reporting moderate to high amounts of
staff recruitment difficulty in April 1974 and December 1974 and
somewhat less in July 1975. A shortage of available personnel
trained in early childhood development was the reason most cited
for this problem. However, some qualitative differences were noted
in the kinds of recruitment problems in the first two years of implementation. Prior to April 1974, difficulties were encountered in

Table 6. Implementation Obstacles Reported by Organization Directors

In your efforts to activate the Early Childhood (EC) Project during the past six months, to what extent and in what instances have you encountered the following difficulties:

	Responses of Fourteen Organization Directors[a]					
	April 1974		*December 1974*		*July 1975*	
	Mean	Standard Deviation	Mean	Standard Deviation	Mean	Standard Deviation
A. *Staff recruitment problems* — finding individuals who are properly qualified for the job? Describe instances.	3.0	1.3	2.9	1.2	2.2	1.2
B. Resistance or *lack of support from other agencies* or community people for the EC Project? Describe instances.	2.6	1.0	2.1	.9	1.7	1.1
C. *Lack of resources* or materials necessary for implementing the EC Project? Describe.	2.6	1.4	2.2	1.1	2.1	1.2
D. Lack of *clarity* about certain *goals* or plans of the EC Project? Describe.	2.5	.8	1.7	.6	2.0	1.1
E. Lack of understanding about *how to implement* certain goals or plans of the EC Project? Describe instances.	2.4	1.2	1.9	.8	1.8	.8
F. *Staff resistance* or lack of motivation to implement the EC Project? Describe instances.	1.8	.9	1.6	.7	1.5	.8
Total Average Implementation Obstacles	*2.6*	*.6*	*2.1*	*.4*	*1.8*	*.7*

[a]The response scale used for all questions was:
1 = None   2 = Little   3 = Some   4 = Much   5 = Great

Note: Measures of the six implementation obstacles were originally developed from a description by Gross, Giacquinta, and Bernstein (1971) of the barriers encountered in introducing educational innovations in elementary schools.

finding staff who resided within a feasible commuting distance. However, in December 1974 and March 1975, the directors noted that an increasing amount of attention and time was needed to train new staff and to screen potentially qualified personnel. This suggests that the directors turned to in-service training of available personnel, after experiencing difficulties in finding professionals in child development in their immediate vicinity.

The second most frequent implementation obstacle was the lack of involvement and support from other agencies in the community for the childcare program. In April 1974 the directors reported that this resulted from skepticism and/or the lack of information regarding the goals and objectives of their programs. During the second year of implementation, the nature of resistance from other community agencies shifted from initial skepticism about the new programs to the problems of other organizations not maintaining their commitments to the childcare organizations. By July 1975, eight directors reported no difficulties in obtaining community support, while several of those who did report difficulties indicated that the lack of support was associated with basic philosophical issues quite independent of the nature of the childcare organizations (for example, dislike of all federally funded programs).

The third obstacle encountered in implementing the new organizations was a lack of resources to supplement the funding provided by the state agency. Three directors indicated considerable difficulty in locating physical sites for their childcare centers or in getting needed improvements completed in available sites (for example, renovating a church basement). Other resource problems included money shortages for equipment, supplies, transportation services, and other technical services, such as professional advice on special problems or developmental norms of children. From April 1974 to July 1975 there was a decrease in the number of directors who reported resource obstacles, particularly problems in locating physical sites and obtaining technical services, supplies, and equipment (many of which were donated to the childcare organizations by civic and religious groups in the local communities). However, problems directly associated with money shortages continued to be a concern for at least four of the childcare organizations in the second year of program implementation. Directors of three of these organizations reported that these money shortages stemmed from a simple lack of available money in their economically depressed counties and that they needed to look to state or federal agencies or to private foundations for assistance.

Lack of clear program goals was reported to decrease between April 1974 and December 1974 but then to increase in July 1975. In April 1974 directors reported problems in three areas: (1) unclear coordination arrangements with other organizations, (2) misunderstandings of the roles and functions employees were expected to perform, and (3) not being clear on what can be achieved by or expected realistically of certain components of services, especially health care services. In December 1974, only the last two problem areas were mentioned, and half the directors reported no ambiguity problems. In March 1975 there was an increase in misunderstandings of staff roles over the previous periods. The open-ended responses of four directors suggested that this problem resulted from personnel turnovers and the confusion caused by losing reports and documents that had been developed at an earlier time. In effect, a new set of problems developed as a consequence of not establishing and updating coordination and control procedures in four of the childcare organizations.

Related to the lack of clear program goals was the lack of knowledge about specific steps to take in implementing goals or program plans. The specific problems mentioned by the directors focused on three issues: (1) developing staff training programs, (2) establishing financial accounting and budgeting procedures, and (3) dealing with inconsistencies between program goals developed during the planning process and the service priorities required by various funding agencies to obtain additional resources. However, with the assistance of the agency specialists and consultants, these problems were resolved, and over time an increasing number of directors reported no difficulties in this area.

Finally, the childcare organization directors reported little or no staff resistance to implementing their programs during the first two years of operation. Where resistance did exist, it was reported to be due to misunderstanding of the program or lack of training rather than to staff opposition or apathy. It is noteworthy that staff resistance was reported as the least significant obstacle to these childcare programs, since it has been reported in other organizational studies as a very significant barrier to introducing planned changed (Gross, Giacquinta, and Bernstein, 1971; Bass, 1970). Our explanations for this are, first, that the childcare organizations were *new;* this meant that preestablished norms or traditions did not have to be changed, and project staffs could get caught up in the excitement of creating a needed childcare service for their communities. Second, these organizations were *small;* this permitted the directors to pay personal attention to the concerns of individual employees. In addition, a core group of employees in many of the organizations was also involved in the planning phases. The greater the participation in planning, the lower were the obstacles in implementing the program (see Table 4).

In summary, there was a considerable decrease in the extent to which the childcare organizations experienced difficulties in implementing their programs over their first two years of operation. Implementation obstacles were found not only to vary in degree but also to take on a qualitatively different character during this period. Furthermore, substantial proportions of the variations in the implementation obstacles encountered are explained by the initial planning processes employed in the programs.

Organization Design and Performance

One should not, of course, attribute all implementation obstacles to the processes initially used in planning the new organizations. Indeed, no program, however well conceived and planned, is likely to be free of implementation obstacles—the actions of individuals, groups, and organizations are interdependent, and each of these actors has limited abilities. Just as it is not possible for any single actor to specify in advance what the particular components or outcomes of a planning process will be, it is unrealistic to try to predict all the obstacles and problems that will be encountered when implementing a new organization. If a set of decision makers were powerful enough to do so, it would still not be desirable because that would foreclose any possibility of learning. It is important, therefore, to examine how implementation obstacles were associated with growth in organizational structure and performance while the childcare programs were being implemented.

Table 7 shows the correlations between the implementation obstacles and the design and performance characteristics of the fourteen childcare organizations during their first two years of operation. Concurrent or cross-sectional correlations within each time period are presented along the diagonal. Time-lagged correlations for April 1974, December 1974, and July 1975 are presented off the diagonal for each relationship. The time-lagged correlations provide much insight into the temporal ordering of the relationships, that is, whether implementation obstacles at an earlier period influence a dimension of structure or performance at a later time period, or whether organization design or performance at an early stage of program implementation affects obstacles at a later stage of implementation.

Scale of Services Provided. In his review of case studies on organizational innovations, Greiner (1970) reports that a common characteristic of unsuccessful innovations is that attempts are made to implement new programs on a large-scale and global basis. In contrast, the successfully implemented innovations began on a small scale, were implemented incrementally, and expanded on the basis of previous success. Beginning on a small-scale basis provides opportunities to evaluate, modify, and improve the design of a new program before having to cope with the administrative burdens of managing a large-scale operation. Therefore it was expected that as the childcare organizations increased in size, number of service sites, and quantity of services provided in their initial stages of implementation, the greater would be the subsequent obstacles to implementing the programs. The correlations in Table 7 show substantial support for this reasoning. The lagged correlations of organization size, number of service sites, and total units of services provided in early stages of implementation are all positively correlated with the obstacles encountered in later stages of implementation. Furthermore, the reverse time-lagged correlations are either negative or near zero. This suggests that the obstacles encountered in early stages of implementation either decrease or are unrelated to the scale of operations of the childcare organizations in later periods of program implementation.

Table 7. Correlations Between Implementation Obstacles and Design and Performance of the Childcare Organizations in First Two Years

	Implementation Obstacles Encountered as Perceived by 14 Project Directors		
	April 1974	December 1974	July 1975
Design of Childcare Organizations			
1. Organization Size (Number of employees)			
—April 1974	.23	.18	.46[a]
—December 1974	-.14	-.06	.30
—July 1975	.14	-.03	.35
2. Number of Service Sites in Community			
—April 1974	.56[a]	.61[a]	.56[a]
—December 1974	.01	.24	.30
—July 1975	.09	.27	.16
3. Formalization of Procedures			
—April 1974	-.32	-.51[a]	.04
—December 1974	-.14	-.09	-.30
—July 1975	.06	.32	-.44[a]
4. Staff Participation in Decisions			
—April 1974	-.08	-.02	-.31
—December 1974	.33	.14	-.08
—July 1975	.09	.13	.18
5. Average Education of Staff			
—April 1974	-.21	-.17	-.27
—December 1974	-.18	-.16	-.47[a]
—July 1975	-.23	-.28	-.55[a]

6. Frequency of Communications with Other Organizations			
—April 1974	$\underline{.20}$	.02	.15
—December 1974	.05	.03	.38
—July 1975	.15	$\underline{.28}$	$\underline{.02}$
Performance of Childcare Organizations			
1. Total Units of Services Provided (All Functions)			
—September 1973 to May 1974	$\underline{.45^a}$	.36	.07
—June 1974 to February 1975	-.06	.14	.30
—March 1975 to November 1975	.05	$-.16$	$\underline{.32}$
2. Efficiency of Childcare Services			
—September 1973 to May 1974	$\underline{-.45^a}$	.14	.12
—June 1974 to February 1975	$-.66^a$	$-.18$	.36
—March 1975 to November 1975	$-.16$	$\underline{-.17}$	$\underline{-.23}$
3. Percent Financial Dependence on State Agency			
—September 1973 to May 1974	$\underline{-.45^a}$	$-.42^a$	$-.23$
—June 1974 to February 1975	.39	$-.48^a$	$-.54^a$
—March 1975 to November 1975	.07	$\underline{.18}$	$\underline{.52^a}$
4. Perceived Effectiveness of Program by Community Organizations			
—Summer 1974	$-.34$	$-.46^a$	.04
—Spring 1975	$-.24$	$-.55^a$	.01
—Fall 1975	$-.04$	$\underline{-.11}$	$\underline{-.38}$

[a]Significant beyond .05 level.

Formalization of Procedures. It was reported above that a new set of implementation obstacles developed in the second year of implementation as a consequence of not establishing or updating procedures to coordinate and control activities within the childcare organizations. Table 7 supports this conclusion of the project directors. Formalization of procedures in early stages of implementation is strongly correlated with decreases in implementation obstacles in the next time period. The structuring of rules, policies, and procedures decreases employees' misunderstandings of their jobs because it specifies the role behavior expected of them.

Staff Participation in Decision Making. A shared approach to power and decision making is advocated by many writers on organizational innovation (Greiner, 1970; Bass, 1970; Delbecq and Van de Ven, 1971; Ackoff, 1974). Participation, they argue, decreases employee resistance to innovation because of the motivational properties embedded in asking people to invest their time and ideas in the creation and implementation of an organizational program. The correlations in Table 7, however, provide little evidence to substantiate this proposition. Although the correlations are in the expected direction, they are relatively small or near zero. One possible reason for these insignificant findings is that the directors reported very little staff resistance during the implementation period; hence, there may be insufficient variation in staff resistance to obtain significant findings.

Educational Level of Employees. The recruitment of qualified staff was the most significant obstacle to implementing the childcare programs reported by the directors. As a substitute to finding staff with required levels of formal education, many of the directors instituted job entry and on-the-job training programs for employees who were hired with a high school education (on the average). This substitution explains the negative correlations between obstacles encountered in early implementation stages and educational levels of staff in subsequent implementation stages. Furthermore, many people. who had been unemployed and on welfare were hired by the childcare centers. Several directors reported that their organizations made an important additional contribution to the community by providing employment to economically deprived citizens. However, the correlations in Table 7 reveal a basic predicament produced by this well-intentioned strategy. The lower the levels of education of employees, the greater the obstacles subsequently encountered in implementing the programs, particularly between December 1974 and July 1975 when several directors chose the strategy of hiring employees from the welfare rolls.

These results exemplify the basic predicaments involved in many of the strategic decisions that directors had to make during the early lives of their organizations. Should one attempt to substantially improve the social and economic well-being of a few individuals on welfare by hiring them and investing significant amounts of time and resources to train them, or should one place greater priority on the overall functioning of the organization and the quality of services to a large number of clients? The alternatives are presented in an either/or way because the level of education of employees is significantly correlated with decreases in the following indicators of performance of the childcare organizations:

1. Efficiency of services provided in all functions ($-.38$).
2. Financial dependence on the state agency ($+.69$).
3. Effectiveness of the childcare organization as perceived by representatives from other community agencies ($-.32$).
4. Quality of childcare services ($-.54$) as judged by a three-person panel of early childhood development experts who made on-site appraisals in each organization (see Van de Ven, 1980).

When the consequences of this hiring decision were presented in a feedback session, they produced three types of reactions from six directors. Two indicated they were not aware of the negative consequences on performance from hiring unqualified people. Three stated they understood some of the trade-offs involved and deliberately chose to hire low-skilled people to minimize labor costs. One director viewed the decision to hire people on welfare as being consistent with the central goals of her organization. She went on to state: "Employers [in the community] have not been fair to blacks [untrained employees]. They make a big fuss when they [untrained employees] do something wrong. They are not willing to pay the costs involved in training people to do basic jobs we take for granted. All learning involves some waste. We forget how much paper was wasted when we had to learn how to write."

Interorganizational Communications. The frequency of interorganizational communications is an indicator of the degree to which the projects worked in coordination with other agencies while implementing their childcare programs. On the one hand, it was expected that the development of interagency relationships would cause loss of autonomy and create a need to respond to the concerns and skepticism of other community agencies about the new childcare organizations, thereby increasing implementation obstacles. On the other hand, it was expected that directors who were experiencing implementation obstacles would seek help from people in other community organizations who initially had participated in planning the programs and would thereby communicate more frequently with other organizations. The correlations in Table 7 between interorganizational communications and implementation obstacles from April to December 1974 are all near zero, while those from December 1974 to July 1975 are somewhat consistent with expectations. Overall, the results are too weak to substantiate any conclusion.

Efficiency of Services Provided. As expected, Table 7 shows that the greater the obstacles encountered in early stages of implementation, the lower was the efficiency of services provided in those and later stages of implementation. Furthermore, the positive directions of the correlations between efficiency in April and December 1974 with implementation obstacles in December 1974 and July 1975 suggest an important point. Overemphasis on service efficiency in the first year of implementation of the new childcare programs may have the negative longer-run consequences of increasing problems and decreasing performance in later stages of program implementation. The findings suggest that the prevalent concern in the public sector with costs per unit of service and other forms of cost-benefit analysis may be self-defeating in the long run. Although efficiency is an important criterion for evaluating mature organizations during periods of restricted resources, overemphasis on this criterion during the initial implementation stage creates new obstacles to overcome in subsequent periods.

Financial Dependence. Obtaining funding to continue the childcare programs after the financial support of the state agency terminated continued to be perceived (but by a decreasing number of directors) as a basic implementation obstacle during the first two years of operation. The data in Table 7 provide additional insight into this problem. As might be expected, the greater the obstacles perceived by the directors in early stages of implementation, the more dependent they remained on the state agency for funding. However, the more financially dependent the organizations were on the state agency in early implementation stages, the fewer the obstacles they encountered in subsequent implementation stages. These results indicate the countervailing pressures on the childcare organizations not to move from dependence to independence, even though it was clear that the state agency would end its funding in August, 1976. Longitudinal research is still in progress to evaluate the behavior and outcomes of the childcare organizations as they passed through this stage.

Summary and Speculations

This research took a behavioral approach to examine the creation of fourteen community childcare organizations at the time of their initial inception in the winter of 1972, during their planning phases from February to August 1973, and throughout their first two years of program implementation until the fall of 1975. Longitudinal research was conducted to explain the development and performance of the new organizations in terms of (1) the planning processes they followed, (2) the implementation obstacles they encountered, and (3) the structural designs that evolved during their first two years of operation. Technically, the research findings are limited to fourteen Texas childcare organizations. In fact, however, these findings throw considerable light on the process of organizational creation in general. Further, my own observations and involvements in the birth of various public and private organizations suggest that the major findings of the study apply equally well to the creation of many other types of organizations.

Important relationships were discovered between the ways in which the childcare organizations were planned and the implementation success they achieved during their first two years of operation. Variations in program implementation success were related in important and different ways to (1) the number of citizens, experts, and community organizations that participated in planning; (2) the involvement of a planning policy board that represented important constituencies in the community; (3) the number of hours worked by planners; (4) the amount of consultation the planners obtained in planning their programs; (5) the levels of education and experience of the planners; and (6) the extent to which the planners deviated from the Program Planning Model (PPM) process. Furthermore, increases in the number of obstacles encountered were consistently associated with decreases in (1) participation, (2) policy board involvement, (3) planning team effort, and (4) expertise of planners; and they were associated with increases in (1) deviations from the PPM process and (2) days of consultation. The latter unexpected relationship was explained by the increase in aspiration levels produced by consultants during planning.

These findings provide substantial evidence to support the major hypothesis of this study, which is that the initial processes in planning new organizations are strongly related to their subsequent implementation success. One basic explanation for this relationship is that a systematic and thorough process of planning can predict, solve, and thereby prevent the complex social, political, and technical problems inherent in creating new organizations. From this perspective, planning is not only a process for technically designing a new organization but also a process for motivating community action and support and for preventing problems from emerging when new organizations are implemented. Indeed, as Kimberly suggests in Chapter Two, the conditions under which an organization is born and the course of its development in infancy have nontrivial consequences for its later life.

However, it would be incorrect to draw the conclusion that implementation success is solely a function of the initial planning process; instead, it is but one of several important contributing factors. Thus, the obstacles encountered during the first two years of implementing the childcare organizations not only varied in degree but also took on a qualitatively different character in subsequent stages of implementations. These quantitative and qualitative variations in implementation obstacles were partially explained by the following structural and performance factors:

1. The childcare organizations that initially attempted to implement their programs on a large-scale basis later experienced serious implementation barriers. In contrast, the programs that began small in size, in number of service sites, and in quantity of services encountered significantly fewer problems in later stages of implementing their childcare organizations.
2. The structuring of formal rules, policies, and procedures in early stages of implementation decreased obstacles and problems in later stages of implementing the childcare organizations.
3. The lower the levels of employee education, the greater the obstacles subsequently encountered in implementing the programs. This result called into question the well-intentioned strategy of hiring individuals on welfare and training them to staff the childcare centers.
4. Overemphasis on service efficiency in the first year of implementation of the new programs had the negative consequences of increasing problems and decreasing performance in later stages of program implementation.
5. Symbolic of the painful stage of moving from dependence to independence, countervailing pressures were experienced by the childcare organizations to become financially independent and at the same time to overcome implementation obstacles. The greater the obstacles experienced in early stages of implementation, the more dependent the childcare organizations remained on the state agency for funding. However, the more financially independent the childcare organizations became, the greater the obstacles they subsequently encountered in later stages of implementation.

The findings presented in this chapter are preliminary because the longitudinal study of the creation and development of the childcare organizations is still in progress. In particular, data continue to be collected for measuring the behavior and performance of the fourteen organizations as they move beyond the creation stage and into a more mature institutionalized stage. Nevertheless, the data presented here provide sufficient evidence to indicate that one can largely explain (and therefore manage) the degree of success in implementing new human service organizations by the strategic choices made regarding planning processes and structural designs during the early phases of organizational creation.

This study leaves in its wake a number of impressions, speculations, and questions about the creation of organizations. They can be mentioned in this conclusion only as "unfinished business," with the hope that they may stimulate future theorizing and research. One concluding impression is that a behavioral approach to the study of organizational creation provides a far richer understanding of the beginnings of collective action than does a structural perspective. Organizational analysts have been enamored with structure because most of their work has centered on mature organizations. Organizational structure provides blueprints (for example, rules, policies, procedures) for performing a set of activities. Structure is useful for managing and coordinating collective action when the means and ends of such action are known. However, in the early stages of organizational creation the means and ends of behavior are often not clear, and the value system on which the organization's structure will be based does not yet exist—there are no structural laws that govern organizational birth in the way that biological laws govern the birth of animals or human beings. Organizational structure is a consequence of the choices people make about the processes they desire to have repeated so that there will be less uncertainty about the consequences of their behavior. Hence, central to an understanding of organizational creation is a focus on the processes of collective action; structure should be allowed to follow and emerge once the consequences of action become known (that is, when processes become repetitive).

This behavioral perspective stimulates three basic questions about organizational creation: (1) *What initiates novel collective behavior?* (2) *What motivates unstructured collective behavior?* (3) *What guides learning so that certain behaviors or processes are filtered out while others are repeated and emerge as the structure of the new organization?* Several points need to be made about these questions.

First, collective, as distinguished from individual, behavior is stressed in these questions because the creation of organizations is not an individual enterprise. Instead, it is a network-building enterprise that centers on the inception, diffusion, and adoption of a set of ideas among a group of people who become sufficiently committed to these ideas to transform them into "good currency" (Schon, 1971). Indeed, a gnawing question is whether one should track the creation of organizations or the life cycle of ideas. Organizations, after all, are but a structural forum in which groups of people institutionalize, harvest, and protect ideas that are in good standing.

The emphasis on collective rather than individual behavior sets this approach apart from that of Kimberly (1979), who, like previous entrepreneurial researchers, emphasizes the personal characteristics of the founder as being largely responsible for the creation of an organization. For example, Kimberly (1979, p. 454) states: "Whether one chooses to call him an entrepreneur, a leader, or a guru, the fact is that his personality, his dreams, his flaws, and his talents were largely responsible for the school's early structure and results." There is no disagreement over the importance of the entrepreneurial role in organizational creation. What is problematic is the misdirected inference that can easily be drawn from such a study. It might be inferred that if one could accurately describe the personality, dreams, flaws, and talents of entrepreneurs, an understanding of the creation of organizations would be achieved. In other words, one might conclude that from the attributes of the founder one can understand the early structure and results of a new organization. But such a conclusion does not take into consideration the processes that go on before an organization assumes a recognizable form and often before an entrepreneur enters the scene. Kimberly recognizes (but does not develop) this problem in his observation that while change in existing organizations occurs in the context of an established culture and an institutionalized set of norms, values, and procedures, this entire context must be created before an organization can be born.

A more direct approach to the three questions asked above may hinge on the distinction made by March and Simon (1958) between *substantive planning*—planning a new performance program—and *procedural planning*—developing programs for the problem-solving process itself. Here, substantive planning would mean the creation of a new organization, while the procedural planning process would be represented by the Program Planning Model (PPM). March and Simon (1958) point out that procedural planning governs substantive planning. A procedural planning model such as the PPM may stimulate a spate of unstructured and ill-defined activity when a new organization is being substantively planned. However, the procedural planning process may itself be routinized to a greater or lesser degree.

Thus, a possible answer to the questions about what factors initiate, motivate, and guide the substantive creation of organizations may be found by examining the procedural planning model employed, which ironically may itself be quite well defined and structured. As a procedural planning model, the PPM offers a relatively simple set of guidelines for initiating, motivating, and guiding the unstructured and ill-defined behavior inherent in substantively planning new organizations. The basic procedural guidelines are to (1) divide the entire process into a series of manageable phases and tasks, (2) involve different groups of people who have the relevant knowledge or expertise on the tasks performed within each phase, and (3) utilize a group decision-making process or strategy that is appropriate for dealing with the tasks and problems unique to each phase.

Indeed, a major impression obtained from observation of the initial planning efforts of the childcare organizations was that the PPM established a far more dynamic social network for creating local community programs than had been anticipated when the study was begun in 1972. Procedural guidelines in the PPM on the entry, exit, and reentry of different constituencies of a community in the planning phases brought about a new organizational entity for community action that did not exist previously—a situation similar to a "rolling federation of alliances" (Clark, 1965) or an "organized anarchy" (Cohen, March, and Olsen, 1972). This rolling federation was created through the voluntary participation of citizens, experts, and community organizations who were involved at different points in time on only those tasks relevant to their self-interests, backgrounds, and skills. In each phase, a different problem-solving strategy was used to guide search, evaluation, and choice; the incremental products of each phase were evaluated and legitimated by a relatively permanent policy board that itself was representative of constituents temporarily involved in each planning phase. Thus, the substantive meaning of action was derived from the social process (Pfeffer, 1977a), and tentative goals were constructed after the action occurred in each phase to "real-ize" and provide order to the behavior (Weich, 1977a).

Use of the PPM makes the locus of power and authority very diffuse initially. The model is based on the voluntary willingness of citizens, experts, and agencies to share and assume responsibility for key community problems that exist within their organizational or occupational domains. The planners and others who assume responsibilities for problems generally do not have authority over those who possess the competence or resources needed to solve the problems. As a result, there is a need to cut across organizational boundaries in the community and to motivate experts and resource controllers to share responsibility for solving the problems by enlisting them in the planning process. Thus, it is out of a specific set of needs to solve problems—by those who assume responsibility for these problems—that a rolling federation of alliances emerges during the early stages of planning, long before a new organization is created or even thought out. In later planning phases, as commitments to an emerging collective program begin to grow in strength relative to the self-interests of the parties involved, the ideas for a human service program begin to take on the characteristics of a formal organization. To the extent that this occurs, the organizational models for decision making, coordination, and control—as developed in administrative theory—become increasingly relevant (Warren, 1971, p. 166).

The PPM partially responds to Cohen, March, and Olsen's (1972) call for a normative theory of decision making for an organized anarchy; that is, for a situation characterized by unclear goals, uncertain technology, and fluid participation, which are typical in the initial planning stages of a new organization. Like the "garbage can" model of Cohen, March, and Olsen (1972), the PPM focuses on procedural guidelines for decision making or problem solving and does not depend on relating current action to goals.

Instead, goals emerge from action. However, the PPM seems to avoid two basic problems present in the garbage can model:

First, decision making by flight or oversight need not be the major feature of the process. Confrontation and resolution of problems in the PPM can and does occur when the issues in the development of a collective entity are decomposed into manageable questions, ordered over time into a meaningful sequence of phases and decision strategies, and addressed by decision makers with the relevant competence and interest. In addition, when specific questions in a particular phase are not confronted or solved, repeating the activities in that phase to resolve these questions may be more efficient and effective in the long run than pressing on in flight or oversight to the questions in the next phase.

Second, decision makers and problems do not track each other as in the garbage can model because different decision makers are matched with different problems or tasks at different points in time in the PPM. The matching of problems with phased strategies and with different participants over time creates significant coordination problems for planners and taxes their process skills. However, it prevents decision makers from falling into a rut and "having the feeling they are always working on the same problems in somewhat different contexts, mostly without results" (Cohen, March, and Olsen, 1972, p. 12). Indeed, planning the creation of community human service organizations involves multiple tasks and decisions, each requiring a different expertise and a different decision strategy. Hence, there is a need for procedural planning models that provide a three-way match among tasks, phased strategies, and participants. PPM is a start in that direction.

5

Environmental Influences on the Creation Process

~~~~~~~~~~~~~~~~~~~~~~~~~~~~~~~~~~~~~

Johannes M. Pennings

The creation of a new organization is one of the most salient moments of its life cycle. Organizational birth is salient not only because it is the starting point of that life cycle but also because it is an overriding factor in molding and constraining the organization's behavior during the subsequent stages of its life cycle. Foundation involves a decision as to location that constrains the organization geographically. The entrepreneur acquires equipment and other assets and selects markets that put further limits on adaptation. The initial stage entails a learning process that results in decision-making patterns, an authority structure, and rules and procedures that are relatively permanent and evoke pressures toward organizational inertia. While organizations undergo modifications and display varying degrees of flexibility, they are cast at birth into a mold that is discernible in all the subsequent stages of their life cycle.

A great deal of organizational theory has dealt with social structure and change of existing organizations, but there has been rather little concern about the creation of new organizations. Many writers simply take the emergence of new organizations for granted and proceed to explain interorganizational differences in structure, adaptation, effectiveness, and so forth. Thus, Hannan and Freeman (1978a) lament the excessive concern for adaptation and the neglect of selection in dealing with organization-environment relationships. Indeed, the most important contributions on organizational birth do not come from organizational theory but from the literature on entrepreneurship. In the case of adaptation, organizations are seen as modifying themselves, such that they are congruent with their environment. Selection-based approaches treat organizations and their attributes as relatively fixed and hold that through selective elimination those organizations prevail which are congruent with their environment.

Entrepreneurship has been a fascinating subject for a wide variety of writers. Some psychologists, for example, have attempted to formulate theoretical statements on the personality traits of entrepreneurs (see McClelland, 1965). They have made comparisons between the attributes of entrepreneurs and those of nonowner managers (Howell, 1972; Litzinger, 1965). Economists see entrepreneurs as agents who disrupt the economic equilibrium by successfully introducing technological, commercial, and organizational innovations (Schumpeter, 1934). Some sociologists have viewed class, race, and ethnicity as barriers to upward mobility that may prompt achievement-oriented individuals to seek alternative, deviant avenues of social mobility (Deeks, 1976; Gould, 1969). Policy makers in Europe, Japan, and the United States have focused on the opportunities that induce individuals to start new firms and have implemented programs to help such individuals in their new ventures.

Entrepreneurs represent a heterogeneous category of individuals. Distinctions can be made between the sophisticated, highly trained scientist who owns a high-technology venture and the low-status, upwardly mobile, self-made entrepreneur, as well as between the lone wolf who approximates the Schumpeterean agent of economic change by triggering a new wave of activity and the mass of imitators whose collective search for a unique opportunity has the appearance of a craze. Certainly, the entrepreneurial individual is an intriguing person whose origins, character, and behavior can be studied from various scientific perspectives.

This chapter, however, attempts to make a different contribution to the study of entrepreneurship, for it shifts the focus away from the entrepreneurial individual and toward the emergence of new organizations. Since the creation of new organizations entails a selection process, it is of interest to explore the environment that is conducive to their creation. Hence, this chapter will focus on urban-contextual factors that promote or inhibit organizational birth. The framework being developed here may be called "ecological" in that it deals with the urban-contextual conditions that are germane for new organizations. Urban environments may be construed as incubators or organizational habitats that display a rich variety of organizational life. They differ in their entrepreneurial conduciveness. The ecological framework delineates the essential elements of urban contexts to explain why new organizations spawn more frequently in some urban environments than in others. It is labeled "ecological" to differentiate it from exclusively economic or psychological approaches, and it resembles certain attempts to explain the urban correlates of human behavior (for example, Spilerman, 1976; Lincoln, 1978). The chapter first discusses organizational birth and the urban context relevant for birth. This is followed by an examination of the attributes that may explain the differential entrepreneurial conduciveness of urban environments. Several hypotheses are formulated and suggestions for future research are provided.

New Organizations and Urban Contexts

Since this chapter is limited to the births of single-establishment organizations, it follows that the creation of new organizations by existing ones is excluded from the discussion. However, there remain several distinctions that have to be made. In the first place, it is important to distinguish between new organizations that represent the first members of a new class or new population of organizations and new organizations that are joining an existing population. The term *population* here refers to an aggregate of organizations that are homogeneous on some relevant dimension—for example, environmental focus, market, size. When the new organization has no precedent, as in the legendary cases of the companies founded by Rockefeller, Carnegie, and Ford, it is convenient to refer to niche theory. Such newcomers enter into an ecological vacuum that others have failed to detect and acquire an initial advantage over imitators. The subsequent entrepreneurial activity triggered by the "first-mover" illustrates organizational birth of the other type: new organizations that join an existing population. In this case, it is possible to refer to the growth or internal selection of organizational populations. For example, the birth of additional contracting firms or an influx of new transatlantic airlines illustrates growth of or replacement within a population of organizations. Clearly, organizational birth can be studied at the level of the single organization or at the level of the organizational population (Hannan and Freeman, 1978a). In the latter case, organizational birth is merely one aspect of a population's growth and decline.

Second, it may also be important to distinguish newness from smallness. There are many classes of organizations that typically consist of small firms. Many such firms are viable because they enjoy a comparative advantage over larger firms. Their optimum efficient size may be small (for example, law firms or bakeries); they may operate in a limited, highly specialized market (for example, engineering services or theatre costume designs); or they may produce specialized parts or components for their industries (Deeks, 1976; Bolton Committee, 1971). Populations that consist of small firms are apt to attract many newcomers because of their low entry barriers, while their "liability of newness" (Stinchcombe, 1965; Williamson, 1975) is less serious than that of new firms in populations whose size distribution is skewed and dispersed. New firms in small-firm populations may simply compete with older small firms, but new firms in skewed-size distributed populations may create disequilibrium by being innovative and by undercutting the established market structure. For example, in an industry dominated by a few very large firms there may be newcomers whose technological breakthrough can upset the previously existing balance in the market. Such considerations suggest that one should also examine the industries to which firms belong—and their markets—when examining births of organizations.

The discussion on organizational populations and organizational birth has already hinted at a metaphoric definition of the environments that are pertinent for the creation of organizations. The term *population* suggests a territorially defined environment because of its association with the biological term *species*. In this chapter I want to stress a spatial delineation of environment by pointing to the urban metropolitan setting within which organizational populations exist. The ecological approach to organizational environments can help resolve the problem of defining such an entity.

The urban metropolitan area presents a convenient means for identifying well-bounded environments of new organizations. Within an urban setting we can detect an array of organizational populations with a distinct collective structure. Urbanization also results in a high concentration of relevant resources that enhances the creation of new organizations. According to Hawley's *Human Ecology* (1950), urban areas accommodate a community of organizational populations whose growth and decline can be traced to the environmental resourcefulness and to the characteristics of their overall organization. There exists a territorial and functional division of labor within such areas. It would then appear that urban areas are highly appropriate for studying organizational birth. This observation is reinforced by contributions from regional economics, most notably developments in location theories. Alonso (1975), for example, has suggested that transportation factors are highly important for the location decisions of entrepreneurs. Additional evidence in support of urban areas as incubators of new firms is supplied by the empirical observation that most new firms are created by native entrepreneurs, that is, by individuals who were born in the city where they began their new ventures (Boswell, 1973). Although this might contradict the view of industrial location economists who stress a gravitation of organizational birth frequencies to those areas that are most attractive economically, Boswell's finding does further signal the importance of local, as opposed to regional or national, considerations.

It is possible, however, to point to the diminishing significance of urban boundaries. For example, taxation and governmental regulations have an impact that cuts across urban boundaries. Legal boundaries often do not coincide with geographical boundaries. Availability of resources such as capital and disposal of outputs often extend beyond urban limits. Furthermore, the urban area is often ill defined and usually includes a central city with its hinterland, as is the case with the concept of a Standard Metropolitan Statistical Area (SMSA). This raises the question of whether suburbs and hinterland are pertinent components of an organizationally relevant environment, particularly when a comparison is made with the environments of supraurban markets and organizational populations that extend beyond urban boundaries and whose attributes would therefore not be included in an urban-ecological explanation of organizational birthrates.

While the delineation of urban boundaries will always remain arbitrary, these difficulties have been partly resolved by Christaller (1966). In his study of urban dispersion in southern Germany, Christaller, concluded that the location of cities is largely determined by some territorially induced division of labor. The spatial differentiation into cities and towns of varying size is largely predicated on their economic role within the larger system. This differentiation follows an hierarchical and inclusive clustering principle according to which successively larger cities supplement each other. This view could suggest that cities are relatively well-bounded elements whose entrepreneurial significance depends on the action radius of a new firm's environment. For example, if availability of skilled labor or transportation costs are irrelevant, the urban context may not be particularly significant. By the same token, Christaller's study would preclude viewing a city as a closed system; rather, it looks upon the city as a territorially defined entity subject to exogenously instigated changes. Therefore, ecological research on birthrates requires a concern not only for the social structure of urban areas but also for the interaction between urban areas and the larger economy. For example, cities that are the hub of an intermetropolitan network may provide better access to entrepreneurially relevant resources than do more peripheral cities.

In summary, this chapter invokes a population ecology view of the urban areas in which organizations come and go; such areas represent a territorially based community of diverse organizations who both compete over limited resources and cooperate with one another. In the next section we shall discuss issues such as competition, resources for sustaining organizational birth, and territorial and functional division of labor. These issues are central in the literature on human ecology.

An important *caveat* is in order, however. The temptation to draw analogies between biological and organizational development is strong because it facilitates the reduction of social complexities to a few parsimonious ordering principles. It is attractive to treat categories of organizations as comparable to species of plants and animals and to draw parallels between the division of labor and competition among organizations, on the one hand, and the symbiosis and competition of living species, on the other. Metaphorically, each population of organizations makes a specialized contribution. This is illustrated by input-output tables (Leontief, 1966), which indicate the proportion of economic output that flows from one industry to another and vice versa. The industries are commonly categorized with devices such as the Standard Industrial Classification, making the analogy with biological species even more obvious.

Unlike plants, however, which show only morphological and functional differentiation among species—except for gradual mutations—industries or other organizational categories are highly diverse. Populations of organizations do not only make interspecific contributions to the collective life of an urban area, region, or national economy but they also become stratified internally. Indeed, the interorganizational structural variations within an organizational population may be so extensive as to challenge the construction of organizational typologies. Within distinct populations, whether they be nursery schools or steel firms, we can notice clear differences in form, function, or other attributes that make the assumption about intraspecific homogeneity of organizations tenuous. The intraspecific differentiation is often so extensive that it becomes problematic to classify organizations ecologically. Even in small-firm populations (for example, law firms, grocery stores, electronic data-processing firms) where competitive pressures should ensure ecological uniformity (Hannan and Freeman, 1978a), it is not difficult to detect widespread diversity in function, type of clients, and so forth. We should therefore supplement the biologically inspired question of Hannan and Freeman (1978a) "Why are there so many different kinds of organizations?" with the question "Why are there so many different kinds of organizations within each of the many kinds of populations?"

Such differences between biotic and organizational ecology considerations cannot simply be dismissed, and in the case of organizational births such differences become particularly problematic. New organizations may join an existing population or they may be so novel and unique in form, function, or any other pertinent attribute that it is impossible to discern similarities between the newcomer and the other organizations. For example, did the implementation of Montessori's ideas result in a new population of nursery schools or did it merely result in an educational innovation that augmented the diversity of nursery schools? Again, Tabasco is a spice made from hot peppers, whose production and packaging process was developed by the entrepreneur Edward McIlhenny (Peterson, 1980). His venture could be viewed as belonging to the population of food manufacturers or to the population of spice manufacturers, or perhaps it is so distinctive that it represents a population of its own. These examples suggest that it is often doubtful whether a new firm is the first member of a new population or an innovative entrant into an existing population. The earlier references to varying types of new firms give added weight to this problem. Perhaps ecological research should examine the structure of that population to which a new organization is akin on some relevant attribute as well as the structure of the set of organizational populations that surround a new firm.

During the following discussion it is always assumed that new firms join existing organizations and that birthrates are part of the succession and/or replacement of elements in growing, stagnant, or declining populations. The urban metropolitan area is a relatively open system, subject to exposure to other urban areas and to the national society in general. New organizations are usually not so radically different as to trigger the rise of new populations. At the urban level it is more likely that new firms will be largely molded after existing firms within the area or that they were triggered by a supraurban trend whose origin should be traced to national rather than urban conditions. The magnitude of intraspecific differentiation, which is so prominent among human organizations, is apt to favor such a research strategy. Ecological research on organizations is bound to be more feasible if we rely on broad but institutionally vested categories such as the industry digit classifications that have been developed by the U.S. Bureau of the Census to group organizations into homogeneous groups. The grouping is usually based on technological and market characteristics, and the number of digits used to classify organizations indicates the inclusivity of each group. A two-digit class (for example, transportation equipment) is very broad, while a four-digit class (for example, aircraft engine parts) is rather specific and by implication contains a more homogeneous set of organizations.

It would be interesting to examine to what extent official classification schemes have resulted in the institutionalization of organizational populations or, conversely, to investigate the need to depart from governmental classifications because they do not fit the ecological typologies of the organizational theorist. These difficulties are particularly salient in the case of multiple-product-line firms where any attempt to establish ecological typologies is doomed to be deficient (see Rumelt, 1974). For example, should Texas Instruments be grouped with Intel since both manufacture electronic chips, or should Texas Instruments be classified with IBM since both produce minicomputers, or should Texas Instruments be lumped together with those firms that make watches. We can continue this kind of questioning almost endlessly. Such considerations suggest that we must search for alternative organizational typologies as well as continue to use existing broad governmental or scientific classifications to explain organizational birth. At present this latter strategy seems to be the more feasible.

Urban Conduciveness for New Firms

Discussion of the urban conduciveness of metropolitan systems has to center on the *ecological organization,* on the one hand, and the availability of *environmental resources,* on the other. During recent years there has been a flurry of debate on the usefulness of "resource-exchange" models (Aldrich and Pfeffer, 1976). These models see organizations as enjoying both variable degrees of flexibility and a discretionary exchange relationship with actors in their environment. This perspective contrasts sharply with that found in selection models. As mentioned earlier, the selection models emphasize organizational inertia and a passive, compliant, and submissive organizational orientation to the environment. Scarcity of environmental resources is a constraint for organizational birth activity. The ecological organization likewise either limits or enhances the emergence and viability of new organizations. It therefore seems plausible to stress environmental constraints in explaining birthrates, even though it is also plausible to impute a high level of flexibility to new firms, which do not yet suffer from the stultifying effects of age. For births, however, it seems fruitful to adapt a perspective of environmental determinism and to explain the frequency of births in reference to the urban environment in which they take place. The relevant attributes of urban environments which I will discuss are as follows:

1. *Urban Level:* Urban size (population density);
   Differentiation (distribution of people, groups, and organizations with respect to attributes such as occupation, industrial output, race, ethnic background, and spatial location); and Ecological change (variations in socioeconomic activities, whether they are trends or random deviations from trends).
2. *Population Level:* Size (volume of output of a population of organizations such as value added or number of production workers);
   Size distribution (the number of organizations within different size categories); and
   Life cycle (the stages of development of the organizational population's technology or output).

3A. *Resourcefulness—Economic:* Availability of savings capital and venture capital; Wage rate; Energy rate;
State, county, and city taxes and subsidies;
Governmental programs (formal attempts to stimulate entrepreneurial activity); and
Governmental regulations (legislative programs aimed at enhancing or reducing the constraints for creating new firms).
3B. *Resourcefulness—Social:* Entrepreneurial climate;
Colleges, universities, and other professional organizations that diffuse innovation;
Quality of life, including economic, political, educational, environmental, and recreational quality of life;
Urban centrality (degree of connection between an urban area and other urban areas within a regional or national network; and
Educational level of the local population.

Ecological Organization of Urban Areas

The creation of new organizations can be investigated by analyzing the effects of the overall ecological organization and by examining the structural characteristics of the population that new organizations are joining. Among the overall organizational aspects we can distinguish size, ecological differentiation, and ecological change. The structural characteristics of the relevant population include size, size distribution, changes in size, stage of the population's life cycle, and the place of the population with respect to its "adjacent" or strategically interdependent populations of organizations.

Urban size or population density is probably the most important predictor of organizational birthrates, and several regional economists have said so (for example, Thompson, 1966; Pred, 1966; Aldrich, 1978b). Thompson (1966) specifies several reasons for the so-called urban size rachet. When cities grow, their industries become more differentiated, and this in turn may induce better than average growth rates. Larger cities also enjoy more influence over state or federal governments than do smaller ones, and a greater proportion of their economic activity is oriented toward customers rather than to sources of supply. Finally, larger cities are more conducive to entrepreneurial activity, since this is largely dependent on innovation and their size alone will ensure a steadier supply of invention and creativity than can be found in smaller cities. Thompson (1966) also deals with a counter trend in urban expansion that is analogous to the issue of organizational growth and the growth of its administrative component (see Berry and Kasarda, 1976). When organizations grow, their administrative components also grow but at a slower rate than the organizations as a whole. Similarly, the size of city governments grows at a decreasing rate in relation to the size of the urban population. Due to size-imposed ceilings, urban areas may reach a point beyond which entrepreneurial activities do not increase as rapidly as before. There may even be an actual decline, and it is ironic that Thompson in 1966 could not envision an absolute drop in city or metropolitan populations. Since 1970 the U.S. census has shown that several cities (for example, Pittsburgh, Cleveland, New York) have experienced actual declines. It is not clear whether longitudinally the relation between urban expansion and organizational birthrates is different from the relation between urban contraction and organizational birthrates. Research on organizational components (for example, Hannan and Freeman, 1978b) has shown that these relations are not mirror images of one another. Perhaps the growth of organizational populations in expanding metropolitan areas cannot be extrapolated to declining urban areas. There are also complications that arise because of urban differentiation and the interdependence among component parts of cities. Before elaborating on this, we will hypothesize that organizational birthrates increase at a decreasing rate as a function of growth in city size or population density.

The relationship between size and differentiation points to empirical and conceptual problems. Size may be a summary variable, that is, size is not only correlated with the supply of resources that sustains the ecology but also with various indicators of urban differentiation. The greater the population density, the larger is the number of economic, occupational, and territorial categories of individuals and organizations. It seems more interesting to focus on these variables, differentiation as this information conveys more and has a greater theoretical significance than city size.

Urban differentiation can be described by reference to the variety of individuals, groups, and organizations in the human ecology. These urban inhabitants are differentiated to the extent that they belong to different overlapping or nonoverlapping segments. For example, the greater the number of occupations and the greater the dispersion of people over these occupations, the higher is the occupational differentiation. Organizationally, urban areas are differentiated to the extent that their organizations can be broken down into categories. This subdividing can be done with such a priori conceptual categories as degree of bureaucratization (Pugh, Hickson, and Hinings, 1969), primary beneficiaries (Blau and Scott, 1962), and technology (Thompson, 1967) or with governmental dimensions such as the Standard Industrial Classification. Categories can also be based on empirical classifications or on patterns of territorial location (Berry and Kasarda, 1977). Any meaningful attribute can be used for partitioning organizations into subsets, but those that describe division of labor are the most interesting ecologically. Type of industry, nature of product, or similar "horizontal" indicators of differentiation are also relevant.

It is hypothesized that urban differentiation is positively associated with organizational birthrates. The relationship is most likely to take the form of an inverted U. Differentiation affects birthrates because the spatial adjacency of organizational populations (and other possible groupings) facilitates mutual exposure and enhances the diffusion of technological and economic innovations (see Stinchcombe, 1965; Thompson, 1966; Hawley, 1950, 1971). Urban differentiation implies the existence of several organizational populations or clusters as well as of other types of clusters, including ethnic and occupational ones. The interaction between clusters creates the roots both for entrepreneurial behavior and for other expressions of nonconventionality.

The existence of clusters is a typical outgrowth of urbanization, since only larger urban systems can accommodate ecological subsystems that are sufficiently large to be viable and to enjoy a certain degree of "critical mass." Indeed, Fisher's (1975) "subcultural theory of urbanism" is predicated on the assumption that the existence of subcultures is made possible by the large economies of scale in metropolitan areas. Fisher sought a synthesis between the ecologists and nonecologists of urban sociology whose debate dealt with the alleged effects of urbanism on human behavior. Gans (1962), for example, pointed to the rich community life at the neighborhood level and saw this as similar to the communal life of rural areas—hence, he was labeled a nonecologist. Wirth (1938), on the contrary, believed that urbanization was one of the most important causes of social disorganization, anomie, and deviance. Fisher's (1975) position is "quasi-ecological." High concentrations of people are associated with subcultures. It is not the total urban system but its subsystems that have consequences for human behavior; those subsystems, however, could only prevail in large urban systems. We can stipulate that it is the propinquity of subcultures that triggers nonconventional behavior: mutual exposure reveals alternative norms and values and produces recombinations of them. This line of reasoning is also meaningful for explaining entrepreneurial activity, since entrepreneurs often are seen as recombining established ways of thinking in some novel fashion.

Presently there is little knowledge about the types of differentiation that are significant for organizational birth. For example, urban areas may be heavily differentiated ethnically or educationally, but such types of differentiation are likely to be less relevant than industrial or occupational differentiation. The urban area may be highly segregated into spatial clusters that enhance the visibility and identity of organizations. This may or may not affect the entrepreneurial conduciveness for certain types of new firms. One may adopt an overall indicator at the urban level, or one may adopt a more restricted, "localized" perspective. In other words, differentiation can refer to the urban area in its totality or it can refer to relatively well-bounded subsystems that are either territorial—for example, central business district and suburbs—or categorical—racial, ethnic, industrial, and educational. The best unit of analysis is difficult to determine here. For example, is educational differentiation more relevant for the rise of new schools and industrial differentiation more relevant for the rise of new electronic component firms? Similarly, there may be indicators of differentiation of inhabitants based, for example, on their employment status and indicators of differentiation of organizations such as the Standard Industrial Classification . In either case it is possible to identify various clusters of elements that fit the notion of "subculture" with its ensuing implications for entrepreneurial activity.

For individual entrepreneurs the urban context can be relevant because (1) they are associated with an entrepreneurially prone subculture whose existence is a typical by-product of urbanism or because (2) they provide liaison between subcultures.

Examples of the first possibility include Jews, Quakers, Cubans in Florida, and Chinese in Indonesia, as well as subcultures of scientists and engineers in certain technological fields (for example, Deeks, 1976; Aris, 1970; Cooper, 1972; Shapero, 1975; Bonacich, 1973). Aris (1975), for example, traces the Jewish propensity to entrepreneurship to historical and cultural facts; thus, Jews "have inherited a whole system of values which, when combined with the environment in which they found themselves, has led them to behave in quite specific and identifiable ways" (p. 232). Presumably, Jews satisfied their desire for independence by establishing their own firms.

Bonacich (1973) provides a more general perspective in her theory of "middleman minorities." Her theory hinges on the temporary settlement of cohesive immigrant groups held together by a strong belief that eventually they will return to their country of origin. Thrift and betterment of their economic status can lead them to realize their long-term objective. The hostile reactions of the host society further reinforce the reluctance of these groups to assimilate and perpetuate their pariah status. The term *middleman* refers to their economic role in society; they typically act as intermediaries between producer and consumer, owner and renter, and elite and masses. The behavior of these groups has to be understood in terms of the role that the host society imposes upon its minorities.

This perspective contrasts sharply with the view of the entrepreneur as a disintegrated, intercultural, marginal man. Collins and Moore (1970) see the entrepreneur as a drifter who is uncommitted and will not be loyal to any organization. For them, he is best illustrated by immigrants and other individuals who have relinquished their ties with their old culture and have not been fully integrated into the new culture. Immigrants have always been likely candidates for entrepreneurship (Peterson, 1977). They seem to fit very well with the Schumpeter (1934) image of the entrepreneur who is at the crossroads of multiple influences and who seeks to combine those influences in some novel fashion. Perhaps the entrepreneur who creates a new type or form of organization fits this description particularly well. In carving out a new niche, he thereby invites imitators and triggers a whole sequence of entrepreneurial activity. Schumpeter considered entrepreneurs as sources of economic change in that they disrupt the equilibrium in an economic society; the description given above invites interesting research at the urban level as to whether new forms of organizations disrupt the social-economic equilibrium and move cities toward new configurations of organizational populations (Peterson, 1980).

The differentiation of urban areas is also pertinent for the analysis of ecological change. It is hypothesized that change in human ecologies is positively related to the creation of new organizations. Unfortunately, however, ecological change in human systems cannot adequately be described with biological metaphors. Ecological change that results from exogenous factors such as the influx of immigrants or increase of demand for goods is rather easy to document. Endogenous changes, however, present serious difficulties. These changes are manifest when the ecology moves from one state of equilibrium to another—for example, when the component parts alter their patterns of complementary relationships or when the available resources are no longer able to accommodate the total system. In biological systems such transitions are rather easily detectable because, unlike organizational populations, biotic populations can be clearly and unambiguously delineated. Likewise, interactions and changes in interactions can be identified in biotic systems, and attempts to model them have been quite successful (see Lotka, 1925; Volterra, 1931). Volterra, for example, examined the predator-prey relationship between two populations—goats and wolves on an imaginary island. According to this study, the growth of the population of wolves is contingent upon their contacts with goats. Thus, it increases proportionately when the number of goats increases, but it declines when the goat supply declines. The growth and decline of the goat population are likewise intertwined with the growth and decline of their predators. Volterra arrived at a system of simultaneous equations in which the number of wolves and goats fluctuates cyclically toward an equilibrium level. An abundance of goats leads to the expansion of the predator population, but this in turn leads to a depletion of goats. Many wolves then starve, after which the dialectical process starts all over again.

While the classification of wolves, goats, and other biological species presents little difficulty, it is very hard to classify organizations into complementary and competing populations. It seems that the application of the Lotka-Volterra paradigm to human ecologies is too ambitious and bound to fail, unless one is willing to sacrifice specific information. For example, economic input-output tables (Leontif, 1966) can be construed as representing wolf-and-goat relationships among economic subsystems. The interindustry demand vector from such tables reveals the resource exchanges among several industrial categories (for example, mining, transportation, and food). Over successive time periods there are changes in the entries of such vectors. These changes can signal an increase or decline in several industries, but they may or may not signal the creation and death of organizations. Although an industry can witness an increase in size, for example, by augmenting the total value added in manufacturing, the increase might accrue to existing organizations and does not necessarily apply to the entry of new organizations. The input-output tables are very broad and are not very interesting at the organizational level of analysis. They are also too macroscopic and aggregative to be suitable for use at the urban level.

Unlike Hannan and Freeman (1978a), I feel that the Lotka-Volterra paradigm is too simplistic for the richness of organizational realities, and I propose a more modest strategy. This strategy would not attempt to examine the mutual influence of expansion and contraction among organizational populations. Rather, it would relate organizational birthrates to such global indicators of urban change as trends in and volatility of economic activity. Trends are stable increments or decrements over time (for example, steady economic growth), while volatility is the patterned or unpatterned deviation from the trend (for example, erratic oscillations in the size of the labor market). The greater the rate of socioeconomic change or the more extreme the ups and downs in economic activity level, the greater the start-up of new organizations. The assumption is that trend and volatility stand for conditions of ecological change. As creators of new organizations, entrepreneurs may be seen as forerunners of ecological change who capitalize on disequilibrium or they may be seen as agents who reestablish equilibrium. Change either erodes the established steady state or represents a move toward a new steady state, and entrepreneurial activity is likely to be reflected by such changes. Peterson (1980) summarizes the mutual influence of entrepreneurship and change rather well when he notes that "each act of equilibriating entrepreneurship has disequilibriating consequences as well" (p. 9).

Among the most salient characteristics of an organizational population is its size distribution. In industrial economics size distribution is often considered the most important aspect of industry or market structure. Size distribution indicates the market proportion that belongs to the four to eight largest firms in an industry. The higher this proportion, the higher the so-called minimum efficient size of firms and the higher the barriers to entry. Populations composed of small firms (for example, welfare agencies, corner stores, bakeries) typically have low concentration ratios. Their capital requirements are small, and it is relatively easy for new entrants to join and to survive. It is therefore almost redundant to hypothesize a negative relationship between concentration ratios and organizational birthrates. In addition, there are obvious differences between biology and economics here. Biologically, it would be absurd to refer to size differences within a population. More significant is the notion of competition. Competition is often absent in highly concentrated industries—particularly among oligopolists. In oligopolies there is a frequent tendency toward market segmentation and other behaviors that reduce cutthroat practices (Pennings, 1980). In biological systems, in contrast, competitive selection usually produces a tendency toward uniformity. Naturally, such conceptual inconsistencies illustrate in a different way that there are limitations in applying ecological frameworks to organizational frameworks.

Apart from economic considerations there are social-psychological reasons for expecting higher birthrates in populations with low concentration ratios. One important reason is the availability of role models. It has already been mentioned that entrepreneurial decisions are often triggered by the availability of role models—a clear example is provided by Shapero (1975) in his description of the electronic industry in Austin, Texas. Since small firms are concrete examples of entrepreneurial feasibility, it is reasonable to expect high birthrates in visible populations with many small firms. Such populations may also increase the detachment of employees in organizations in which their need for innovation and creativity is frustrated (Peterson, 1980).

The size distribution of firms is often associated with the life cycle of organizational populations. The life cycle can be derived from the developmental stages of the products or services; that is, the product life cycle is reflected in the life cycle of the population and vice versa. Populations that are in relatively early stages are frequently associated with so-called high-technology industries (for example, electronic components or aerospace instruments), but this is not always the case—witness, for example, the popular music industry, which is subject to fads and major changes in taste (Peterson and Berger, 1975).

The early stages of an industry's life cycle are characterized by innovativeness and high levels of birth activity. However, during later stages there is often a consolidation of the industry into an oligopolistic structure. Although the ensuing entry barriers discourage or frustrate potential entrepreneurs, economists have also suggested that the later stages of a product's life cycle often create a vacuum that makes possible the emergence of new firms. Scherer (1967: 390-394), for example, suggests that during these later stages firms often make defensive research and development investments: their patent system promotes a monopolistic position that can be strengthened by fencing in the field of technology covered by the patents. Organizations thus retreat into their established market segments and protect them through status quo research and by acquiring licenses. Elsewhere, Scherer (1970) asserted that such defensive research and development strategies may be stultifying. If oligopolistic firms rely on conservative research, outsiders may be attracted to their markets. Paradoxically, while high levels of research and development create large entry barriers, they may also produce lack of flexibility and inertia with the result that potential entrepreneurs detect vacuums that they can then fill.

Unfortunately, the life cycles of populations or of their output apply more to national or international levels than they do to local, urban levels; for present purposes, therefore, this concept is relatively insignificant. There are also many difficulties with the life cycle concept itself since many organizational populations have extraordinary longevities (for example, religious and military organizations), while the concept implies a development toward death.

Finally, research should examine the immediate relationship between individual organizational populations and the populations they interact with. This approach would be analogous to the "organizational set" approach to the study of organization-environment relationships (Evan, 1972), as well as to economic research on so-called external economics (James and Struyk, 1975). External economics is illustrated by the establishment of a new firm that invites others to follow suit and to serve it in a complementary or symbiotic fashion. James and Struyk (1975) tested the hypothesis that urban areas are incubators of new firms by examining the external economics of central business districts. It was assumed that industries would be located in central business districts because of the availability of services, suppliers, and rental production facilities. The lack of support for the incubator hypothesis was explained by the availability of suburban sites with sufficient external economics for new firms. Nevertheless, James and Struyk's study illustrates the feasibility of investigating the transactional relationships among members of different organizational populations and the implications of these relationships for new establishment.

Resourcefulness

The review of ecological organization and birthrates would make little sense if we were to ignore the resourcefulness of the human ecology. The supply of pertinent human resources determines the "carrying capacity" (Hannan and Freeman, 1978a) of the ecology. Other things being equal, a rich environment reinforces the birth potential of urban areas, while a lean environment lessens their birth potential. Urban areas are not closed systems but instead interact heavily with other systems. Thus, economic self-sufficiency may or may not have important implications for organizational births. The importance of this factor depends largely on whether the organizations in question have supply or output requirements that extend beyond the urban boundaries and on their transportation requirements. Social, that is, noneconomic, resourcefulness may similarly affect birthrates, depending on whether the new firms have a "cosmopolitan" or a "local" mission.

Resourcefulness overlaps considerably with ecological organization. This is particularly clear if we make a distinction between commensalistic and symbiotic relationships among populations of organizations (Berry and Kasarda, 1977). Commensalistic relationships exist among competing populations (for example, breweries, drinking water companies, and utility firms that compete for water or breweries and soft drink manufacturers that compete for sales outlets). Symbiotic relationships exist among complementary populations (for example, breweries and grain dealers). For new firms, relevant resources include generic ones for which every firm and every population of firms compete (land, location, and some raw materials) and resources that originate from other populations of organizations (ideas, trained specialists, capital, and so forth).

It would not make much sense to distinguish resourcefulness from ecological organization if one wanted to explain the total number of new firms in an urban area. However, if one is interested in· explaining the birthrates in a specific category (for example, firms in the electronic industry, trading firms, or firms producing mousetraps), then it appears more fruitful to treat the demand and supply of the other populations or industries as a pool of economic and social resources from which the population under study can draw. Economic resourcefulness includes the availability of savings and venture capital, wage and energy rates, taxation systems, and governmental regulations and economic development programs. Social resourcefulness includes the presence of economic and technological innovation, availability of relevant occupational groups, and social attributes of the inhabitants-at-large. While the limitations of this chapter prevent an encyclopedic description of these attributes, the present discussion will highlight their most important aspects.

Economic Resourcefulness: It is obvious that birth levels are associated with the availability of wealth. Capital resources such as savings capital are crucial for economic advancement. Although entrepreneurs take risks when they start a new venture, the risks are often limited to the funds invested. Historical evidence suggests that during the change from mercantile to industrial capitalism the legal basis of firms changed from full to limited responsibility, thus enabling entrepreneurs to make use of unsecured (for example, nonmortgaged) capital (Aldrich, 1978b). This change was followed by an upswing of entrepreneurial activity. Banks and other financial institutions, however, are often reluctant to provide capital funds to entrepreneurs. Therefore, it is important for entrepreneurs to identify other segments in the capital market that are less averse to taking risks. Venture capital firms, for example, specialize in risky new investments. It is somewhat paradoxical, however, that providers of venture capital are often not particularly instrumental prior to or during start-up of a new business but instead postpone their commitment until the business has accomplished a certain level of solvency and viability (Johnson, 1978). It appears that entrepreneurs often have to rely on such additional sources as kinship groups, friends, and wealthy individuals.

Wage and energy costs are clearly important in their impact on the creation of new firms. Carlton (1978) found that for energy-intensive industries the price of energy was strongly related to birth activity, although it was not as sensitive a predicator as the cost of labor. Carlton found little relationship between taxation variables and entrepreneurship, perhaps because, unlike wage and energy costs, income taxes are mostly associated with state or national levels, while property taxes are highly contingent upon local assessment procedures. Although the impact of taxation systems is difficult to delineate, it seems intuitively plausible to expect that urban areas with favorable corporate taxes induce higher organizational birth rates. Taxation and governmental subsidies that are specifically geared to stimulate local economic development may be instrumental for increased birthrates, and many studies on entrepreneurship endorse an active governmental role to increase the establishment of new firms (Thompson, 1966; Boswell, 1973; Deeks, 1976; Peterson, 1977; Bolton Committee, 1971). Recommendations include changes in legislation on inheritance taxes, guaranteed bank loans, small-business development centers, industrial location policies, improvement of regional infrastructures, and formation of cooperative ventures.

Social Resourcefulness. Social resourcefulness is either tangible or intangible. Intangible resourcefulness includes the "climate" of entrepreneurial spirit that may prevail in a particular urban-metropolitan region. Also intangible is the "public" confidence in future economic developments, as this confidence is revealed by surveys. Such intangible conditions may affect the propensity of potential entrepreneurs to begin new businesses.

The supply of professional groups pertinent for certain types of new firms illustrates a tangible aspect of social resourcefulness. Naturally, this supply could be labeled "economic" in that it indicates the availability of know-how as a production factor of new firms. I prefer to label it "social" in that such professional groups are often the source of novel ideas that initiate the start-up of new firms. This kind of resourcefulness is also indicated by the presence of colleges and universities, or at least their proximity has been a strong stimulator for science-based business start-ups. Well-known examples include "Route 158" in Boston (Harvard University and M.I.T.) and the San Francisco Peninsula (Stanford University). Anecdotal evidence suggests that the presence of such centers of innovation promotes an entrepreneurial conduciveness for technologically based industries in particular. Such centers are notoriously known as providers of potential entrepreneurs (Shapero, 1975), but they are also the hubs of information networks that stimulate local birth activity. The importance of entrepreneurially significant diffusion from centers of research can be measured by the number of graduate students enrolled in specific engineering, chemical, biological, and medical university departments or by the number of research grants awarded to those departments.

The social quality of life is an important but more general factor in the creation of organizations (Liu, 1974). Indicators for quality of life include environmental, educational, and political components and assess the attractiveness of the urban areas in terms of how well they meet general needs of the population.

It is important to refer to an aspect of urban areas that is germane to resourcefulness but that applies primarily to the relationship between urban areas and their external, regional, or national environment. This kind of resourcefulness is contingent upon the centrality of cities in their interurban network. Central cities not only provide resources locally but also obtain resources from other cities. Compared with more peripheral cities, they are the meeting place or intersection of regional or national economic and social segments, and this centrality augments their entrepreneurial conduciveness. All urban areas are exposed to exogenous influences, and it seems reasonable to argue that central metropolitan areas provide an especially favorable environment for new firms, particularly to new firms that have a national, cosmopolitan mission or whose demands for resources are not limited to the confines of their urban environment. Central cities are indicated by the presence of national head offices, by prominence within the transportation infrastructure, and so forth (Abrahamson and Dubick, 1977; Christaller, 1966).

Finally, the educational level of the local labor force is an important factor in organizational creation. Not only is the size of the pool of potential entrepreneurs directly related to the educational qualifications of the local population, but so also are aspects of workers' competence and occupational commitment. Stinchcombe (1965) considers conditions such as schooling and workers' inclinations toward professional organizations, labor unions, and the professional-occupational standards they maintain as having a strong impact on the creation of new organizations. Some aspects such as unionization may have more negative than positive consequences in that they increase wages and other labor costs, while other aspects such as professional associations and schooling enhance the diffusion of information and the information-processing capabilities of the infrastructure. They also reinforce the saliency and visibility of role models.

As mentioned before, these conditions of economic and social richness may be correlated with the ecological variables noted earlier. An urban area with a pronounced mosaic of ethnic, racial, occupational, and industrial entities presents a wealth of stimulants for new organizations. Such urban areas are likely to be richer in such generalized resources as availability of capital, scientists and engineers, and favorable governmental dispositions. Although urban size, differentiation, and change are probable determinants of organizational birth rates, we can expect that economic and social resources in themselves have a significant impact on birth rates. In fact research should isolate the extent to which environmental resourcefulness contributes to organizational birth rates over and beyond the explanatory power of size, differentiation, and change. Resourcefulness in itself may explain a great amount of the variance in frequency of births, and several documents draw conclusions to that effect (Bolton Committee, 1971; Boswell, 1973; Deeks, 1976). In this chapter, however, I have stressed the joint consideration of ecological organization and the availability of entrepreneurially relevant resources. I hope that this discussion has identified avenues of research that will help isolate the effects of structural variables as well as the effects of resources on the frequency of organizational births.

Conclusion

This chapter has provided an ecological framework of entrepreneurship. It has stressed that structural and process dimensions of urban systems, as well as the availability of resources, explain differences in organizational birthrates. The most important urban structural attributes are size, differentiation, and change. Attributes of the organizational population include size, size distribution, life cycle, and aspects of the population set. Economic and social resourcefulness are reflected in wage and energy costs, availability of venture capital, taxation systems, professional groups and associations, universities and other centers of diffusion of relevant information, quality of life, and national prominence. Research ought to be undertaken to determine the validity of the hypothesis that these attributes are related to the level of entrepreneurial vigor of an urban-metropolitan area. The personal backgrounds of entrepreneurs, their achievement orientation, and other motivational aspects can be important, but they may be insignificant compared to the contextual area from which their new business firms emerge.

Ideally, research on organizational birthrates should be complemented with research on the rise and decline of new firms. The first years of a new organization are among the most important of its life cycle, but little information exists about the reasons for success, decline, or death. We need theoretical developments on the death rates of organizations—including aspects of the human ecology as a set of antecedents of organizational mortality. New or small firms engage comparatively little in deliberate long-range planning of their external operations. They seem to be more preoccupied with reactive adaptation to their environments than with proactive manipulation of them (Deeks, 1976). New firms also show a remarkable decline in performance and a greater likelihood of bankruptcy when the entrepreneur leaves and is succeeded by others, whether relatives, employees, or outsiders, and his presence thus seems crucial for the initial life stages of the firm (Boswell, 1972). Information on the role of entrepreneurs in safeguarding new ventures against a hostile environment should therefore also be considered in trying to understand the early existence of new firms. Such research may also move organizational research away from an almost exclusive cross-sectional approach toward longitudinal designs in which the historical antecedents of organizational behavior become central.

PART II

Transformation of Organizations

Once created, organizations go through a variety of transformations. Some die relatively quickly. Others prosper and continue relatively unchanged for decades, even centuries. Still others undergo one or more relatively dramatic changes in mission or structure or both. The range of possibilities is vast, but the central question is what happens to organizations as they "mature" and how can we begin to understand that process.

The four chapters in this section of the book begin to address this central question. In Chapter Six Tichy starts with the assertion that the notion of organizational life cycles "is seductively simple. . . . Organizations do not follow predictable biosocial stages of development. They share some common properties with biological systems. . . . However, they also have unique capacities. . . . The laws of social systems are not the same as those of biological systems." Tichy sees all organizations as confronted by three ongoing dilemmas: the technical design problem—how desired output is generated; the political allocation problem—how power is distributed; and the ideological and cultural mix problem—how ascendant values are determined. He argues that none of these problems is ever solved in any ultimate sense. Solutions are inevita-

161

bly partial and temporary. At particular points in time, however, one or the other of these problems is organizationally salient and energy is directed toward its solution. What is cyclic is that the solutions to one problem contain "triggers" for the others. The three ebb and flow interdependently, and the problem faced by management is which cycle to deal with when.

Tichy also develops the idea, which he illustrates with his experience with the Martin Luther King Health Center, that the shape and content of organizational futures may be partly determined by *which* problem is dominant when the organization is created and by how well it is solved at that time. Although Tichy does not actually say so, the implication is that relatively ineffectual problem solving at birth may be inordinately costly to an organization for reasons that are both obvious and not so obvious.

In Chapter Seven Lodahl and Mitchell introduce the concept of "organizational drift"—the gap between founders' ideals and intentions, on the one hand, and the enacted organization, on the other—in their analysis of the transformation of two innovative universities. Founders of organizations must have both technical and institutional skills. Institutional skills are particularly important in the founding of innovative organizations where uniqueness may be an inviting target for unfriendly critics. Founders "must create symbols, language, ritual, and organizational structures" and "must move beyond the merely formal, rational, planned, and utilitarian aspects of structure . . . to deal with the vast institutional substrate out of which all human organizations are born." In the two universities they studied, however, Lodahl and Mitchell found that, over time, technical skills displaced institutional skills as the basis for operation and that this process created organizational drift. Drift, they argue, is inevitable in innovative organizations unless a "cycle of vigilance" can be developed and maintained to counteract pervasive tendencies toward the familiar, the established, and the routine.

Walton's Chapter Eight explores the factors and forces that shape the fate of new work structures. Based on his experiences in four organizational settings over a period of ten years, it represents an effort to create a developmental theory that encompasses both creation and transformation but that ultimately focuses on success. The four organizational systems developed quite differently, and Walton set for himself the task of accounting for these differences.

Many of the themes found in earlier chapters reappear in

Walton's detailed account of the evolution of the four settings he observed. Particularly noteworthy are the difficulties encountered in maintaining high levels of commitment to the new structures over time and the tendency toward drift and away from innovation. Regarding maturation, Walton observes that "work structures do not really become established until both the requisite human resources and task technology are well developed," although in the four cases these developed at quite different rates. He also describes a key dilemma for new work structures in terms of survival: "External relations are important to the survival of a high-commitment work system to the extent that its ideology deviates from the prevailing norms in the larger system. . . . Deviance creates interest on the part of external parties, some of whom probably will find the deviant system threatening to their roles, their skills, their status, or their ideologies." The "liability of uniqueness" can be overcome, but only through careful planning and replanning.

The level of analysis shifts in Chapter Nine. Brittain and Freeman are interested in the phenomenon of organizational proliferation; that is, the development of new organizational forms and the expansion of the organizational populations in which they are observable. Their analysis unfolds at the industry, the organizational, and the individual levels. In their view, "industries develop, opening new niches that represent opportunities. Organizations and the individuals who populate them move into these niches in ways that reflect both past histories of organizational growth or decline and personal careers." The themes that they broach are ones that appear in various forms in other chapters. Organizational birth and development are influenced by a combination of external problems, external opportunities, and internal events that are shaped by the experiences and aspirations of key individuals. They illustrate their arguments with examples from the semiconductor industry—an industry that has experienced extraordinarily rapid growth and has thus created the possibility for widespread proliferation of a variety of organizational forms. But in spite of their reliance on only one industry for examples, they take the position that "the basic ecological dynamic prevails in all organizational populations, with the outcome in any industry specific to the environmental conditions under which organizational forms seek to exercise their relative advantages."

6

Problem Cycles in Organizations and the Management of Change

Noel M. Tichy

The notion that organizations have life cycles is seductively simple. It is true that we can talk about organizations being born and going through a creation phase and that we can refer to organization growth over time. However, the biological analogy of a system going through predictable phases of development does not hold up to empirical scrutiny. Organizations do not follow predictable biosocial stages of development. They share some common properties with biological systems—for example, they are born, they import energy, transform it and produce an output, and are differentiated and are functionally specialized. However, they also have unique capacities such as negentropy (Katz and Kahn, 1966) and go through changes that are explained more by such factors as environmental threats, opportunities, size, and technology than by unfolding maturational processes. Organizations are not easily catergorized by such labels as "childhood," "adolescence," and so on. The laws of social systems are not the same as those of biological systems.

This chapter argues that organizations have three interrelated cycles. These cycles are not based on maturational processes but on the dynamics of social systems surviving and making adjustments in various contexts. Organizations must make cyclical adjustments over time. These adjustments come about as the organization attempts to resolve three basic ongoing dilemmas.

The first dilemma is the *technical design problem.* Here, the organization faces a production problem; that is, social and technical resources must be arranged so that the organization produces some desired output. The second is the *political allocation problem* or, in other words, the problem of allocating power and resources. The uses to which the organization will be put, as well as who will reap the benefits from the organization, must be determined. The third is the *ideological and cultural mix problem.* As social tools, organizations are, in part, held together by normative glue, that is, by the sharing of certain important beliefs by its members. Hence, the organization must determine what values need to be held by what people.

Because organizations are dynamic and always undergoing shifts and changes, none of these problems is ever resolved—they are ongoing dilemmas. At different points in time any one of them may be in need of adjustment. Adjustments in each of these three problem areas are conceptualized in cyclical terms; thus, there are technical, political, and cultural adjustment cycles. Organizations vary over time in the amount of energy invested in making adjustments in each of these cycles.

All three cycles overlap and interact with each other in ways that may be beneficial or problematic for the organization. Figure 1 graphically portrays the cycles in terms of peaks and valleys. A peak represents a high need for adjustment in one of the three problem areas, while a valley indicates a smooth, nonproblematic time for that cycle. The left axis of the figure includes two dimensions: (1)

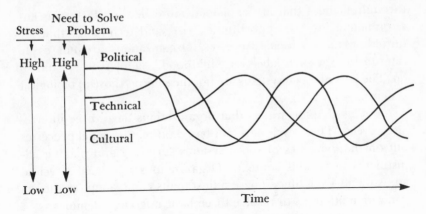

Figure 1. Organizational Cycles

amount of stress or tension created in the organization with regard to a particular problem area, and (2) the need for adjustment to manage the particular cycle. Thus, the peaks represent both high stress and high need for adjustment. Each cycle has associated with it a different set of problem-solving and managerial actions. The adjustments are managed by strategies that range from benign neglect or purposeful avoidance of the problem to such direct means as unilateral leadership decisions, group task forces, bargaining among competing interest groups, or showdown fights.

Each cycle has its own type of uncertainty. Technical uncertainty is related to uncertainty regarding production issues. Thus, when the organization is faced with less information than it needs to make work decisions, uncertainty is high. The major contributors to high technical uncertainty are rapid changes in the environment, complex tasks, and highly interdependent tasks. Support for this argument is found in the information-processing perspective on organization design (Tushman and Nadler, 1978). When there are increases in any one of these sources of uncertainty or in some combination of them, the technical cycle begins to peak.

A peak in a technical cycle occurred in the health center case that will be presented more fully later in this chapter. The technical cycle peaked during this center's early years of development as a result of several changes. First, the environment became less munificent; that is, resource limitations were put on the organization. The Department of Health, Education, and Welfare (HEW) cut back on grants, and this move forced the center to be more efficient in the provision of health care and to demonstrate greater cost effectiveness. In addition, as the organization grew, the complex task of delivering comprehensive and team-oriented community health care came to require an organizational design capable of high levels of information processing—one that could incorporate social, family, and medical input into health decisions. The center's rather *laissez-faire* leadership and loose management structure did not provide the necessary levels of information processing. Thus, the technical cycle reached a peak, and the organization had to make adjustments. The organizational and managerial adjustments entailed the development of greater information-processing capacity and resulted in the redesign of the health teams and the introduction of a matrix form of organizational structure.

Political uncertainty relates to uncertainty over who has the power to allocate rewards and to decide on the goals of the organization. When there is high uncertainty in this area, the political cycle peaks. Thus, a political peak occurred at the health center when a coalition of external community board members attempted to influence managerial actions inside the health center and to effect the hiring of people of their choosing rather than of management's. This resulted in the formation of a counter coalition of community workers in the health center, and this coalition attempted to fend off the external community board members and to maintain the power to allocate resources and decide on the goals of the organization internally. The result was a great deal of political uncertainty. The organizational adjustment in this case involved weakening the external board and thus reducing uncertainty.

Cultural uncertainty is related to differences among organization members with regard to their values and ideology. The health center began at a peak of cultural uncertainty. A group of outside professionals came into a poverty area of the South Bronx of New York with a particular ideology about health care and community development. Since this ideology was not familiar to or shared by community members, the major problem at the start of the organization was to develop an ideologically homogeneous coalition of outsiders and key community people. Once this coalition was formed, the cultural cycle gradually moved toward a valley of low uncertainty.

Conceptual Background

Before the health center case is presented to illustrate how cycles functioned over time in one organization, several additional concepts need to be introduced along with some propositions about the functioning of organizational cycles. The first paragraph of this chapter argues against thinking in terms of developmental phases. But there is one exception to this argument: all organizations do go through a developmental stage of birth, that is, a start-up or creation phase. Furthermore, there are some core issues that all organizations must resolve during this phase. There must be a way to mobilize people to invest energy in the organization, and decisions must be made about the form of the organization. But organizational cycles play a key determinant role even at this stage.

Depending on which cycle or cycles are dominant at the organization's birth, different organizational adjustments will take place. An organization that starts with a cultural cycle peak will focus a great deal of its time and energy on questions of values. Often this cycle will be dominated by the actions of a highly cohesive core group and its charismatic leader. An organization that starts with a technical cycle peak, as might be the case with a business that wants to produce a new kind of widget, will be characterized by a great deal of activity aimed at solving technical production problems—for example, how best to organize the work, capital, and management to produce widgets. A political peak at the beginning of an organization's life will involve a great deal of coalitional bargaining and exchange activity to determine who will have the power to allocate resources and to decide on the organizational goals. Thus, one of the propositions about organizational cycles is:

Proposition 1: The resolution of early, birth-stage problems in an organization is largely determined by which cycle or cycles are dominant.

Two types of events trigger uncertainty and thus cause organizational cycles to peak. One set represents events and activities that occur independently of the cycles. The second set involves the cycles themselves, which trigger one another in a dialectical process; that is, a peak in one cycle will eventually trigger a peak in one or both of the other cycles. Regardless of which set of events causes a cycle to peak, the process is the same. Some core group in the organization experiences uncertainty and responds to it; the results are stress and a felt need for adjustment.

The first set of triggers include:

1. Environmental changes, such as increased complexity and unpredictability.
2. Technological changes that result in the potential for new products or services and/or new methodologies for producing existing products and services.
3. Shifts in agreement among organization members over the goals of the organization; for example, when splits erupt among members of the dominant coalition regarding the future mission of the organization.
4. Shifts in agreement among organization members over the means of getting the work done in the organization; for example, when different factions support different forms of production or of organizational structure.
5. Changes in people; that is, bringing new recruits into the organization, especially ones who differ in some significant way from existing members; examples here would be women and minorities brought into white, male-dominated organizations.

Figure 2 presents these trigger events. It is proposed that disturbance or uncertainty created by a trigger leads to a need for adjustment in one or more of the cycles. The shaded cells in Figure 2 represent the cycles that are influenced most strongly by each of the triggers. Note that the environment influences all three simultaneously. This means that a major uncertainty in the environment often leads to stress and to a need for simultaneous adjustments in the technical, political, and cultural cycles. This does not mean that the organization will attempt to make such adjustments simultaneously, simply that the peaks may occur at the same time.

The various triggers are hypothesized to affect the cycles in different ways. For example, technological triggers affect the technical cycle more than they affect the other two cycles. But shifts in agreement over goals and means both impact the political cycle and cause it to peak.

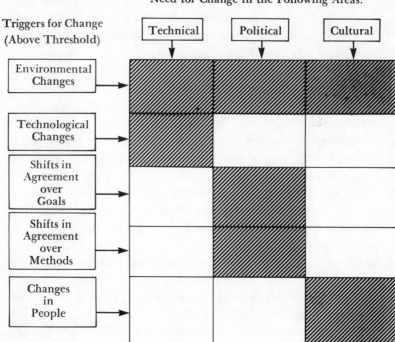

Note: Shaded areas indicate major expected impact from a particular trigger.

Source: Tichy (forthcoming).

Figure 2. Triggering the Change Process

Proposition 2: Uncertainty-creating events have differential impact on the three organizational cycles.

The second set of triggering events for cycles are the cycles themselves. Except for major environmental triggers, events start by creating uncertainty in one cycle. But since the cycles are dialectical in nature, they cause counterreactions in one another. A major technical adjustment often triggers a political realignment, as when an organization is designed and the careers and power bases of various individuals are altered. This in turn can trigger a cultural cycle that will alter the member's values and norms to fit with the changed technical and political environment.

Proposition 3: Organizational cycles are dialectical and trigger one another.

The *technical cycle* is managed by applying conceptual tools that help solve the production problem. The information-processing model of organization design (Tushman and Nadler, 1978) represents one set of tools. The basic premise is that an organization is effective to the degree that there is a match between the amount of uncertainty it faces and its capacity to process information for dealing with the uncertainty. Technical uncertainty is defined as the difference between information required to complete a task and information actually possessed.

The *political cycle* is managed by applying conceptual tools that help solve the political problem. The uncertainty that is important here does not involve task accomplishment but rather the power to allocate resources and decide on organizational goals. Political uncertainty is defined as the degree of stability and predictability of the bargaining and exchange relations among interest groups in relation to the allocation of resources, power, and prestige. As political uncertainty increases, so does the need for political bargaining and exchange in order to manage this uncertainty.

The *cultural cycle* is managed by applying conceptual tools for resolving the *ideological and cultural mix problem.* Organizations are able to manage this problem to the extent that inconsistencies in cultural values are matched with a capacity for making adjustments in these values among members. The cultural cycle can be triggered when there are shifts in cultural values in the environment or when new people enter the organization.

Proposition 4: Each cycle has associated with it a distinct set of conceptual tools for dealing with uncertainty; the technical cycle is managed by applying conceptual tools to resolve the production problem; the political cycle is managed by applying conceptual tools to resolve the political allocation problem; and the cultural cycle is managed by applying conceptual tools to resolve the ideological and cultural mix problem.

The Change Process

The change process is described in terms of how the three cycles affect the overall organization. The overall organization is thought of in terms of the model presented in Figure 3. This model is built on the assumption that organizational effectiveness (output) is a function of the characteristics of each of the components as well as of the way that the components interrelate or fit together within a system. Thus, descriptions of the components, as well as of the interrelationships among them, are necessary for analysis. Figure 3 briefly defines each of the components of the organizational model.

The model portrays organizations as more than a set of static components. Organizations are systems that are in dynamic interplay with their environment and that have multiple and dynamic interdependencies among parts. The dynamic interrelationships among the parts of the organization and the degree to which the organization fits with its environment must be simultaneously analyzed from the technical, political, and cultural perspectives. The analysis can be thought of as generating answers to the following four questions:

1. Assuming that the organization exists to maximize effectiveness and efficiency, that is, assuming a technical-instrumental perspective, how well do its parts fit together?
2. Assuming that the organization exists to allocate resources among various interest groups, that is, assuming a political economy perspective, how well do its parts mesh?
3. Assuming that the organization exists to perpetuate and reinforce value and ideological systems, that is, assuming a cultural perspective, how well do its parts fit together?
4. How congruent are the three perspectives—technical, political, and cultural—with one another for the organization at this point in time?

The management of change consists of predicting, channeling, guiding, and altering the three cycles. These adjustments, which can be seen as forces that carry the organization through time, are cyclical in nature. The pattern of these forces varies from situation to situation, but the predictable patterns are that (1) these forces oscillate and have a tendency to regress to the mean, and that (2) they tend to set up counterreactions; that is, an extreme

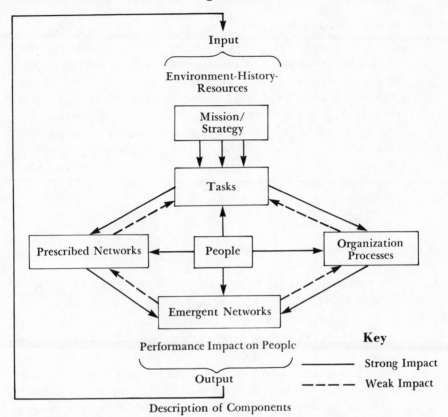

Input

Environment-History-
Resources

Mission/
Strategy

Tasks

Prescribed Networks ← People → Organization Processes

Emergent Networks

Performance Impact on People

Output

Key

―――― Strong Impact

― ― ― Weak Impact

Description of Components

Mission/Strategy: This includes the organization's reason for being, its basic approach to carrying out its mission, its strategy, and its criteria for effectiveness, namely the objectives.

Tasks: This refers to the technology or technologies by which the organization's work is accomplished.

People: This includes the characteristics of the members of the organization: background, motivational patterns, managerial style, and so forth.

Prescribed Networks: This refers to the explicitly designed social structure of the organization. It includes the organization of subunits, communication, and authority networks, as well as structural mechanisms for integrating the organization.

Organizational Processes: These are the mechanisms (communication, decision making, conflict management, control and reward) that enable the prescribed networks to carry out the dynamics of work.

Emergent Networks: These are the structures and processes that, while not planned or formally prescribed, inevitably emerge in the organization.

Figure 3. Organization Model

technical focus will create pressure on both the cultural and political cycles. Successful change must rely on the ability to predict cycles and to channel and guide them. This means that a change manager will at times be a political builder of coalitions, a power broker, and an influence manipulator coping with the political cycles. At other times he or she will be solving problems rationally, relying on "scientific" data and principles to cope with the technical cycle. And at other times he or she will be an ideological leader. At still other times he or she may be doing all three simultaneously. Therein lies the need for change management to be built on a deeper awareness of organizational cycles.

A Case Illustration

The Dr. Martin Luther King Jr. Health Center (MLK), a neighborhood health center located in the South Bronx of New York, serves one of the most blighted urban areas in the United States. The problems of deteriorating housing, widespread unemployment, lack of educational opportunity, crime, and drugs have contributed to a complex of socially related health problems that defy conventional medical solutions. The center was founded in 1966 by a federal grant administered by the Montefiore Hospital and Medical Center. MLK has grown into a health care center with a staff of close to 400 employees, who serve 39,000 residents of a section of the Bronx that has 75,000 residents. The center is known for its innovations in primary health care. It developed the family-oriented primary health care team, employed community health workers, utilized nurse practitioners in unique ways, and developed a matrix organization design, as well as an internal structure managed all the way to the top by community members.

The MLK case is presented in order to illustrate how organizational cycles operated in one setting over a ten-year period. The discussion of the case is divided into four phases. These are not to be construed as developmental stages but as *post hoc* descriptions of phases that the organization went through. The title of each phase is meant to reflect the major activity during that time period in the organization's life.

Start-Up

The dominant cycle in the start-up phase for MLK was the cultural cycle. This cycle was triggered by a major opportunity provided by the environment. The Office of Economic Opportunity (OEO), which was established in the mid-1960s, made large grants available to build neighborhood health centers. The availability of this resource led Harold Wise, a physician, to develop an ideology for organizing a critical mass of people to start the center. Wise's ideology was anchored in a view of health care as a right of all citizens and of health constituting physical, psychological, and social well being. He believed that health care should be controlled by the community and that the health center should be managed by community members. Since this core group started with only a vague image of some future organization, the key problem to solve was the value and ideological problem; that is, Wise and the core group had to develop a common ideology and a sense of mission for the center. People were recruited to join the new culture on the basis of its mission.

Next, the core group saw it as its moral duty to move into the community and organize it around this ideology. The professional outsiders identified the informal community leaders and built an alliance with them. The outsiders were highly committed to their ideology and formed a social contract, an implicit agreement, with the community members to carry out this ideology. For the community members, the ideological commitment was preceded by a desire for jobs for themselves.

The conditions that facilitated cultural cycle problem solving included a munificent environment (money was readily available), a highly charismatic leader, and an organization with a great deal of fluidity. The first year saw the health center begin as a social movement. The exercise of authority was through normative rewards to members who had made highly personal and moral commitments to the intrinsic value and mission of the organization (Etzioni, 1961).

During the center's first year, Wise, as its leader and founder, energized people to do "their own thing," that is, to get projects started and to try things out and not worry about how well they would work or who would pay for them. The organization was dominated by the moral feeling that what its members were doing was right and that innovation was the correct mode of operation.

During this phase, however, there was increased political uncertainty. Although the community board was a benign factor during the first two years of the center, conflict began to develop between board and staff over control of the center and patronage (jobs for family and friends of board members) during the third year. At this point, the major conflicts among the board, the middle-class professional staff, and the community workers began to emerge. Since the community was poor in institutions as well as in other resources, the MLK board became one of the few forums for political activities. It therefore attracted a variety of community activists with various political agendas. One of the major issues on the board was the struggle for power between blacks and Puerto Ricans. Thus, the political cycle began climbing toward a peak after several years.

The situation within the center was different from that facing the board. Community workers and professionals had become increasingly concerned with health delivery and less involved with broad political and social problems in the community. Although the majority of the center's workers were black, ethnic conflicts were muted because of the ties that developed between blacks and Puerto Ricans as a result of on-the-job comradeship. But there was increasing divergence between board members and community workers. Initially, they had held a common point of view. As the workers became more technically competent and career oriented, however, they began to view the board members, who served part time without pay, as uninformed about health matters and unqualified to make decisions about the center. Furthermore, the workers wanted to cool down ethnic conflict and regarded the playing out of the struggle between Puerto Ricans and blacks on the board as a threat to the center.

Wise and the community workers developed a political strategy for the eventual takeover of the center by the community; that is, the community workers would eventually become the managers. Thus, rather than having its control turned over to an external board, MLK would develop an internal cadre of community workers. This strategy required a coalition of community workers and professionals who would resist the control of the external community board. The coalition was formed, and the external board became a weak political force at MLK for most of the following ten years.

The emphasis on the cultural and political cycles triggered the technical cycle. By the end of the start-up phase, there was a crisis that included confusion, frustration, and feelings of ambivalence toward the charismatic leadership. This crisis did not get resolved without pressure from both external and internal sources. Two young physicians and a management professor from M.I.T. were major conduits for external pressure, each telegraphing the message that the ship was not in good order and required a technical overhaul. The resolution of the crisis in Phase II was facilitated by the investment of managerial attention and energy in rational problem solving. The technical organizational cycle had been triggered, and this resulted in the explicit and systematic reexamination of mission and strategy, system design, development, and implementation. The information-processing capacity of the organization was increased to match uncertainty, especially at the level of the health teams, where a much more organic system than previously existed was designed, including a matrix organizational structure. But the start-up phase had ended with the organization facing confusion, internal conflicts, and frustration. The dominance of cultural, then political, concerns had left little attention for the technical concerns, even though the technical cycle had reached a peak.

Systems Development

The second phase of MLK's development was dominated by the technical problem, that is, by the need to rationalize and develop managerial practice and procedures and thus provide a semblance of order from the confusion created during Phase I. The organization made a heavy investment in developing systems and procedures. The conditions that facilitated development in Phase I—experimenting, creativity, entrepreneurial leadership— actually hindered development during the second phase. The decision-making and leadership required in Phase II was a rational planning mode, along with a less participative and forceful managerial style.

The pressure for change was of sufficient intensity for Wise to seek outside help, and he turned to Richard Beckhard from the Sloan School of Management at M.I.T. Beckhard brought management and organization design expertise to MLK, thus providing the group with new models for dealing with their problems. Beckhard worked with the top management and the community heirs apparent, Deloris Smith and Sonia Valdez, in clarifying MLK's mission and strategy. Once this was done, it was clear to Beckhard and the MLK managers that the center's structure and management were ineffective. It did not provide effective team-oriented health care with maximum community and worker involvement and control.

Beckhard proposed a new organization design and management structure. The result was that MLK came to have a matrix type of structure; team development and planning work were carried out within each team, and plans were developed for training and preparing the community leaders to take over the center. Problems in the technical component were managed in the systems development phase; the result was a reduction of confusion, frustration, and feelings of ambivalence.

The implementation of these plans was left to the leadership of Dr. Edward Martin, the director of health services. He was determined to make MLK follow its new plans and carry its own financial weight while at the same time providing quality health care.

By the end of Phase II the organization had been driven hard. Not only had new systems been designed and implemented but the community managers were trained and had moved into positions of authority. The organization experienced a sense of accomplishment as well as a sense of having had to work hard to achieve it. The technical cycle was descending into a valley. Despite these feelings of accomplishment, however, the organization had been pushed too hard and power had become more centralized, resulting in a reaction against control and in cynicism about management. A greater we/they dynamic between managers and workers set in. Even though the technical cycle was dominant during this phase, the political cycle was triggered and started climbing when attention was directed to developing community managers to take over the center. The cultural cycle remained stable throughout this period.

Stabilization and Consolidation

This phase provided MLK with a time to test the newly designed and implemented technical solutions to the production and efficiency problem, as well as to make necessary minor alterations and improvements. At MLK this phase had the added significance of testing the newly promoted community managers, who were now given total responsibility for managing the center. Organizational activities for the most part involved making small adjustments and changes. The cultural problem was minimally focused on as people became increasingly preoccupied with career considerations and instrumental rather than ideological concerns.

By the end of this phase, however, the political area began to require attention. The cycle was leading toward another peak because of growing pressure from HEW (the grant was shifted to HEW when OEO was dismantled) and Montefiore to turn the center over to a community board. This meant that new community managers had to deal with the political uncertainty of creating a working board. This was difficult because the existing board had some powerful members who were not very supportive of the existing management, and there was the very real danger that a community board would alter the center's goals and replace key managers. The community managers justifiably feared that their jobs might be in danger if the currently constituted board took over. Over a period of several years a reconstituted board was put together, and it became a working board with total responsibility for the center. Montefiore turned over all control for the center to the community board early in 1978.

Self-Renewal

Overlapping with the transition to a new board was a tremendous pressure from the environment for cost effectiveness, coupled with an emigration of patients from the MLK service area and a reduction in federal grants given to MLK to cover deficits. This phase triggered a struggle for survival in an increasingly hostile environment, and both the technical and political cycles began peaking. The center faced two problems: (1) how to manage more efficiently and effectively and (2) how to capture greater allocation of HEW and other resources for MLK and the South Bronx. The managerial response under such circumstances can be to trigger political or technical activities or both. Political activities focus on attempting to capture additional financial resources from various government agencies. Technical activities focus on mapping the environment through marketing and financial studies, reformulating the organization's mission and strategy, and mobilizing it for action around the redesign and change of strategy. MLK focused first on the technical theme. However, the political cycle also began to peak during this phase, with the major political uncertainty being the balance of power between the internal community managers and the external community board.

At the writing of this chapter, the two cycles—political and technical—were at a peak simultaneously. The organization faced a major problem: how to survive with tighter financial resources. At the same time the external board had for political reasons forced the resignation of the director, a community manager who was very competent technically. This mobilized an internal coalition of community workers to fight the external board. Another rather ominous sign was that the cultural cycle was rising at this point too. In other words, there was increasing value and ideological heterogeneity among the staff. One group represented a radical Marxist ideology, another was still committed to the ideology of community-based preventive health care, and another group focused on instrumental material gain, that is, how to make more money. The simultaneous peaking of two cycles creates enormous strain on an organization. If all three cycles peak simultaneously, it is questionable whether an organization can cope. But this may happen at MLK.

Conclusion

The concept of organizational cycles was introduced as a means for thinking more systematically about organizational change and adaptation in a continuous fashion rather than in discrete separate points in time fashion. The three cycles—technical, political, and cultural—were derived from what was proposed to be three core characteristics of all organizations; namely, that the organization must deal with a production problem, a political allocation problem, and a cultural and ideological problem. Furthermore, these problems are never solved in any permanent way but remain in continuous flux. In analyzing organizational change, it is important to be able to separate these three cycles, much as one might separate the strands of a rope, in order to understand the functioning of each.

The three strands of the rope must be understood not only individually but also in relation to one another. This chapter attempted to lay the conceptual groundwork for analyzing both the individual cycles and their interdependencies. A number of propositions were introduced that require empirical investigation and conceptual revision.

Proposition 1: The resolution of early, birth-stage problems in an organization is largely determined by which cycle or cycles are dominant.

In the MLK case the cultural cycle was dominant. This meant that the organization was mobilized and built around a core set of values and beliefs. In such organizations, as indicated in some of the other chapters in this volume, it is not unusual to see confusion and frustration emerge a few years later because of the lack of initial solutions to the production problem. This proposition predicts that an organization born with a dominant technical cycle would have different birth problems. A first step in investigating this proposition would be to find additional case examples of each type of organization at birth—a technical one such as a new business firm, a political one such as a new political party or union, a cultural one such as a new ideologically driven social, education, or health organization. Carrying out in-depth qualitative analyses such as in the MLK case would be the most fruitful research strategy at this early exploratory phase. Such analyses could be followed by larger-scale comparative studies.

Proposition 2: Uncertainty-creating events have differential impact on the three organizational cycles.

A great deal of both conceptual and research work is needed to begin investigating this proposition. The trigger events that were presented in Figure 2 must be operationalized by answering the questions, What is an environmental change and how is it measured? Then it will be necessary to develop operational definitions and measures of technical, political, and cultural uncertainty. Third, ways need to be devised to link specific trigger events with uncertainty in each of the cycles. Again, at such early exploratory stages it seems useful to begin with good qualitative case examples and field studies. These can be followed by comparative longitudinal studies.

Proposition 3: Organizational cycles are dialectical and trigger one another.

In the MLK case it was argued that cycles were triggered both by external factors and by one another. Some interesting avenues for research include investigating whether or not there are any predictable patterns to the intercycle triggering. For example, do technical cycles tend to trigger political or cultural cycles? It might be empirically investigated whether the political and technical cycles tend to precede the cultural cycle. Again, an initial research strategy should be to do comparative analyses of longitudinal case studies.

Proposition 4: Each cycle has associated with it a distinct set of conceptual tools for dealing with uncertainty.

The final proposition calls for lines of research in the political and cultural area that parallel efforts done on contingency and information-processing views of organizational design and structure (Tushman and Nadler, 1978). In other words, the relationship of environmental uncertainty, goals uncertainty, and uncertainty over the means of production needs to be empirically measured and related to methods for reducing political uncertainty in an organization. In the cultural area, value and ideological heterogeneity needs to be studied in relation to organizational attempts to manage such uncertainty. It is hoped that these propositions will stimulate further investigation into the technical, political, and cultural nature of organizations.

7

Drift in the Development of Innovative Organizations

*Thomas M. Lodahl
Stephen M. Mitchell*

Maturity in an organization is signaled by its ability to reproduce. It reaches this point when it exhibits historicity and control; that is, when its values and ideals, which serve as templates for interpreting experiences and taking action, can be passed down through successive generations so that the organization "exists" independently of those who currently embody it. The innovative organization which we define as one trying to do something new or different from others of its kind, has special problems in reaching this stage. It must not only function efficiently but it must also legitimize itself to the world—and to its backers and followers—because of its uniqueness. As it passes through successive stages of

184

development, ideals and values are formed in relation to unmet needs, perceived problems, and timely opportunities, as well as sponsors' wishes. Somehow the founders must fashion an organizational design and create an atmosphere in which their unique ideas can be reinforced and understood in relation to past experience or other innovative attempts. In other words, the institutional, largely unwritten side of the organization must be developed along with formal structure and process.

Evidence in this study, however, suggests that institutional processes are still too vaguely understood to be managed effectively. Without special attention, they tend to develop independently of formal structures and intentions—to drift off on their own. The term *organizational drift* refers to the gap between founders' ideals and intentions and the enacted organization (the organization as experienced). In this chapter we will examine the foundation of two innovative universities in an effort to delineate the factors that contribute to organizational drift. If we can pinpoint exactly what events or processes cause an organization to become other than what it was intended to be, then perhaps we will be able to suggest how to create an organization that remains what it was intended to be.

Institutional Skills

Basically, what we are arguing is that the creation of an innovative organization requires two distinct types of skills. The first set is composed of technical skills. These are the standard managerial techniques that will enable the founders to solicit funds, find appropriate contractors, hire personnel with the necessary qualifications, set up effective procedures, and so forth. These problems have been reasonably well documented (Starbuck, 1965, 1971).

The second set of skills, however, has received less attention. These may be labeled "institutional skills," and they involve the manipulation of structure and process to ensure that the organization becomes an institution. They are used to design the organization in such a way that the values and ideals of the founders are embedded in the reality of the organization. We should note that our definition of an institution focuses on the phenomenology of the actors in the organization, that is, an institution is an organization that is able to ensure consensus as to values and ideals across generations of workers. A phenomenological perspective assumes that perceptions are influenced by the context in which the actor is located. This is why the manipulation of structure and process is crucial to the utilization of institutional skills, for it is through such a manipulation that the ideology of the organization comes to be represented in the reality of the work context.

Insofar as ideology emerges wherever there is a break with the past (Geertz, 1974), it becomes a central feature of the innovative organization. The ideology summarizes the values and ideals that the founders intended the new organization to epitomize. However, the deliberately innovative organization is an inviting target for those who worked their way up by mastering the subtleties and enduring the trivia of the status quo. Pioneers attract unfriendly critics. In order to maintain their thrust and their members' energy, such pioneers are forced to rise above mundane preoccupations with accounting, finance, materials, and methods. They must create symbols, language, ritual, and organizational structures, not knowing to what degree they might support or subvert the intended innovations. Thus the founders of innovative organizations must move beyond the merely formal, rational, planned, and utilitarian aspects of structure that make up the "girders and rivets" school of organizational design to deal with the vast institutional substrate into which all human organizations are born. (Lodahl, 1974). Put another way, founders must link the formal and more "objective" aspects of the creation of structure with the institutional, largely subjective or phenomenal aspects of organizational life. They must utilize institutional skills.

Bringing an organization into existence is an exercise in the creation and maintenance of meaning. It is important to remember that the image that marks the start of an organization is produced in a specific historical context (Stinchcombe, 1965). Any new organization must allow for some degree of fit into the historical and cultural forces of which it is a part. There is a limit to the degree of innovation, and the successful organization usually represents "an idea whose time has come." For the founders of an innovative organization, this means that they must take account of the status quo with which they are confronted, especially as it relates to the institutional aspects of the organization's birth. It is the successful manipulation of the institutional processes that enables the image of the innovative organization to become a reality, for it is through the use of institutional skills that value is infused into social machinery (Selznick, 1957) and commitment to the new organization is achieved.

The generation of commitment through the use of institutional skills requires that the potential member be disengaged from preexisting attachments, that is, from the status quo. Then, by stressing the ideals and values of the new organization, that is, by using the ideology as a resource, the founders of the organization may be able to generate total commitment on instrumental, affective, and moral levels (Kanter, 1972), while also fostering the value consensus that is crucial to the legitimation of authority and organization. We assume that commitment is important, especially to an innovative organization that must stress its uniqueness to all its members. In this regard, the importance of ideology and its infusion into the structure and process of the organization cannot be overemphasized. "Ideology names the structure of situations in such a way that the attitude toward them is one of commitment" (Geertz, 1974, p. 231). An innovative organization must try to instill an almost religious fervor into its members. A spiritual commitment to the ideology is called for. The danger of organizational drift is that a shift in the type of commitment will occur from one based on ideology to one based on techniques, departments, or self-interest. While this shift in commitment may be tolerable for an organization that desires routine performance, for the innovative organization, in which peak performance must be the goal, such a shift is deadly. The founders must do whatever they can to ensure that the ideology is realized in practice; in other words, they must strive to prevent organizational drift.

Three factors can be used to enhance this process. The first is the founder himself. As a charismatic leader, the founder may serve as a significant source of identity. His actions may become the basis of ritual and myth (Pettigrew, 1976), and his overall behavior guides the new organization through the turmoils of birth (see Chapter Two). Second is the use of organizational structure. A structure should be designed that reinforces the ideology and serves as a source of reaffirmation of the organizational values. In all cases the values of the ideology must be reaffirmed, while the proper structure to achieve these values is left open. Finally, the social processes of the organization must also reinforce the ideology if commitment is to be assured. Since "the ideals and purposes that initially bring men together constitute the unifying bonds of the groups they form" (Blau, 1964, p. 50), the innovative organization must not allow these ideological resources to be lost.

In this chapter, we discuss factors leading to organizational drift along with various alternatives for coping with it, in relation to data from case studies of the founding of two new universities in England in the 1960s.

What Drift Is

Conceptually, drift may be defined as the difference between the ideals as enunciated in the ideology and the perceived operations of the organization in practice—operations that result from the structure and processes employed. Another factor, the members' own view of the value or ideal in question, is also of interest. We may define commitment as the agreement between the ideal as enunciated and the members' own view of that ideal. In essence, our study centers on the relationship between these three factors (ideology, perceptions of the organizational reality in practice, members' own views) and the variables affecting these relationships. Since we are studying the founding of innovative organizations, we presume that ideology is both a stable and a focal factor. For an innovative organization to become an institution, the organization in practice and the members' own views of it must be congruent with the ideology as enunciated. Organizational drift and lack of commitment result from an incongruence between (1) ideology and the organization in practice and (2) the members' own views of the organization. We are attempting to isolate the variables that contribute to the development of such incongruence.

In both of the universities studied, there was an "interdisciplinary ideal"—a belief that British university departments had become overspecialized and their heads too despotic. For both, there was an immediate structural consequence: the universities were organized according to functionally defined "schools of study" rather than specialist-oriented departments. This was enacted in a number of ways in both schools; both had, for example, "Schools of European Studies," in which languages, history, literature, and other relevant subjects were combined into a common syllabus. Drift would occur, then, if members felt that certain specialist groups were taking over or that there was "secret departmentalism." We believe we captured the outcomes of these perceptions by measuring "ideals," "actuals," and "own views." We saw these as measuring ideology, the enacted structure, and personal commitment to the ideal, respectively.

In Figure 1, data on the three variables listed above are graphed according to the *year of arrival* of the respondents at Alpha university. Statements of ideals were taken from published documents of each university; respondents were asked to indicate how consistent the statement was with:

1. The ideals usually put forth by this university.
2. The way things were actually done here.
3. Your own personal views.

Drift is the difference between 1 and 2; commitment is indexed by the difference between 1 and 3. (For Figure 1, the trend for "ideals" is not significant; for "university does," $p = .09$, and for "own views," $p < .005$).

Figure 1 shows that drift is greater for late arrivals than for early; all *know* the ideal almost perfectly; early arrivals see the universities as carrying through the ideal, but later ones don't. The divergence is even greater between ideal and respondents' own views, that is, commitment is less, as the new organization ages. Why?

We believe that there are compelling practical reasons for this. Early arrivals were recruited more carefully than were later ones, with greater attention to fit with ideals. Contact between founders and later members decreased, and as founders' energies inevitably waned, their initial charisma dimmed. Control over institutional climate (and socialization) passed to the wider group of colleagues-at-large; to the degree that enacted structure departed

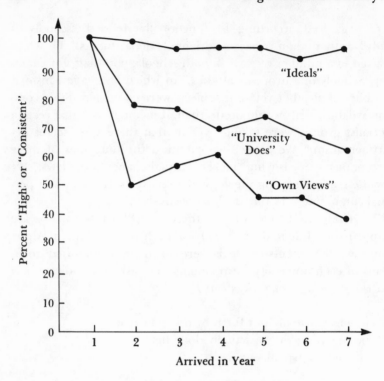

Figure 1. Organizational Drift

from the ideal, disillusionment and counterdependence increased. Finally, the most recent recruits, who showed the highest level of commitment (that is, whose own views were the most congruent with the ideals as enunciated) after that of the early founders, found an exhausted group of founders and an already-formalized organization that provided them with little opportunity to make innovative contributions of their own. Dissatisfaction and disillusionment were the result and led to a widening between "ideals" and "own views." We shall illustrate these ideas by referring to data on recruitment processes, contact with founders, the dynamics of social activity, and the effects of formalization.

Setting and Method

In order to deal with expected increases in student numbers, the University Grants Committee (UGC), which oversaw expenditures for British higher education, decided to expand the number of new universities. Between 1958 and 1965, the UGC approved the founding of nine new universities, seven of them in England. All were to have a minimum site size of 200 acres, and almost all the cost would be borne by the government. All were encouraged to be innovative in the structure of courses, curriculum content, teaching methods, and governance. A better setting in which to study the founding of innovative organizations can hardly be imagined. We have a group of people with a mandate to start organizations that will break with past tradition (that is, will be innovative), and who have been given all the resources necessary to overcome the preliminary technical problems that confront the founders of all organizations. This freedom from technical constraints allowed the founders to concentrate on the development of institutions, thereby highlighting the importance of institutional skills. Further, because several universities were started in a short period of time, the basis for a comparative analysis was present. Finally, since much of the initial development has been well documented (Daiches, 1970), we have a solid foundation on which to begin an investigation.

The two eldest of these foundations were studied after they had been in existence for seven and eight years. By that point in time, Alpha university (the older) had achieved considerable institutional success; Beta, only a moderate amount. Alpha was already high on the preference lists of matriculants, had a distinguished staff in many fields, and had little difficulty in placing its graduates. Beta, somewhat more remote from London, was considered by its staff to have lesser reputation in many fields (Beyer and Lodahl, 1976), was lower on preference lists, and had not grown as fast. In describing their founding processes, we used three main data sources: records and archives, personal interviews with founders and current members, and a mail questionnaire that achieved a 73 percent response rate after two follow-ups.

Recruitment Processes

One way of minimizing the differences between innovative ideals and the preexisting ideas of new members is to organize the recruitment process so as to attract those who favor the innovations and to select only those whose ideas are most likely to fit in with the innovative enterprise. A great deal of attention was paid to recruitment in the early days of both universities, both publicized their innovative plans (Alpha more than Beta), and both sought faculty who themselves had multidisciplinary backgrounds. Table 1 plots recruitment variables according to the year of arrival of the respondent. We see, for example, that at Alpha, 40 percent of those who arrived in the first year said they were highly aware of the university before they were interviewed; 100 percent said the university emphasized its differences from others a "great deal"; and zero percent of the respondents said the university emphasized their subject matter competence over their fit with the new ideas. All three variables shift a good deal by year of arrival, but perhaps the most spectacular change is in the drift away from emphasizing the difference between these and existing universities.

This is all the more serious because there are definite relationships between recruitment practices and acceptance of the in-

Table 1. Initial Conditions for New Members

| Variable | University | Arrived in Year | | | | | | | p^a | p^b |
		1	2	3	4	5	6	7		
Awareness of this university (percent "high")	Alpha	40	33	30	36	26	38	35	.02	NS[c]
	Beta	$(+)^d$	66	36	19	5	17	19		.04
How much university emphasized differences (percent "great deal")	Alpha	100	52	57	50	55	31	40	NS	.04
	Beta	$(+)$	78	50	52	26	49	26		.05
University emphasized subject matter competence over new ideas (percent "heavily or lean toward subject matter")	Alpha	0	43	56	37	54	60	65	NS	NS
	Beta	$(+)$	33	64	67	72	54	58		NS

[a]Significance levels for overall differences (between universities).
[b]Significance levels for trend (within universities).
[c]NS = not significant.
[d](+) = N too small to calculate percentages.

novative ideals. Table 2 shows correlations between recruitment variables and three aspects of the interdisciplinary ideology espoused by both schools. These are further broken down by the three socialization variables mentioned earlier: awareness of the ideal ("ideal"), what the university is really doing with respect to this ideal ("actual"), and what the respondent really believes with regard to this ideal ("own view").

Recruitment variables (the columns of Table 2) are the same as Table 1, except that the third variable is reversed; that is, a positive score means that the university emphasized ideas over subject matter competence. The results show that at Alpha twenty of twenty-seven correlations between recruitment and ideology are significant beyond .05, and at Beta ten of twenty-seven. Looking inside the table, we note that at Alpha the strongest correlations are with "own views," suggesting that recruitment acts directly to select those whose views accord with the ideals, rather then being mediated through communication processes or perceptions of structure.

Table 2. Correlations Between Recruitment Variables and Interdisciplinary Ideology

Ideology Variables		Recruitment Variables					
		Alpha			Beta		
		1^a	2^b	3^c	1^a	2^b	3^c
Single-subject	Ideal:	.06	.13	.23	.04	.10	00
degree too	Actual:	.12	.15	.23	.17	.10	.19
narrow	Own view:	.17	.29	.29	.08	.12	.06
Contextual	Ideal:	.06	.18	.13	.11	.17	.06
(nonspecial-	Actual:	.10	.16	.20	.20	.11	.14
ized) study	Own view:	.14	.18	.16	.22	.04	.08
Interdisci-	Ideal:	.02	.13	.03	.22	.18	.07
plinary	Actual:	.13	.11	.24	.22	.14	.17
schools	Own view:	.28	.25	.24	.23	.11	.18

Note: Pearson correlations: Alpha: $r_p < .05 = .13$; Beta: $r_p < .05 = .17$.
[a]Awareness of this new university.
[b]University emphasized differences from older ones.
[c]University emphasized ideas over subject matter competence.

Thus, we have demonstrated the importance of recruitment in controlling socialization in the infant organization, and we have concrete evidence on how neglect or other changes in recruitment emphases can lead to organizational drift and lack of commitment. Founders of innovative organizations cannot afford to relax their vigilance over the selection of new members; they might keep in mind that even in mature institutions many academic administrators devote a major share of time and attention to this key process.

Socialization

However, founders of new universities have a special problem: while they can't be everywhere at once, they nevertheless must pay attention to the new problems that emerge constantly as the university grows. The close, clublike atmosphere of the first few years, which provides important contact between new members and the founder-entrepreneurs, gives way to the remoteness of the harried administrator, rarely present except at ceremonial occasions. Our data show that the percentage of respondents reporting "no contact" with founding vice-chancellors and pro-vice-chancellors increases from 30 percent to 80 percent between the first and seventh years (significance was .001). If the maintenance of charisma depends on direct personal contact, we can see why it decays in the growing organizations.

Inevitably, participation in a new and innovative enterprise entails risk and potential sacrifice by members; identification with charismatic and dedicated founders helps justify early hardships. Without some degree of contact, such identification is unlikely, and disillusionment lurks close by. Of course, if the founders are able to select deans who are equally dedicated to the ideals, perhaps some of this direct, personal socialization can be delegated. At Beta, however, there were a number of *negative* correlations between contact with deans and agreement with ideals, suggesting that the personal influence of the deans worked the wrong way from the founders' point of view. In terms of our operationalizations, contact with the founders is a means of ensuring commitment to the organization, that is, it improves the probability that the members' own views will be congruent with the ideal as enunciated by the founders. However, as the organization grows, the founder is placed under increasing time constraints and becomes subject to "founder burnout." Structures and processes must therefore be developed to replace the contact with the founder as a basis of ensuring commitment. Delegation of socialization responsibilities is one possibility, but one that will succeed only if the new contacts transfer the ideals of the university. We have seen that this is not always the case. These contacts can provide the new member with exposure to the ideals as enunciated and with the opportunity to see the ideals in action, that is, they can contribute to perceptions of the organizational reality. But insofar as delegation of socialization to unreliable hands results in perceptions of the organizational reality that are incongruent with the ideals, it can also contribute to organizational drift.

If recruitment falters, if founders lose contact and charisma, and if deans can't be trusted, who ends up controlling the socialization process in the innovative organization? Respondents were asked to indicate how useful a variety of information sources were in "learning the ropes" when they came to the new university. These sources are shown in Table 3, broken down according to when the respondent arrived at the university (first three years versus last four or five). High-interaction settings (faculty meetings and interaction with colleagues) lead the list, underscoring their importance in creating the meaning-context for the new ideals. Deans are third on the list of sources in both universities, with formal attempts at socialization (handbooks and structured orientations) bringing up the rear.

It is extremely significant that the only socializing agent to *increase* in importance over time (in both places) is interaction with colleagues. Together with evidence presented above, this strongly suggests that, *very early on*, control over socialization passes from the founders to the group of colleagues-at-large; from the province of formal design to that of the informal, institutional, and largely uncontrollable. To some degree, this is probably an inevitable result of the process of growth. As the organization grows and encounters increasing specialization, not only is a time constraint placed on the founders but political subunits are created. It is these subunits that become the source of socialization. The problem is

Table 3. Early and Late Socializing Agents

Rank	Alpha		Beta	
	First 3 Years	Last 5 Years	First 3 Years	Last 4 Years
1. Faculty meetings	61	44	76	46
2. Colleagues	61	70	66	72
3. Deans	31	17	55	23
4. Try changing something	31	26	44	37
5. Nonacademic administrators	21	12	16	10
6. Conversations with students	20	10	6	12
7. Vice-Chancellor, Pro-Vice-Chancellor	27	4	19	3
8. Handbook	10	7	16	10
9. Formal orientation	4	1	8	0

Note: Numbers represent percent of respondents who indicated that an information source was "very useful."

that "the purposes of this group become far more primary than the purposes of the larger setting" (Sarason, 1972, p. 93), the results being a commitment to the subunit rather than to the ideal and a perception of the organization that is incongruent with its ideology. The question is whether the successful use of institutional skills can prevent or hinder these kinds of organizational drift.

Founders have only a short time in which to place their unique stamp on the way things are done—shorter, perhaps, than anyone might have imagined. Here, in what was perhaps the most favorable environment for innovation in the long history of university foundations, we see organizational drift setting in clearly by the fourth year. Shaping new behaviors in academia is clearly no easy task.

Formalization

Still another method is available to the founder who would prevent organizational drift: formalization. If organizational structures and processes can be created to guide members' behavior in the direction of the ideals, perhaps the other sources of drift can be controlled or minimized. Indeed, the challenge in the development and utilization of institutional skills is to design structures and processes that will ensure the maintenance of the ideals. "The extent of the discrepancy between intent and accomplishment is in large part a function of how one defines the services and the criteria of its quality" (Sarason, 1972, p. 100). In general, the more concrete the ideals are, that is, the more they relate to specifics rather than generalities, the easier they are to put into practice and to test (Edelman, 1971). The difficulty here is that for the innovative organization especially, the relationships between structures and outcomes are largely a matter of guesswork. At Alpha, for example, with its tutorial ideal, no lecture halls were built for the social sciences for the first three years of the university. Also, as one wag pointed out, the dustbins behind the School of Molecular Sciences at Beta were labeled "Chemistry."

Even where structural arrangements in keeping with the ideal are utilized, there is no guarantee that the members will have the skills required to function within these structures (this is one point where institutional and technical skills interact). To illustrate, while seminars were in keeping with the ideal, no one at either university was experienced in running seminars. As such, it was a dysfunctional structural arrangement. Decisions might be made in interdisciplinary meetings, but much personnel planning was done by single-discipline groups. Rules and procedures seem the surest way of achieving some ideals; for example, degree requirements ensure breadth of exposure to more than one field of study, and inclusion of junior faculty in the academic senate ensures more widespread participation in governance. This does not mean, however, that senior faculty will not be suspected of running everything, or that students will put equal effort into their noncentral courses. The question is how to develop an effective control mechanism for institutional factors. Unfortunately, it is a question that has never really been addressed.

Formalization also closes doors to those later arrivals who would still innovate in their own areas. In our study, respondents were asked, as an index of formalization, to indicate how open the university was to their ideas for trying new approaches. The results are shown in Figure 2, again tabulated by year of arrival. There is a precipitous drop in openness over the first three years at Beta, and a more gradual, but equally conclusive drop at Alpha. (Overall trend is significant beyond .05.) To the degree that formalization decisions are irreversible, they severely limit the open-endedness of the organization. As Selznick (1957) has pointed out, "premature formalization . . . may seal off leadership during the early stages of organization-building, when it is most needed. As a result, leadership decisions such as those affecting the institutional core and the social base may be left to uncontrolled adaptation" (p. 107). If this happens, socialization passes back to colleagues-at-large, as noted above.

Although exhausted founders might rebel at leaving any questions open, the consequences of not doing so are severe. We correlated answers to the "openness" question with three items that measured satisfaction with the present university. The results showed that perceived openness of the university is highly and positively correlated with satisfaction with the present university ($r=.36$), and negatively with preference for another university or intentions to apply for a different post ($-.20$ and $.18$). These find-

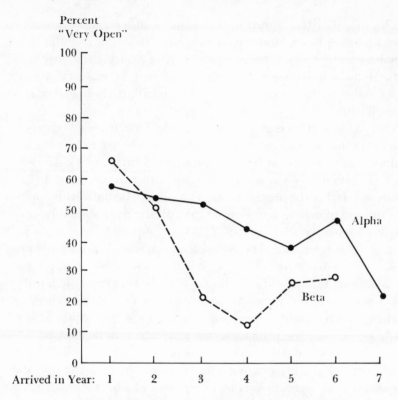

Figure 2. Flexibility: "How Open Was the University to
Your Ideas for Trying New Things?"

ings were supported by interviews that showed extreme amounts of
alienation and disillusionment among those junior faculty recruited within the two years before the study was done.

Thus, formalization is a two-edged sword. It might be a
tempting weapon to use against organizational drift, but it clearly
blunts important sources of energy and ideas among recent arrivals. The irony is that among these people were some of those most
committed to the original founding ideals. Looking at their pre-
decessors, however, they saw either exhausted founders or hypo-
critical climbers who came because of chances for faster promotion.
Their own mobility appeared blocked, their pay was low, and their
idealism was thwarted. In many ways their only chance at professional survival was to revert to the traditional research and writing

roles that they had hoped to transcend or at least supplement by participating in an innovative enterprise. To the degree that formalization prevented these members from realizing the ideal that they felt the university represented, what may have been intended as a hedge against organizational drift ended up causing organizational drift.

At least two points need to be made. First, while all organizations require some degree of formalization to ensure coordination among members, formalization also carries with it implicit dangers. The question is, What is the minimum structure necessary to ensure survival of the organization? That should be the starting point of organizational design. Beyond that, all structure should be considered tentative (Sarason, 1972). This is especially true in an innovative organization, where the challenge is to create a structure that will embody the ideology. When the structure hinders the realization of the ideology, it should be replaced. Obviously, a problem arises insofar as people are reluctant to change, especially when they contributed to establishment of the status quo. This is one reason why the primacy of the ideology must be stressed.

The second point concerns the rewards offered to individual members of the organization. As Sarason (1972) points out, the leaders of the organization must keep track of what they can do for members. Organizational reality is created through the actions of its members, and the members do what they are rewarded for. Institutional skills should stress rewards for behavior in keeping with the ideology. As we have seen, it is too easy for the organization to create a situation in which the only rewards available are those from the status quo. The maintenance of commitment and the prevention of organization drift require that the structure and process of the organization reward actions that are congruent with the ideal, even if this means questioning the structure and processes that are the source of rewards.

Organizations and Institutions

In retrospect, our results do not paint a very happy picture for those who would found and try to maintain an innovative organization. We are confronted with an example of what Kimberly in Chapter Two calls the "paradox of success": in order to succeed, the innovative organization must sacrifice the very things that made it innovative. It is not enough, however, to note the apparent lack of power an innovative organization has in relation to the larger context in which it is born. We must try to pinpoint more precisely the reasons for this apparent paradox so that an effort can be made to deal with it and thus ensure that the innovative organization will be an institutional as well as an organizational success (Selznick, 1957).

We believe that in the distinction between organizational and institutional success lies the answer to our dilemma. As noted earlier, two distinct sets of skills are needed in order to bring an innovative organization into being. One is a set of technical managerial skills, the other a set of skills related to the institutional process. Organizational drift and lack of commitment result when technical matters are given priority over institutional ones. When an innovative organization is created, both are given equal weight. But as the organization grows in size, it becomes more differentiated and begins to attract attention from the guardians of the status quo. The members of the organization are confronted with a continual flow of technical details that demand constant attention if the uncertainty of organizational life is to be decreased. In such circumstances, it is all too natural not to want to tamper with what has already been created. Since the meaning we attribute to an organization is grounded in the mundane reality of everyday life (Silverman, 1971), technical skills increasingly come to shape this meaning.

The result of this shift in the relative weight given to the two sets of problems can be seen by considering how technical and institutional skills deal with the processes of recruitment, socialization, leadership, and formalization. We have already seen that these processes are closely linked to organizational drift and member commitment. What we are arguing here is that the changes that occurred in the performance of these processes as the organization developed resulted from a shift in priorities in skill use, with technical skills displacing institutional skills as a basis for operation. For example, recruitment, when performed according to technical criteria, requires that the person selected have the necessary technical qualifications for his position. Job postings and other standard methods of soliciting new members are appropriate. In contrast, recruitment under institutional criteria calls for the selection of new members based on a congruence of their values with the ideology of the innovative organization. This is best performed through the use of interpersonal networks and direct contacts.

Similarly, socialization, when based on technical criteria, requires that the new member be introduced to the rules and regulations of the organization. This can best be handled by the persons he will work most closely with, that is, his colleagues. When socialization is performed according to institutional criteria, however, the emphasis is on the generation of commitment and adherence to the meaning of the innovative ideology. This is brought about through the use of rituals, symbols, and myths, as well as by contact with the charismatic leadership of the founder or head of the organization. Here we run into yet more evidence of the alteration in priority of skill use. Charismatic leadership, which stresses the importance of the innovative ideology both by example and through creation of a broad image of the organization, is required for institutional leadership, while technical leadership is geared to the more mundane operational skills of management and is meant to handle specific, detailed problems. To some extent, the pressures of a growing organization will probably force the leader to confront technical managerial matters. We saw that while it is possible to delegate responsibility for socialization to others, this can result in a socialization away from the universal ideology to particularistic criteria supported by a specific department. The possibility of delegating the technical responsibilities, while maintaining institutional skills in the leader, did not arise in our studies.

Finally, technical skills call for the adoption of structural constraints through formalization in order to reduce uncertainty. In contrast, according to institutional criteria, structure is necessarily subservient to ideology. The values in the ideology must be reaffirmed, while the structure used to achieve them is left tentative. This means that the organization must be continually open to innovation and that it must have a way of allowing members to critique the old methods or structures and suggest new ones. Meetings that allow for admissions of weakness on the part of the organization can bring out the common bonds of the organization, lessen conflict, and strengthen social integration.

The point is not that technical skills are evil or unnecessary—the organization cannot survive without them. But with only technical skills in operation, the organization will succeed only as an organization. If it is to succeed as an institution, equal weight must be given to institutional skills. Unfortunately, current managerial education lays heavy emphasis on technical and managerial skills, little or no emphasis on institutional skills. As a result, the creation and maintenance of an innovative organization awaits the presence of an individual with intuitive institutional skills— the individual we have come to call the entrepreneur (see Chapter Two).

Figure 3 summarizes the variables we have considered in our discussion of organizational drift. In the figure, we note that an organization begins as an idea that is then transformed into a set of guiding ideals. From this point on, two distinct skills come into play, one institutional and the other technical. Institutional skills elaborate the ideals into an ideology; technical skills use the ideals to formulate organizational goals. As noted above, the two sets of skills then operate differentially on recruitment, leadership, socialization, and formalization. All these processes interact to produce the meaning of the organization as perceived by its members.

The organization is a success as an institution to the degree that it exhibits authenticity, functionality, and flexibility across generations. Authenticity requires that the organization embody its ideals, functionality requires that the organization work, and flexibility requires that the organization be receptive to the inputs and suggestions of its members. If these tests are met, the organization will also evidence a high degree of commitment by its members. Overall, an organization that is an institutional success can be characterized as having a sense of group commonality and togetherness. In contrast, if institutional skills are not utilized while technical skills are in operation, the organization may well be an organizational success but an institutional failure. In that case, there will be evidence of organizational drift and disillusionment. Such an organization will be characterized by individual self-interest,

Institutional Processes	Idea	Technical Processes
Creation, Elaboration of Ideology	Founding Ideals	Statement of Organizational Goals
Use of Personal Networks; Selection Based on Values and Ideals	Recruitment	Broad Search; Use of Universalistic Criteria
Face-to-Face Contact with Founders; Sharing Rituals, Symbols	Socialization	Rules and Procedures Learned Through Colleagues
Charismatic, Mythic Images (Transforming)	Leadership	Problem Solving and Consensus Making (Transactional)
Ideals Paramount; Structure Tentative	Formalization	Early Routinization; Uncertainty Reduction

Figure 3. Institutional and Technical Processes

differentiation, and technical efficiency. Again, it is important to note that we are concerned here with innovative organizations in which ideology is a primacy resource. For other organizations, ideology may not be so important; in those cases, achieving organizational success may be all that is desired.

The Cycle of Vigilance

We should, then, pay more attention to the importance of institutional skills in innovative organizations. But the phenomenon of organizational drift also implies that we take the idea of a "science of administration" seriously. Specifically, it requires that we treat any innovative organization as a hypothesis about its environment. This means that the design of the organization must be tested by operationalizing it in the environment. It also requires that we monitor the technical and institutional aspects of the organization not only at birth but also during its development. What we are suggesting is that an organization's development cannot proceed along a unidirectional path, but must allow for some kind of feedback, that is, for processes that will monitor the current state of the ideals and suggest self-correcting action through actions on both the technical and institutional sides of the enterprise.

The importance of some cycle of vigilance, while especially apparent in an innovative organization, is applicable to all organizations. Every organization has some image of a future reality that it would like to experience. Organizations implement various structures and processes in an effort to make the image come true. The crucial point occurs when the fantasized setting is matched with reality (Sarason, 1972). What a cycle of vigilance allows for is a structured time in which to make a comparison between the image and the reality and to ponder the possibilities for future action. Since we are dealing with innovative organizations, we have argued for the primacy of ideology and suggested that the structure and processes of such organizations should be called into question when there is evidence of organizational drift or lack of commitment. It is also possible for the ideology to be called into question. It may be that an organization could be quite content with its current structure and process, despite the fact that the organizational reality is incongruent with the espoused ideal. In such a case, the ideology may need to be replaced.

Reduced to simplistic terms, our argument is that any organization, in order to be a success as an institution, must exhibit a congruence among its ideology, the perceptions of the organizational reality, and the members' own views of the ideal. Since any decision or action resulting from a decision in an organization is made in ignorance of the future (Berger, 1974), it is subject to unintended consequences (Merton, 1968; Selznick, 1957) that may produce organizational drift or lack of commitment. While some of these unintended consequences may result from aging and others from growth and differentiation, the important point is the incongruities that they represent. (Indeed, insofar as these incongruities result from forces in the social and historical context in which the organization exists, undue use of such biological metaphors as "growth" and "aging" may obfuscate more than clarify). The cycle of vigilance is a mechanism for handling such incongruities.

During an early verbal presentation of these findings, one observer commented: "Maybe the excitement is in the building of the university; we should divide the campus into four parts, and let each incoming class build its own structure. When they graduate we bulldoze it down and a new group starts over." While such a cycle of building, destruction, and rebirth would be unworkable, the idea behind it is important. Given the looseness of the coupling between ideals and supporting structure and process, we must either continuously invent and discard, as in the bulldozing suggestion, or we must be able to monitor the adequacy of both the ideals and their supporting structures. Such a systematic process of self-examination and continuous revision would allow for organizational learning, maintain openness, and tighten the connection between ideal and structure.

Such a process did take place at Alpha, but not at Beta. This process may be in part responsible for the relatively shallow decline in openness at Alpha, at least through its sixth year. Both universities produced an organizational plan immediately before the students arrived. At Alpha, an assistant registrar instigated a yearly revision of the "organization" document during which growth in student and faculty members was anticipated, committees were formed, augmented, or eliminated, authority lines were revised, new schools were planned, and so on. In these and supporting documents, which will be the focus of a future study, little explicit attention was paid to the maintenance of the ideals and symbols of the university; nonetheless, they provided a systematic, frank self-appraisal in which participation of the founders was thoughtful and broad. Despite these efforts, role pressures on founders, deans, committee heads, and senior faculty had become so intense by the sixth year of the university, that a management consulting firm was brought in to study the situation and suggest simplifications. Considerable streamlining was achieved at little expense to the founding ideals, despite great faculty skepticism about use of management consultants.

There was thus a willingness to submit the organization to critical scrutiny in an effort to improve its success as an institution, that is, to ensure that the organization in practice did not drift too far from the innovative ideology. In the words of one founder-member (Daiches, 1970): "We have learned that it is not enough to work out a blueprint and to assume that all that is then necessary is to implement it. The implementation involves complex problems of human as well as subject relationships, and these are never solved but need to be repeatedly looked at" (p. iv.).

8

Establishing and Maintaining High Commitment Work Systems

❤❤❤❤❤❤❤❤❤❤❤

Richard E. Walton

During the past decade an increasing number of companies have used new facility start-ups to implement innovative work structures. These innovations represent pioneer attempts to achieve a creative synthesis of task management techniques and healthy work environments. Because they can serve as models for future new facilities, their importance goes beyond their meaning for the employees involved and their value to the sponsoring firms. They also provide concrete alternatives toward which established facilities might be transformed over time, especially as expansion occurs or new technology is introduced. The rate of growth of these innovations in the United States appears to be accelerating. Their effectiveness has ranged from spectacular success to dismal failure, but there is as yet no reliable body of knowledge about how to successfully develop these work systems.

How does an innovative work structure develop during its early years? What developmental processes and dilemmas, if any, characterize those years? What factors drive and pace their growth and shape the distinctive lines along which they develop? Which of these factors are exogenous, and which can be influenced by members of the organization? These are the questions that this chapter addresses.

Part One: Definitional Concepts

The new organizations analyzed here are examples of what, for many years, I have called "innovative work systems." I propose here a theoretical definition of these work systems, referring to them by one of their key ingredients, namely, high commitment by members. The distinguishing feature of "high-commitment work systems" is *not* merely that commitment is sought by planners to promote a productive and healthy work place, for that would also be true of more conventionally structured work organizations. Rather, the distinguishing feature of these systems is that high commitment by workers is presumed in the basic design of the work structure. Thus, a high-commitment work system is one that is designed to *generate* high commitment, to fully *utilize* high commitment for gains (human and business), and to *depend* upon high commitment for its effectiveness. If high commitment is not forthcoming, the system is vulnerable.

By way of contrast, a conventional plant that provides close supervision, simplified tasks, narrow job descriptions, detailed procedures, and relies heavily on formal controls, is designed to function adequately even when member commitment is moderate to low. It provides relatively few ways for the organization to benefit from high commitment, and it has relatively low power to elicit such commitment.

The implications of the definition given above must be understood by all participants in a high-commitment work system. A sensitive interdependence exists between organization structure and human involvement. On the one hand, members will remain highly committed to the work system if, and only if, it satisfies the work criteria that are important for them—involvement in decision making, equity, dignity, security, job challenge, autonomy, and so on. On the other hand, the management planners of the work system will continue many of the features of the structure found to be attractive, if, and only if, the work system proves to be highly effective in economic terms. In the longer run, if either the human or business benefits are not forthcoming, the work structure will be revised toward a more conventional form. Thus, high-commitment work systems must, to an exceptional degree, meet the needs of both members and the organization.

Innovative work systems are sometimes defined by the structural designs they employ—for example, work teams, delegation of responsibility, or challenging work. And sometimes they are defined by their underlying ideals, such as "equity," "security," "individualism," and "democracy." The plants analyzed here could be defined in either of these ways, but, for present purposes, the particular design and ideals are less important than that they were selected in order to inspire, sustain, and utilize high member commitment. To be sure, some design elements are commonly relied upon to produce these work systems. One such element is provision for participation. Member participation in management activities is often powerful in generating commitment and virtually essential if the organization is to realize the contributions of which committed members are capable. Other attributes that are important in maintaining high commitment are mutual trust and open communication.

The broad concept "level of commitment" is comprised of four types of member involvement, which vary in terms of evaluative orientation and intensity. The most positive (highest level) involvement is "moral," reflecting a sense that what one is doing is morally correct, perhaps morally superior. Positive, but less intense, is "spontaneous-expressive" involvement, which conveys the idea that what one is doing is enjoyable, gratifying, even fun. Relatively neutral involvement is "calculative"; it is accompanied by low affect. The most negative (lowest level) is "alienative" involvement. (Etzioni, 1961, identified moral, calculative, and alienative involvement. My work has required the addition of spontaneous-expressive involvement.) Involvement at the highest and lowest levels is most intensely felt. Each type of involvement can be visualized as either adding to or subtracting from overall commitment.

Viewed in these terms, high-commitment work systems are ones that are characterized by spontaneous-expressive involvement and may even be seen by members as morally superior; they are marked by moderate amounts of calculative behavior and relatively little alienative feeling. The rationale for creating high commitment is that it tends to be accompanied by motivational energy, by responsiveness to the needs of the business and fellow employees, by identification with unit members and goals, and by other attributes favorable to both business indexes and the quality of work life.

Although this type of work system has certain benefits, it is not an option equally available in all settings. Some task technologies give workers more chances to apply high-level skills and provide more benefits to the organization by making workers attentive to variances in the production process. They thus offer more opportunity to generate and utilize high commitment than do other technologies. Similarly, some workers are more inclined than others to respond positively to greater work flexibility and responsibility, more participation in decision making, and more variety in work routines.

In the present conception of a "work system" four analytical components are especially important: task technology, human resources, work structure, and meaning. Task technology includes the material and physical equipment utilized, the basic steps or stages in the production process, and the operational requirements inherent in the material, equipment, and production process. Human resources are the technical and organizational skills extant in the organization. The work structure is composed of the patterned methods for accomplishing the organization's tasks. Those methods include definitions of roles and rules and provisions for training and information; they also include systems for compensating participants and supervising work. Thus a work structure represents a particular solution for combining human resources and task technology. Alternative work structures usually can be designed to accomplish the same work.

The fourth component of a work system is the meaning that people come to attribute to the work structure. Some aspects of meaning that characterized most of the work systems reported here are illustrative of high-commitment work systems generally:

Autonomy:	"Not having a foreman looking over your shoulder."
Openness:	"You can say what you think to anyone without fear of recrimination."
Mutuality:	"People help each other, follow a good-neighbor policy."
Achievement orientation:	"People try hard to meet goals."
Influence:	"People's opinions make a difference here."
Challenge:	"What we do is a challenge. You never stop learning."
Pioneering:	"This work system is leading the way."
Elitism:	"We have a special work force."
Objectivity:	"We must look at issues from a team-wide or plant-wide viewpoint and apply objective standards in dealing with pay issues."
Self-discipline and peer pressure:	"It's up to us to see that people don't abuse privileges."

These meanings deal with how people ought to be treated and with members' responsibilities to the organization. "Meaning" also includes members' answers to questions such as the following: Is the work structure significant or insignificant in their lives? Do they feel good, bad, or indifferent about it? Do they expect that the features they approve will endure or not? Manifestly different work structures tend to generate different meanings for participants. But different meanings (or organizational ideologies) can be associated with similar work structures, because actual meanings also are influenced by the stated philosophies of those who orient new members or who explain subsequent modifications of the work structure.

The work structure determines the limits on how members *can* be engaged by the organization, but meanings determine how they *will* become involved. My treatment of the development of a work system sees the system's structure and its meaning as each moving through its own developmental cycle. Consider the work structure. I assume it normally passes through a number of developmental "processes." It is (1) conceived or planned; (2) formed or initiated when people are hired, trained, and begin working; (3) established in the form of routines; (4) maintained through practice and reinforcement; (5) and terminated at some point or replanned in part, setting the whole cycle in motion again until the changed part comes to be established and maintained.

Similarly, I assume that meanings are formed, develop, and change over time. (1) Meanings, like structure, may be planned or at least implicitly intended by the planners; and prospective members have preconceptions, often based on prior work experiences. (2) Preconceptions change to expectations as a result of cues found in the work setting—words, actions, direct experiences. Meanings at this stage are tentatively held hypotheses. (3) There will be some period in which hypotheses about the organization culture are tested and strengthened (or weakened and replaced by other hypotheses). Over time, beliefs about the organization become more or less firmly imprinted in the minds of its members. (4) Established meanings are then maintained by experience, until (5) for some reason they are replaced or disappear along with the work structure.

The processes tend to occur in the sequence listed and to characterize phases of the developing organization, but there will be certain types of exceptions to this tendency. First, one process will not end before another begins; therefore, at best a "phase" refers to the dominance of a process at a point in time. Second, replanning and termination processes can be initiated at any time, thereby starting a recycling through the earlier phases. Repetitions of these developmental cycles of both structure and meaning may continue to occur over the entire life of an organization. This chapter treats those that occur during the more formative years.

Part Two: Comparative Analysis of Four Work Systems

The four manufacturing plants to be reported on here are:

1. Topeka: General Foods' Topeka, Kansas, dry dog food plant hired a work force late in 1970 and started operations in 1971. It was observed from its beginning through 1976. The plant's work force remained at less than 100 employees over the six years of observation.

2. Salem: This sunbelt plant, which machines ball bearings, is part of a large diversified manufacturing company. Employment at the plant, which started up in 1975, grew to slightly under 300 and remained at that level through 1978, with capacity for additional growth in volume and employment.

3. Goshen: This northern plant machines parts for diesel engines and assembles engines. The plant began hiring production workers in 1975, and by early 1979 the plant employed 550. Employment in the existing facility was expected to grow to over 2,000.

4. Derry: This plant, located in the Midwest and belonging to a large manufacturing firm, fabricates and assembles grain-drying implements. It started up in 1976, and by 1979 the plant and machinery were fully employed by a production work force of 130.

I participated as a consultant in planning and development of the work innovations in all four plants. (Except for Topeka, which has already been identified in published material, the plants have disguised names.) Here, however, I am a social scientist describing and interpreting these experiences and generalizing from them. My judgments of the trend lines of commitment in each of these four systems are presented in Figure 1. These judgments are based on clinical observations, which will be detailed a little later. Although the observational data could be related to the strength of each type of involvement discussed earlier—from moral to alienative—what is presented here is a judgment of the overall strength of member commitment. "Moderate commitment" in Figure 1 is intended to describe the kind of commitment found in a conventional plant that is generally well managed and is progressive in its personnel problems and practices. A "moderate" level of commitment is below what I judge to be adequate to sustain over the long term the types of work structure employed by these four

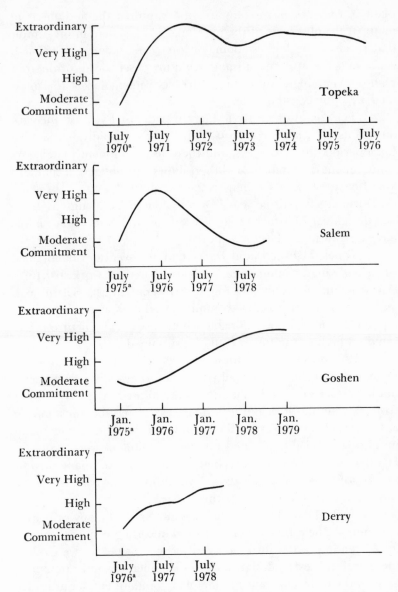

^aThese dates give approximate times when start-up crews were hired, marking the beginning of work system with members at all levels from plant manager to workers.

Figure 1. Patterns of Development of Member Commitment in Four New Manufacturing Plants

plants. "Extraordinary commitment" captures the judgment of many of the observers of the particular work system in my sample that reached the highest point on my scale, namely, Topeka. It represents the uppermost standard in my observations of the four plants. "Very high" and "high" are convenient labels for intermediate points on the scale.

The commitment trend lines over the first years at the various plants offer many contrasts. Topeka's rises rapidly, is sustained for a period, dips, recovers, and then declines somewhat. Salem's commitment rises initially and then shows a prolonged decline to a low after three years. Goshen's is flat initially and then climbs steadily. During its first three years, Derry's commitment curve is directionally similar to Topeka's but is less dramatic in its rate of initial increase and in the level it achieves.

Topeka, Goshen, and Derry had achieved and maintained sufficiently high commitment levels to make their work structures effective, but the trend lines follow different patterns. Salem's pattern is the most divergent—commitment there having declined to a point that made it questionable whether a work structure predicated on high commitment could be sustained.

How do we explain these differences? The four plants had many commonalities. They all were built to provide new capacity, not to replace existing facilities; all were located in towns far away from existing facilities and headquarters; all became important or at least visible employers in their communities. The managements in all cases explicitly planned a high-commitment work system, a fact that gave them special visibility in their own companies. None was represented by organized labor, although in Salem a union campaign occurred during its third year.

While the four work structures also applied many principles in common, the actual designs differed in certain respects, and the implementing tactics differed even more. But before we explore these differences in design and implementation and attempt to explain the different trends in member commitment, let us return to the question of the types of field data that these trend lines are intended to reflect.

During my periodic visits to each plant over its life history, I interviewed, as well as worked and mingled with, fairly representative samples of the plant population and observed a variety of ongoing activities that characterized the plant's day-to-day working patterns. The data provided me with evidence related to the following types of questions:

- Were employees conscious of a particular philosophy at the plant?
- Did their references to that philosophy indicate strong approval and inspiration?
- Did they compare the plant's operative philosophy favorably with philosophies encountered in previous employment?
- Were employees deeply engaged in many of their work-related tasks?
- Did they indicate that they personally cared about the performance of their unit and that they had taken initiatives to improve it?
- Did employees' engagement and initiative appear to be readily forthcoming, voluntary, and spontaneous, rather than simply compliant with directives of superiors?
- Did they indicate that they found gratification in the total work situation?
- Were they optimistic that the aspects of the work situation that they liked would be established and sustained over time?

Affirmative evidence to these questions and similar ones indicated high commitment, whereas negative evidence was indicative of low commitment. Affirmative answers to the following illustrative questions lowered my estimates of the commitment level:

- Did employees make cynical remarks about the work system philosophy or management intentions?
- Did they report that games were being played between supervisors and workers?
- Did members of the organization refer to possible punishments (including blame) in explaining why they did not engage in certain work-related activities?
- Did they indicate that their present job was "just a job, nothing special"?

The periodicity of my visits stimulated members of the organization to make statements about changes in their perceptions and feelings in the intervals between my visits. For example, workers would indicate that they had become more or less confident of management's commitment to the stated philosophy. Management would report evidence of more or less spontaneous achievements by workers. Moreover, I could detect any shifts in the amount of comments reflecting hope versus despair about the work system and pride versus disappointment in the quality of participation activities. The trends for each plant portrayed in Figure 1 were confirmed by informed members of the plant, and discussions of such trends often formed the basis for actions by management.

The fact that I was similarly involved in these four plants and other new plants that were attempting to create high-commitment work systems has permitted me to make comparisons among plants with confidence. Thus, if I have not managed to completely avoid bias introduced by my personal involvement, that bias should not affect either the interperiod comparisons of a plant or the comparisons among plants. Naturally I wanted all four work systems to succeed.

Topeka Dog Food Plant

General Food's radically innovative plant was conceived in 1968 and started up in January 1971. (The following account is adapted from Walton, 1978.) This study treats the original plant built on the Topeka site, which produced dry dog food primarily out of grain ingredients. A second plant for canning dog food with meat ingredients was built on the same site several years later. It was not included in the study.

Commitment and Results. During the first year and a half, commitment was built to an extraordinary level at the Topeka plant and continued at a relatively high level over the next five years. There was, however, a significant decline and recovery centering on the system's third birthday, and there was a gradual but perceptible decline thereafter.

The new work system was very effective in both human and economic terms over the period covered by this study. A study by the Ford Foundation in 1973 found high levels of worker participation in decisions, freedom to communicate, expressions of warmth among the workers, commitment to the job, and individual self-esteem. Another study of Topeka in 1974 confirmed this positive view (Lawler, Jenkins, and Herline, 1974). The head researcher of that study, Edward Lawler, stated in personal correspondence to me: "Our data . . . show high levels of satisfaction and involvement in all parts of the organization. In fact they show the highest levels we have found in any organization we have sampled. I specifically compared it with other small organizations and still found it superior."

Work Structure Elements. In the front half of the work flow, referred to as "processing," plant personnel received, unloaded, and stored raw materials, including grain, tallow, and vitamins, which were then mixed, formed, baked, cooled, coated, and fed into a surge tank, all by continuous process technology. This process was controlled in part by local instruments and valves placed on the many pieces of separate equipment that were distributed throughout various floors and work areas. It was also partly controlled by a central instrument room that monitored the entire process. The second half of the work flow, referred to as "packaging," involved feeding the product into several packaging lines, operating the packaging equipment, transferring packages to the warehouse, and shipping the product by rail cars.

The entire system was vulnerable to a breakdown in performance at any stage of the work flow. Variability in the characteristics of agricultural raw materials required operators to continually adjust other elements, including heat and moisture, in order to turn out a product to constant specifications in a cost-effective way. Compared with the other manufacturing systems studied, the "process" tasks at Topeka were moderately difficult to master, while the "packaging" tasks were of average difficulty.

Three rotating shifts were used to operate the plant twenty-four hours a day, five days a week. On each shift, one self-managing team was responsible for the "process" segment of production and another for the "packaging" segment. The teams numbered from seven to fourteen operators, large enough to embrace a set of interrelated tasks and small enough to permit face-to-face meetings for making decisions and for coordination.

Activities usually performed by separate units—maintenance, quality control, custodianship, industrial engineering, and personnel—were built into the responsibilities of each team. For example, team members screened job applicants for replacements on their own team.

An attempt was made to design every set of tasks to include both manual skills and mental functions, such as diagnosing mechanical problems and planning. The aim was to make all sets of team tasks equally challenging, although each set would involve unique demands. Consistent with this aim was a single job classification for all operators. Pay increases depended on the mastery of an increasing number of skills. The fact that there were no limits on how many members of a team could qualify for higher pay brackets encouraged employees to teach one another any skills they had mastered.

Operators were given the data and guidelines to make production decisions ordinarily made at higher levels. The role of the first-line supervisor, called the "team leader," was to facilitate the team's decision making. As for plant rules, management refrained from specifying any in advance. Rules evolved over time from collective experience. The technology and architecture of the plant were designed to permit rather than discourage informal gatherings of team members during working hours. Status symbols were minimized—for example, a single entrance led into both the administrative office and the plant.

Management assumed that workers with certain profiles of skills and attitudes would be more likely to prosper in the structure just outlined. These would be workers who had higher needs for influence, more interest and skill in dealing with people, and above-average mechanical aptitude and analytical abilities. A relatively favorable supply of labor in the area, combined with public announcements that an innovative work system was planned for the new General Foods plant, permitted management to screen as many as ten applicants for every job it needed to fill. Management naturally attempted to select the best applicants in terms of the particular requirements of the innovative work structure. However, because of the limited state of the art in employee selection generally and because the supervisors who screened applicants at Topeka were relatively inexperienced interviewers, it remains an open question whether the final sample of employees differed in any systematic way from that which would have been selected for a new plant with a more conventional work structure. A more important effect of the final screening process was its impact on the attitudes and self-perceptions of the newly recruited work force—an effect to be discussed later.

Planning (1968 to July 1970). During this period, the four persons who were to manage the plant designed the work structure. They were assisted by the division operations manager to whom the plant would report and by a consultant. These six men were determined to avoid the worker dissatisfaction that had developed in the company's existing pet food facilities. They were inspired by the possibility of bringing about exceptional worker involvement in the new plant.

The division operations manager played an important role in raising the sights of the design team and in absorbing as far as possible the organizational risks associated with pioneering a new plant design. The consultant drew upon his experiences and his knowledge of behavioral science to contribute to the design and to identify other innovative organizations that the design team might visit. However, the actual design grew naturally from the past experiences and beliefs of the four men who would manage the plant. The important condition was that they were permitted to start with a clean sheet of paper and were given a generous amount of lead time so that they could be both inventive and thorough in their design activity.

Forming (July to December 1970). Well before start-up, team leaders were hired and included in the work of planning, training, and team building. Lead time was allowed for new concepts to be articulated, debated, and translated into work procedures and structures. Managers had time to develop insights into human behavior and to coalesce as a group. Team leaders screened candidates, choosing about 70 from more than 600 applicants, to form a relatively talented and receptive work force.

Certain procedures helped establish the new work culture. The process for screening team leaders included role playing and group discussion and provided a unique, involving, and even anxiety-provoking initiation. According to one observer, this initial experience created a sense of hardiness, uniqueness, and elitism among team leaders. These leaders, in turn, utilized similar methods in screening workers, thereby transmitting the same spirit to the work force. Though healthy skepticism existed, these experiences created a readiness among workers to give the innovations a fair trial. Thus, woven into the formation processes, there was a concerted effort to communicate the desired work culture and indeed to begin to establish it.

Establishing a Culture and a Work Structure (1971). The first year of operations was marked by a variety of minor "tests" of the system and by the development of potent group phenomena. During the first few weeks, some cash was taken from an open change box. Workers and managers alike were ready to dig into their own pockets to replace the missing cash and maintain the open cash box that was used to make change for the vending machines. This readiness symbolically confirmed the system's premise of trustworthiness.

After a number of weeks, the operators felt they were ready for their first pay increase, based on mastery of their first job. The fact that management had not anticipated this early development of expectations both reinforced the doubt of the skeptics and weakened the confidence of the believers. But when management ultimately agreed to review the qualifications of the operators for increases, they reaffirmed the responsiveness of the system.

Soon after, a railroad strike tested the capacity of the teams to solve new work problems, and this they did effectively. By interrupting regular production, the strike also tested management's commitment to provide secure employment. Plant management tried to resist corporate pressures to make layoffs. The occasion once again crystallized fears and hopes about the system. As it happened, however, the strike ended before there was a definitive answer to the question of employment security.

Developments within each of the six work teams largely determined how a given person viewed the work system. At times team leaders provided too much structure and thereby seemed to contradict the stated philosophy. At other times, they provided too little structure and seemed to dramatize the impracticality of worker participation. Nevertheless, sooner or later the groups coalesced. They became the most powerful factor in forming and enforcing the system's norms about cooperation, openness, involvement, and responsibility.

In brief, 1971 was a time of building technical and social skills and of testing employees' preliminary understanding of the premises of the system. Those who were initially receptive became more committed and, with a few exceptions, the skeptical decided to "buy in." They had gained a temporarily stable understanding of the meaning of the work system and had evolved effective ways of performing the tasks involved in the start-up of the plant. But this equilibrium was short-lived.

Push for Output (1972). In 1972, the developed skills, knowledge, attitudes, and relationships were put to work in a demanding way. Pressure for production volume, resisted during 1971, now had to be met, but this maximum production effort had unfortunate side effects. First, quality suffered, undermining one source of pride. Second, with the plant now "humming," there was less immediate need for group problem solving and less time for meetings. This reduced the social maintenance within groups. Third, teams began yielding to the temptation to improve their own performance at the expense of the next shift.

A management change at a higher level also troubled the Topeka managers. The division manager to whom the plant reported and who had held an umbrella over the fledgling system during the past year was replaced by a person less sympathetic to Topeka. Doubts grew about the company's commitment to the Topeka innovation. Topeka had come to be viewed by some line and staff groups at headquarters as uncooperative. These groups resisted the plant's claims to autonomy and its requests to be excepted from certain corporate policies and procedures.

Still the plant was performing well, reaching capacity output with about 70 people (compared with the 110 originally estimated as needed on the basis of standard industrial engineering principles). Substantial savings from lower overhead, fewer quality rejects, and other factors were attributed to the work system. Participants felt proud of their accomplishments, and the plant had become perhaps the most publicized example in the United States of a solution to what the media were calling the "blue-collar blues." A

journalist's account of his visit to the plant had been featured on
the front page of the *New York Times* on February 3, 1973. Along
with work innovations at Volvo, it was the subject of NBC's "First
Tuesday" program—sixty minutes of prime television time. An
article analyzing this "prototype" plant and its initial successes
reached over 100,000 subscribers of the *Harvard Business Review*
(Walton, 1972). This publicity added yet another meaning to the
work system for its members.

All things considered, however, this was a period when
commitment leveled off. If the production year of 1972 is compared with the start-up year of 1971, "participation" and "openness" generally went down. Nevertheless, the impressive production results increased optimism among workers and managers that
the system would survive. Thus, although the commitment level
had been maintained through the second year of operation, the
components of that commitment had been realigned. The work
structure was somewhat less attractive to operators under full
production than under start-up conditions, but the perceived
viability of the system climbed as a result of its demonstrated
effectiveness.

Replanning: Turmoil, Decline, and Reversal (1973). A trough
had been reached during the summer of 1973 in various indexes of
the system's health. This trough was followed by a steady improvement during the fall. During the first half of 1973, however,
the emphasis on production volume continued, along with heavy
overtime, few team meetings, and intershift rivalry. The negative
effects were cumulative, changing the meaning of work for members to the point that basic commitments began to weaken. Without
meetings, trust and openness were declining. The prolonged push
for maximum production also deferred the movement of workers
from one team to another, a movement that could occur after an
operator had learned all of the jobs on the team and therefore had
earned "team rate." This delay, which postponed the date at which
an employee could earn "plant rate " (by demonstrating mastery of
all jobs in the plant), tended to undermine commitment.

When interteam movement was finally okayed, a large
number of transfers occurred between packaging and processing
units. At about the same time, thirteen team members and two

team leaders were chosen to form the nucleus for a new canned pet food plant being built on the same site. This wholesale movement alleviated some problems but created others. Many members felt "deserted" by those who left for the new plant. The original teams often had identified themselves closely with their team leaders, whose personal styles varied widely. Now team leaders were faced with new teams and vice versa.

Team leaders who were trying to build a team for the second time often could not muster the same enthusiasm for the task. They felt unfairly resisted by the new teams and often received contradictory requests from two subgroups within a team—one asking for more direction, the other for less. Perhaps to avoid these crosscurrents, team leaders held fewer team meetings and became more absorbed in plant-wide projects.

The absence of team meetings had a dramatically negative effect. Members needed to cooperate hourly in their tasks and weekly in learning from one another but had not developed the necessary mutual confidence to do so. Moreover, the recently hired employees were not learning about their rights and obligations in the system, and many were not developing commitment during the critical first months.

By the summer of 1973, the site manager, previously preoccupied by his strained relations with the corporation, started attending to the issues that troubled the Topeka organization. Workers and managers became aware that they had neglected the acculturation of new members and the development of newly formed teams. They resolved to rework these issues, and there were definite upward trends in openness, trust, and commitment in the fall of 1973. Another indication of strength was the fact that managers were working themselves out of their jobs by developing their subordinates. One level of the hierarchy was eliminated when the manufacturing manager became a consultant to other parts of the corporation, as well as to the Topeka plants. Also there was growing interest in decreasing the number of team leaders.

Notwithstanding the restored commitment and other favorable developments reported above, some long-term transformations had occurred and some other weaknesses had begun to appear by late 1973. It is true that by the end of 1971 the initial work structure was firmly in place, geared to the start-up task conditions in which equipment was running part-time and down part-time and in which joint problem solving, experimentation, and learning were required and permitted. This work structure, in both design and implementation, was experienced as highly consistent with what management had offered initially as the desired work culture. Thus, less than two years after the organization had been formed, both a structure and a set of meanings were well established.

But then in 1972 and 1973 the task had changed significantly from one of starting up and debugging equipment to one of producing efficiently and in volume. This change required a revision of the work structure in a direction that made it less attractive to members, even after the temporary pattern of neglect was corrected and the effects of changes were absorbed. Three weaknesses had become evident.

First, the system had not developed problem-solving mechanisms for the whole plant that were as effective as those used in the face-to-face teams. The problem was illustrated by two plant-wide issues in the fall of 1973: (1) differences of opinion about the selection criteria for a spare-parts coordinator, and (2) whether the pay system for office employees should be revised along lines different from those of the factory pay system. Representative plant committees dealing with these issues were given only limited confidence. The norm had developed that employees did not support solutions shaped by problem-solving groups in which they had not been directly involved. This reflected a strong preference for "participatory democracy" over a "representative" form of self-government. As a result, committee actions were not truly accepted by the larger work force.

Second, although there was unusual frankness among all employees, there was also concern whether the amount of openness and objectivity at the plant was adequate given the stringent requirements of the work design. For the system to work, an individual had to be candid in contributing to problem solving, conscientious in judging an idea on its merits, and objective in evaluating the qualifications of peers for higher pay rates. A strong desire by participants to increase these attributes, especially objectivity in making evaluations, was observed. When peer evaluations were "not honest," pay increases were given that were not justified (creating inequities), and individuals were assumed to have qualifications they did not possess (forcing others to do their work). Objective criticism was muted when a person feared he would be ostracized by a clique. Because influence was vested more in lateral than in hierarchical relations, workers were more concerned about the judgment of peers than of superiors. Furthermore, there was no quantifiable, stable, and automatic basis such as seniority for a worker's security. One worker explained that the tenuous basis of his security made him continuously concerned about his relations with the many people who could help or hurt him in the future. Another worker said, "The match in the gasoline is pay." He explained that decisions about the worth and pay of members were starkly real. The result was a moderate tendency for workers to ease up on standards—for example, shrinking from hard, exacting evaluation of a worker's mastery of all tasks in the plant before awarding him the plant rate. People tended toward reciprocation, each giving the other the benefit of the doubt.

More impressive than the moderate gap between ideal and actual behavior were the high ideals themselves. The system had idealized influence based on expertise rather than on formal authority or political power. Participants felt guilty whenever they did not live up to the ideals.

Besides the inadequacy of plant problem-solving mechanisms and the difficulty of being objective, there was a third weakness, namely an absence of mutual support and trust among team leaders. The team leaders had a norm of self-sacrifice relative to their teams, but they did not seek needed changes in their own situations. As one team leader said, "I never did think the 'Topeka system' applied to team leaders themselves." Team leaders were expected to engage in frequently exhausting dialogue with operators, and it had not been made legitimate for team leaders to put limits on their own accessibility.

Thus, Topeka moved in two main directions in 1973. The top managers reversed the dramatic decline in commitment by rebalancing two routines—production-task routines and team-building routines. At the same time, however, new problems were developing that the system was aware of but was not necessarily attacking in imaginative ways.

Steady State with Traces of Erosion (1974 to 1976). During this three-year period the work structure itself was maintained with very little change. However, the meaning of the work system for its members underwent change. By November 1976, a number of elements in the positive work culture had declined, reducing somewhat the attractiveness of the work system and members' commitment.

By general agreement it was still a very productive plant and a superior place to work, but the "quality of work life" had slipped. And while the majority still supported—by their own behavior— the unique strengths of the "Topeka work system," an increasing minority did not. Slippage occurred across a broad front of attributes: openness and candor; helping among team members; identification with plant management; confidence in General Foods; perceived upward influence; effective leadership within teams; and cooperation among shifts. In addition, there continued to be serious doubt about the ability of teams to make objective judgments of members' qualifications for pay increases. Team members now accepted the subjectivity and other imperfections as facts of life, and clique behavior became more pronounced.

Following 1973 a concerted effort had been made to improve relations among team leaders and to increase their influence over matters affecting them. In addition, their number was reduced from six to three. However, by 1976, the position of team leader had again become ambiguous and unsatisfying. Team leaders were discouraged about prospects for advancement, a feeling sharpened by the fact that their plant-wide assignments had broadened their abilities and raised their aspirations. Moreover, team members provided them with more grief than satisfaction. Team leaders, not unlike foremen in other plants, felt that they belonged neither to the work force nor to management. They complained that they were not backed by management. As a result, the position failed to attract the most talented team members.

A number of other factors had had depressing effects on the work system during the period from 1974 through 1976. Three of the four managers most responsible for the Topeka system left General Foods, and the fourth moved from the original dry food plant to the canned pet food plant, which was managed as an independent entity. Many thought that the managers who left had been treated unfairly by the company; indeed, the managers themselves considered their pioneering work a loss rather than a gain in their General Foods careers. These original managers had been committed to the Topeka philosophy and were willing to "go to bat" to protect the system, but the workers could not assume that their successors would develop the same commitment. Some people at the plant held a contrasting view, however. They believed that the departing managers had been too aggressive, thereby contributing to the strained relations with the corporate hierarchy, isolating the Topeka innovation, and hurting their own and others' career opportunities in General Foods.

Another depressant was the neighboring canned food plant. It lived under a cloud of uncertainty for three years—it would gear up for a national launching of a new product only to have the plan canceled when the product did not prove out in market tests. Two layoffs had occurred in this plant in 1975. However, beginning in the summer of 1976, the product sold well, and the plant began a highly accelerated start-up, moving quickly to three shifts and a six-day schedule. In order to get the plant on stream in the shortest possible time, management deferred the introduction of many aspects of the innovative structure utilized in the dry plant, such as pay geared to the learning of multiple jobs. This was interpreted by members of the dry plant as a lack of commitment to the "Topeka system." Besides, there were no new task challenges of significance in the dry plant during the period from 1974 to 1976. A major expansion had been planned but did not take place. New products requiring process changes were contemplated but not introduced. The technical and social skills that had accumulated were no longer being challenged, and the result was complacency.

Perhaps an even more significant cause of drift was the lack of capacity for self-renewal. As noted earlier, the work system had not dealt effectively with plant-wide issues. Representative committees had treated a few specific issues, but seldom, if ever, had gained the full confidence of the employees. Moreover, there were no regular plant-wide forums in which issues could be raised. In the absence of a plant-wide mechanism to which it could respond, management needed to take the initiative in assessing the health of the system, reviewing existing procedures and roles, setting goals for organization development, and proposing innovative solutions. But they had done little of this since 1973 except in relation to a proposed bonus scheme.

The plant community had lost its sense that the work system would need to evolve continually. Rather, within the work force there was a widely shared and deeply felt responsibility to *protect* and *preserve* the work system launched in 1970. Similarly, the managers who replaced the founding management team appeared to be awed by the system's impressive capabilities and more concerned to avoid disturbing a good thing than to evolve it to a still higher state of excellence in human and business terms. Vigorous, proactive leadership was required if the plant was to more fully realize its potential.

Salem Bearing Plant

The plant began hiring in July 1975, started production in October with a small crew, and increased employment over the next twenty months to slightly under 300. It operated on a seven-day, twenty-four-hour schedule. In addition to participating in the initial design process and making periodic visits to the plant during its history, my consulting activities provided two major observational points in the Salem plant. These systematic diagnoses of organization strengths and weaknesses were conducted at the end of one year and then again at two and a half years, each conducted by a team of three or more persons external to the plant, including myself. Members of these study teams interviewed over one third of the plant population each time and presented their findings to a cross-sectional sample of the plant to check the validity of their observations.

Commitment and Results. Salem offers the sharpest of contrasts with Topeka. The Topeka story is one of success through its first six and one-half years, but with some accumulating clouds of uncertainty as of my last reading. Salem is a story of relative failure through its first three and one-half years, with some possible hope generated by a change in plant managers in 1978. The commitment trend line reached a very high level at an early date, but then steadily declined until mid 1978, where it bottomed out at a level below that required to sustain the type of work structure employed at Salem.

Salem's economic performance compared satisfactorily with the division's older plants, but for competitive reasons, this new plant needed to excel. Even if one discounts some of its unrealistic goals, it fell far below its potential. Poor performance was reflected in volume, quality, cost, and housekeeping. While both commitment and effectiveness were disappointing, their trend lines differed importantly. Commitment increased during the first eight months, but this was not reflected in improved task performance, primarily because of shortcomings in design and implementation. Poor performance continued and eventually dragged down commitment.

Why did the Salem work system fail to develop as planned or along the lines of Topeka?

Planning (1974 to June 1975). There were no major differences between Topeka and Salem in the spirit or forms of the planning activities. Moreover, many conditions favorable to the high-commitment work system at Topeka also existed at Salem. It drew workers from a plentiful labor market. The work force was receptive to work and open-minded about the philosophy communicated to them. The technology provided plenty of challenges to those who would need to master it and operate it efficiently. It also afforded high leverage for worker skills and attitudes to affect quality, volume, and yields. The plant manager and his staff were selected early enough to allow them to plan the new work structure. Salem's innovations, in fact, received more philosophical support from corporate headquarters than Topeka's. Salem's plant management team, even more than Topeka's, utilized consultation and training relevant to its innovative efforts.

The design for Salem had many similarities to the Topeka work structure, which Salem's planning team had reviewed. Major similarities were work teams, pay geared to increased mastery, and participative mechanisms. There were also some notable differences. Salem, for example, adopted a different shift assignment pattern. Whereas Topeka utilized rotating shifts, Salem created three fixed shifts, and thus a worker assigned to days always worked days. Salem management recognized that rotating shifts had certain advantages and would in particular promote equality—no shifts could regard themselves as second class, and all would be equally exposed to the managers and staff on the day shift. Also, rotating shifts provided more stability in that there would be no movement from less desirable night shifts to day shifts. However, management doubted that rotating shifts would be acceptable to the work force in the Salem area.

Salem also chose a different supervisory strategy. It started with a one-to-three ratio of supervisors to work teams versus Topeka's one-to-one ratio during start-up. In addition, the work teams were to manage themselves from the outset with a minimum of assistance from supervisors, in contrast to Topeka's pattern of heavier supervisory direction at the outset and gradual withdrawal of this direction as teams gained more technical and organizational skills. The Salem planners wanted to avoid completely any tendency for teams to become dependent on supervisors and for supervisors to become accustomed to a directive role.

Formation Processes (July 1975 to February 1976). This period includes the hiring and training of workers in the second half of 1975, the start of production in October 1975, and continued increases in the work force during the first quarter of 1976. Commitment was climbing, and optimism was as yet untarnished. Evidence of subsequent difficulties had not yet been detected.

Like the planning processes, the early formation processes at Salem were, on the face of it, as effectively conceived as those in the comparable period at Topeka. They began at Salem during a preemployment training period of eighty hours (paid for by the state) in which potential employees were trained in various machining skills to enable them to set up and operate several basic machines. The training program introduced the unique philosophy of the plant's work system. By the time these employees entered the plant, they had a high sense of excitement and some shared visions.

The employees in each of several waves were trained together, entered the plant together, and then worked together on teams. Each new group started up a new operating unit further downstream in the work flow until all departments were manned for the first-shift operation, a process that was repeated six weeks later for the second shift. The addition of a third shift followed a different pattern—workers were brought in individually and without advance training.

These later formation processes were less effective than the earlier ones. Whereas Topeka started up a fully equipped plant with a full complement of 70 production workers, Salem increased from 55 to 225 workers over a year in increments of from ten to twenty per month. Salem's developmental task was more difficult. Employees who entered the plant directly without benefit of a separate training program did not gain a clear sense of the philosophy underlying the work structure. Their early impressions of what it would mean to be part of the organization varied in both content and forcefulness. A complicated work schedule, which we shall examine shortly, further retarded the establishment of stable shared meanings.

Despite some employees' imprecise conception of the work system, however, the overall level of commitment was very high by February 1976, when the plant population numbered about 175. Despite production shortfalls, management was encouraged by the enthusiasm, cooperative spirit, and "can do" attitude manifested by the work force. Moreover, supervisors' uncertainty about their roles was accepted as natural at this stage of development. Although it was clear that neither the technical start-up nor the social start-up would be easy, plant management, division management, and their consultants assumed that there were no fundamental problems that could not be worked out during the next year. This confidence was soon to be shaken by the "technical assistant episode" described below.

Decline (March 1976 to July 1978). During this period, the structure and meaning of the work system failed to stabilize. Structural defects were discovered but not remedied. A decline in commitment was reflected by discontent, abuses of the salary system, "goofing off," and so on. From mid 1977 on, division managers lost confidence in plant management. They increasingly viewed corrective actions as "too little and too late." When a union compaign in the spring of 1978 received the interest of some employees, this was taken as further evidence of weak plant management. But it was the technical assistant episode that was most symptomatic of the plant's enduring problems.

By March 1976, management had become concerned about the lack of trained people at key manufacturing points in the plant.

To help fill the gap, management identified a handful of employees within the work force who they believed had superior skills and assigned them to the new role of technical assistant. Promoted to the top pay grade, technical assistants could be called upon to move around to trouble spots. But when the decision was announced, "all hell broke loose." The action was seen as contrary to two premises of the work system, specifically that people would have an opportunity to influence those decisions that would affect them and that pay increases would be related to certain predetermined levels of mastery. (It was widely recognized that the persons tapped as technical assistants did not remotely possess the skills prescribed for the top pay grade.) Management, which had acted in good faith, later appreciated that creating technical assistants was not a good solution or one appropriately executed. Thus, whereas at Topeka the early tests had resulted in strengthening the premises of the system, this incident in Salem had precisely the opposite effect.

Although the incident raised doubts about management's intentions, workers nevertheless continued to hope for the success of the Salem work system, which was called the "team concept." This hope sustained a flat level of commitment for another six months. After that the cumulative effects of a number of factors steadily depressed performance and in turn commitment.

First, there was a persistent "skill gap." The plant management initially and repeatedly underestimated by a wide margin the experience and skill required to achieve normal efficiency in turning out products. The equipment employed to machine bearings was highly complex and sensitive, the product had to meet very close tolerances, and the economics of the business required high-speed operations. The local work force had few, if any, of the required machining skills. In the division's other plants the skills of operating, supervisory, and engineering personnel had been built up over decades, and Salem management simply underestimated the many invisible forms that experience and knowledge can take. The division had grown in the past by acquisition and had had no prior experience in new plant start-ups.

Management finally concluded that preemployment training, which had focused on setting up and operating basic machine tasks, should have given more emphasis to preparing workers to diagnose and adjust mass production equipment. Two departments in particular—turning lines and grinding lines—used equipment that is recognized in the industry as very difficult to keep in tolerance at high speeds. And because all the products flowed through these two units, the plant's output could be no better than the worst of the two.

Generally, the managers shared this retrospective diagnosis of the skill gap. They acknowledged past errors of judgment and took corrective steps to bring in additional technical resources, only to discover that their corrective steps were far too small. The misjudgments appeared to be related to "wishful thinking" about the effects of their organizational approach. The skill gap was further increased during the second year when a change in product mix required even more sophisticated operator skills than those required by the mix of products originally planned for the plant.

Second, there was an enduring pattern of unduly ambitious forecasts. The plant was continuously committed to goals that bore no relationship to current achievements. Management's lack of prior experience with a start-up helps explain the initial overestimation. After that, Salem plant pride created a reluctance to admit that the plant could not follow the originally projected learning curve. There was, however, some disagreement about who was making these unrealistic forecasts. Plant management thought that the division had imposed these overly optimistic forecasts; division management believed that the plant had entered into these commitments freely. This is but one reflection of a more general "noise factor" in the communication between plant and division.

The continual failure to reach goals had several effects. It raised concerns at the division level, it created a sense of psychological failure rather than success and pride, and it encouraged short-term actions designed to get production up immediately. To illustrate, during the first three years, the founding plant manager would invariably tell a phone caller how well the plant was doing, in terms of throughput that day, at any time of the day! And, analogously, machine adjustments for the short term were being made by operators.

Third, two interrelated design elements—work teams and

supervision—were either poorly conceived or misunderstood. The team concept had come to be understood by team members to mean "getting along" with other members and "autonomy" of supervision, whereas originally it was intended to emphasize the interdependence of members' tasks, joint problem solving, and mutual help. In retrospect, it appears that the "human relations" connotation of the team concept was fostered inadvertently during the training in team skills that members received after joining the organization. After eighteen months, when the problem had become clear, management found it exceedingly difficult to correct the meaning of the team concept.

There was, in addition, need for more supervisory direction during this period. The supervisory role was ambiguous, but was generally viewed as facilitative rather than directive. Supervisors, each of whom had responsibility for several different teams, were viewed as separate from the teams, not as members of the teams. Often they were excluded from team meetings. Moreover, the majority of teams were not coalescing on their own into effective coordinative units. Over time supervisory ranks were increased to provide nearly a one-to-one ratio of supervisors to work teams. However, strengthening the role of supervisors proceeded very slowly, in part because of the "autonomy" meaning of the team concept and in part because few supervisors had credible technical or leadership skills. As some team members said, "What do they bring to the party?"

Fourth, the pattern utilized for manning the seven-day, twenty-four-hour schedule had certain adverse effects. Originally, the new plant had been justified on the basis of a three-shift, five-day work schedule. During the planning process in 1975, however, the design team came up with an assignment pattern that it thought would make seven-day operation acceptable to employees. The team proposed seven-day operation to realize a better return on capital employed, increasing its projections of performance by about 40 percent.

Within a team on a particular shift, team members were permitted to determine which days each member would work as long as the team provided the required manning on all seven days. Thus, to take a simplified example, a seven-member team would determine which five members would be working each day. This latitude for individual schedules did make the seven-day schedule more acceptable, but it also produced a continually changing team composition. Management made one corrective adjustment on the grind lines in requiring that three-person work teams be formed and that they choose identical work schedules. While this stability helped the grind lines, transfers from the off-shifts to the more desirable day shifts further increased the instability of the teams' working relationships. This general churning of team membership hindered the formation of trusting relationships, the ability of team members to learn from one another and from team mistakes, and the development of group problem-solving skills.

The management structure proved to be too thin and too unstable to manage the seven-day operation during start-up. The original management organization, based on five days, had not been revised when the plan was changed to seven-day operation. Moreover, the instability of supervisory relationships greatly confounded the management task. For example, while teams remained on the same shift, supervisors rotated from one shift to another every six months. This feature, which the supervisors preferred because none of them wanted to stay on the less desirable shifts, nevertheless made it difficult for them to strengthen their role in relation to the teams. Each time the supervisors rotated, time was required before they became familiar with the team; and then, as the six-month assignment drew to a close, they were increasingly in a "lame duck" status. Although the disadvantages of this structural element were understood by management, there was a reluctance to force a change on the supervisors. This kind of cautiousness, in fact, manifested itself in many ways and prevented management from implementing corrective changes.

Fifth, the pay scheme lost its original meaning. The assignment of technical assistants to the top grade had begun what became a common pattern of compromising the standards for advancement from one pay grade to the next.

Sixth, the capacity existed to diagnose problems but not to remedy them. Salem's mechanisms for identifying and diagnosing problems included steering committees formed to study a problem and recommend changes, outside consultation, and major studies of strengths and weaknesses—one study conducted after a year and another after two and a half years. But corrective action did not occur, because planning and implementation processes broke down. Plant management was relatively cautious and lacked implementation skills. It was also handicapped by the seven-day schedule and the emphasis on near term results created by the continual failure to meet production goals, and it therefore never mustered the management time necessary to make basic changes.

Although certain management beliefs have already been referred to above, they will be summarized here because they underlay many of the problems. One such belief was "wishful thinking." More precisely, this was a belief that placed too much faith in the power of deep commitment to meet any challenge and thus encouraged an underestimation of the need for technical skills and management systems. Another mental habit was "either/or" thinking, which can be illustrated by the reasoning, "If we are trying to create a positive motivational climate, we cannot think in terms of direction, rules, evaluation, and discipline. They will just lead us back to a conventional bureaucratic organization." No one literally uttered this sentence, but such an assumption seemed to thread its way through management thinking well into 1977. This led management to a pattern of permissiveness that actually undermined the credibility and attractiveness of the work structure.

After management concluded that there were too few standards and too little discipline in enforcing the standards, it began using punishment. Unfortunately, however, it was inclined to generalize the point too broadly, and imposed punishment for poor performance even when the concern about performance may have been positive. Thus, there remained too little appreciation of the particular types of behavior to which punishment could be constructively applied.

Key managers also seemed to believe that member commitment was tenuous or fragile and would be withdrawn completely if major corrective changes were made. The alternative view, which I happened to share, was that the existing commitment was sufficiently robust for management to take whatever initiatives were required, provided that there was a process for discussing how the changes supported the philosophy of the high-commitment work system. Management gained insight into the "either/or" and "wishful thinking" patterns and their consequences sometime during 1977 and began to study the corrective changes that needed to be made. But the "fragile" hypothesis kept interfering with management's resolve to actually make the changes.

Replanning and Change (mid 1978 to present). A review and change process began on the plant's third birthday. It was led by a new plant manager brought in to replace the original manager, who had left the company. The union campaign was underway when the new manager entered the plant, but the work teams had instinctively avoided polarizing their members' differences regarding the advantages and disadvantages of a union. The new plant manager encouraged open acceptance of such differences. Apparently discouraged by the small amount of support that the campaign had generated, the union organizer ended it September 1978.

The early effects of the new manager on people's hopes and expectations were positive, and the preliminary substantive changes in the work structure that he made in the fall of 1978 were reasonably well received. Within a few months, he initiated many changes, including the following:

- Responsibility for quality was moved from line units to a separate unit reporting to a staff manager. This change recognized the urgent need to ensure that quality got more attention.
- More specialization in set-up work was instituted in two bottleneck units in an effort to get these units onto a reasonable learning curve. In the turning unit, this was seen as probably a temporary measure, because proficiency in setting up the equipment could reasonably be acquired by a high percentage of the unit's employees. In the grinding unit, it was thought that the added specialization would become permanent.
- Supervisors were required to attend team meetings and to write and distribute minutes of these meetings. This move was intended to clarify that supervisors were expected to become more involved in team matters and to help ensure that this happened.
- Shift assignments of supervisors were stabilized. The practice of rotating across shifts every six months, with its disruptive effects, was abolished.

These were changes that increased the soundness of the design at that time and in fact were long overdue. They were needed to inject more competence and more order into the work structure.

The changes—especially the first three—could be perceived in either of two ways: (1) as a progressive dismantling of the innovative work structure or (2) as a series of corrective measures intended to make the work system succeed within the same philosophy—indeed as an effort to preserve the founding philosophy.

I am uncertain whether these changes in work structure were implemented within the framework of the same general philosophy that guided the original design. This could well have been the case. But at the other extreme, the general philosophy might at some point be explicitly abandoned—the work system formally terminated and the work structure replaced with one that does not depend so greatly on worker commitment—one, that is, that can operate with significantly lower commitment levels. At this writing, I would not care to predict whether or not the plant will be successfully developed into an effective unit in the next few years.

Goshen Engine Plant

The Goshen plant was purchased in 1974, and the first production workers were hired in 1975. The work force had grown to 550 by early 1979 and was expected to grow until it reached 2,000 employees. Goshen was an industrial community and, although marked by a history of labor unrest, it offered a work force generally possessing high industrial skills and pride in those skills. Thus, the plant could, and did, hire many workers who already possessed a high level of technical skill (in contrast to Salem).

Commitment and Results. Commitment of the work force in early 1975 was moderate and flat because a slowdown in the engine business had clouded the plant's future. Commitment rose in 1976 and 1977 and was maintained through 1978 at a very high level. Among work teams in the plant and office, the commitment level ranged from moderate to extraordinarily high. Because of the continual entry of new people and the periodic introduction of new lines, overall plant commitment was an aggregate of changing elements.

Goshen's early performance compared favorably with the company's other plants, including another new plant with a similarly innovative structure. The plant manager was duly cautious when, in January 1979, he said, "It is too early to tell how we will be doing ten years from now, but current performance is in the right direction."

Goshen's impressive performance was reflected by many comparative indicators: low turnover and absentee rates, excellent delivery, favorable costs, better quality within the plant and better warranty cost performance on engines in the field. The safety record was poor initially, but it improved to become average. In January 1979, the plant was surpassing corporate production records on certain expensive equipment. It was also projected that Goshen would require 10 to 20 percent fewer people than sister plants in the labor-intensive assembly area. Top management chose to assign Goshen a new engine that would be highly cost competitive. In short, the Goshen plant was gaining an image as an exceptionally good supplier.

Internally, performance varied widely from one team to another; thus, supervisory reassignments and other changes were made periodically in an effort to upgrade machining lines, support groups, or assembly work teams that were performing poorly. Because of the functional independence of most teams, the weak production areas in Goshen did not affect overall plant production as they did at Salem. Similarly, the overall plant commitment level was not dragged down to the lowest common denominator as it tended to be in Salem. The economic effectiveness of the plant, like the commitment trend line, generally increased over the four years studied.

Conceptual Planning (1974). Even before the new plant site had been selected, the plant manager, his boss, and an internal consultant had agreed that this new plant would utilize an innovative work system. They asked me to join the planning effort and I accepted. A few years earlier, another engine plant in the company had started up with an innovative work structure. We expected to learn from the mistakes and achievements of the other plant.

In 1974, the plant was purchased, building renovation was started, and several key managers were selected. Each of these managers had experienced the start-up of a previous plant (not the innovative plant) and understood the technical challenge before them. By January 1975 they had a general philosophy. "Trust," "growth," "equity," and "excellence" were the four major principles by which the plant would be organized and managed.

Forming, More Planning, and Marking Time (1975). The firm's business slowed down dramatically and unexpectedly in 1975. Renovation of the building continued, but with less time pressure. The hiatus created an air of uncertainty as well as an opportunity for further articulation of philosophy, policies, and practices. The dozen managers hired in early 1975 were assigned the task of translating the four principles into job design, plant layout, pay systems, and guidelines for managing such matters as overtime and plant security. This activity enabled a growing number of managers to internalize the management philosophy.

The plant's original mission was to machine foundry castings into engine parts. Each part was machined by a separate line of heavy, complex, automated equipment. Thus, the basic task technology of the plant was envisioned as comprised of twenty or so independent machining lines, all sharing some common facilities, such as shipping, receiving, storage, and sand blasting. The plan called for these lines to be grouped into four or five administrative units called "businesses," each as self-sufficient as possible in terms of possessing the engineering, maintenance, finance, and personnel support required to be accountable for results. The individual lines were to be started up in the plant one by one over many years. Teams were to be the basic building blocks of the structure. Teams of seven to twenty-five operators would be responsible for an entire machining line (for example, the piston line) or for some central support activity.

In its use of work teams and in most other respects, Goshen's work structure was similar to that described in the Topeka case. But its pay and advancement system was different from Goshen's. Conceptually, the pay system linked pay level to skill acquisition, but there was a minimum fixed schedule for increases. In effect, unless someone was not performing adequately, he would move up from the entering rate to the top operator rate step by step after predetermined intervals. As it turned out, this relatively weak linkage between pay and skill development allowed Goshen to avoid certain problems that plagued the pay system in Salem (failure to maintain standards) and Topeka (tension related to peer evaluation).

The work structure included an elaborate "developmental review system." Subordinates were to propose future "growth" modules (skill and knowledge acquisition), and supervisors were to discuss, modify, and approve such career plans and evaluate subordinates' progress. In practice, the system's prescribed procedures were ignored as often as they were observed. However, because the pay increases, with few exceptions, were awarded on a scheduled basis, the fact that the review system was not operating as intended had few practical consequences. People deepened and broadened their skills very much in the spirit of the pay system. In 1978, the formal review plan was simplified and revised in an effort to make it more workable.

Forming Work Teams by Trial and Error (1976). The first three machining lines were started up and support groups were formed in late 1975 and early 1976. As in Topeka and Salem, the philosophy behind the work structure was communicated to work team members in ways intended to arouse intense interest and anticipation. By the end of 1976, the plant employed 150 people, and management had gained experience in orienting new members and in developing work teams. But two major difficulties developed at this stage.

First, most of the supervisors, called "team advisers," felt ineffective. They were bypassed by team members from below and by business managers from above. They lacked legitimate authority in areas such as discipline. It became apparent that the planners had gone too far in minimizing the directive role of supervision, especially with teams of newly formed employees. Therefore, the supervisory role was given more support as a distinct level in the hierarchy, and supervisors were provided training in the techniques for developing teams.

Second, a number of employees were hired who were acknowledged by the interviewers to have been marginally employable but, it was hoped, "trainable." As it turned out, these new employees were not able to meet the structure's requirements, namely, perform multiple tasks, take initiative, and exercise self-discipline. These employees continued to be a problem, but the lesson was learned and applied in future hiring. It came to be appreciated that in the early life of this plant, it would be better to err on the side of overqualified rather than underqualified workers. The "qualified" and "overqualified" would be challenged by the relatively demanding task structure, would make that structure work, and would also form a pool from which supervisors could be drawn as the plant grew. These are illustrative of the effective adjustments made during this period, although not all the "errors" that surfaced were addressed, and there were others that only appeared later.

Managing Diversity and Making Mid-Course Corrections (1977 to 1979). Describing this period is difficult because of the diversity of work experiences within the plant. Indeed, diversity continued to be a major conditioning factor. For example, the continual infusion of new people meant that employees differed vastly in their familiarity with the unique features of the Goshen system, as well as in their capabilities. Thus, by the end of 1978, there were eight machining lines at eight different stages of maturity, ranging from the formation phase to the maintenance phase. Several others were in the planning phase.

The difference between manufacturing and office work also brought special problems at Goshen. Compared with the other three plants studied, Goshen required much larger office and professional work forces. Earlier, the planners had found it relatively difficult to conceive innovative work structures for office and professional personnel that would be especially attractive to them. During this period, dissatisfaction expressed by these groups triggered a replanning process.

Then there was the diversity caused by a corporate decision to make the plant an engine assembly facility as well as a machining facility. The technologies of machining and assembly impose different constraints and offer opportunities for different types of work structure. Under the new plan, one third of the floor space and one half of the eventual work population would be devoted to assembly. Assembly began with thirty workers in June 1977, and the daily output and manning levels were expected to increase to capacity in five years.

An impressive aspect of Goshen's culture emerged during this period—its capacity to make corrective adjustments. Although initially there was too little distinction between the structure required for start-up and that desired for steady-state conditions (like Salem), there was a capacity to correct design errors (unlike Salem). The most important adjustments, according to the plant manager, related to an upgrading of the concept of "excellence." The more people-oriented aspects of the structure were emphasized during the earlier periods. But during 1977 and 1978 more emphasis was placed on economic goal setting and reporting systems, which provided teams with cost-per-piece data and enabled them to track their performance. A more balanced emphasis changed the meaning of the work system but did not make it less attractive; if anything, the work structure became *more* attractive—and more credible to workers.

Other adjustments during 1977 and 1978 were made in particular elements of the work structure and in particular meanings. For instance, when an earlier formulation of team members' rights and obligations regarding team assignments was discovered to have disadvantages to the business, the policies were modified. Similarly, there was initially a strong reluctance to use discipline—for example, for abuses of the salary system—but management gradually realized that lax standards depressed rather than enhanced morale. One team—as a team—was permitted to interview a candidate for the position of its supervisor. When the candidate reported feeling harassed because of the number of interviewers and the procedures they employed, this participative procedure was dropped as inappropriate at the current stage of development of teams.

The "growth" concept, as articulated, had created unrealistic expectations, especially among those performing secretarial duties and bookkeeping. Indeed, some experienced secretaries felt "guilty" because they were not learning new skills and were not encouraged to take pride in practicing secretarial skills they already possessed. An effort was made to change "growth" from a concept that implied breadth into one that also embraced depth of mastery and the maintenance of existing skills. This revision of meaning progressed slowly but surely. Orientation activity was also found to have created higher expectations for promotion than could be met. It took a long time to act on this diagnostic insight. Nevertheless, by 1979, orientation was being modified.

Goshen's ability to continue to modify its structure through the first four years of its life was enhanced by the fact that in 1979 it had reached less than half its projected size. Thus, there was a general feeling that the organization was still in a formative stage. There was also the more practical judgment that the majority of the people who would be affected by the structure were still to be hired and that changes could therefore be made more easily now than later. Other factors contributed to Goshen's adaptive, innovative capacity. The plant manager, from the beginning, had emphasized that the structure would evolve and that changes would be necessary. Moreover, participation by those who would be affected by the changes increased both the soundness and the legitimacy of the replanning process.

During 1978, the president of the company visited the plant and came away deeply impressed. This confirmation strengthened commitment. It also increased the number of visitors coming to inspect the plant. The plant management tried to play down the idea that Goshen's work structure had any necessary relevance for the firm's older plants, but there still was a risk that the combination of Goshen's high performance and the president's endorsement would create resentment toward the plant and pressure to decrease its autonomy, as did happen at Topeka.

But this did not seem very likely at Goshen, assuming that plant management would continue to handle relationships with headquarters as in the past. Strikingly, the plant manager built open and mutually responsive relations with corporate staff groups, including finance, personnel, and engineering. He welcomed regular visits and advice from these groups; and, when he needed to influence them—for example, to gain an exception to a policy—he took great pains to present his case with well-reasoned logic and documented evidence. By 1979, the presence of many highly effective teams reassured management that it was on the right track. Still, some engineers and other professionals were not convinced that the work structure would succeed. Commitment among some members of the plant community was exceptionally high; among others, it was only moderate.

One task of the Goshen organization was particularly difficult in view of the targeted size of the plant; namely, how to ensure that the steadily growing number of managers were managing in a way consistent with the plant's philosophy. I have already noted that in 1975 the founding managers had an opportunity to internalize this philosophy. Later, a series of two-day, off-site meetings were used to educate groups of twenty to thirty managers and professionals in the rationale for the work structure and the practical implications of managing this type of structure. Another method, more idiosyncratic to the plant manager's style, was what he called his "agitator" role. He spent time talking with people at all levels of the organization. When he learned that a work team had encountered problems, such as stagnation at some level of development, he would start agitating them to confront their supervisors.

Despite its demonstrated capabilities up to 1979, one had to be cautious in projecting how Goshen would evolve. Certain issues could be anticipated. For example, individual teams were given latitude in the starting time of shifts. In machining, where the work teams would remain independent, this might continue to be acceptable even in a large plant under heavy production pressure. In contrast, under conditions of high volume production in the assembly area the functionally organized teams of the assembly area would become more dependent on each other. In this case the latitude of individual teams might become impractical and would therefore be decreased.

Another issue was whether one could devise an effective productivity-sharing system for the plant, given its size, complexity, and vulnerability to external economic conditions. Management regarded such a system in strategic terms and thought that it should take effect as the plant matured and as salaries, which increased steeply during the first few years of employment, began flattening out.

Other conditions added uncertainty. The plant would grow much larger than its present size and possibly at a very rapid rate. Though individual machining lines had already shifted from start-up modes to all-out production, the assembly units had not, and it was certain that assembly work at high volumes (300 engines a day) would significantly affect the work structure and its meaning to workers. Finally, if the plant manager were to be replaced before the work system became more institutionalized, that change would create a particularly serious source of uncertainty.

Derry Equipment Plant

The Derry plant manufactures grain-drying implements. It was planned in the first half of 1976, started up in July 1976, and expanded rapidly over the next year. By January 1979, the plant and equipment were fully employed by a work force of 130 persons who worked two shifts five days a week.

Commitment and Results. The plant was effective from the start. The work system developed much as management had envisioned, proved satisfying to its members, and exceeded business plans. Although the first few years of this plant provide a success story, it is not as dramatic as Topeka's. Commitment at Derry was high, but it did not climb as rapidly as at Topeka or reach Topeka's extraordinarily high level during a comparable period. Still, Derry did not experience decline in commitment comparable to the trough in the third year at Topeka.

In January 1979, management stated that, using appropriate comparisons, the plant was judged 20 percent more productive in terms of output per employee and 35 percent more profitable than the firm's other plants. This favorable performance was attributed to (1) cost-conscious attitudes and habits that produced low expense rates for machinery repairs, tooling, and supplies; (2) lean manning practices at all levels requiring everyone to wear many "hats"; (3) the effective development of task skills and coordination mechanisms; and (4) a generally positive motivational climate.

The safety record had been initially worse than that of the firm's average, but it improved to the point where it was average. Product quality during the first year was no better than that of the firm's other plants. Because of the usage pattern of grain-drying products, plant personnel did not receive any customer feedback on the first year's production until September 1977, when the grain-drying season was in full swing. However, when farmers did find quality problems in the field, their feedback produced a dramatic and immediate improvement. The quality record became better than that of comparable plants within the firm.

The absenteeism rate of 2 percent was regarded as very good by management. The annual attrition rate was running 15 percent. However, when the reasons for the terminations and quittings were examined, this could be judged near the optimum rate for the period in question. Located in a rural area, the plant had drawn primarily young workers with little industrial work experience. The general work ethic was assumed to be favorable, but selectivity had been limited by a low unemployment rate in the local labor market.

The plant's products required fabrication of light metal with a considerable amount of welding, painting, and assembly. Manufacturing required some specialized operations, such as machining and balancing fan blades, assembly of electrical control boxes, and testing of completed units. The task technology was easier to master than that of Topeka, Salem, and the machining lines at Goshen. The parts of the manufacturing system were also less tightly coupled than in Topeka, Salem, and the assembly lines at Goshen. An error or a stoppage at any stage in the work flow was less disruptive in the Derry plant than in the other plants.

Planning (First Half of 1976). For several months prior to plant start-up, which occurred in mid 1976, the plant manager and the division personnel manager planned the work system, adapting many ideas that characterized previous plant innovations, including work teams, pay based on skills acquired, and progressive delegation of self-management responsibilities. In this planning effort they were assisted by key subordinates as they were brought on board and by myself. They had the explicit support of the division manager to whom the plant would report.

Forming (Second Half of 1976). During the second half of 1976, a work force of about sixty was hired, the plant began production, and the basic organizational structure was formed. The gradualness of the rise in commitment at Derry reflected Derry's strategy for the inculcation of meaning. This strategy differed from that of the other plants. Management philosophy became apparent through actions rather than words, although management did tell employees the following at the time of hiring: "We are going to manage this plant in a very participative way. You will be highly involved. Everyone will be expected to learn the total manufacturing process and to know the total product. We will invest in a lot of training to develop your skills and knowledge. And, finally, we will expect a lot from you."

There were several reasons why these ideas did not immediately signal to employees that they were involved in something special. Management did not coin any phrases or concepts designed to capture employees' imagination and did not contrast this mode of operation with that of traditionally managed plants. Moreover, many of the young employees hired did not have sufficient prior factory work experience to fully appreciate the differences themselves.

A major commitment to training workers in a variety of task and team skills was a key element of the plan. Management's actual delivery on its promise of training programs was one of the more important incidents in the plant's early life, and it served to convince workers of management's seriousness about the work system that had been described in orientation.

Expansion and Associated Problems (January to September 1977). The first three quarters of 1977 were marked by a very rapid expansion of the work force—from 60 to 215 employees, including more than 100 temporary workers during the summer period. According to the plant manager, this period of build-up caused the plant "to pay a toll" by decreasing team meetings and management contact with workers, by taxing the available tooling and engineering support, and by lowering the quality of working conditions. He labeled it a period of "treading water." The presence of temporary workers caused some regression in team development, as meetings became more perfunctory and members became more inhibited in discussing problems they were having among themselves. Temporary workers were also more apt than permanent ones to test the discipline boundaries, with disruptive effects on the plant community. The period was very successful economically, but management felt that it had not made headway in establishing the longer-term work structure and its potential meaning.

Evolving Structure and Meaning (September 1977 to September 1978). After the bulge of temporary workers was behind the organization, management continued to add to its permanent payroll and gradually build the plant's capacity. During this period the organizational structure evolved and became more established. Teams were relatively small (three to ten members), and their membership was stable for blocks of time. But team membership lacked longer-term stability because workers were required to rotate every six months from one department to another, such as from assembly to fabricating. The pay system had four basic levels, reflecting a combination of breadth and depth of skills. There were limits on the numbers who could be awarded the top two rates. For example, only 15 percent could achieve the third level—that of technician.

It was intended from the beginning that teams would be relatively self-managing, although this aspect was not emphasized as much in the orientation at Derry as it had been in the three plants already analyzed. Step by step, the teams assumed progressively more responsibility for such functions as maintenance, testing, hiring, discipline, and promotions. A schedule of weekly team meetings was strictly adhered to—they could not be canceled or deferred.

The plant started out with only two supervisors and continued this way well into the period when plant workers exceeded 150, including many temporary employees. Management then found it necessary to double the number of supervisors. By September 1978, there were four supervisors, two of them covering 75 workers on the day shift and two covering 25 workers on the night shift.

No rules were published. But there was a well-developed code of acceptable conduct, communicated verbally, that covered such matters as attendance, horseplay, and fighting. These codes grew out of experience. The plant manager initiated prompt remedial action when organizational norms were violated. Apparently, employees supported this pattern partly because the actions were consistent with widely shared norms and partly because the plant manager took great pains to explain to the entire work force the facts and reasoning upon which his final disciplinary or corrective action was based. There was also a plant-wide advisory council that met with and advised the plant manager. This forum was widely regarded as effective.

Several other elements of the work structure are worth noting. A number of plant-wide tasks were shared very widely. For example, everyone, the plant manager included, took his or her turn making coffee, cleaning the lunch room, and raising and lowering the flag. Everyone, again including the plant manager, participated in a ritual of complaining about having to do these tasks. The sharing of these chores appeared to have a "leveling" effect and also an "integrating" consequence for the plant community as a whole. A related element of the work system was an active calendar of plant-wide social functions.

Management was committed to provide employment that would be as stable as possible; the implication was that it would make more than conventional efforts to avoid layoffs. The credibility of this commitment was boosted in the summer of 1978, when management placed elsewhere a number of temporary workers who no longer were required in the Derry plant but who had expected three more weeks of summer employment.

Steady State (September 1978 to present). By late 1978 the work system was marked by a highly stable membership, continued productivity improvement, relatively stable total employment level (decreasing slightly by attrition to reflect productivity increases), and a relatively stable work structure and meaning. Management expected to turn out new products in the future and also expected to introduce some cost and information procedures that would enable the work force to fine tune the work system. The plant manager was also convinced that the number of supervisors could and should be reduced in the future, given the relatively stable work force and its expanding capabilities. But none of these changes would necessarily cause any basic rethinking of either structure or meaning. One significant change was contemplated—a plant-wide productivity bonus. Without such a gain-sharing scheme, management projected that commitment would taper off moderately in the coming years.

Similarities with Topeka suggested themselves to the Derry management. It is true that Derry had not built commitment and expectations to the same level as characterized Topeka when it entered its third year, but they were very high. Management was determined to find a way to keep organizational renewal as a way of life in this work system. Time will reveal the success of this attempt.

Part Three: Theoretical Propositions and Illustrations

Set forth below are propositions about high-commitment work systems and their development. Parts of this developmental theory are particular to high-commitment work systems, others apply to work organizations generally. Some have been induced from the cases discussed above. Others have been derived by deductive processes or adapted from other theories, but they also receive support from the case analyses. By the term *developmental theory* I mean systematic answers to these questions: What facilitates the creation of high-commitment work systems? Why do some develop effectively while others do not? More particularly, what factors determine the soundness of the structure and the level of commitment? What influences how rapidly these systems mature and whether or not they adapt?

Before detailing the theory, I have outlined its five major structural points:

1. High-commitment systems are more likely to be initiated in new settings when founding managers perceive a need for exceptional task performance, care directly about the work life of members, assume certain favorable conditions to exist in the current technology and potential work force, and believe they can muster the extra resources required early in such systems.

2. Effectiveness of the work systems studied here is defined in terms of positive human and business results. Effectiveness results from two factors—the level of commitment and the soundness of the work structure. In the short run, defective structures utilize poorly the energy associated with high commitment. In the longer run, defective structures reduce the commitment level itself. If a structure oriented to high commitment is sound, then effectiveness will vary directly with the commitment level achieved.

3. What affects the soundness of a structure designed for high commitment? A sound structure is one that fits the task technology and human resources. This idea applies to all work structures, but some unique design dilemmas occur in the high-commitment structure. Because these dilemmas change over time, they are important aspects of developmental theory.

4. What determines the level of commitment, which we have defined as the summation of four types of involvement (moral, spontaneous-expressive, calculative, and alienative)? The amount of each type of involvement is a function of basic predispositions of members, including their needs and preferences; the work structure itself; and the meanings of the work structure. The strength of the more positive types of involvement is especially affected by two aspects of the meaning of structure, namely, its attractiveness to members and its apparent viability.

5. What affects the rate at which work systems mature, that is, move through earlier developmental processes? What affects their ability to survive, adapt, and change? The maturation rate of structure is influenced by the initial fit between requirements of the task technology and available skills, by elements of instability in either technology or work force, and by the capability of the work system to detect errors in design. The rate at which meanings become established is influenced in part by the same factors but also by activities consciously designed to accelerate the establishment of meanings. The ability to change elements of structure and meaning is related to several factors, including clarity about underlying values and mechanisms for identifying problems and legitimizing solutions.

1. Facilitating Conditions in the Prehistory Period

A complete theory of the development of high-commitment work systems would explain why this alternative is created in lieu of more conventional work systems in some new settings but not others. Because the four cases studied are all positive examples, they do not offer contrast in this respect. Nevertheless, some hypotheses can be offered, based on the four positive cases reported here and on other instances where management consciously opted *not* to create a high-commitment work system in a new setting.

It is conducive to the creation process if those in a position to strongly influence the design of a new work system:

1.1 Perceive an urgent need to excel in task performance.
1.2 Directly value the social and psychological health of members.

1.3 Can visualize structures and meanings that could enhance task performance and the human experience at work. This potentiality is greater when technology renders performance more dependent upon human skills and attitudes and when potential workers are receptive to participation and possess relevant technical and social skills.

1.4 Can negotiate resources for the extra investment required in the initial development of a high-commitment work system. These resources include planning time, consulting, training, permission for a possibly longer start-up curve than usual, and political support to absorb the risks associated with innovations.

These conditions affect not only the decision to create but also effectiveness during subsequent developmental phases. They were generally present among the systems studied, except that Topeka would have benefited from more political support and Goshen from a greater desire to excel in task performance at an earlier date.

2. Effectiveness of Work Systems

"Effectiveness" of high-commitment work systems refers to both favorable human and task outcomes, unless one particular type of result is indicated:

2.1 Effectiveness will be determined by a combination of the level of commitment achieved and the soundness of the structure.

2.2 Work system planners presuppose a range of member commitment and design the structure accordingly. High-commitment work systems are those where the minimum of that range is high commitment. Assuming actual commitment falls within the planned range, then effectiveness will vary directly with the soundness of the structure.

2.3 Assume that a sound structure exists. Effectiveness will vary directly and proportionally to the amount of commitment, provided it falls within the range of commitment contemplated. Should commitment fall below that range, the work structure will rapidly decline in effectiveness and the structure will probably be revised (for example, to rely on more coercion and tighter rules). Should it rise above that range, it

*will have relatively little influence on effectiveness, because the struc-
ture has not provided ways to utilize extra involvement for the benefit of
either the task or the individual.*

2.4 *Task effectiveness, in turn, is a determinant of commitment, its strength
depending upon the role that task achievement plays in the meaning of
the work system.*

The relationship between soundness of structure and effectiveness was most dramatically illustrated by the Salem case, where
our analysis implicated a number of separate aspects of design and
implementation. Goshen's initial structure was corrected in a
number of ways, but there was little direct evidence that design
errors had any significant effects. The Topeka situation was subtle.
The error there was one of omission; that is, there were few, if any,
modifications of the initial work structure.

In my analyses of the four cases, the hypothesized relationship between effectiveness and commitment were most apparent
in: (1) the progressively increasing commitment and steadily improving effectiveness in Derry; (2) the rapid learning and
problem-solving during the high-commitment start-ups in Topeka
and Goshen; (3) the relatively high rate of both commitment and
effectiveness in certain Goshen teams; and (4) the moderate decline
in commitment and effectiveness (relative to potential) in Topeka in
later years.

Even my long-term exposure to these cases does not enable
me to be certain about the predominant direction of causality in all
the relationships noted above. I do know that in Salem the poor
effectiveness lowered commitment more than lack of commitment
lowered effectiveness. In this case the structure fell below the
necessary threshold of soundness.

One period in Topeka's history fails to confirm that effectiveness and commitment are tightly coupled. Topeka's temporary
dip in commitment after several years did not result in a discernible
decline in task performance, although human satisfaction was
down. The cases do not contain any illustration of commitment
levels that exceeded the planned range. A borderline example of
commitment that fell below the range occurred in the Salem case.

3. Soundness of Structure—Its Fit with Evolving Technology and Human Resources

This section and the next treat aspects of work structure. The next section deals with the incentives that generate organizational energy. Here we deal with the roles and rules that channel that energy. The next section explains why members reflect different levels of commitment; this section analyzes the soundness of the structure that utilizes commitment.

My approach to building this part of the theory is (1) to hypothesize how three analytically distinct components of a work system (technology, human resources, and structure) relate to each other; (2) to hypothesize the developmental tendencies unique to each component; (3) to analyze the dilemmas created by the opposing developmental trends among certain components; and (4) to trace out the further implications of how these dilemmas are managed.

In identifying major alternative patterns by which work roles and rules can be structured, I will utilize the distinctions between "mechanistic" and "organic" structures made by Burns and Stalker (1961). "Mechanistic" work structures are characterized by functional specialization, precise definition of roles and authority, hierarchical structure of control and communication, and operations governed by instructions issued by superiors. This type of structure is appropriate where the task is relatively predictable and where knowledge and expertise are concentrated in the management hierarchy. In "organic" work structures individual task definitions are contingent upon the total situation. There is a network structure of control and communication, operations tend to be governed by operators themselves, and vertical communications often take the form of information and advice. Organic structures become more appropriate as uncertainty increases and task knowledge and problem-solving expertise become more widely dispersed in the work system. Thus, we can speak of these developmental tendencies:

3.1 The development of the work structure, in terms of the organic-mechanistic spectrum, is related to task technology and human resource capabilities, which follow their own developmental patterns. Therefore, structure, the most manipulable element, tends to be consciously evolved in ways that take into account these developmental patterns.

3.2 *From initial start-up to normal operation, the task technology evolves from uncertainty to relative certainty, from requiring greater to lesser problem-solving capability. An organization design aligned with this development of task technology would evolve from an organic to a mechanistic form.*

3.3 *In contrast, the human resources system develops from lesser to greater technical skills and knowledge and from lesser to greater group problem-solving capacities. This developmental pattern of human resources would indicate a design that evolves from mechanistic to organic.*

In what ways does the human resources system evolve toward greater skills and knowledge in a new setting with a new work force? The relevant technical skills must be acquired. Knowledge of desired product characteristics and the manufacturing system must be gained. Trust, respect, and the ability to communicate efficiently take some time to develop. The more developed the human resources, the more one can rely upon a flexible and open work structure, that is, an organic one. Thus, to be strictly consistent with the development of human resources in new settings, one would start with more hierarchical direction and control and more prescribed procedures, decreasing these over time. The human experience would be one of going from narrower latitude to broader latitude, from less complex problem-solving challenges to greater ones.

Why does the task technology in a new setting evolve toward more certainty? During start-up, pieces of equipment have to be adjusted and debugged, and their idiosyncrasies have to be learned. This process occurs over a period of time, during which each piece of equipment becomes progressively more reliable. Balancing interdependent parts of the production process presents another level of problems, the solutions to which also get worked out over time. The more uneven the rates of debugging, mastery, and control of functionally interdependent parts of the system, the more complex the balancing problems. After a task technology has been started up and stabilized, there are fewer operating variables, and adjustments typically occur within narrower ranges. Decision rules have evolved to handle many of the more common variations. The task technologies in the four plants studied would never evolve to the point where no new problem solving was required, but without new product configuration, new process technologies, or new raw material substitutions, the problem-solving requirements would be minimal.

The more operationally developed the task technology, the more the structure needs to emphasize control, efficiency, and structured problem solving rather than learning and unstructured problem solving, and a relatively mechanistic structure with prescribed input procedures becomes appropriate. Thus, if it is to match the development of the task technology in each of these new settings, the initial structure should be relatively organic and move toward greater definition and constraint.

Of course, the task technology does not always follow the simple characteristic pattern of evolution mentioned here. In Topeka and Derry, it did, although at Derry the introduction of new products in the second year caused the work system to jump from a more advanced state on the original experience curve to a less advanced state on the experience curve for the new products. In Salem, the competitive role of the plant shifted somewhat just after start-up when products different from those assumed in the original plan were assigned to the plant. Unfortunately, they were even more difficult to learn how to manufacture effectively. Had the system already been well on its way to mastering the original products, the new products might have provided a useful challenge.

If the above discussion is valid, it follows that differences in the uncertainty inherent in the task technologies must be taken into account in the development of high-commitment work systems. Uncertainty in the task technologies derives from (1) the difficulty of performing individual tasks under production conditions and (2) the tightness and complexity of the interdependence of parts. These conditions lengthen the time required to master and stabilize the technology.

In Salem, which had the most uncertain technology, both of these conditions were present. Two departments employed equipment that was very difficult to keep in tolerance at high speeds. The plant's output could be no better than the worst of these two steps in the work flow. Topeka, which was also organized functionally, was similarly vulnerable to a bottleneck operation at any stage of the work flow. Because it had a continuous flow technology, its parts were even more tightly coupled than Salem's, but the equipment itself was less uncertain and more readily mastered. Goshen's manufacturing technology was similar to Salem's except that Goshen's plant was comprised of many smaller parallel machining lines that varied in complexity. Most lines did not include equipment as temperamental as that in the two most difficult units at Salem; in any event, the Goshen plant's overall state of development was more an average of the parallel and *independent* lines than the same as the least developed line. In Goshen's assembly operations, mastery did not take long, but interdependence among its parts was moderately high. Derry, with the least difficult technology, neither represented a tightly coupled system nor employed equipment and assembly operations as complex as those generally found in the other plants.

The contradictory implications of the development patterns for human resources and task technology create dilemmas for structural design:

3.4 *The evolving structure usually represents a series of compromises, in which some "human resources gap" is created during early start-up and some "human resources surplus" is generated once normal operations have been established.*

3.5 *How contradictory the initial status of the task technology and human resources will be depends upon the uncertainty inherent in the start-up of the technology compared with the level of skills of the newly recruited work force.*

3.6 *The "human resources gap" refers to the extent to which the current work structure is consistent with higher skills, attitudes, and group problem-solving capacities than those that actually exist. One effect of this gap is to induce development through trial-and-error learning. One risk associated with the gap is that effectiveness will suffer, frustration will mount, and the credibility of the structure will decline.*

3.7 *The "human resources surplus" refers to the extent to which higher skills and problem-solving capacities have been developed during start-up than are required for normal operation. One adverse consequence of this underutilization during normal operation is that loss of challenge will detract from the attractiveness of the work system and hence from commitment to it.*

These dilemmas and their consequences are illustrated by the four cases. In Topeka, for instance, there was a human resource gap initially because the loose structure was designed to fit the technology start-up task; after the human resources had come to be well developed, they actually exceeded the amount required to function in the more certain environment (see Figure 2). The effect of the "human resources gap" was that the rate of start-up was slower; in other words, immediate output was forgone in the interest of learning. The effect of the later "human resources surplus" was that the sense of challenge and achievement on the part of members suffered and some letdown occurred along with a moderate erosion of interest.

The pattern of work structure development at Topeka dealt reasonably well with the opposing developmental trends of the task technology and the human resources. The human resources gap in the first year was considerable, but not excessive. Supervisors at first consciously provided moderate direction and then decreased it as skills, knowledge, and working relationships increased. This human resources gap was planned, and the market demand for the product was resisted to allow for learning to take place. Then, at a certain point, the structural trend was moderately reversed, and more mechanistic features were introduced in response to the imperativeness of volume operation. In the meantime, human capacities continued to develop. The result now was an underutilization of resources and a certain amount of disappointment, but neither was so serious as to cancel the earlier meaning attributed to the work system.

In Salem the initial open structure fit the uncertainty of the start-up task but neglected the fact that the skills and problem-solving abilities required to make the structure work would take considerable time to develop. If Salem is contrasted with Topeka in terms of Figure 2, Salem's initial structure was more organic and its

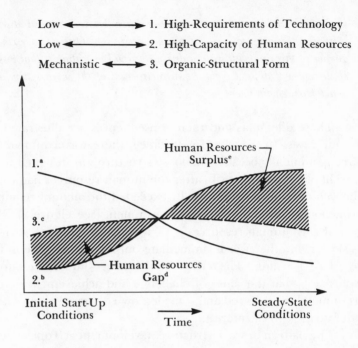

Low ◄───────► 1. High-Requirements of Technology

Low ◄───────► 2. High-Capacity of Human Resources

Mechanistic ◄───► 3. Organic-Structural Form

1.ᵃ

Human Resources Surplusᵉ

3.ᶜ

Human Resources Gapᵈ

2.ᵇ

Initial Start-Up Conditions

Steady-State Conditions

Time

ᵃRefers to the amount of human skill and problem-solving capability *required* by the task technology. It is shown to have declined after technology is debugged and stabilized. It is the "task technology" variable.

ᵇRefers to the amount of human skill and problem-solving capability *possessed* by the work force operating the technology. The "human resources" are shown to rise as a result of learning.

ᶜIdentifies the degree to which the structure includes organic versus mechanistic elements. It is shown to have become increasingly organic (as skills developed) during start-up period and then to have reversed its trend, as more mechanistic elements were introduced under normal operating conditions.

ᵈReflects the extent to which the current structure "assumes" greater skills and problem-solving capability than currently exist. This concept focuses on the "net" human resources gap which exists after taking into account the structural solution, rather than the "gross" discrepancy between the skill requirements of the technology and the skill bank currently possessed by the work force. The same distinction applies to our conception of the Human Resources Surplus.

ᵉReflects the extent to which greater human capabilities exist than are "assumed" by the current structure.

Figure 2. Developmental Patterns and Dilemmas at Topeka

initial stock of skills and other human resources was lower—a combination of factors that created a larger human resources gap. Moreover, Salem's curve showing the inherent need for technical problem-solving started out higher. This is a more systematic way of visualizing the excessive gap between actual skills and those presumed by the structure, a skill gap that figured so importantly in Salem's problems.

Goshen differed from Salem in two fortunate respects. Its initial technology required less problem-solving capacity than did Salem's two difficult departments, and the work force brought more relevant skills. Therefore, although the initial structure at Goshen was too organic, creating a sizable human resources gap, it was not as serious as at Salem. In Goshen, management promptly recognized that it had underestimated the need for supervisory direction. After increasing directiveness in a remedial step, Goshen then began to gradually decrease it until steady-state operation on a particular line was achieved.

Derry had almost as large a human resource gap as Topeka. While its task requirements were less difficult, less supervisory direction was provided. Recall the very low ratio of supervisors to workers. The Derry plant manager was especially concerned about the anticipated underutilization of human resources.

The interrelationships among human resources, structure, and technology found in the four cases just discussed also illustrates two other propositions:

3.8 At any given level of development of human resources, a particular amount of difficulty in the task technology is optimal. Because the capacities of human resources increase, this optimal amount of challenge rises.

Contrasting examples illustrate this proposition. On the one hand, stagnation of the Topeka work system after four years would have been less likely had the system been confronted with the need to manage change—new types of equipment, major additions, or a stream of new products. On the other hand, had Salem's starting inventory of technical skills and problem solving been greater or had its technology been less temperamental, then Salem's work system might have developed in a way similar to Goshen's.

3.9 At any given level of development of human resources, there is an optimum amount of mechanistic versus organic structural attributes.

Several design errors are illustrative of this: An error in Goshen and Salem was that the role of supervision was defined too minimally at the formation stage of the work structure. In Goshen the ratio of supervisors to team members was appropriate; but because their role was viewed as strictly facilitative, supervisors had little basis for influence other than the power of their personalities. The teams floundered until a concerted effort was made to define the supervisors' authority. Supervisors then were able to provide the needed task structure for the work, lead the group in problem solving, and promote the appropriate team norms. In Salem the problem was more severe. Not only was the role defined even more minimally but also the ratio of supervisors to workers was much lower. Finally, supervisors were selected with relatively modest skills and little experience directly relevant to the Salem plant.

A related design error was in the method chosen for manning the twenty-four-hour, seven-day operations in Salem. Because the method provided too little structure, too little stability, it arrested the rate of development toward established meanings and established work routines.

The design of an evolving structure, including its implications for the size of the skill gap and surplus that are created, must take into account the short-term and longer-term trade-offs described above. A lack of structural soundness results when misjudgments occur here, but these misjudgments can be minimized if two kinds of planning are carried out.

The first planning task is to visualize a work structure that will be appropriate when the task technology has become operational under steady-state conditions and when human skills, attitudes, and relationships have been well developed. The product of this planning is the "steady-state design." The second planning task includes provision in the work structure for stimulating the development of appropriate skills, attitudes, and relationships. It also includes planning the initial (transitional) work structure—a structure that will take into account the planned rate of development of human resources and the anticipated maturation pattern of the task technology. A decision to align the structure more closely with the human development pattern rather than the task development pattern must be made consciously after weighing the consequences discussed earlier.

Many instances of unsound design relate to the confusion between (1) the design characteristics of the steady-state structure that planners want to create and (2) the design of the transitional structure of the organization. Certain elements that are feasible in a developed high-commitment work system are much less feasible in a newly formed organization. These elements include recruitment of people with modest technical skills, minimal supervisory roles in managing work teams, reliance on peer pressure for controlling abuses of policies predicated on trustworthiness, and self-selected work schedules to cover seven-day operations.

4. Commitment Generated by the Structure and Meaning of Incentives

Earlier, I proposed that effectiveness is a function of soundness of design and the level of commitment attained. The level of commitment has been defined as the summation of various types of member involvement. Three factors determine this level: (1) the work structure incentives offered by the organization, (2) members' predispositions for different types of involvement, and (3) the meaning members attribute to the incentives they encounter.

These factors can be elaborated briefly. The most basic point is that different types of incentives tend to elicit different types of involvement, some more positively oriented than others. However, this tendency is weakened when employees are strongly predisposed to a type of involvement different from the type sought by the incentives employed. Moreover, members' involvement is influenced not only by the structure of incentives but also by the meanings these incentives come to have for them.

The propositions dealing with incentives and involvement in high-commitment work systems that are proposed here involve a revision and extension of the paradigm set forth by Etzioni (1961). Etzioni distinguished three types of incentives that organizations employ to ensure member compliance with organizational requirements, namely, coercion, remuneration, and norms. And, as previously noted, he also identified three types of member involvement in organizations—alienative, calculative, and moral. He observed that different types of institutions could be defined in

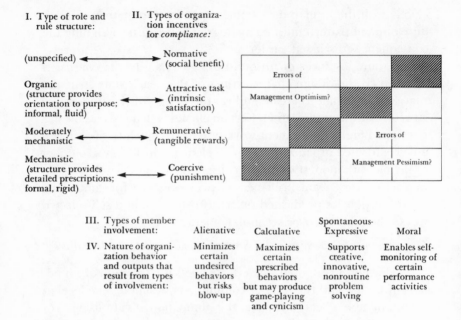

I. Type of role and
    rule structure:

II. Types of organiza-
    tion incentives
    for *compliance:*

(unspecified) ⟵⟶ Normative
(social benefit)

Organic
(structure provides
orientation to purpose;
informal, fluid) ⟵⟶ Attractive task
(intrinsic
satisfaction)

Moderately
mechanistic ⟵⟶ Remunerative
(tangible rewards)

Mechanistic
(structure provides
detailed prescriptions;
formal, rigid) ⟵⟶ Coercive
(punishment)

Errors of
Management Optimism?

Errors of
Management Pessimism?

III. Types of member involvement:	Alienative	Calculative	Spontaneous-Expressive	Moral
IV. Nature of organization behavior and outputs that result from types of involvement:	Minimizes certain undesired behaviors but risks blow-up	Maximizes certain prescribed behaviors but may produce game-playing and cynicism	Supports creative, innovative, nonroutine problem solving	Enables self-monitoring of certain performance activities

Figure 3. Dimensions of Work Structure

terms of their reliance upon certain types of incentives and the ways in which members were involved. There are basically three types of institutions, illustrated by prisons, business organizations, and churches. Each represents a particular congruent combination of the types of incentives and involvement.

My research findings require a revision of the Etzioni paradigm, and I propose an additional type of member involvement, namely, spontaneous-expressive involvement, which I have already introduced. I also propose an additional category of incentives, namely, the eliciting power of intrinsically attractive tasks and task environments. The elaborated paradigm is in Figure 3. The categories I have added are those that most characterize the high-commitment work systems studied. Also, the basic paradigm developed by Etzioni and adapted here has certain implications not discussed by Etzioni. As derived and proposed here, it is based on deductive reasoning but is also consistent with field observations.

My present interests are different from those of Etzioni. While he was distinguishing among a broad range of institutions in society, I am interested in finer distinctions among work organizations in industry, particularly in the relative emphasis given to the various incentives employed by different plants at different points in developing work systems:

4.1 *There are four types of incentives that a work organization may offer its members to comply with organizational goals or requirements. These incentives are punishment, tangible rewards, intrinsically satisfying work environments, and perceived social good. Other elements of the work structure tend to correlate with the type of incentive employed (see columns I and II in Figure 3.) For example, there is a tendency for punishment schemes to be accompanied by highly formalized rules and specifically defined roles and for intrinsically attractive tasks to be accompanied by a more open and flexible definition of roles and rules.*

4.2 *Individual members can be involved with an organization in four different modes—ranging from a very negative "alienation" to a very positive "moral" involvement. The type of "human involvement" will influence the patterns of organization behavior and performance. (See rows III and IV in Figure 3.) For example, a "spontaneous-expressive" involvement is more likely than a "calculative" involvement to produce creativity. Similarly a "moral" involvement yields behavior that is self-monitoring and will continue without organizational recognition or accounting.*

4.3 *The central hypothesis of this section is that while mathematically there are sixteen possible combinations of organizational incentives and types of member involvement, only four combinations are stable: alienation and punishment, calculative involvement and remunerative incentives, spontaneous-expressive involvement and intrinsically attractive tasks, and moral involvement and normative incentives. These four combinations are more likely to occur than the other twelve.*

In Figure 3 the types of incentives and involvement have been arranged in matrix form with the combinations just cited falling along a diagonal, ascending from the most negative to the most positive form of involvement. Thus, referring to the matrix, one can say that there are only four equilibrium points—all on the diagonal from lower left to upper right.

At any given point in time, however, the situation may be off-diagonal. Consider a plant where management has relied upon punishment to enforce discipline and piece work to elicit effort and where workers are involved in their work in an alienated and calculative manner. Suppose management reached three conclusions: that too much worker energy is devoted to beating the system and too much management effort to maintaining it; that a more spontaneous-expressive involvement by workers would produce both more and better work, more effective problem-solving, and a healthier organizational climate; and that at some basic level these workers would prefer the spontaneous-expressive type of involvement. To achieve this latter type of involvement, management might initiate the redefinition of work tasks to make them intrinsically more attractive to workers. However, unless the initiative results in a shift to spontaneous-expressive involvement by workers immediately—a result that is unlikely—the situation is temporarily out of equilibrium. Over time management will either succeed in achieving the higher equilibrium desired or will have to return to the earlier coercive and remunerative incentives.

Such situations, which are off-diagonal in the upper left region of Figure 3, may be characterized as "errors of management optimism" whenever the organization's superior does not fully recognize the nature of the subordinates' involvement (members are more alienated or calculative than the manager appreciates) or when he naively assumes that the level of involvement can be easily changed. But, as the example just cited illustrates, these off-diagonal situations are not necessarily "errors." They can be a disequilibrium stage in a planned process of upgrading the commitment level of the organization. They are not "errors" when the superior is prepared to deal with the difficulties involved in upgrading the equilibrium and understands that he risks failure.

A situation can also be off-diagonal in the other direction, often representing an "error of pessimism" by management. These pessimistic errors may have a greater tendency to be self-fulfilling than errors on the side of optimism. For example, if one shifts to major reliance on punishment in a work situation where the involvement has been primarily spontaneous-expressive, there will be a strong tendency for involvement to become more alienative.

Taken by itself, the paradigm outlined above might suggest that high commitment would be assured if one could design an intrinsically attractive work structure. But logic suggests, and field studies confirm, the need to consider another variable, namely, the potential interest on the part of members to be involved in a spontaneous-expressive way. More generally, it is proposed:

4.4 *The actual involvement of members is partly determined by their predispositions for involvement and partly by the organizational incentives they encounter.*

Thus, if the members recruited to the work system are strongly predisposed to be involved in an alienative or calculative way and they encounter an intrinsically attractive work environment, both forces will be acting to influence their actual involvement. And if the predispositions to lower levels of involvement are strong enough, the incentives will have to be revised downward to match the involvement.

A particular type of institution may be generally characterized by a particular incentive-involvement profile. For example, as Etzioni points out, business institutions are usually characterized by remunerative incentives and calculative involvement. But viewed at close range, a particular organization can be found to be relying simultaneously on several types of compliance mechanisms and sometimes on all four:

4.5 *While an organization can be said to reflect a central tendency in terms of a particular incentive-involvement combination, the organization actually utilizes a mix of incentives, and any member is involved in different ways in different organizational activities. Moreover, individual workers will have central tendencies of involvement that may vary from the organization's central tendency. Some may be characteristically involved at a higher level, others at a lower level.*

The four case studies are generally interpretable within the four-by-four matrix paradigm proposed here. The analyses of the four plants confirmed the need for the additional categories of incentives and involvement and supported the propositions that relate incentives and involvement. They also illustrated that organization incentives are mixed, that there may be multiple levels of involvement for any single member, and that there is a diversity among members in types of involvement.

All four work systems achieved, at least temporarily, high member commitment. In each case the higher levels of involvement resulted in large part from the way that the work structure was designed and implemented. Following are some of the features that were intended to be intrinsically attractive and that in fact did promote spontaneous-expressive involvement:

- Tasks were designed to include challenge and variety.
- Training and job movement were scheduled to provide individual growth.
- Work units were structured to provide membership in primary groups and to receive delegated responsibilities for self-management.
- Status differentials were minimized to decrease social distance.
- Plant-wide activities were provided to build a sense of community.
- Forums were provided to give employees a voice.
- Communications were set up to keep employees informed.
- Feedback systems were designed to give employees a sense of accomplishment.
- Screening methods were used that would enable work teams to feel committed to new employees and the latter to feel "chosen."

Employee reactions to changes made in the structural elements noted above sometimes demonstrated how these elements and spontaneous-expressive involvement had been linked. This can be illustrated by Salem. Originally team members were allowed to decide which days they would work, as long as the overall manning requirements were met. When it became apparent that the lack of stability of the three-person teams operating the grind lines was seriously retarding the learning curve on this equipment, management decreased the individual's latitude by requiring that three-member teams choose the same schedule. Members experienced this as an important loss.

In three of the four cases—Topeka, Salem, and Goshen— the work structure was tied explicitly to human as well as economic values and the moral superiority of this system was asserted—the intent was to elicit some moral involvement on the part of members. This level of involvement developed in all three cases, especially at Topeka, where the media publicized the system as a solution to a social problem. Thus, where the work systems were viewed as morally superior, the equilibrium of incentives and involvement covered the far upper right-hand cell on the diagonal of the matrix in Figure 3. Derry's work system was cast in moral terms to a lesser extent.

In all cases there was some use of punishments. However, at Derry, boundaries on behavior were clarified and enforced earlier than in the other three cases, and this was done in a way that I regard as realistic and constructive. In the other cases there was a tendency to assume that punishment would be unnecessary. This reflected a moderate error of optimism regarding the general level of involvement of some members or the particular level of involvement of members in some aspect of the work structure, especially provisions governing attendance. These three work structures failed to acknowledge fully that, although the incentive-involvement equilibrium has a central tendency, this tendency is comprised of a diverse set of more particular equilibria.

For example, even at Topeka, where the complete work force was hired at the same time, members were "buying in" to the system according to their own timing. This reflected the fact that some were more favorably disposed initially than others to respond to the intrinsic incentives. A few were so predisposed to calculative or alienative involvement that they left or were forced to leave the organization.

Other examples show how individuals were involved in different ways when complying with different organizational requirements. For most groups, attending to quality was spontaneous-expressive, but being punctual was more calculative;

that is, it was related to the fact that members were rewarded or punished for punctuality. Or, to take another example, one member might be involved in joint problem-solving in a spontaneous-expressive way but involved in required overtime in a calculative or alienative way—both during the same work day. Compliance with some types of requirements, like reliable attendance, may be exceedingly difficult to achieve without explicit rewards or the potential for punishment. But managers in Goshen and especially in Salem were overly concerned that utilizing punishment to enforce any type of requirement would degrade the *entire* system.

Thus, although Proposition 4.2 asserts that incentives pitched at a lower level than the current member involvement tend to have the effect of degrading the level of involvement, I am now prepared to argue that it is possible to have several levels of incentives operative or potentially operative at the same time and related to the same type of behavior without *necessarily* degrading the current level of involvement to match the lowest incentives, as long as these incentives are internally consistent and some other conditions are met. I am not yet sure what these other conditions are, but I believe they involve the meanings of work systems.

There are two (opposing) tendencies for the equilibrium to shift during the early years:

4.6 *The tendency for some actual behavior patterns, especially those reinforced by attractive socializing agents, to become normative and internalized moves the equilibrium related to those behavior patterns upward.*

This developmental trend can best be illustrated by postulating a sequence of incentives and involvement employed in other socialization situations. A parent may initially punish a child for not sharing toys with a sibling, then shift to rewarding instances of sharing. At some point the child may come to find that sharing is fun and finally come to believe that sharing within the family is morally right. Similarly, patterns of mutual assistance at work and of reliable attendance may be responsive to reward and punishment incentives at one stage but then later become normative and internalized as "right" in the work system in question. This pattern is illustrated by Derry, where the plant manager defined limits on counterproductive behavior—limits that were not written but were well understood and increasingly accepted and enforced by almost all members of the plant community.

4.7 The declining difficulty in the task and the rising skills referred to earlier and interpreted within the matrix framework of incentives and involvement indicate a tendency for the equilibrium to move downward. There are related but additional downward tendencies that occur when the newness of the total experience of membership in a high-commitment work system wears off, when compensation curves flatten, and when the efficacy of the system is demonstrated. These factors tend to produce an "equity gap."

Two commitment patterns most clearly illustrated by Topeka— peaking at the end of the start-up period and a gradual erosion of commitment during the later years—are consistent with this proposition.

During conditions of a successful start-up, the task challenges the workers. Their ever-changing achievements provide relatively high intrinsic satisfaction. Moreover, in a high-commitment work system, the ambitious development and utilization of organizational skills provide additional satisfaction. If the pay scheme rewards skill acquisition, as was the case in all four plants, there is a relatively rapid rate of individual pay advancement during the first three to five years. Thus, both intrinsic and extrinsic rewards tend to create a sense of equity—heavy contributions are matched by generous rewards.

But the calculus changes as time passes. The routineness of the steady-state operations, the flattening of the social and technical learning curves, the corresponding slowdown of individual pay increases—all these work toward a perception of decreasing rewards. Moreover, if the plant is performing exceptionally well, as Topeka was after three years, Derry was after two and one-half years, and Goshen could be projected to be, then members perceive

their contributions more clearly. Thus, a perceived unbalance between contributions and rewards is likely to develop unless there is
a means for increasing the rewards at this stage. A sense of inequity
will directly undermine the perception of the moral superiority of
the work system. Equity has in fact become an increasingly salient
issue in the three plants, although it has not yet become a significant concern, as I had earlier expected.

The planners of all four high-commitment systems recognized the long-term difficulty of basing their systems too heavily on
spontaneous-expressive involvement in that they planned to eventually add a plant-wide gain-sharing scheme. A gain-sharing
scheme contains at least three levels of incentive; it inceases (1) the
rewards for performance, (2) the attractiveness of the task environment, and (3) equity in the work system and hence its claims to
moral superiority. For a variety of reasons noted in the cases themselves, however, none of the plants has yet introduced such a gain-
sharing system.

I have discussed member involvement as a response to incentives designed into the work structure. No allowance was made
for the range of possible interpretations of these design elements.
Yet it is members' interpretations of these elements that finally
determine their responses. Meanings are shaped not only by the
incentives themselves but also by events that occur in the plant and
the rhetoric used to refer to these events.

It is possible for the meanings associated with each level of
incentive to be more potent or less potent than one might have
expected on the basis of the incentive structure alone. With respect
to each level of incentive provided by the organization, members
are in effect making personal judgments of two kinds: "In view of
events, rhetoric, and my predispositions, how attractive to me are
these elements of structure, and how likely are they to be sustained?" In aggregation, these judgments determine overall commitment:

4.8 *Overall commitment is primarily a multiplicative function of two as-*
sessments by the employees in question: (1) the actual attractiveness to
them of the many types of incentives and (2) the credibility or viability
of the work system as perceived by them. This formulation turns out to

be structurally analogous to the idea that the expected value of a future event is a function of its utility and the subjective probability that it will occur. Indeed, commitment corresponds closely to the "expected value" of the system to the members.

The work structure sets general limits on the way participants can feasibly be engaged in an organization, but the meaning that workers attribute to the work system will determine how they actually become involved. Thus, managers of high-commitment work systems must not only manage structure, coping with all the dilemmas and potential pitfalls described above, but must also be concerned about the development of meaning. Ideally they will conceive an "intended meaning" that is both consistent with the planned work structure and is as compelling as possible, and then develop the meanings sensitively and skillfully.

The types of meanings contemplated by the planners of these high-commitment work systems generally include the following elements:

1. Members will be inspired by viewing the ideals represented by the work system—be inspired by what they regard as its moral superiority.
2. Members will find the work intrinsically attractive because of the content of their tasks, the memberships and relations integral to their work activities, and their influence over matters affecting them.
3. Members will be reinforced by compensation and other rewards contingent upon their positive contribution.
4. Members will perceive that while there is individual freedom, latitude, and flexibility in many respects, there are recognizable limits that will be enforced with penalties.

This statement of intended meanings corresponds to my four levels of incentives. None of the planning teams explicitly intended the four meanings contained in these statements. Derry gave less emphasis than the other plants to the first and more to the fourth. The fourth, related to discipline, entered into Salem and Goshen late. But all four plants emphasized that intrinsically attractive work would provide the cornerstone of meaning for the work system.

Meanings are not always those intended. Consider an example of a design element that took on unintended meanings. Work teams at Salem came to take on such meanings as "good human relations, freedom from supervision, and individual autonomy" rather than the more appropriate and intended meaning of "cooperativeness in the pursuit of independent tasks." Although these alternative interpretations of work teams may originally have had equal potential for being attractive to the newly hired employees, the "human relations-individual autonomy" meaning was much less viable than "cooperativeness," given the task technology. At some point members came to appreciate that work teams as they understood them might not be sustainable. Unfortunately, they tended to interpret negatively management's attempt to change the concept of work teams.

Our cases provide many other examples where management found that meanings needed to be revised. At Goshen the meaning of "growth" was revised as it applied to job design and skill development, and "task excellence" was upgraded relative to quality of work life. At Topeka, there was a need to legitimate decision making through representative forums as well as through participative mechanisms. Also, the work system as a whole needed to be seen as evolving rather than merely requiring protection. In some cases the revisions were needed to increase the attractiveness of the work system, in other cases its credibility. Efforts to revise meanings involved articulating the different meanings and exploring the rationale for new meanings. They also involved taking initiatives consistent with the new meanings.

I said earlier that events can shape meanings, whether intentionally or unintentionally. At Salem management's decision in the celebrated "technical assistant episode" to act unilaterally and with disregard for pay classification standards tarnished the meaning of the participation principle and blurred the meaning of pay for acquired skills. Topeka participants reinforced trust when there was widespread readiness to replace the missing cash in the open change box. The efforts of Derry's management to locate jobs for their temporary employees who otherwise would not have a full summer's employment were symbolically important in reassuring permanent employees that employment security was important to management. Proposition 4.8 related commitment to both the perceived attractiveness and the perceived viability of the work structure. The cases contained at least three issues about viability. Does local management mean what it says? If so, will higher management support local management? Will the work system be effective and hence validate the founding rationale? The first two questions were especially important during plant start-up, whereas the third became more important after the system was operational.

With respect to consistency between stated philosophy and management action, Topeka and Salem offered the sharpest contrasts. The handling of certain critical issues by Topeka's management tended to confirm its espoused philosophy. In contrast, the actions of Salem's management's often hurt its credibility. As for support from higher management, I have already discussed the major contrasts between Goshen, where higher level support was assiduously developed, and Topeka, which lacked that support. The perception that Topeka managers who left General Foods had not been fairly treated by the company detracted slightly from the perceived viability of the work system, but because the system was manifestly so effective, this event and the cynicism it generated detracted more from its attractiveness than from its credibility.

Now for the question, "Will the work system be effective?" At Topeka and Goshen impressive performance after start-up did more than anything else to convince people that the work system would probably be continued. Conversely, in Salem, the most significant adverse influence on both attractiveness and viability was performance shortfalls. The experience of the Salem plant illustrates how short-falls can create a downward movement in the incentive-involvement matrix. One might have expected that lack of performance would have prompted management to rely less heavily on an attractive design and more heavily on rewards and punishments, and that member commitment would have been scaled back in response to management's revision of incentives. Instead, the lack of performance seemed to be demoralizing and to act directly on member commitment. Management revision of incentives was a response to both low performance and already depressed member commitment. Commitment declined because performance shortfalls directly affected the attractiveness of the work structure and the perceptions of its viability.

5. *Work System Maturation, Adaptation, and Survival*

A number of developmental processes—planning, forming, establishing, maintaining, and replanning—apply to both the development of work structures and the development of meaning. These processes do not necessarily constitute distinct phases, and the sequence can be interrupted at any stage in the process.

"Maturation" and "establishing the work system" refer to movement from the planning phase through the establishment phase. Several propositions in this section will deal with the rate of establishing the structure, others with the rate of establishing meaning. "Adaptation" refers to the capacity to replan when conditions warrant. A number of ingredients are hypothesized to enhance the adaptive capability of high-commitment work systems. "Survival" refers to the continued existence of the work system as a high-commitment system. The factors affecting survival include adaptation, just mentioned, and soundness and commitment, which have already been analyzed. An influencing factor not yet treated is external relations, which we shall explore below.

The four cases exhibited different maturation rates. First, Salem was still in a state of flux after three and one-half years. After a highly accelerated rate of "formation," the processes by which work structure and meaning became established had proceeded at a very slow rate and had been interrupted by replanning—both redesign of the work structure and redefinition of the meaning of the work system. Establishment had not taken place to any significant extent.

Establishment and maintenance had occurred in Goshen's machining lines where membership was stable and the technology had been brought under control, but other teams were still in the process of formation. Moreover, while some elements of meaning and structure were well established in the plant as a whole, others were clearly following a highly evolutionary pattern. Topeka moved steadily toward the establishment of structure, although it experienced a hitch after three years during transition from start-up to steady-state operations. Derry had an established structure in a relatively short period of time. There was no recycling required to revise either structures or meaning in the transition from start-up to steady-state operating conditions.

How do we account for these broad differences and other more subtle ones? The following propositions are based on the observation that work structures do not really become established until both the requisite human resources and task technology are well developed:

5.1 *The greater the differences between the inventory of human resources at the time of forming the structure and the human resources required to support the work structure planned for steady-state conditions, the longer it will take for the work structure to mature. Relatively large differences can be the result of any of several factors: a planned structure that is highly organic, inherently difficult task technologies, low skill levels possessed by workers at the time they are hired, and predispositions to lower-level involvement.*

5.2 *The more changes that occur in the character of the task technology during the period of formation, the longer the time required to establish a work structure.*

5.3 *The more membership instability, the slower the maturation rate. Instability can result from continuously infusing new employees as part of a longer versus shorter build-up of the complete work force, instability of relationships and assignments, and turnover.*

Consider how propositions 5.1 and 5.2 apply to the four cases:

The rapid maturation of Derry's structure was aided by the fact that the task technology was the least difficult to master. Goshen's experiences illustrate these propositions in several respects. One distinctive characteristic there was the generally high level of technical skills possessed by those newly hired into the work force. This worked favorably toward establishing the work structure. Working in the opposite direction was the introduction of the assembly task in the third year, which required replanning of certain rights and obligations of employees and a revision of job design criteria. Also, the periodic addition of new machining lines kept slowing down the average level of maturation of the, overall structure as well as adding to its total complexity. This required elaborations of the work structure, especially of its supervisory and coordinative functions.

In Salem, the work force's lack of machining skills and the difficult technology in two departments worked against the establishment of the work structure. Other factors, contained in the hypotheses that follow, worked in the same direction to completely frustrate development of the work structure. Topeka's experience does not lend any support to propositions 5.1 and 5.2. Topeka's planned work structure was ambitiously organic, and the task technology was as difficult as that of Goshen's, yet there was a relatively rapid establishment of the work structure. The explanation is to be found in propositions 5.3 and 5.4 (given later); stability of membership and good error detection during the early years favored rapid development.

For proposition 5.3, the evidence is generally consistent with the membership instability hypothesis. In Topeka's start-up the complete work force was hired and assigned to shifts and teams at the outset. This factor helped simplify the establishment of the work structure. Derry's hiring of the complete permanent work force took more than a year. During this period a very large temporary work force had come and gone. The required rotation of members among departments every six months created changes in assignments and relationships. These factors slowed what otherwise could have been an extremely rapid maturation rate.

Goshen clearly represents the longest period of build-up, but internally the stability of assignments and relationships ranged from high to moderate. These mixed causal factors were matched by the mixed maturation record described earlier. Salem's build-up period produced only slightly more instability than Derry's and much less than Goshen's. However, the scheduling and assignment methods allowed for an enormous amount of "churning" in terms of the daily membership of working units. In addition, turnover, especially on the third shifts in the two bottleneck departments, was a source of further instability. Overall, Salem manifested the most instability and was the slowest to mature.

5.4 The poorer the ability of the work system for error detection and corrective action, the slower the rate toward establishment of the structure and the less likely the continual replanning or rejuvenation of the work structure once established.

In Salem the existing work structure could not stabilize, and yet the necessary replanning did not occur until the new plant manager arrived. Management's ability to take corrective action was handicapped by certain beliefs—for example, that commitment was fragile—as well as by poor implementation skills. In Goshen the readiness and ability to replan kept the system moving toward a viable, stable work structure. Interestingly, the prospect of future growth and the slow movement toward an established structure tended to lower the threshold for initiating replanning of the work structure.

The Topeka case provides a complex illustration of the proposition considered here. While there was adequate problem-solving capability to move relatively quickly to a stable structure, there was not a capacity to initiate more fundamental replanning in years three to six, which was a period marked by unnecessarily early aging.

The following set of propositions deals with the maturation of meaning in high-commitment work systems:

5.5 The rate of establishment of meaning will be influenced by the rate of the development of the work structure, since the structure itself is a major determinant of meaning. Hence, the factors hypothesized to influence the rate of structural development are also hypothesized to influence the development of meaning.
But other factors operate to shape meaning:
5.6 In high-commitment work systems there is a tendency for planners to deliberately accelerate the establishment of meaning.

5.7 Accelerated meanings in high-commitment work systems tend to produce a rapid rise in commitment.

5.8 Accelerated meanings increase the risk that unintended definitions of the work structure will emerge or that intended meanings will turn out to be unrealistic. Hence, this strategy of establishing meaning places great demands on the adaptive capability of work systems.

Compared to planners of other work systems, planners of high-commitment systems are more conscious of the meaning dimension of a work system and more deliberate in planning for its development. One aspect of this planning is a tendency to initiate a different timing for the developmental steps of meaning relative to developmental steps of the work structure. In the start-up of most work organizations that do not include a high-commitment objective, there is little planning for the type of culture that key members want to develop. The "meaning" of the work system therefore tends to develop and become apparent after the fact. Hence the establishment of the work structure tends to precede the establishment of meaning—the second occurring in bits and pieces.

Derry represented a moderate departure from this typical pattern. Although the plant manager had a clear idea of the organizational ideology he wanted to develop, he usually communicated this conception first by his actions and then by his words. The words gave additional meaning to the structure already experienced, and the manifest structure itself ensured a correspondence between intended and attributed meanings.

In the other three of our cases, management took more initiative in establishing meaning. These cases show that the development of meaning can have an important bearing on the degree of commitment. High levels of commitment were achieved by a strategy of early, careful, and full communication to new members of the planners' hopes and expectations for the high-commitment work system. These plants established a highly attractive meaning for the work structure well in advance of establishing the work structure itself. This aggressive strategy is hypothesized to have had several specific effects along lines actually anticipated by the planners of Topeka, Salem, and Goshen. First, these three managements had assumed that if the potential for involvement were to be fully realized, it would be necessary to alter the expectations of the new work force that were based on prior industrial work, beginning with the worker's first contact with the organization. Second, they realized that the motivational energy, identification, creativity, and other attributes associated with high commitment could become available immediately for the plants' tasks, accelerate the development of social relations, and tend to promote a culture consistent with these developments. Third, they believed that once people seriously entertain a dream or a set of hopes, they will work to make that dream or those hopes a reality. The creation of these expectations would help to ensure that the system was moving toward its ideals, as it in fact did in Topeka for three or four years and in Goshen to date. In these two cases leadership created a constituency that in turn became a source of pressure to live up to the ideals. This third rationale for the strategy would appear to be more compelling in larger organizations, such as Goshen, where the planners' personal influences are less direct and less pervasive.

Several types of risks observed in our cases are hypothesized as inherent in the strategy of accelerated establishment of meaning. One risk is that the meaning established early will fit the start-up task structure better than the steady-state one, as happened in Topeka. Another risk is that meaning will be discrepant with the initial structure, as "growth" was in the office context at Goshen. And still another risk is that when one is dealing with an abstract concept such as "teams" without yet having a concrete manifestation of the concept, it may take on unintended meanings, as happened at Salem. Management permitted, perhaps encouraged, the role of supervisors to be defined outside of the initially formed teams. Their subsequent redefinition as an integral part of teams was extremely difficult to implement and had not been achieved when the new plant manager took over. Thus, the risks of an accelerated establishment of meaning are that unintended definitions will emerge or that intended meanings will eventually turn out to be unrealistic. Subsequent efforts to redefine meanings may be unsuccessful or successful only at the cost of disappointment or even cynism if they are interpreted as a shift in philosophy rather than as a necessary corrective adjustment.

Adaptive capability is an especially strategic function in high-commitment work systems for many reasons. To the extent that there is less accumulated knowledge about designing and implementing plant-level structures that assume higher commitment than conventional ones, there will be a need to make course corrections, especially during the first several years. To the extent that the first several years create high commitment—a result that they often seem to have—then the high expectations can only be met over time if there is a strong capability for adaptation, innovation, and renewal:

5.9 *Several ingredients of high-commitment work systems, if present, enhance their ability to revise their structure and meaning: clarity of values, an evolutionary view of structure, change mechanisms, and optimism about the capacity for change.*

In both Topeka and Salem I detected a frozenness to the work structure and its meaning. In the case of Salem this lack of adaptation was nearly fatal to its high-commitment work system in the early years. In the case of Topeka, it accelerated the aging (without growth) of the work system in the three-to-six-year period.

The most important ingredient here is that meaning itself is clearly related to the human well-being and economic efficiency values that underlie the work structure rather than to some aspect of structure itself, such as teams. In Salem, both management and workers tended to fixate on the team concept rather than on underlying values.

The second most important ingredient is the general expectation that many structural elements will be revised in the light of experience and/or changing conditions. This expectation helps to avoid defining the meaning of the system in terms of its particular structural elements. It also helps ensure that changes made to preserve the work system will be so interpreted rather than automatically assumed to represent an abandoning or a backing away from the work system philosophy. Topeka lost this expectation, and Salem's management failed to foster it.

A third element is the existence of forums or other mechanisms for amplifying concerns, for testing the adequacy of proposed changes, and for legitimating these changes. Salem had plant-wide forums, but Topeka did not. A fourth element is a realistic appreciation of the robustness of high-commitment work systems. We saw an underestimation of this in Topeka (*after* new management in years four to six) and in Salem (*until* new management arrived after three years) and hence a tentativeness based on intimidation by the system or unfamiliarity with it.

External relations are important to the survival of a high-commitment work system to the extent that its ideology deviates from the prevailing norms in the larger system of which the unit is a part. Deviance creates interest on the part of external parties, some of whom probably will find the deviant system threatening to their roles, their skills, their status, or their ideologies. Contrasts between Topeka and Salem, on the one hand, and Goshen and Derry, on the other, illustrate the importance of external relations, although these contrasts have not provided the basis for deriving a general proposition.

Friction developed between Topeka management and the line hierarchy and staff groups at headquarters. Topeka management was viewed as dogmatic and uncooperative. Topeka management in turn viewed the staff groups as hostile to the work system philosophy. Topeka thus became isolated, increasing its defensiveness and its lack of adaptation. Although Salem management was confident of hierarchical support for its work system, it failed to establish an appropriate pattern of mutual influence between the plant and the division. To division management, it appeared that plant management either stubbornly resisted influence or overreacted by uncritically accepting ideas advanced by the division. Given such a relationship, it is not surprising that the plant became committed to unrealistic forecasts, made rash decisions in some areas, and was unresponsive to some potentially useful ideas from division management.

In contrast, in the case of Derry, the plant-division relationship was managed effectively, in part because the division personnel manager was a direct collaborator in planning and implementing the work system. However, Goshen represents an even more striking contrast to Topeka and Salem in terms of the management of the external relations. As noted earlier, the Goshen plant manager deliberately and expertly developed a pattern of mutual responsiveness with groups at headquarters. In terms of work structure, he was able to gain and maintain the autonomy that the plant needed in some areas and yet to accept certain unavoidable constraints without letting them demoralize Goshen's managers and workers.

Thus, although I have no proposition to offer, I can formulate contrasting external strategies for the work system whose structure and meaning makes it deviant in the larger organization. One strategy attempts to create a mutually responsive relationship with external parties or to co-opt them. The other strategy attempts to buffer the work system from external influences. With either strategy, the deviant work system must be effective in a business sense.

Topeka failed to gain the support of higher management not because of a lack of performance but because management was antagonized by the plant's bid for autonomy and its assertion of the moral superiority of the work system. Topeka's management may have chosen to confront more issues with corporate groups than were required to preserve the work system. Salem lost the confidence of higher management not because of a lack of sympathy for its philosophy but because of Salem's lack of performance. Salem's management may also have failed to confront a critical issue with division management, namely, forecasts of production.

Conclusion

My attempt to summarize the cases will of necessity be selective, and I will make the summary through a brief examination of leadership. The importance of leadership manifests itself in many, if not all, of the other work system factors isolated in the theoretical analysis. For example, the significant tasks of leadership include gauging and managing the alignment among task technology, human capacities, work structure, and meaning, as well as managing the development of each. Some contrasts and comparisons may be helpful in indicating the role of leadership.

In Topeka the original leaders effectively modeled the intended meaning of the work system, sensitively handled situations that became symbolic tests of the work system, buffered the organization from distracting friction with external parties, and yet decreased the organization's continued dependence on themselves. But after the more influential leaders departed, there was, nevertheless, a leadership vacuum. There was no vision of what the work system could become or how it could evolve; there was not the boldness to create ad hoc challenges to the system; and there was not an appreciation of the need to institutionalize some self-renewal mechanisms. The result was a work system that, although performing effectively, was stagnant in developmental terms.

In Salem, the original leaders had the imagination and boldness to plan an innovative work structure. Their charisma as well as their tactical plan for the formation of the organization created the high commitment necessary to launch the work structure. But their lapses offset their strengths. They repeatedly let faith in the motivational effects of an attractive work system divert them from a realistic assessment of the soundness of certain aspects of that work structure. This led them to commit themselves to unrealistic forecasts and to underestimate the technical resources required to start up and operate the plant, the need for more managerial direction initially until the self-direction capacities of workers had developed, and the need for punishment as an available response to individual abuses. At a later stage, recognizing that they had erred in the ways just indicated, they let still another belief prevent them from pursuing bold and imaginative *changes* in the work structure. This time the belief was in the fragility of commitment. Their fear was that an attempt to redefine the autonomy of teams would be perceived by members as an abandonment of the work system ideals and would decrease their commitment. The prophecy was potentially a self-fulfilling one. In any event, my discussions with members of the work force and my experiences with other high-commitment work systems led me to conclude that the Salem work system was robust, at least through January 1978. It took a new plant manager to initiate changes in the direction required.

In Goshen, effective leadership was concentrated in the plant manager and a few others for several years; it came gradually to be shared by some other members of his staff. The plant manager was highly respected by people at all levels of the Goshen organization, even by persons who disagreed with him on certain matters. He had been unswerving in his belief that such a system could be developed in the Goshen plant. This belief was expressed without jargon and without unwarranted faith in thé motivational power of an attractive work structure. His leadership style included what he described as agitating workers to work toward change and development.

In Derry, the plant manager had himself embodied the plant system—his confidence in people was balanced by a capacity to take decisive action when, in individual cases, that confidence was not confirmed. He had remained in a very high-profile role—a role that was feasible in a small plant. He had let his actions speak for themselves. At the same time he had developed participative mechanisms that kept him in intimate touch with the rank and file and that enabled the rank and file to influence decisions with plant-wide effect.

Identification of the role of managerial leadership in the development of the work systems studied here raised the question of other roles, such as the role of organizational consultation. Just as the management leadership role is discussed in this chapter largely in terms of influencing structure, meaning, and the other factors that comprise the present theory, so too can we conceive the consultants' roles. Theoretically, there is no necessary requirement for organizational consultation as such. Practically, in the cases studied here, the consultants, including myself, assisted in the following ways: (1) substantive contributions in planning the design and the subsequent developmental strategies and tactics, and (2) periodic assessments of progress toward organizational ideals. I assume that some personal qualities conditioned the consultants' influence and that there was some symbolic significance to their participation, but I am uncertain about the nature of these influences.

In these cases, my own involvement certainly had initially encouraged management to embrace work system ideas that were ambitious in terms of delegating supervisory functions to work teams. Later, in three or four cases, I often found myself in a more conservative posture than management, cautioning against what I regarded as premature or potentially unwise acts of delegation.

The general propositions presented earlier help explain the differences among the four plants studied and the changes that occurred within the plants. The case studies can only illustrate the propositions; they cannot prove them. When these theoretical propositions are applied to still other high-commitment work systems, we may gain or lose confidence in the propositions stated here. Undoubtedly the propositions will require modification.

Certain parts of the theory were most helpful in explaining the empirical findings. These parts, which also seem more significant than other aspects of the theory, especially warrant further testing. One significant set of propositions includes those based on the idea that the opposing evolutionary tendencies of task technology and human resources create a predictable pattern of dilemmas over the early years and that, although these dilemmas are present in the start-up of all work organizations, they are amplified in the case of high-commitment work systems and are the source of many of the structural weaknesses observed in our cases. We can then ask, Will the management of the "human resources surplus" during steady-state conditions prove to be a general problem and an important one when the development patterns of other high-commitment work systems are analyzed?

Another potentially important set of propositions includes those that relate member involvement to the incentive structure and the meanings attributed to the incentives. These propositions articulate what was asserted at the outset to be the sensitive interdependence between organization structure and human response in high-commitment work systems. In planning and managing these particular types of work systems, one must not only reach for the higher levels of involvement that we have called moral and spontaneous-expressive but one must also acknowledge that with respect to some organizational requirements, such as attendance and punctuality, member involvement can be expected to be calculative, even alienative. Therefore, not only is the central tendency of such systems higher in terms of our matrix of incentives and involvement, but the systems must orchestrate a broader range (the full range) of incentives and involvement. The propositions offer some insights into this phenomenon—for example, how meanings help members interpret elements of the incentive structure. Nevertheless, additional findings are needed to answer certain questions. How, for example, can punishment be employed without undermining the effects of those incentives that elicit spontaneous-expressive involvement?

Another question is, How do high-commitment work systems deal with diversity among employees in terms of their central tendency for involvement? Conventional organizations deal with this problem by the "lowest-common-denominator" approach, which means in effect that they simply ignore the potential that exists for higher levels of involvement. Thus ignored, any potential that may have existed tends to disappear. Self-fulfilling tendencies of what we call the "errors of pessimism" take care of that. At the same time, however, high-commitment work systems cannot simply ignore the diversity of involvement, as Salem helped demonstrate. The self-fulfilling tendency of "errors of optimism" is not strong enough to overcome the effects of diversity by itself.

A third set of potentially important propositions deals with a question seldom addressed in organization theory, namely, the rate at which the work system matures. These propositions help explain why Topeka matured rapidly and then failed to evolve further, why Salem never established a stable structure and set of meanings during the three-and-one-half-year period of observation, and why Goshen matured at an intermediate rate and also continued to evolve over the four years of the study. The propositions that explain these differences incorporate contextual factors like the uncertainty of the technology and the initial inventory of human skills, start-up strategies that affect personnel stability, and management systems that help detect and correct design errors. Even if the propositions presented are valid, the explanation of this important phenomenon remains partial and invites the attention of further researchers. I hope that invitation is accepted!

9

Organizational Proliferation and Density Dependent Selection

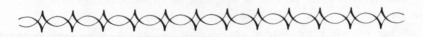

Jack W. Brittain
John H. Freeman

Organizational theory has long been preoccupied with the adaptation of single organizations to their environments. However, theorists have largely ignored the broader social system of which organizations are a part and the patterned ways in which populations of organizations expand in response to changes in that broader system. Previous work by Hannan and Freeman (1974;

Note: This research was supported by NSF grant SOC78-12315. The authors would like to acknowledge their intellectual debt to Michael Hannan, as well as thank him for his valuable comments on an earlier draft. They also wish to thank Howard Aldrich, Glenn Carroll, Robert Harris, and Douglas Wholey for their comments on earlier drafts, and Carolyn Brittain for providing research assistance.

291

1978a) suggested that selection among populations of organizations may play a major role in determining the composition of organizational communities, but did not deal specifically with the development of such organizational systems. This chapter attempts to extend their framework in two basic ways. First, we present some ways in which organizations with a given set of structural features become more numerous, a process we have labelled "proliferation." Second, we examine some of the consequences of this expansion of an organizational form for related organizational forms, how these consequences change over time, and what their impact is on the development of organizational systems.

The ecological perspective presented by Hannan and Freeman relies on Stinchcombe's (1965) notion of waves of organizing over time and space as a source of variability in organizational structure. Stinchcombe argues that the conditions prevailing at a given moment in time put their stamp on new organizations and that, due to the inertial properties of organizational structure, these organizational characteristics persist as long as the organizations survive. If this is true, then the variability that one observes at any moment in time reflects variations in founding conditions and—according to the selection logic of ecological theory—in the processes by which organizations with certain characteristics have survival advantages over organizations with other characteristics. According to this perspective, bureaucratic organizations exist, for instance, not simply because they operate in static environments (as much of modern contingency theory would suggest), but because such organizations were founded during a period in which bureaucratic features predominated and bureaucratic structure gave them survival advantages over other kinds of organizations.

While Stinchcombe emphasized the diversity produced in organizational populations by variations in the period of founding, Hannan and Freeman's (1978a) focus is on the selection mechanism as a process resulting in the dominance of certain organizational forms in particular environments. Selection in organizational ecology is based on differential advantage among organizational forms in competition for scarce resources. This perspective presumes high density populations, but such is clearly not always the case. One significant period when density is not a factor is the interval during which organizational populations are being created to take advantage of newly created resources, that is, when new organizational forms and populations are being created. Mammoth construction projects like the Alaskan oil pipeline and the development of entire cities in the Middle East have provided the resource base for just this kind of proliferation. In both instances a large number of organizations were founded in a short time, with success for some kinds of organizations more a function of timely arrival than their ability to outcompete other forms. In this chapter we reconsider the process whereby organizations are founded and forms proliferate, with an emphasis on the causes and consequences of temporal variations in population density.

It seems to us that it would be profitable to conceptualize this phenomenon at three levels of analysis: industry, organization, and individual. (In this chapter we consider each of these separately, but note that the same empirical events occur regardless of the level at which attention is momentarily focused.) We define "industry" as a set of organizations that may be divided into populations characterized by different organizational forms but are interrelated on the basis of characteristic resources and basic usage technologies. In this sense we may speak of a steel industry or an education industry, each of which is distinguishable from other industries in terms of the "resource space" it occupies. The industry designation implies neither a multiplicity of form nor a particularly significant interaction among forms, except as the interdependence among forms is related to the defining resources. Our interest here is in the relative availability of various resources, such as money, market segments, people, energy, physical space, and physical substances, and the various combinations in which they are used.

The resource space that defines an industry may include a variety of resource combinations, each with a specific pattern of temporal availability, that could potentially support an organizational population. For many kinds of industries, including profit- and service-oriented ones, the partitioning of the resource space centers on a distinction between price-sensitive and quality-conscious market segments. Other possible bases for dividing the resource space include hours of operation, convenience of location, servicing agreements, and specialization of function. Any particular combination, or set of combinations, of resource utilization that distinguishes one organizational population from another is what we will call a "niche." An industry, then, may include a number of distinct niches, filled to varying degrees by specific organizational populations. Each niche is a resource base that supports a population with a given form, but the resources involved are not necessarily exclusive to any single niche; niches may overlap on various resource dimensions. As one could infer from our definition of industries as relatively distinct resource spaces, the overlap between organizational populations within an industry is much greater than the overlap of organizational populations across industries.

We use the terms *industry, resource space,* and *niche* to underscore the evolutionary importance of technologies in organizational population dynamics. The advantages accruing to organizational populations from technical changes, process innovations, and organization innovations derive from changes in the resource base on which the population depends. Contingency and strategic choice models treat such dislocations in the resource base as atypical, but we argue that such modification is the rule rather than the exception in many organizational populations (for a similar view, see Pfeffer and Salancik, 1978). In their competitive and cooperative interrelationships, human organizations generate new technologies with attendant new resources. Furthermore, they try to organize stability in the supply of resources that might otherwise be available only haphazardly, thus making previously impractical technical innovations feasible.

At the organizational level of analysis, populations of organizations appear, flourish, and disappear during the normal course of population dynamics. The time frame in which this happens may be extremely protracted in some instances, but on the whole it happens much more quickly than is generally assumed. In the present instance, we are mainly concerned with the manner in which organizational forms first appear and become common. We wish to show that the prior history of organizational growth and development can be expected to have effects on the rate of organizational founding as individuals leave one organization to found another.

Finally, we can consider the process of development and

proliferation as it is manifested at the individual level. Many of the differences among forms involve demographic differences in the participants that affect the likelihood of entrepreneurial activities in the industry. They also affect the ease or difficulty with which people move from one organization to another and, hence, the ease with which new organizations may be founded.

In each of the three sections that follow, we have mainly drawn our examples from the semiconductor industry (although we have used other types of examples where they seemed appropriate). "Semiconductor" refers to the electrical properties of the materials (primarily germanium and silicon) used in the production of diodes, transistors, and integrated circuits, the major components in solid-state electronics. We find the industry producing these devices interesting because it is relatively new, because it has grown rapidly through a series of technical revolutions, each of which had recognizable consequences for the organizations in question, and because it has experienced continuous and dramatic increases in production and sales. Given our interest in the development of organizational systems and the proliferation of organizational forms, these characteristics of the industry offer several distinct advantages. First, the rate of organizational founding appears to be inversely related to the age of the industry and level of capital required for entry and directly related to the industry's growth rate; the semiconductor industry—especially during the 1960s—offers provocative examples in each of these respects. Second, since the industry's growth is based on a whole series of technical innovations, the ecological processes of founding and failure have been greatly accelerated. Third, the examination of profit-making organizations is in general advantageous because their failures tend to be much more easily discerned than are those of non-profit organizations, which may experience long periods of latency.

The Development of Industries

Industries develop, opening new niches, when *technologies* change to permit novel ways of combining resources either in the product or service produced or in the method of its production. Besides product and process innovations, such technical innovations may include changes in transportation systems or changes in the supply of critical resources. Such technical innovations may occur regularly, sporadically, or only once, and each of these patterns of change have different implications for organizational populations. When they occur often, a niche may exist where organizations compete to realize the "first-mover" advantages that result in excess initial profits. Such excess "profits" are not confined to business firms. For example, the charitable fund-raising organizations that staged the first "walkathons" and "bikeathons" were able to exploit public enthusiasm for the events that was later diluted as such events came into common use. Depending on the pattern of innovation, a separate niche may exist that includes organizations that compete through production efficiences in an attempt to lower per-unit costs. Later we will argue that these niches presume different patterns of resource availability over time with varying consequences for different organizational forms.

In addition to purely technical innovations, changes in the social system can affect both the relative availability of resources and the level of competition among organizational forms. Unexploited resource spaces sometimes appear when changes in the broader social system encourage the use of technologies already available. This change may occur in the sense that organizational populations in different industries change in such a way that they provide a market for products not previously marketable, or because normative constraints on the application of existing technologies are lifted. Collins (1979) has studied the cycles of expansion and contraction in European higher education, and he contends that such cycles are primarily the consequence of attempts to build political cultures conducive to the development of state power. Essentially, he refers to a process by which one industry (education) expands and contracts in response to parallel processes in another population (government agencies and bureaus). Aldrich (1979) examines both technological and social system effects on rates of organizational proliferation, pointing out that political revolutions and technological innovations are both major sources of waves of organization-founding.

Along the same lines, shifts in the human population may lead to combinations of resources which were previously not available, creating the potential for new industries, or new niches within existing industries. The migration from east to west in the United States in the middle of the nineteenth century created resource combinations not previously available, providing a basis, for instance, for the establishment of transcontinental rail service. Likewise, the current explosion in the number of Mexican restaurants in the United States obviously has something to do with the in-migration of Mexicans and the diffusion of their cuisine into the broader cultural system.

Finally, characteristics of organizations themselves may contribute to the creation of new technologies and new modes of organizing. Some types of organizations are more conducive to originating innovations which lead to the development of entirely new industries while other types are more successful at implementing innovations (Aldrich, 1979). Some organizations self-destruct in ways which open the door to new organizational forms based on new technologies. And often, the development of one industry, with its attendant pattern of niches and organizational forms, generates others that use different technologies to occupy distinctly different places in the flow of resources through the broader social system. It is on this basis that the military industry with its populations of armies, navies, and the like generates an arms industry comprised of private firms, government laboratories and armories, and so forth.

Development of the Semiconductor Industry

The first point contact transistor was constructed at Bell Laboratories in 1947. This feat was such an important technical accomplishment that it resulted in a 1956 Nobel Prize for the three inventor-scientists involved in the development of the device— Walter Brattain, John Bardeen, and William Shockley. While this particular event was critical in the sense that it uncovered the basic principles underlying the functioning of all semiconductors, it did not have immediate commercial significance. After the basic research on the transistor was completed in 1948, the project was turned over to a team at Western Electric, the manufacturing division of American Telephone and Telegraph (A.T. & T.), for further development (Weiner, 1973).

The basic innovations that led to the first commerical production of the transistor were developed at Western Electric in 1950 and 1951. This involved developing a process technology for growing germanium crystals with the proper balance of purities and impurities and perfecting the junction transistor, which had the durability and consistency that made the commercial use of the transistor feasible. While these developments were taking place, A.T. & T. was involved in an antitrust suit that was instituted by the federal government in 1949 and that sought to force A.T. & T. to sell Western Electric. This case was settled in 1956 when A.T. & T. made several concessions—including agreeing to stay out of the commercial semiconductor market—in exchange for retaining Western Electric. Tilton (1971) speculates that this litigation was a major reason why Western Electric chose to tread lightly in the electronics industry.

Western Electric began licensing its transistor technology in 1951, going so far as to bring all the licensees together at one time to transmit details of the production process. Among the original producers were such industrial giants as RCA, General Electric, Raytheon, Motorola, CBS, and Sylvania, as well as several small, virtually unknown firms such as Texas Instruments and Transitron. By 1954 there were eighteen firms manufacturing transistors in the United States (Tilton, 1971, pp. 52–53).

The original demand for semiconductors was quite limited. The major difficulty was price: the average price for receiving tubes at that time was about $.70 (Electronic Industries Association, 1976, p. 86), while the price of germanium transistors ranged from $10 to $16 (McDonald, 1961). The one advantage semiconductors had over tubes at this time was size, and as a result they were only widely used in hearing aids. In an effort to create a market for its rapidly expanding productive capacity, Texas Instruments invested $2 million in a joint venture with an independent radio manufacturer to develop a portable radio that could use the germanium transistor. This development subsequently defined the major consumer market for discrete semiconductor components well into the sixties.

Although several firms in the industry were actively trying to develop applications for the transistor, they were hindered by germanium's heat intolerance. This constraint was particularly vexing since the military and the arms industry—large potential users of semiconductors even if their price relative to tubes remained high—needed devices that could tolerate extreme heat. Though engineers at all the major manufacturers had experimented with silicon (which can tolerate higher temperatures than germanium) transistors, problems in crystal fabrication continued to thwart further development. In 1954, however, Texas Instruments began the first commercial production of silicon transistors, getting a significant jump on all the other transistor manufacturers; no major competitors began producing silicon transistors until 1958. From 1950 to 1960, Texas Instruments' total sales expanded from $7.6 million to $232.7 million for an average yearly growth rate of 40 percent, with earnings rising from $348,000 to $15.5 million (McDonald, 1961). Since Texas Instruments is a fairly diversified business, semiconductors were not solely responsible for this expansion; nevertheless, the company's involvement in electronic components went from zero to approximately 50 percent in this period, and its other product lines—most notably military electronics and silicon production—benefited a great deal from the "spillover" (Mansfield, 1968) produced by its involvement in semiconductors.

Another major breakthrough in product and process occurred in 1961, when Texas Instruments and Fairchild Semiconductor jointly announced production of the integrated circuit. The government had supported research at Westinghouse and RCA for several years in an effort to develop a semiconductor chip that included all the components of a standard circuit. The major obstacle to production was the absence of a process technology for fabricating the chips. In 1960, however, Fairchild announced the development of the planar process, which allowed for the design of multi layer chips. Because Texas Instruments held crucial patents on the integrated circuit, a cross-licensing arrangement was worked out so that both firms could enter the market. The development of the integrated circuit was pivotal for the industry because it defined the production processes fundamental to the most advanced current devices and because it established the direction of the industry, which was to put the greatest number of circuits possible on each chip.

Figure 1 shows how important the integrated circuit has been in the development of the industry. The total dollar value represented by integrated circuits in Figure 1 is even more impressive when one considers the fact that the average selling price for some of the devices dropped by as much as 90 percent over the product life cycle.

Another fundamental design breakthrough was made in 1971 when Intel started selling the microprocessor. Intel had previously used financial muscle to edge out several smaller competitors

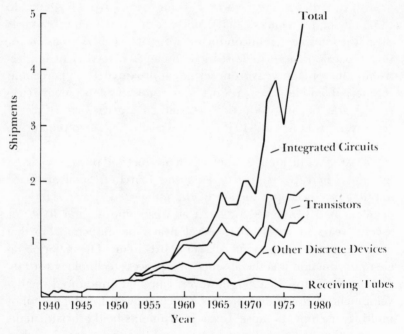

Sources: Webbink, 1977, pp. 11 and 169; Semiconductor Industry Association, 1979.

Figure 1. Value of Shipments of Electronic Components, 1939–1978 (in billions of dollars)

in the race for dominance in large-scale integrated (LSI) circuits. According to Zaks (1977), the first microprocessor was actually designed under contract as the main component in a desk calculator produced by a Japanese manufacturer, and its success as a component was largely unexpected by Intel's management. Prior to the development of the microprocessor, the industry was oriented toward designing specific circuitry for each application, and industry leaders such as Texas Instruments were worried about how to efficiently produce small batches of specialized integrated circuits. The microprocessor had the advantage of applicability to a wide range of uses at a much lower cost than specially designed circuits. With its success in memory chips and microprocessors, Intel grew from a firm with 42 employees and $2,672 in sales in 1968 to a firm with 1,000 employees and sales of $23.4 million in 1972. From 1972 to 1973, it expanded further to 2,550 employees and sales of $60 million (Bylinsky, 1973).

At the present time, several companies are working on the very large-scale integrated (VLSI) circuit, which incorporates more than 100,000 functions on a single chip. Unlike previous advances in chip densities, the use of VLSIs is expected to be quite limited— principally to computer memories—simply because the number of functions it incorporates falls beyond the range of typical usage. Furthermore, some industry experts argue that chip technology is rapidly approaching the point where concerns about servicing, maintenance, and design complexity are becoming more important than increased chip density (Moore, 1979). Whether this is in fact true remains to be seen: after all, in 1970 people in the industry made the same claim about LSI technology, which is now taken for granted.

It is important to emphasize that while the sequence of innovations from discrete semiconductors through VLSI has defined the direction of product development in the industry, these are by no means the only innovations that have occurred. The numerous process developments that have been associated with each product innovation have been of equal importance in fueling the growth of the industry. Improvements in process technologies have in fact been a major source of the continuous downward adjustment of prices that characterizes the industry. In addition, improvements in equipment and raw materials have contributed to lowered costs, which have produced a further lowering of prices.

The principal consequence of decreasing prices has been a rapid expansion in applications of the most current technologies. The tremendous expansion of consumer electronics in the past few years was largely the result of just such phenomena. The decreasing price of electronic components has allowed electronic devices to virtually eliminate the mechanical devices that have traditionally dominated such instruments as watches and calculators. In addition, the development of computer technology and of microelectronics has been inexorably linked, with computer manufacturers currently purchasing the major share of the most advanced devices.

Within the framework of our definition of industry, then, the semiconductor industry consists of the organizational populations engaged in the manufacture of various electronic components—for example, transistors, diodes, rectifiers, integrated circuits, and microprocessors—that require the same basic raw materials, production processes, and design technology. Many of the personnel that work in the industry are also highly interchangeable in terms of their basic skill contributions. Also, all the organizations that are involved in the industry produce for some common customer pool that, although segmented in terms of usage, could potentially substitute one firm's output for another's.

Our description up to this point has treated each innovation as an isolated event, but our real concern is with the temporal pattern on innovation and technical discovery and how this pattern affects the proliferation and succession of organizational forms. A wide variety of firms are engaged in semiconductor production. There are large, diversified firms such as RCA and Motorola; there are extremely competitive but not especially innovative firms such as National Semiconductor; there are firms that specialize in single product groups (for example, Signetics and American Microsystems); and there are a variety of small firms, as well as various "captive" producers—for example, the semiconductor operations at IBM and Western Electric. The success of these firms has varied enormously across product groups and over time, with no one type of firm dominating the entire industry. For instance, in 1953, when tubes still dominated, the leading producers of electronic components were RCA, Sylvania, General Electric, Raytheon, and Westinghouse (Mackintosh, 1978). By 1960, when discrete semiconductors were becoming the dominant factors in components, two newcomers, Texas Instruments and Transitron, were the market leaders, followed by Philco, General Electric, and RCA (Mackintosh, 1978). The industry had gone through another change in leadership by 1965, with Texas Instruments still topping the industry in sales but now followed by Motorola, Fairchild Semiconductor, General Instrument, and General Electric (Mackintosh, 1978). By the time that the industry had completed its transition to the integrated circuit in the mid seventies, RCA was the only one of the original ten major tube manufacturers still producing semiconductor devices. In 1975 the dominant producers of integrated circuits were Texas Instruments, Fairchild Semiconductor, National Semiconductor, Intel, and Motorola.

This variation in success over time is largely a function of the rapid rate of technical innovation in the industry and the performance pressures it creates for different organizational populations. In addition, the general munificence of the environment in which the industry operates has contributed to the diversity of organizational forms observed. The almost continuous stream of product and process innovations in semiconductors has resulted in tremendous improvements in quality and large decreases in price for standard semiconductor devices, and both of these factors have contributed to the exponential growth in semiconductor sales. Performance improvements have generally preceded price decreases in major product innovations, largely because the military market, space program, and to some extent the computer industry have been extremely quality conscious in their buying. This has in turn fueled the willingness of firms to engage in speculative development. The rapid rate at which prices for new devices have fallen subsequent to their introduction reflects the significant learning economies that characterize the industry (Webbink, 1977), as well as its relatively competitive nature. Such rapid price declines have encouraged further application of microelectronic technology in industrial and consumer devices, providing the vigorously expanding demand that has maintained the industry's growth.

This combination of continued growth and simultaneous variation in success may seem inconsistent to some readers. The general assumption is that munificent environments do not impose constraints on organizational success and that such environments are not competitive. But such may not be the case if one adopts a population perspective. The conditions that create environmental richness may very well limit the viability of some populations, while allowing other populations to expand seemingly without limit. The munificence created by decreasing prices and ongoing innovation in semiconductors is extremely rewarding for those organizations that are heavily involved in product and process development, but many other organizational types may find the scale required to use plentiful resources beyond them. In addition, there is a great deal of uncertainty in the expected outcomes of investment decisions under such rapidly changing conditions. While the payoffs for some innovations are very high, others may become obsolete before they get into production or may never achieve the production economies necessary to compete with less sophisticated devices.

One of the major consequences of the rapidly evolving technology in semiconductor electronics has been the development of "first-mover" advantages. These arise for several reasons. First, the version of a product that is introduced earliest and adopted by consuming organizations becomes the technical and design standard to which all subsequent variations must adapt. This forces firms with different versions of the same product to engage in costly redesign work to make their devices compatible with the first entrant. Since this redesign work consumes time, the initial entrant can develop significant pricing advantages from acquired production experience, that is, from the "learning curve." The learning economies that characterize semiconductor production have their root in the basically empirical approach taken in the implementation of process technologies. Many of the technical refinements that increase the yields of good devices are not made prior to introduction mainly because of the pressures for early entry but also because they require cumulative experience (for example, it takes time to determine the exact processing temperature for achieving optimal performance characteristics). The final component of the first mover advantage is the economic profits that a firm can exploit while other organizations are redesigning and attempting to overtake the innovator on the experience curve. These monopoly profits can be used to increase capacity, a step that gives the first mover a greater opportunity to dominate the market as it develops.

In many cases, the crucial element in gaining a first-mover advantage is the development of the materials technology. The success Texas Instruments derived from being first with the silicon transistor was based on the development of a method for producing silicon crystals. The promise of silicon as a potential material was well known throughout the industry (McDonald, 1961; Braun and MacDonald, 1978). Similarly, the basic patent covering the integrated circuit was filed in 1959 by Texas Instruments, but the device did not become commercially feasible until the process technology was developed at Fairchild Semiconductor in 1960.

Clearly, not every firm in semiconductors is a major innovator, but every such firm does have to deal with technical change as a fact of business in the industry. Thus far we have paid no attention to the fluctuations in demand for devices over time. If demand for a new product is very high from the time of its introduction, then it is quite likely that the organization making the introduction will not be able to meet initial demand. Intel's success in large-scale memory products was in part due to the failure of the first entrant, Advanced Memory Systems, as a mass-producer. A second characteristic of the demand situation that is relevant to the survival of organizational forms is the historic susceptibility of semiconductors to recessions. The significant declines in sales in 1960–1961, 1967–1968, 1970–1971, and 1974–1975 (see Figure 1) were exacerbated by cost cutting attempts designed to maintain market share. As we can see in Figure 2, these years produced significant numbers of failures in the industry, while the years in between the downturns were characterized by high founding rates. In many cases, those factors that contribute to innovative success may also result in an inability to withstand fluctuations in demand. For example, devoting a high proportion of earnings to research and development activities, new production capacity, and technical talent may make a firm a temporary industry leader, but it is the firm's ability to weather hard times that determines if it will remain

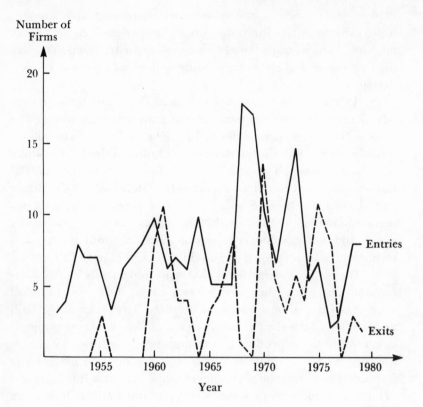

Sources: Hoefler, 1968, 1976; Tilton, 1971; Braun and MacDonald, 1978.

**Figure 2. Number of Producers Entering and Number
Failed or Acquired**

in such a position very long. This ability to withstand resource constriction is, in fact, a quite general requirement for survival in ecological processes.

So far we have identified four consequences of the rapid rate of technical change in semiconductors, all of which relate to the general competitive situation in the industry. First-mover advantages go to those firms that successfully introduce new products or new processes that increase the quality or decrease the price of existing products. The fact that many of the critical innovations leading to major successes have involved processes rather than product conceptualizations means that most individuals in the industry have been aware of what needed to be accomplished at any point in time and that any of a number of research teams could have come up with a crucial discovery. In order for firms not involved in innovations to enter new markets, it is necessary that they have a production capability that allows them to respond quickly to changes. This ability to change may involve "slack resources" (Cyert and March, 1963), or it may involve a gradual substitution of one product for another as demand develops over time. Finally, because innovation is ongoing and demand is constantly fluctuating, continued success in the industry demands an ability to survive bad times and remain aggressively competitive with regard to anticipatory price cutting on long-term contracts and cutting costs with each increment of increased production.

The preceding paragraphs should give some indication that success in semiconductor manufacturing requires much more than simply having the newest gadget. Texas Instruments, Fairchild Semiconductor, and Intel all entered the components industry as small, unknown firms, and each has had tremendous success based on a major innovation. But they are the exceptions: the average life-span of a small firm in the industry during the 1960s was approximately two years (Tilton, 1971), and it would be surprising to find that it is substantially longer now.

In his case analysis of diffusion in the electronics industry, Tilton (1971) argued that small, entrepreneurial firms have been central to the development of the industry and its rapid innovation rate. During the early years of the industry, production was not dominated by the large manufacturers of receiving tubes, which is what one might suspect given the tube companies' central position in the electronics industry of the time. These companies had a vested interest in the existing technology and did not move quickly into semiconductor production. In ecological terms, their adaptability was limited by the structural inertia (Hannan and Freeman, 1978a) created by their commitments to existing technology. If we refer back to Figure 1, it is obvious that tube sales were far higher than semiconductor sales until about 1958. Clearly, the posture adopted by the tube firms was not, from a short-run revenue maximization viewpoint, such a bad strategy. However, once sales in semiconductors began to expand very rapidly, those firms that had been more heavily involved in semiconductor manufacturing were better equipped to take advantage of the boom.

A very similar pattern occurred in integrated circuits with the development of the metal-oxide semiconductor (MOS). Texas Instruments and Fairchild dominated the development of integrated circuits at the time that the MOS technology was introduced. They apparently did not think that this slower-speed but lower-cost technology was particularly appealing. Unfortunately for them, such was not the case, and their late entry gave several small firms a big jump in process technology and productive capacity.

A major advantage that new, small-scale innovators have over larger firms is that they do not have to invest heavily in research and development. Because innovation in production requires a certain level of sophistication in electronics, it is virtually impossible to enter the industry without prior experience. Not coincidentally, the most useful kind of experience is in developmental engineering. In California's Santa Clara Valley (also known as "Silicon Valley"), the leading development group during the sixties and early seventies was at Fairchild Semiconductor. From 1960 to 1978, twenty-three of the sixty-four newly founded semiconductor manufacturing firms were direct offshoots of Fairchild; these included National Semiconductor, Rheem Semiconductor, and Intel. Each of these in turn fostered their own group of progeny. We will consider the dynamics of such proliferation and the niche structure of industries in the following section.

The Proliferation of Organizations

As industrial technologies develop, niches open and close, thus creating turmoil in organizational populations. Organizations enter the industry with new departments and divisions. Entrepreneurs create new firms and attempt to develop them in ways that will provide competitive advantages. Success breeds imitation, and spectacular success is frequently followed by equally spectacular failure. In addition to bankruptcy, new organizations "fail" in the sense that they are often acquired by larger organizations seeking to take over what has become a mode of organizing with demonstrated potential for success.

Although this chapter focuses on the semiconductor industry, which is composed of profit-making firms, we should be clear that success calls forth imitation in other kinds of organizations as well. A new kind of army unit designed to exploit a new technology generates imitations just as profit-making firms do. The same can be said for voluntary associations.

The following discussion blends three lines of reasoning. First, we review the discussion by Hannan and Freeman (1978a) of specialism and generalism to show how patterns of environmental variation may be expected to result in differences in viability for various organizational forms. Second, we analyze the shifting advantages and disadvantages accruing to organizations as new niches open and a sparse level of population is replaced by a more intensive level of population, with a resulting increase in competition. Finally, we consider the economic advantages that various organizational forms derive from dynamic proliferation processes. One consequence of rapid technological change is that small numbers bargaining becomes inescapable. This tends to create the first-mover advantages that open the door to specialist firms, as well as an inevitable conflict between the individual self-interest of potential entrepreneurs and the interests of the organizations in which they participate. Put simply, when organizations are structured so as to encourage innovation, the measures that reduce opportunism are more difficult to apply. Individuals then face a choice between opportunism within the organization, which results in an excise tax on innovation, and opportunism in the broader industry, which is called entrepreneurship.

Specialism and Generalism

Hannan and Freeman (1978a) analyzed organizational population ecology in terms of three kinds of environmental variables. The first of these is *uncertainty*. If we conceptualize environments as shifting among a set of resource states, then the probability of being in any one of these resource states at a given moment in time can be used to define uncertainty. If the probability of being in any particular resource state is low, we conclude that uncertainty is high. Alternatively, the degree of certainty in any particular resource environment may be expressed as the degree of serial correlation between successive periods of resource availability. In general, more specialized organizational forms should do better when uncertainty is low.

A second variable is the convexity/concavity of environmental variations, or the *compatibility of environmental states*. Given that environments shift among resource states, the differences among these states may be more or less hospitable to any given organizational form. For example, just as climatic fluctuations may be severe or temperate through the seasons, so boom and bust periods in the business cycle may be more or less severe in different industries. When these periods or states are mutually incompatible, so that it is difficult to devise a mode of organizing that does well in all states, the situation is defined as being characterized by a "concave fitness set." When the states are compatible, so that an organization can survive in all of them, the fitness set is described as "convex" (Levins, 1968).

Finally, the environment's *grain* is defined as the frequency of changes among states over time. A fine-grained environment is one in which changes are fairly common. The reverse is a coarse-grained environment. Grain is especially important when the issue is whether organizations can persist by riding out unfavorable periods.

Specialist organizations are those that concentrate their capacities in ways that exploit only a narrow range of the available resources. In terms of product markets, such firms concentrate on a particular price—quality range—Rolls-Royce is an obvious example. An alternative, or generalist, approach, is to try to offer something for everyone—General Motors is a good example of this. We do not mean to imply, however, that size is necessarily correlated with generalism. A "mom and pop" diner is a generalist organization from this point of view, whereas a Boston lobster house, seating fifteen hundred people, is a large specialist.

Hannan and Freeman argued that specialist organizations are likely to appear whenever and wherever uncertainty is low. They also argued that specialists will prevail where uncertainty is high and is found with concave fitness sets in fine-grained environments. These environments vary among such different states that it is difficult to devise an organization that will do well in each of them. At the same time, changes are so frequent that it is possible to do very well when conditions are right, while muddling through when they are not. In all other conditions generalists are expected to be the most prevalent form.

The major issue of concern in past ecological formulations has been whether specialists will outcompete generalists or vice versa. Given any persistent pattern of environmental variation, however, we can expect to see changing population distributions as the temporary advantages of one form wane and the population shrinks because of the appearance of organizations with competitive characteristics that have long-run advantages.

Density Dependence

One of the basic conceptions that population biologists use to model growth of populations in finite environments is the Verhulst-Pearl logistic growth equation:

$$\frac{dX}{dt} = rX\left(\frac{K - X}{K}\right)$$

In this equation the rate of change of a population with size X is a function of some rate of natural increase r, and an upper limit, or carrying capacity, K. Ecologists sometimes describe alternative modes of selection—or strategies for survival—in terms of the parameters of this equation: r and K (MacArthur and Wilson, 1967).

Pure r-strategists, on the one hand, are organizations that move quickly to exploit resources as they first become available. Their structure makes them relatively inexpensive to set up; that is, they concentrate on activities that require low levels of capital investment and simple structures. They are called r-strategists because they trade on speed of expansion. Their success depends heavily on first-mover advantages, which makes them high-risk and high payoff organizations that gain maximally from temporarily rich environments. Such organizations persist only where the pattern of resource availability is highly uncertain and resources are dispersed over time or space (Pianka, 1970, 1978). Where critical resources are available with any certainty, exploitive strategies will usually fail when faced with organizations emphasizing competitive efficiency. Thus, industries that are unchanging should not have r-strategists.

K-strategists, on the other hand, are organizations that are structured to compete successfully in densely settled environments. They may be either specialized or generalized in the variety of resources and resource levels that they can take advantage of. K-strategist organizations generally expand more slowly into new resource spaces than r-strategists because the structures generating competitive efficiency frequently preclude the rapid adjustments necessary to capture first-mover advantages. Competition on the basis of efficiency generally involves higher levels of investment in plant and equipment and more elaborate organizational structures. Given a resource space generated by some technical innovation (for example, a new product), we can expect K-strategists to outcompete r-strategists after some time if population density reaches a point near the environment's carrying capacity for the total population of organizations. When r-strategists enter an industry, seeking to exploit some open resource space, they may expand so quickly that they attract counteradaptations. K-strategists pursuing these counterstrategies often force r-strategists out of the resource space. If they are to continue existing in such a situation, r-strategists must modify their structures to become K-strategists, which is highly unlikely given any degree of structural inertia (Hannan and Freeman, 1978a).

Given that r- and K-strategies exhibit different levels of fitness with respect to increased population density and the corresponding increased competitiveness, then selection at any point in time is *density-dependent*. As organizational populations proliferate in a newly opened resource space and total population begins to approach the environment's carrying capacity (K), then we can expect to see continued success in survival and proliferation for K-strategists at the expense of r-strategists that may have moved into the resource space early and initially appeared dominant.

Whether K-strategists dominate an entire industry, however, depends on the dynamics of resource availability across potential niches. It is not correct to argue that r-strategists are competitively inferior. Rather, they compete by being able to exploit available resources before density makes their survival problematic. This means that r-strategists must actively pursue first-mover advantages. In industries with rapidly changing products (the high fashion segment of the apparel industry), developing technologies, or highly variable market munificence (egg producers), a pattern of resource availability may exist within the resource space that inhibits the development of high population density, thereby allowing r-strategists to survive. Furthermore, the resource pattern over time may in fact be structured such that r-strategists have particular survival advantages within their niche, a point we will develop in greater detail in a subsequent section.

Economics of Organizing

A number of concepts commonly used by economists have figured prominently in this discussion. Students of industrial organization have devoted considerable attention to such issues as the conditions under which firms practice vertical integration, developing productive capacity in the supply of raw materials or in organizing channels of product distribution. These economists seem preoccupied with issues of relative firm size and industrial concentration. One of the subissues of theoretical interest as well as of policy relevance is whether large firms spend more on research and development than small firms do, and whether oligopolists spend more than firms in more competitive markets. Economists have also discussed the conditions under which first-mover advantages characterize market structure.

The work that is particularly relevant to our present concern is Williamson's (1975) analysis of the economic logic of organizing. He is primarily interested in the issue of whether combinations of productive activities are carried out within the boundaries of single firms and coordinated through authority structures, or whether they are carried out by formally autonomous firms and coordinated through market mechanisms. He argues that this question is not answerable in terms of technology and the economies of scale that it generates. Various specialized parts of the production process are usually divisible in such a way that various forms of contracting could be used to combine them. When they are not so divided, it is because the transaction costs imposed by imperfectly operating markets are greater than the transaction costs imposed by the organizational hierarchy.

This is to say that organizations can, under some circumstances, combine those specialties more cheaply than markets can. In particular, this is the case when conditions of "information impactedness" and small numbers bargaining obtain. The former occurs when exchange parties are not equally well informed about the consequences to be expected from a particular transaction. Such a condition exists when a used car dealer tells a potential customer that the vehicle recently brought to his lot by an unsuccessful stock car driver was in fact the proud possession of a matronly schoolteacher. Information impactedness also occurs when both parties together have inadequate information with which to forecast the ultimate costs and benefits of the transaction. Information impactedness is particularly important when the number of participants in a market is so small that some of them can in fact have a recognizable influence on prices. If one assumes that these participants will act opportunistically, taking advantage of the aforementioned structural characteristics (by lying, for instance), market mechanisms can be expected to be rather costly. Williamson argues that organizations can better control this opportunistic behavior than can markets, and can therefore more reliably and cheaply provide themselves with the products and services they would otherwise obtain through contracting in the market.

It seems obvious that business firms, as well as other kinds of organizations, may choose to be involved in activities that offer various mixes of small-numbers and large-numbers bargaining situations. Productive capacity relative to market size is not the only desideratum of bargaining combinations. A single resource environment (many resource environments can only be artificially viewed as "markets") may limit the number of organizations that become parties to a transaction. Social institutions, for example, may make participation by many possible suppliers of a service illegitimate by imposing licensing requirements. The rate of technological change may impose similar constraints. A rapidly changing product technology may offer continuously appearing advantages of short duration to organizations prepared to move quickly.

Williamson does not ignore the role of technological advances, but he does treat "science-based" industries as "possible" exceptions to his assertion that "firms and markets coexist in symbiotic equilibrium" (1975, p. 176). He sees such industries as exceptional to the extent that exogenous technological change significantly determines market structure. Continuous innovation, from this viewpoint, creates markets that exist independently of transactional economies, allowing firms to engage in economically exploitative activities. It seems likely that this kind of environmental change is continuously distributed across industries; it is certainly not clear that it is confined to "science-based" productive technologies. For example, constantly changing fashion patterns in the apparel industry allow firms to reap monopoly profits from highly popular designs in much the same way that pharmaceutical houses benefit from major drug discoveries.

Williamson's analysis effectively deals with the advantages accruing to individual organizations from vertical integration, but we find this framework deficient for *our* purposes in at least one respect. This deficiency lies in Williamson's treatment of the environment—particularly those resource segments known as markets—as static. Certainly, for Williamson's purposes it is reasonable to consider the development of organizational hierarchies in the context of unchanging resource environments, but it is just such an approach that creates difficulties with the so-called science-based industries. The supposed benefits of integration depend on implicit assumptions of stability in demand and technology; but if stability varies widely across industries, as we contend, then so must the benefits of organizational expansion into vertically related markets. The issue of interest from an ecological viewpoint is whether integration provides any survival advantages given a pattern of environmental change; we expect that in some cases integration may actually lower fitness.

We have argued that conditions of relative certainty will favor populations of specialist forms that seek to dominate a relatively narrow niche (see Hannan and Freeman, 1978a, for a discussion of niche breadth). We expect organizational subunits to have a specialized function relative to the market and expect that the transactional benefits accruing to an organization from having such a subunit will vary with the dynamics of the resource environment.

In other words, from an ecological position, we would expect that success in the kind of integration that Williamson discusses is subject to selection pressures. Certainly, if one observes only profit-making organizations, then one would expect to find that the basis of selection will lean heavily toward transactional benefits. But the underlying issue is how an organizational population may most effectively gather the resources that will ensure its viability. The more general nature of the ecological perspective, then, allows us to deal with organizations as a broad class of social entities. However, we would agree with Williamson that profits and the contribution to profits are at least to some degree more observable than "resources." Also, we do not mean to imply that we think Williamson's analysis is erroneous; we simply think that the treatment he offers is too narrow.

Focusing on economic organizations, we expect that where factor markets are stable, or change with relative certainty, the selection criterion that determines the success of captive producers is their efficiency relative to the market. This is the case that Williamson has dealt with in such detail, and we have little new to say about it. In this case, efficiencies may derive from the consumer's (parent firm's) ability to plan in advance on a supply and to gear production to its own products with less uncertainty. Similarly, product design can be coordinated with developing technologies, creating usage efficiencies that are not available from standard inputs. As we have already pointed out, the success of vertical integration in uncertain environments is much more problematic than in certain ones, depending in large part on the frequency of changes.

One consequence of a high level of coordination is that captive producers must modify their technical choices to reflect the preferences of the parent firm. Instead of pursuing technical leads where they appear to offer the most potential, they follow those leads that appear most in accord with the parent firm's plans. Unless the parent firm derives significant "spillover" in its main products from innovation, the rapid movement into recently opened or recognized resource spaces that r-strategies presume is generally precluded. Vertical integration thus makes it unlikely that captive producers will be technological leaders. As a result, the parent firm often commits itself to less than state-of-the-art components but may realize an overall benefit from using older designs more efficiently.

Captive production and the existence of markets are significant factors in the proliferation of organizational forms. The degree to which consumption is captive determines what kinds of organizations we can expect to find in an industry and is a major influence on the success of autonomous forms. By casting the economics of integration in ecological terms, we can consider issues of integration and viability at the same time.

Ecological Dynamics, Market Structure, and Organization

In the preceding sections, we have introduced and reviewed a number of conceptual schemes but have made no effort to integrate them. Up to this point we have discussed factors contributing to innovation in organizational systems, population ecology, density-dependent population growth and the economics of integration. This section attempts to create a theoretical framework that encompasses each of these perspectives.

We argue that as new resource sets appear through technical innovations or changes in the social system, opportunities are created for the expansion of existing (and founding of new) organizational populations. To the degree that established organizations exhibit properties of structural inertia and are organized relative to existing resource availability, they are unlikely to recognize what may initially seem to be a minor change in their resource environment.

Stinchcombe (1965) argued that knowledge about organizational opportunities and access to the resources needed to set up organizations are not uniformly distributed throughout the population. Opportunities usually come to individuals at key informational loci, and most often these loci are situated in existing organizations. The recognition of opportunities generally requires some degree of specialized knowledge about their existence and how they may be exploited; it also requires access to resources (especially financial) that may be used to create new organizations and new organizational forms.

The organizational forms that operate within an industry

may be more or less conducive to innovations that subsequently create opportunities for organizational proliferation. In Aldrich's (1979) treatment, organizations that are loosely coupled and are structured to reduce the restrictive influence of centrally controlled discipline are more likely than others to generate innovations. In so arguing, he follows a long-standing tradition stemming from such writings as Burns and Stalker's (1961) work on innovation and environmental change, Simon's (1962) analysis of partially decomposable systems, Blau and Scott's (1962) "dilemmas," Cohen, March and Olsen's (1972) "garbage can model," and Weick's (1976) discussion of loose coupling. Most theorists would agree that innovative solutions to problems are more likely when organizations are loosely structured. It also seems true, however, that organizations structured in this way experience more difficulty implementing decisions, that is, in putting to use the innovations they are so proficient at developing. As Lenin well understood, one does not make revolution with a loosely coupled band of freethinkers.

In some industries, such as semiconductors, much of the innovation comes from small firms organized by entrepreneurs, whose organizations tend to be as highly centralized and as tightly joined as their managers can make them. We argue that such organizations are frequently spawned by large, loosely joined organizations that generate new ideas but have difficulty making use of them. Blau and Scott (1962) recognized this dilemma long ago. To generate new ideas, one needs a loosely-coupled and decentralized system: to implement those ideas one needs the opposite. While there is no simple solution to this dilemma, we argue that, from the perspective of a developing industry, *one* solution is the implementation of new ideas through the founding of new organizations. For this to occur, new niches must open or old ones must become more munificent. This appears to be what happens when the technology on which the industry is based develops rapidly and demand for the industry's products or services also increases, which is one reason we find the semiconductor industry so intriguing.

Niche theory plays a central role in ecological theories of organizations (Hannan and Freeman, 1978a) and is crucial to the ideas about the development of organizational systems we are presenting here. As we have previously defined it, the organizational niche is the set of combinations of resources necessary to sustain a specific organizational population. In adopting this view we argue (as did Hannan and Freeman, 1978a) that every organizational population occupies a distinct niche. The fitness of any particular organizational form, defined here as the probability of that form's persistence, varies across the full range of its niche, decreasing where increasingly marginal resources are utilized. Figure 3 shows a plot of hypothetical fitness functions for three populations, A, B, and C, along a single environmental resource gradient, E. Given a lack of competition from A and C, population B will expand to the full range of resource utilization represented by its *fundamental niche* (the area between points a and b). But with competition, the area of niche overlap where the other populations' fitness is dominant will result in B being constrained to the *realized niche* (the area between points m and n), and we can only expect to observe B if environmental resources are available to support the realized niche requirements.

If we view the entire resource gradient in Figure 3 as a linear representation of the resource space defining an industry, then we can use niche theory to evaluate the fitness of various organizational populations relative to the patterns of resource availability within the resource space. In Figure 3, population A uses a relatively narrow range of resources compared to the broader range that B utilizes; A is more specialized than B. The entire resource space of an industry could be partitioned among many populations of specialists, but the ultimate determinant of whether specialists or generalists will prevail within any subspace is how resources are distributed over time, or in some cases, over space (see Hannan and Freeman, 1978a). If E represents a single critical resource (for example, a continuum from price-sensitive to quality-conscious markets, a possible resource variable differentiating forms within an industry), then whether we observe multiple populations within an industry depends on whether the industry has combinations of vital resources with differential patterns of availability. We have argued already that factors like technical and product change often create new resource combinations that are differentiated from existing ones. The question of whether specialists or generalists will capture the new resources and, thus, whether the resource space is

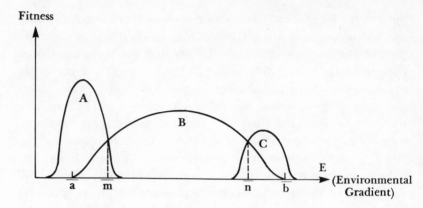

Figure 3. Fitness Functions of Three Populations

dominated by one form or the other is exactly the issue Hannan and Freeman (1978a) discuss.

Whenever new resources and new patterns of resource availability are created, which is often the case with major technological breakthroughs, new niches are opened and the potential for organizational opportunism exists. The potential for opening new niches is not solely confined to the creation of new resource spaces but is also possible within an existing industry where for social, technical, or institutional reasons a specific resource set was not previously available. A good example of such a situation is presently taking place in China, where recent liberalization trends could lead to the regeneration of fashion-oriented apparel. The critical factor in whether new resources will result in new niches is the pattern of resource availability, just as this is the critical factor in whether we will observe multiple populations within a resource space. If the pattern of resource availability over time for new resources matches the pattern of utilization of current populations, then it is very unlikely that a new organizational form will have any competitive advantages, especially considering the disadvantages posed by the "liabilities of newness" (Stinchcombe, 1965). From the perspective of niche theory this means either that the potential new form's niche is included and subordinate to that of the existing form (its fitness is everywhere less than that of the existing form) or that the new resources are still within the range of the existing population's realized niche (for instance, within C's niche but to the left of point n). In either case the new form is expected to fail.

When we developed the idea of density-dependent selection, we argued that opportunities for r-strategists are created by uncertainty and dispersed resources and that such environmental conditions are produced by mechanisms like technical change and highly cyclical product markets. A single technical innovation creates only temporary opportunities for r-strategists that soon disappear as densities develop. The same is true for changes that occur only sporadically. For r-strategists to remain viable the pattern of resource availability must shift frequently and with some uncertainty. In more conventional niche terms, then, the pattern of change must be *fine-grained*. Furthermore, technological change and similar change processes through successive fitness states are uncertain almost by definition.

The competitive conditions that affect the success of new organizational populations when they invade previously unoccupied resource spaces are quite different from those considered in prior ecological formulations (Hannan and Freeman, 1974, 1978a). In particular, such situations are characterized by low population density, which we have argued is conducive to the establishment of r-strategists. Occupying a niche within a newly established resource space is usually a very risky proposition: resource environments are often changing rapidly, there are significant liabilities of newness associated with any organizational innovations, and both future innovation and future competition present significant threats to continued viability. In addition, new resources typically are created at the edges of currently occupied niches, putting a premium on specialism, and likewise creating the context for exploitative success. In general, we can say that the specialism generated by uncertainty predicted by Hannan and Freeman (1978a) will be r-specialism where environmental change is through progressive fitness states rather than the alternation between two fitness states that they describe.

Resource environments that change rapidly and alternate among relatively incompatible states create situations that have precisely the advantages for opportunism discussed by Williamson (1975). Because of first-mover advantages and the advantages accruing to specialized knowledge, small numbers bargaining and information impactedness cannot be avoided in such situations. Vertical integration presents a significant competitive threat to r-specialists, especially if the resource environment becomes relatively stable after a series of changes, thereby reducing the basis for the information impactedness that allows r-specialists to pursue exploitive strategies.

When change is not so radical that it requires new organizational solutions (convex fitness set), generalist organizations should dominate. The advantage that the generalist form has over the specialist form is its adequate performance in more environmental states, that is, its ability to exploit a wide range of resources. This is only an advantage where future states are relatively uncertain and change is structured in such a way that internal resources can be easily shifted to take advantage of environmental changes. In fine-grained environments (where we would expect to find r-generalists) such adjustments would have to be relatively rapid. This suggests that r-generalists would likely employ labor-intensive technologies. However, where change is more coarse grained (resulting in K-generalists), organizations can afford to develop sunk costs in capital-intensive production methods. A variant of generalism results from coarse-grained change among concave fitness states. In this case we would expect that changes, particularly technical changes, would be implemented quite gradually, with productive capacity slowly shifted to current technologies or areas of high demand. This type of generalism is termed *polymorphism* (Hannan and Freeman, 1978a).

The economic niches in which K-generalists should be the prevalent form include markets dominated by mature product groups or by products that undergo changes that do not make old products or production technologies obsolete. Even under these conditions, sparsely populated niches may arise that allow r-strategists to temporarily exploit some market segment. However, as product groups mature and production technologies become well established, the structure of changes in the environment evolve from fine- to coarse-grained. Often, after major process improvements are discovered, only minor changes can be expected in the future. As densities develop, K-generalists should eventually become the dominant form. However, if environments become too coarse-grained (to the point of approaching certainty) specialist organizations may develop advantages that pose a significant threat to K-generalists.

We have already given considerable attention to K-specialism in captive environments in the preceding section. The captive producer gains the advantage of a buffer against uncertainty as a result of the parent firm's successful adaptation to the broader environment. This is an adaptation represented by its factor and product markets, and the parent firm's likely greater experience in management. Organizations in captive structures typically receive at least some of their resources from the parent firm in ways that constrain their structures and management and therefore make it extremely difficult to even contemplate a strategy other than K-specialism.

In general, given a relatively certain environment, we expect to find a preponderance of K-specialists. Whether these specialists will be merchant or captive probably depends largely upon the kinds of transactional economies that exist and whether there are significant market imperfections. K-strategists are also subject to liabilities of newness because of their greater investment costs. When an organization competes on the basis of efficiency, rather than on the basis of first-mover advantages, it is extremely important that organizational members in highly interdependent positions coordinate their work well. Furthermore, in order to acquire the resources necessary for more capital-intensive production, these organizations must have reputations for success. In many cases K-strategists, especially captives, have evolved from earlier r-strategists on this basis. We generally expect such structural changes to be confined to the early part of the organizational life cycle, when structural inertia is first developing, and to be largely irreversible (Hannan, Freeman, and Tuma, 1978).

It seems likely that consumers who are seeking the transactional advantages of integration into factor markets dominated by r-specialists will seek successful r-strategists with a demonstrated capacity to fill a recognized and proven niche. If they do, the risks of r-strategies are compounded. If they do not fail in such a conventional term as bankruptcy, they are likely to fail in the sense of being bought out or taken over in a way which changes strategy and form. In either case the organizational configuration fails. The consumption requirements imposed by the parent firm cannot help but transform the captive producer into a K-specialist after acquisition.

Besides the merchant and captive K-specialism we have been discussing, there is another variant of K-specialism that centers on obsolete technologies, which in some cases are the result of "disintegration" of captive production. As one technology is replaced by another, the volume of production associated with the old technology becomes less and less attractive for large producers. When this is the case, the technology may be sold to a smaller producer willing to continue with the product through to its disappearance.

We have identified five major organizational forms (along with several variants) that seem to fit into the framework of ecological expectations described earlier (see Hannan and Freeman, 1978a, for more details) and to have the economic advantages expected in our modified version of Williamson's (1975) arguments. Each of these types is prominently related to the speed with which organizations move into new niches, and the efficiency tradeoffs they must handle.

First, the *r-specialist* moves into niches rapidly when they open. This kind of organization is adapted to environments which are uncertain, have concave fitness sets, and in which variation is fine grained. We contend that new niches are frequently like this. Rapidly developing technologies produce many such niches and, consequently, r-specialists are extremely common in the periods of rapid industrial change.

The second form is the *r-generalist*, which, like the r-specialist, trades on its ability to recognize newly opening niches. The basis of differentiation between the r-specialist and r-generalist is the structure of the fitness set in the environment in which they operate. For the generalist form, the fitness set is convex. Since r-strategists are mainly found in environments where competitive efficiencies are not particularly important, they may both be present in a given resource space even though the niche of the specialist form is included in the generalist niche.

Third, the *K-generalist* attempts to exploit as many of a niche's variant conditions as possible. Profit-making firms of this kind offer diverse product lines. They compete on the basis of productive efficiency and marketing skill, and they attempt to develop product designs and marketing strategies that will stretch out the period over which their product line can be sold and that will delay obsolescence. Because they must maintain excess capacity in order to offer a wider variety of products and because their emphasis on productive efficiency usually results in higher capital intensity, these organizations are usually more expensive to set up and slower to adapt than are *r*-specialists.

The fourth type is the variant of generalism known as *polymorphism*. This form is expected to be dominant in environments with coarse-grained change patterns, concave fitness sets, and uncertainty. It maintains residual structures to deal with the problem of widely ranging fitness contingencies. An example of this type of organization is the modern university, which expands or shrinks departments according to long-term changes in demand but seldom eliminates departments.

Finally, there are three kinds of *K-specialists*. Independent producers rely on productive efficiency in relatively stable environments to outcompete generalists on the basis of lower coordination costs. This form will be unlikely when market inefficiencies are high. Captive producers are organizations that are subsidiaries of larger firms, frequently having been absorbed by other organizations in vertical integration acquisitions and mergers. Such organizations are buffered from uncertainty by the parent firm. This lack of uncertainty permits specialism that takes the form of product development tailored for specific input requirements of the parent firms. These captive producers may be *r*-specialists that have been purchased in order to provide predictable supplies of an especially crucial raw material or component. Subordinate producers are organizations that have acquired an obsolete but still viable technology. As one technology replaces another, the older variant is frequently still useful for some purposes but in low enough demand that it does not pay *K*-generalists to continue its production.

As these strategies develop, opportunities for individuals are modified in predictable ways. The structures of firms and the demographic distribution of their staffs encourage people at various levels to either stay or to leave. Such consequences figure importantly in the processes by which organizational forms proliferate. In the next section we examine the niche structure of the semiconductor industry, and in the following section we consider the role of individuals in proliferation.

Niche Structure and the Dynamics of Proliferation in Semiconductors

As we noted earlier, there are three basic components in the competitive structure of the semiconductor industry: (1) technical innovation, which includes product and process developments; (2) first mover advantages, which include becoming the industry standard, having production capabilities that make rapid response to innovations possible, being further along in the "learning curve," and the initial economic profits that allow for the rapid development of capacity; and (3) superior survival characteristics, including the ability to withstand demand fluctuations. Incorporating these characteristics into a structural strategy may be very beneficial in some instances but may entail negative consequences in others. Ultimately, the survival value of any particular strategy depends on how it is related to the way resources are distributed in the environment.

The semiconductor industry clearly includes several niches that are distinguishable from each other in terms of uncertainty, convexity/concavity, and grain. These niches are interdependent in a rather complex manner; thus, a certain organizational form may create the conditions that a second form needs for survival, while a third form may slowly outcompete the second given a different environmental structure.

We understand the industry to have four basic forms: (1) the producer of state-of-the-art devices; (2) subunits of larger firms producing standard components for the "merchant" market; (3) the independent producer of standard components for the merchant market; and (4) the captive producer. Given the structure of innovation in the industry, each of these types of firms can be expected to have competitive advantages in certain situations. One might assume that these structural strategies merely represent the contingencies imposed by the particular market in which a firm chooses to operate at a given time. But this does not appear to be the case: supposedly well-managed firms have made some tremendous blunders proceeding on just such an assumption.

In Tilton's (1971) work on the diffusion of innovation through small firm proliferation he argued that innovations can be more easily adopted by firms that do not have any vested interest in an old technology and that, once these firms adopt a new technology, they force other firms to do likewise. This line of thought, however, assumes a lack of product differentiation and the existence of a single niche. Furthermore, it is entirely static in its conceptualization.

Given the fine-grained uncertainty at the leading edge of the semiconductor industry, we would expect to find firms specializing in the rapid implementation of innovation. This does not mean that a particular r-strategist has to be the source of the innovation, only that such an organization be ready to take advantage of innovations when they appear. Intel's early domination of the LSI memory chip market came about because the firm that introduced the device, Advanced Memory Systems, could not supply the initial demand because of production problems associated with getting adequate yields of acceptable devices. As a result, Intel's device, which appeared slightly later, was adopted by fifteen of the eighteen worldwide computer manufacturers. It became the industry standard, catapulting Intel into the ranks of the industry leaders and produced a gradual decline in Advanced Memory Systems through 1976, when it merged into Intersil. Intel also pioneered the microprocessor, and at the time of this writing was working on the development of VLSI memory devices (Moore, 1979).

Because the production and design of semiconductors require a relatively large amount of technical knowledge, information about opportunities is basically confined to those working within the industry. It has often been the case that new technologies are developed in established firms but due to inertia are not immediately implemented. This was the case with metal-oxide-semiconductor (MOS) technology. Major producers like Texas Instruments and Fairchild initially ignored the possibilities of MOS, choosing instead to devote their attention to faster, bipolar devices. Because of this, a number of firms specializing in MOS technology were started up by former employees of Fairchild—firms such as General Micro-Electronics and General Instrument.

We have argued that r-specialists should do quite well initially but that their success often invites entry by other forms. When it became apparent from the viability of specialized firms like General Micro-Electronics and General Instrument that MOS technology had some potential, a number of other firms, including Fairchild and Texas Instruments, entered the market. After the MOS market became more competitive, the r-specialists in the market began to experience financial difficulties: both General Micro-Electronics and General Instrument were acquired by Philco-Ford, which attempted to get a foothold in the integrated circuit market. As a consequence of the Philco-Ford purchase, a number of employees of General Micro-Electronics broke off and set up American Microsystems, which specializes in the production of MOS integrated circuits. Pursuing a K-strategy of producing aggressively priced standard components enabled American Microsystems to become one of the largest integrated circuit producers in the industry (Webbink, 1977).

Captive firms are a major factor in semiconductor manufacturing. In a 1977 Federal Trade Commission report on the semiconductor industry, IBM and Western Electric were estimated to be, respectively, the third and fourth largest semiconductor manufacturers in the world. Although these firms do not produce for the merchant market, their productive capacity is a significant factor, especially when they shift from buying a chip externally to producing it internally. There are also a large number of captive producers that operate on a much more modest scale, including divisions of Hewlett-Packard, Xerox, General Motors (Delco), National Cash Register, and Zenith Electronics. These firms all use large numbers of both standard and specialized devices, and on the basis of Williamson's (1975) thesis it is thought that they derive substantial transactional economies from internal production.

Given these economies, one would expect that autonomous K-specialists would be squeezed out of the market, but this is not the case. The significant learning economies that characterize the industry are largely responsible for the niches available to K-specialists. Small- and medium-scale users cannot establish internal operations that are large enough to lower their internal transaction costs below the market level. The result is that the prevalence of learning economies (or information impactedness) constitutes a barrier to entry for all but the largest firms.

Another variant of K-specialism dominates a niche that is characterized by a highly certain (although still competitive) situation: obsolete technologies. Other industries may have niches that are characterized by a high degree of certainty (for example, highly standardized merchandise in markets with relatively fixed market shares), but any industry with a rapid rate of technological change will probably leave marginal markets in its wake. An example of this kind of firm is Germanium Power Devices Corp., which produces germanium transistors (Iversen, 1979). This firm recently acquired Texas Instruments' line of germanium devices after Texas Instruments decided that it was no longer practical for it to continue serving such a small market. Germanium Power Devices has also acquired the germanium lines of Bendix, Honeywell, and General Electric. This market is rapidly disappearing, but there is still some residual demand because a number of military devices were designed with germanium transistors. Two other firms, Lansdale Transistor and Silicon Transistor, also operate in this market, which amounts to about \$25 million a year.

The complex interdependencies that exist in the industry involve the relationship between the two major types of specialists and the large, diversified manufacturers. Firms like RCA, General Electric, and North American Rockwell have only a segment of their total business in semiconductors and are generalized into a wide variety of situations. They have significant financial advantages over smaller firms and prefer to use those advantages in developing market shares in established product lines with large scale production and competitive pricing. These firms are all K-generalists, but they do not pursue strategies that lead them to compete in a direct way with r-specialists. These firms use their financial resources and production capacity to meet large orders for standardized products. In many instances this includes nearly obsolete products like receiving tubes, which RCA continued to manufacture up through 1976 (Webbink, 1977). These firms can also capitalize on their financial resources by bidding aggressively on large scale contracts that require very long production runs if substantial profits are to result. One rapidly developing situation that will be characterized by just these kind of conditions is the production of solid-state circuits for the automobile industry.

These large diversified firms reflect the polymorphism that Hannan and Freeman (1978a) have argued characterizes universities and other kinds of organizations that operate in environments that vary radically over time but experience changes over only very long periods (coarse-grained, concave fitness set). Because of their emphasis on competitive efficiencies, there is always some danger that a general environmental shift will put a segment of these organizations into direct competition with K-specialists in a relatively certain environment. In such a case, we would expect the polymorphic generalist to simply abandon that particular segment of its niche. Such was the case when General Electric dropped its germanium line to Germanium Power Devices and when Westinghouse conceded defeat in the integrated circuit market after trying to make its way in as a late entrant.

The second kind of diversified firm in the industry is typified by Texas Instruments and Fairchild Semiconductor; both are diversified into other areas, but the largest component of their business is in semiconductors. The consequence of this high degree of involvement is that these firms are much more vulnerable to technological changes than are more broadly diversified firms and as a result are more keenly aware of the threat posed by r-specialists. As an example, Philco Electronics responded to the development of the transistor by investing heavily in a mechanized process that promised to result in very efficient production. Unfortunately, by the time Philco was ready for full production the device became obsolete. Philco did not immediately recognize this, being quite content with its 70 percent market share in what had become an obsolete product. The consequences were the rapid disintegration of Philco's financial resources and its acquisition by Ford in 1961.

Texas Instruments has been able to deal with the threat posed by technical change because of its quite efficient production capabilities and because it maintains excess productive capacity, which allows rapid entry into developing markets. By putting an emphasis on being able to fulfill growing demand for highly sought-after products, such firms can frequently squeeze out small r-specialists, which typically have difficulties meeting initial demand for major innovations. It is also possible for these generalists to try to leapfrog new innovations with slightly larger or faster devices, a strategy that Texas Instruments used effectively in its late entry into microprocessor production. National Semiconductor, which is currently among the top three producers in the commercial market, has relied heavily on such aggressive tactics as pricing its current output at levels that anticipate future efficiencies and selling below cost to build its market share and force specialists to abandon products much earlier than might be expected.

As we argued in previous sections, we expect to see a proliferation of these various forms at different points in an industry's developmental history. It seems perfectly reasonable to say that shifts in the structure of the resource environment can have a profound impact on the distribution of firms within an industry because these shifts cause niches to close. The number of firms highly diversified outside the components industry declined steeply in the 1950s as the pace of innovation accelerated, but it is again rising as multinationals like Siemens and Philips buy into the industry in mature product areas. Indeed, the importance of innovation and technical change in determining the diversity of forms that we have observed can clearly be seen if one examines the European semiconductor industry, which does not contribute to technical change in the industry and is primarily involved in licensing technologies as they become available. This industry is dominated by large, diversified multinationals (Tilton, 1971; Braun and MacDonald, 1978).

Individuals and Organizational Proliferation

How do organizational forms spread to fill a niche? To work out a fully developed population ecology of organizations would require a theory of organizational life cycles in which both birth and death processes were carefully described; we are not yet ready for such a task, but we can analyze some of the ways in which organizations are founded and how the pattern of industrial development has predictable effects on organizational structures that can in turn be expected to have predictable effects on the founding of new firms.

When individuals start new organizations, they are likely to seek ways to avoid the task of custom designing each organizational role. Obviously anyone involved in an entrepreneurial act will be short on time and heavily burdened by the absence of organization through which responsibility can be delegated. It is to be expected, then, that such individuals will seek models to imitate in designing the new organization. Such models are found in the individual's own experience and in the experience of his or her colleagues. These models of course may be negative in the sense that features of past experience may serve as design options to be avoided in the present. Our point is that new organizations do not spring from the minds of entrepreneurs as totally original creations. Rather, it is likely that in most respects such organizational designers will copy what seems to have worked well in their past experience. Thus, people with military experience can be expected to design organizations differently from those whose experience is, let us say, in universities.

Stinchcombe (1965) has argued that duplicating aspects of organizational structure from already existing organizations in many ways mitigates the liabilities of newness. If he is correct, then we would expect organizations joining a small population not only to reflect the founders' experiences but also to emulate the population's most (apparently) successful members. In doing so, organizations take advantage of preexisting role relationships, that is, of the fact that a pool of participants exists to serve as models for teaching others those roles and to generate confidence in other organizations that supply necessary resources. Finally, when such organizations are set up, crucial internal interdependencies may be managed by filling positions with individuals who have previously known each other and who may be expected to exhibit the kind of trust that strangers would find it difficult to develop among themselves. This means that one of the central mechanisms by which organizational forms proliferate is through the mobility of individuals. This mobility is patterned by the histories of the organizations from which they come, by the careers that they have followed up to that point, and by personal considerations related to the stratification system and mode of family organization.

The industry's growth rate has a number of implications for organizational founding. First, the rate of growth is likely to be correlated with the rate at which new niches open up. As new products and production processes are developed, new resource requirements emerge and create opportunities. r-strategist organizations can be expected to jump into these niches quickly. But since r-strategists are inexpensive to set up, it is frequently almost as easy for a manager with experience in the industry to organize a new entrant as it is for an already established organization to shift from preexisting niches to a new one, and entrepreneurial rewards provide a significant incentive for following such a course. The inclination of existing r-strategists to move into a new niche will depend in part on the level of density in the niches they already occupy. If K-strategists have not yet appeared, r-strategists may be able to compete successfully; in addition, their first mover advantages may not yet have been exhausted.

At the organizational level, the prior rate of growth of a particular organization affects its current structure. Organizations that grow in spurts generate bulges in their age distributions. This means that people hired at the end of, or just following, a period of rapid growth, look above them in the hierarchy and see people of about their own age. This suggests to them that promotion will be slower than normal. Particularly aggressive, technically proficient people are likely to leave the organization under these circumstances. One of the many ways in which success breeds failure, then, is that it structures the organization so that those individuals with the most potential for making contributions to the organization will depart at a critical time in the organizational life cycle (Hannan, Freeman, and Tuma, 1978).

In addition to the age distribution, other organizational features affect the likelihood of exiting (that individuals will leave a given firm). Tall hierarchies with many levels offer more promotion possibilities than flat hierarchies. In high-technology industries in which professionalized work forces predominate, tall hierarchies are common. The greater number of hierarchical levels that organizations of this kind are likely to have mitigates the effect of age bulges. In addition, the strategy being pursued by the organization in question, as well as by others in its niche, affects the tendency of individuals to pursue new technical leads as the industry expands.

We have argued that K-strategists in general compete on the basis of efficiency. This mode of organization stresses discipline at the expense of flexibility. K-strategists in captive markets subordinate the pursuit of new technical leads to the efficient production of inputs for the parent firm's production systems. Such organizations tend to spin off personnel whose training and organizational role puts them in a position to know where new niches are opening. This process depends heavily on the rate of change in the industry and on the barriers to entry that have been erected by current-population members or that are inherent in the technology.

At any rate, r-strategists whose efforts are concentrated on expanding rapidly enough to fully capture first-mover advantages run the risk of failure as entrepreneurially oriented management and technical staff leave to pursue the opportunities that they have learned about by participating in the firm's technical development. They are also imperiled by technical obsolescence in their staffs. This occurs partly because of the exiting behavior just mentioned, and partly because of the tendency for technically trained professionals to lose their state of the art knowledge.

Engineers and scientists frequently become obsolete because most companies are unwilling to retrain them in remedial programs. This unwillingness has a number of causes. In a highly uncertain environment, when r-strategists abound, investing resources in individuals who may exit and take their skills with them, is unwise. Also, salaries are only partly dependent on technical skills. Seniority has much to do with wage rates in virtually every industry. It is simply more expensive to retrain someone with high seniority (and high salary) than it is to replace that person with someone more recently trained. Such problems and the moral issues they imply are very likely to become particularly salient in industries with histories of rapid growth, once that growth tapers off. K-strategists may likewise find themselves falling behind technically because of aging technical staffs. The distribution of technical staffs across the pure continuum from research to applications engineering is important here. Obsolescence can be expected to set in most rapidly among those doing the process application. For them, alternatives are often a question of managerial talent. Those without it either become glorified draftsmen or lose their jobs entirely.

Remember that the rate of technical change is not perfectly correlated with the rate of product market expansion. The latter may generate either employment growth or organizational proliferation and concomitant r-strategist opportunities. K-strategist organizations in environments that change rapidly in both technology and market growth can bury their obsolete staffs in less technically demanding organizational roles and can renew themselves technically by constant hiring and expansion. Firms facing changing technologies but static total demand do not have such a luxury.

The age distribution within organizations is also important since the likelihood of exiting to found new organizations is almost sure to be correlated with a person's age. Older employees are probably less willing to split off than younger ones. At the same time, however, the ability to accumulate the requisite resources and the experience that success frequently requires is often not found in new employees. It is probably the case, then, that the likelihood of exiting to form new organizations is an inverted U-shaped function of age and seniority.

One of the important ways that organizational forms spread to fill a niche is through a process by which people leave already operating organizations, carrying with them experiences and ideas that lead to nonrandom structural patterns in the organizations they found. Rapidly expanding industries create opportunities for such entrepreneurial activity, with past rates of growth in both technological development and product markets producing waves of organizing in which niches are filled.

As we have emphasized, entry into the semiconductor industry requires a great deal of specialized knowledge about both technical matters and the opportunity structure of product markets. A great many of the most respected technical people in the industry have doctorates in physics or chemistry, and many had prestigious academic careers before they entered private industry. But—even given the quality of the individuals involved in the industry—we do not know of anyone who has started a firm without having been previously employed by another firm in the industry.

A significant number of firms that were started during the early years of the industry were either founded by or organized around former Bell Laboratories personnel (Braun and Mac-Donald, 1978). The two most significant of these organizations were Texas Instruments and Shockley Transistor. Texas Instruments enticed Gordon Teal, a crystal specialist, to leave Bell Labs in 1952. According to Braun and MacDonald (1978), Teal was having difficulty getting support from Bell Laboratories for his research interest in growing silicon crystals with specific patterns of impurity distribution, largely because such an approach was considered commercially unviable. Teal accepted an offer from Texas Instruments (then known as Geophysical Services, Inc.) because he was a native Texan and preferred to return to his home state (McDonald, 1961). At Texas Instruments, he developed a method for growing silicon crystals that could be commercially exploited for transistor production—an innovation that made a major contribution to the success of Texas Instruments.

Shockley Transistor was founded by one of the discoverers of the transistor, William Shockley, with the backing of a large electronics firm, Beckman Instruments. Shockley recruited a large number of the best scientists of the time to work for him, setting up shop in Palo Alto, California. For reasons that are not particularly clear, Shockley's operation was subject to a considerable amount of internal dissent, and eight of Shockley's employees eventually left to start Fairchild Semiconductor with the backing of Fairchild Camera and Instruments. Fairchild Semiconductor eventually hired almost everyone who had ever worked for Shockley, thereby becoming the beneficiary of Shockley's recruiting efforts. According to Braun and MacDonald (1978), forty-one semiconductor manufacturing firms have since been founded by former Fairchild employees. It is principally because of this large number of spin-offs that so many major firms are located in "Silicon Valley" in California.

There is a great deal of interfirm mobility among personnel working in the semiconductor industry. In his study of diffusion processes, Tilton (1971) cited this level of mobility as one of the major reasons that American firms have been so dominant in the development of semiconductor technology. We expect that such high levels of job mobility and common founding sources will result in a great deal of structural similarity among related firms, but we cannot say with any certainty whether this will be the case.

The American semiconductor industry has experienced a tremendous amount of growth in the past twenty years. One consequence of this growth has been an employee-age distribution that is highly skewed toward the young. Since there has been no leveling out of this growth, we can only speculate that this uneven age distribution is eventually going to have a significant impact on the careers of individuals in the industry. This empirical issue is certainly well worth future study (Pfeffer, 1979).

Conclusion

The development of new organizational forms, along with the expansion of the organizational populations in which they are observable, can be studied as the intersection of two processes. On the one hand, industries develop, opening new niches which represent opportunities. On the other hand, organizations and the individuals who populate them move into these niches in ways that reflect both past histories of organizational growth/decline and personal careers.

Research of this type seems to hold great promise for building links with other disciplines. The so-called new institutional economics is an area from which much can be learned and, we hope, to which something can be contributed. In sociology, the contemporary isolation of organizational research from other specialized interests in social organization is to be deplored. When organizational sociologists have nothing to say of interest to specialists in stratification, political sociology, and urban sociology, the field's relevance to the operation of modern societies is open to doubt. A focus on the material conditions that link individual opportunity and social change would offer some hope of strengthening those ties that were so important in the early development of organizational sociology.

We have relied heavily in this chapter on the semiconductor industry as an extended example to illustrate our arguments. In doing so, we did not mean to imply that we think the industry is typical in any particular way: what we suspect, in fact, is just the opposite. The semiconductor industry is interesting because it is growing and changing at a tremendous rate, with significant consequences for organizational populations. The result of this rapid change and growth has been a great diversity in available organizational niches, along with a corresponding diversity in organizational forms, certainly not the situation in many other industries. Nevertheless, we think that the basic ecological dynamic prevails in all organizational populations, with the outcome in any industry specific to the environmental conditions under which organizational forms seek to exercise their relative advantages. In the food processing industry, for example, we would expect to find neither a great deal of organizational diversity nor the use of r-strategies. In the apparel industry, however, with its constantly changing fashions and high level of competition, we would expect to find a level of diversity similar to that in semiconductors and a sizable population of r-specialists.

While the research reported here has been both qualitative and highly speculative, this need not always characterize this sort of study. In many cases, one can gather quantitative data on both the organizations and the individuals who set them up. Data of this kind are regularly gathered by trade associations and by financial institutions. We intend to turn in that direction in pursuing our current line of research.

PART III

Decline of
Organizations

⬦⬦⬦⬦⬦⬦⬦⬦⬦⬦⬦⬦⬦⬦⬦

All organizations face the possibility of decline, and many face the possibility of termination. The three chapters in this final section of the book deal with these possibilities, although the questions addressed by each are quite different.

In Chapter Ten Whetten focuses on organizational decline, a phase that may occur in any stage in the life cycle of an organization and that involves either an absolute decline or a marked decrease in the rate of its performance. Because he focuses on decline, rather than on the ultimate termination of organizations, the insights that Whetten develops should be helpful to individuals confronted with the prospect of managing organizations under conditions of scarcity or revitalizing organizations that have become stagnant as a result of their own inertia. His approach is to develop some general typologies of the sources, processes, responses, and outcomes of organizational decline that may be used to guide research. In so doing, he raises a number of important issues. For instance, he separates organizational decline into the two categories of cutback and stagnation and argues that they tend

339

to be caused by different environmental conditions—cutback by scarcity and stagnation by abundance. He speculates that vulnerability to decline will be different for rapid-growth than for slow-growth organizations and specifies general typologies for both the causes of decline and the managerial responses to decline. Finally, he urges future researchers to be particularly sensitive to the implications of decline for both public- and private-sector organizations.

In one important sense, Niv's treatment of the kibbutz in Chapter Eleven anticipates Ouchi's discussion in Chapter Twelve of the failure of clans. Niv observes that communal forms of organizations are notorious for their inability to survive. Their disintegration, he believes, begins with the choice of ultimate purpose made during their creation. If that purpose is to create and rigidly maintain a certain ideology, the process of disintegration by stagnation is joined. To preserve its core ideology, this type of commune closes its boundaries to influences from the outside and thereby places limits on the resources and markets that it needs for survival.

If, by contrast, the commune's chosen purpose is to propagate and disseminate its unique ideology into the environmental elements with which it has exchanges, disintegration will follow a different route. The commune's ideological base will erode gradually through the process of assimilation into the conventional world that it hoped to change. In either case, the fundamental ideological goal of the commune will cease to be achieved or maintained and, on this ground, the communal organization will be judged to have failed.

Niv presents us with two different operational definitions of failure. Under conditions of communal disintegration by stagnation, he observes, the organization will cease to exist. Its activities will halt, and its members will disperse for want of resources to continue. In contrast, under conditions of disintegration by assimilation, the commune's people and activities may remain intact, even flourish. Failure here is of a social, not a technical, nature. Only the ideological basis upon which the communal organization was founded has dissolved; otherwise, the organization is very much alive.

Ouchi in Chapter Twelve treats an organization as any stable pattern of exchange relationships between individuals engaged in cooperative action. He identifies three types of organizations on the basis of the mechanisms that each employs to facilitate a stable pattern of transactions among task-interdependent parties: markets (prices), bureaucracies (formal authority), and clans (socialization of members). He then describes the conditions under which each type of organization will succeed or fail.

Under conditions where performances of the parties may be audited with precision, but where goal congruence between parties is minimal, markets will succeed; when performance becomes unmeasurable, however, markets will fail. Under conditions where performances of the parties cannot be measured unambiguously but where goal congruence between parties is complete, clans will succeed; they will fail, however, if opportunism erodes goal congruence. When neither extreme condition exists (that is, when neither performance measurability nor goal congruence can be assured), markets and clans can be expected to give way to the rules of formal authority provided by the bureaucratic form of organization. One is then led to conclude that bureaucracies are more robust than either markets or clans, both of which rely on extreme conditions that obtain only rarely in collective activity.

Ouchi also observes that the occurrence of transactional inefficiency does not necessarily imply that an organization actually will close its doors and go out of business. Indeed, Ouchi believes that, "to a greater or lesser degree, all organizations are in a state of at least partial failure." The fact that permits organizations to carry on in the absence of transactional efficiency is that they may be able to pass on their inefficiencies to society-at-large if it accepts their legitimacy. "Ultimately," says Ouchi, "organizational failure will occur only when the society deems the basic objectives of the organization to be unworthy of continued support." Thus, although transactional efficiency is the basis for assessing the relative effectiveness of economic organizational forms, Ouchi concedes that their ultimate success or failure rests with their ability to justify their existence. If they are successful in achieving legitimacy in society (as in the case of schools and churches), organizations may not need to defend their relative efficiency.

10

Sources, Responses, and Effects of Organizational Decline

∿∿∿∿∿∿∿∿∿∿∿

David A. Whetten

Managing declining organizations and coping with the consequences of retrenchment are pressing societal problems. Evidence
of decline is pervasive. Schools have cut back because of decreasing
enrollments, industry has laid off record numbers in response to
recessionary pressures; the military had to scale down its operations after the Vietnam War; many churches have been forced to
close their doors due to lack of support; and municipal services
have been curtailed as a result of declining revenues. The consequences of decline are far reaching. Families suffer the effects of
unemployment, and the morale of the remaining workers deterio-
rates as they are forced to fight over smaller and smaller resource
pools. When an entire industry retrenches, the effects are felt

throughout society. For example, the displacement of thirty million farm workers due to increased mechanization in agriculture is claimed by some to represent the genesis of our contemporary urban problems (Boulding, 1974).

So alarming are the potential consequences of widespread organizational decline that several scholars have proposed radically new forms of government and commerce to meet this impending crisis (Benveniste, 1977; Heilbronner, 1976; Commoner, 1976). Whether or not these proposals will be adopted, it is clear that our society is ill prepared to cope with decline. Since the Second World War our country has enjoyed unprecedented growth, and, as Kenneth Boulding (1974) has noted, all our institutions have become adapted to survival under conditions of rapid growth. The need to adapt to emerging conditions of scarcity represents a significant challenge at the individual, organizational, and professional levels.

At the individual level, decline runs counter to our strong success ethic. During our golden era of abundance, the values of optimism and self-assurance have reigned unchallenged (Sutton and others, 1956). The ease with which people are able to live in an expanding economy encourages an ego-centered orientation (Fox, 1967). With few threats to collective interests, individuals are free to pursue personal accomplishment. However, under conditions of munificence, ease is confused with effort, and success with accomplishment. During this age of "the power of positive thinking" (Peale, 1952), when we are instructed to "think and grow rich" (Hill, 1967), it is the norm to ascribe success to personal accomplishment. The dark side of this philosophy that success can be willed is its implication that failure reflects personal incompetence. This logical trap is also reflected in the tendency to treat organizational growth as evidence of youth and vitality; decline then becomes equated with old age and senility. So powerful is the association between growth and success and between decline and failure in our society that Scott (1976) has proposed that the chief issue in the management of declining organizations is not whether managers are capable of saving them but whether they are willing to make the attempt. The best hands are generally the first to abandon a sinking ship, and it is difficult to sign on a new crew for a ship that is taking on water (Argenti, 1976; Hirschman, 1970).

The success ethic is engrained in our culture to such an

extent that, when individuals must discuss a failure experience, they tend to describe it as though it were a personal success. Personal credit is taken for being: perceptive enough to recognize that a marriage partner was ruining our life; capable enough to keep a business from losing any more than it did before we had sense enough to bail out; so ethical, smart, or experienced that our former boss felt threatened by our presence in the organization.

During a period of economic expansion, there are of course more organizational births than deaths, and there is more growth than decline. For example, between 1950 and 1975 there were 2.2 million business starts and only 100,000 deaths (Statistical Abstract. . . , 1976). In this kind of expansionary period, decline and death are discomforting anomalies that are explained away as examples of failure to implement properly fundamental management principles. Because growth has been the norm in our country for decades, the experiences of managers in declining organizations have not been widely documented (Smith, 1963). Thus, as we enter a period of economic slowdown during which a larger number of organizations will experience decline, their managers will have relatively few precedents or guidelines to rely on (Bogue, 1972). Recognizing this problem, Boulding (1974) has called for the establishment of clearinghouses to facilitate the exchange of ideas and suggestions among managers coping with decline.

At the professional level, organizational behavior teachers and researchers are ill prepared to provide the necessary support services for administrators in declining organizations because the field is dominated by a growth paradigm (Scott, 1974; Whetten, 1979c). For example, few courses are taught on management in declining organizations or under crisis conditions. Further, many of the models used to teach administration assume conditions of expansion. A typical textbook discussion of conflict management instructs students to resolve conflicts over resource allocation by formulating a "win-win" alternative. When munificence prevails, this is a realistic prescription, since offers of side payments or promises of larger portions in the future can be made. However, when the total resource pie is shrinking, the "win-win" option becomes less plausible since current losses are not likely to be made up in future allocations.

Organizational research has also been dominated by studies

on growth-related topics. The work of Blau and his associates (Blau, 1968, 1970; Blau and Schoenherr, 1971) dealt primarily with the problem of maintaining coordination in an expanding organization. This line of research spawned numerous studies on administrative ratios (Pondy, 1969; Rushing, 1967; Indik, 1964) and the relationship between control strategies and such other organizational properties as innovation (Hage and Aiken, 1967) and professionalization (Hall, 1968). While interest in this line of research has waned, the growth-oriented paradigm it represented remains strong (Benson, 1977; Kotter and Sathe, 1978).

A strong growth orientation is also reflected in the literature on organizational development (Greiner, 1972). One of the most frequently stated reasons for a so-called organizational development intervention is that workers have become alienated due to the negative effects of increasing organizational size. The use of profit centers, interdepartment integrators, team building, and humanistic leadership practices represent attempts to infuse an intimate, supportive, and tractable environment into large, complex organizations.

While our society as a whole is ill prepared to cope with widespread decline, we have few options (Boulding, 1973; Daly, 1973, 1977). The industrial complex has been forced to cut back in response to double-digit inflation and an aroused public's concern about the rapid depletion of our natural resources (Schumacher, 1973; Commoner, 1976; Meadows and others, 1972); educational institutions, as already noted, have been forced to retrench because of declining enrollments (Trow, 1975; Green, 1974; Cartter, 1970); and the legitimacy and resource base of government have been eroded by a taxpayers' revolt over poor services and high taxes (Smith and Hague, 1971; Dvorin and Simmons, 1972; Whetten, 1979b; Fenno, 1966). The purpose of this chapter is to call attention to the need for an intensive examination of organizational decline and to begin to sketch out the research domain involved.

Decline as a Concept

The word *decline* has two principal meanings in the organizational literature. First, it is used to denote a cutback in the size of an organization's work force, profits, budget, clients, and so forth. In this case, an organization's command over environmental resources has been reduced as the result of either decreased competitive advantage (the organization has a smaller share of the market) or decreased environmental munificence (the total market has shrunk). A decrease in market share might reflect poor management, but a shrinking market generally does not. The erosion of an inner city's tax base, a decrease in a school district's enrollment, or the scarcity of oil during an embargo all reflect drastic changes in environmental munificence that are beyond the control of a city department head, school superintendent, or gasoline retailer. The best an organization can do under these conditions is to anticipate a downturn and buffer the production technology from its effects by stockpiling raw materials, diversifying services or product lines, or expanding into recession-resistent markets. The object is to reduce the element of crisis in decline through the use of forecasting techniques, diversification, and contingency plans for rationing (Thompson, 1967).

The term *decline* is also used to describe the general climate, or orientation, in an organization. Using a life cycle model, some authors speak of mature organizations that become stagnant, bureaucratic, and passive, as evidenced by their insensitivity to new product developments, workers' interests, and customers' preferences. This condition of deterioration may or may not result in a loss of revenues. One of the traditional arguments against monopolistic markets is that they allow firms to become stagnant without experiencing serious repercussions. Similar observations have been made about the consequences of a lack of competition in the public sector (Roessner, 1979). Kolarska and Aldrich (1978), Ansoff (1970), and Cyert and March (1963) argue that under competitive conditions a decline in revenues triggers a revitalization cycle in the organization.

It is important to note that decline-as-stagnation does not necessarily imply an absolute decrease in income, whereas decline-as-cutback does. Stagnation is more often reflected as a decrease in the rate of increase than as an actual decrease. This distinction is useful because it highlights the fact that it is decline-as-cutback, not decline-as-stagnation, that is the emerging crisis ushered in by an era of scarcity. The problem of stagnating organizations, which has been around for generations, is actually less likely to occur during periods of scarcity since the two forms of decline are activated by opposing environmental conditions. Stagnation is more likely to occur during periods of abundance, whereas cutbacks are more likely during times of scarcity. The focus of this paper will be primarily on decline-as-cutback.

Literature on Organizational Decline

The literature related to organizational decline is very broad and diverse. Unfortunately, very little of this material reports empirical research. Instead the literature is dominated by case-study descriptions of declining organizations, armchair analyses of the causes of decline based on reviews of published case studies, and prescriptive guidelines for preventing or coping with decline. In the literature, decline has been examined at two levels of analysis: (1) within a population of organizations and (2) in individual organizations. Conceptual and empirical work focused at each level will be discussed in turn.

Population Level

The dominant theoretical orientation in this area is the natural selection model (Aldrich, 1979; Aldrich and Pfeffer, 1976; Campbell, 1969; Hannan and Freeman, 1978a). Its principal components are three ecological processes that proponents argue occur in all biological and sociological populations. These processes, or stages, are variation, selection, and retention. In a population of organizations variation in member characteristics occurs as a result of either planned or unplanned actions. Consequently, the model does not require the assumption of administrative rationality or intentionality. Applications of this model have tended to overlook the historical development of variations and have concentrated primarily on their effect on survival. The second stage, selection, reflects a differential rate of survival within a population. As certain variations are reinforced by the environment, some members develop a superior competitive advantage. The retention stage signifies that certain positively valued characteristics have been preserved, duplicated, or reproduced in the population. Thus, the focus of the natural selection model is primarily on the birthrate (rather than on the death rate as many suppose) of a mutant strain (Stebbins, 1965). The competitive advantage of a species does not appear suddenly in one generation; instead, it emerges gradually over several generations as the number of its members possessing a positively valued characteristic increases geometrically.

This model has been strongly advocated by Kaufman (1973, 1975). He argues that most models of organizational processes are overly rational: "Our pride in personal accomplishment seems exaggerated" (1975, p. 145). He reasons that the evolutionary model explains everything that can be treated by rational models, plus a great deal more. In reviewing rational models, Kaufman (1975) asks, "Why do some organizations adhere to practices that caused others to die? Why isn't the world filled with old organizations? Why don't organizations with the smartest people always survive the longest?" (pp. 144–145).

While several other authors have noted the difficulties of applying the natural selection model literally to the study of organizations (Aldrich and Pfeffer, 1976; Weick, 1969; Aldrich, 1979; Stebbins, 1965; Child, 1972), it is clearly a useful conceptual tool for analyzing changes in the composition of a population of organizations over time. Examples of research using this approach include Nielsen and Hannan (1977), Aldrich and Reiss (1976), Freeman and Hannan (1975), and Hannan and Freeman (1978b).

There are several researchable questions emerging from this literature that warrant further investigation. We will examine two. First, "What organizational characteristics will enhance adaptability to the environmental conditions anticipated in the future?" This question represents the heart of the organizational growth and decline issue. But in order to understand the processes of growth and decline, one must first understand the conditions that determine the more fundamental states of survival and death.

There is an extensive body of literature that predicts future environmental conditions. Some futurists have argued that our pluralistic, decentralized, capitalistic system is doomed. As it becomes more and more evident that contemporary institutions are unable to respond adequately to the increasing turbulence and complexity of their environment, they will be replaced with centralized planning and a socialist economy that will foster a more equalitarian distribution of increasingly scarce resources (Heilbronner, 1976; Commoner, 1976). Other futurists, however, have proposed that the present trend toward increased complexity and centralization will eventually be checked because it is antithetical to the American spirit. As a result, there will be even greater emphasis placed on individualistic enterprise and mediating structures (Miles, 1976; Berger and Neuhaus, 1977). For the most part, however, it is assumed that organizations in the future will be located in turbulent, centralized, and highly complex environments (Bennis, 1966; Vacca, 1973; Kaufman, 1973; Chadwick, 1977; Ansoff, 1965).

There has been considerably more disagreement over the ideal organizational characteristics for these environmental conditions. There is clearly not unanimous agreement regarding the characteristics that will be selected out by the anticipated turbulent and complex environmental conditions of the future. The most widely discussed organizational characteristics are size, age, auspices, internal control, and structural complexity. Although these have been included in many cross-sectional organizational studies, they lend themselves to population ecology research. Some have argued that large size and old age are liabilities under turbulent environmental conditions. As an organization increases in size and grows older, it tends to become more bureaucratic and inefficient; it finds it more difficult to change quickly; it makes more enemies as it encroaches on a greater number of sacred domains; it becomes a larger target for militants and regulators alike; and it has fewer options for expansion as it reaches the maximum share of its markets allowed by law (Rubin, 1979; Bennis and Slater, 1968).

Others have argued that small, young organizations will have the greatest difficulty surviving because they are inexperienced. The consequences of a bad decision or a sudden downturn in the economy are intensified in a small organization due to a lack of slack resources; and the negative effects of interpersonal conflict are more difficult to contain than in a large organization (Stinchcombe, 1965; Levine, 1978; Kaufman, 1975; Boswell, 1973; Perrow, 1979). There is also considerable disagreement over the advantages of centralization versus decentralization in turbulent environments. Burns and Stalker (1961), Aldrich (1978a), and Porter and Olsen (1976) have argued in favor of decentralization. For example, Porter and Olsen maintain that a generalist in an outpost office is more responsive to changing environmental conditions than a specialist in a centralized headquarters. But Hawley and Rogers (1974), Yarmolinsky (1975), and Rubin (1979) have countered that decentralization can immobilize a system facing a turbulent environment. Yarmolinsky uses the term *institutional paralysis* to describe the inability of universities to change, because no one interest group has sufficient power to alter the organization's course.

There is considerably more agreement about the adaptive value of "loose coupling." This concept addresses the extent to which units in an organization must interact with one another in order to perform their systemic functions. While loose coupling is generally associated with decentralization, there is a difference between the two concepts. Generally, when we think in terms of centralization and decentralization, we are treating the organization as an integrated whole. The parts of the organization are assumed to be working in concert toward common objectives, and the extent to which power is delegated is an indication of the number of people involved in making strategic plans for reaching these objectives.

A decoupled system is quite different. Its components share a low level of interdependence, as shown by Thompson's (1967) concept of pooled interdependence. A business conglomerate exemplifies this concept, as each subsidiary has considerable power to select product lines, adjust prices, and alter its operating structure, as long as these decisions do not adversely affect profits. Several authors have argued that this type of institutional structure facilitates long-term adaptability (Weick, 1976; Aldrich, 1979; Glassman, 1973). Not only is this structural configuration highly flexible and therefore responsive, but the freedom given each unit to respond to its unique environment also tends to produce a large pool of internal variety over time. This diversity makes the organization robust by preventing it from being adversely affected by changes in one sector of its environment (Ashby, 1956; Hedberg, Nystrom, and Starbuck, 1976; Rubin, 1979). The principal liability of this design is that it is extremely difficult for the organization as a whole to make purposive coordinated changes if those become necessary.

The operating units strongly resist the usurption of their autonomy, and their response to programs initiated by the central office varies from foot dragging to defiant opposition.

A loosely coupled structure is therefore best suited for organizations whose units do not need to respond to environmental changes in unison. The institutional paralysis in the face of massive environmental change, discussed by Yarmolinsky (1975), results when an organization that consists of sequentially or reciprocally interdependent parts (Thompson, 1967) adopts the structure of a holding company simply because this design is compatible with the institution's values of autonomy and self-governance.

There is also considerable agreement regarding the effect of auspices on organizational responsiveness. Many authors have noted the lack of incentives for innovation in the public sector, and Rainey, Backoff, and Levine (1976) have identified several key differences between public and private organizations. Compared to private organizations, public organizations have less market exposure, more environmental constraints, and are more subject to political influences that affect their internal operations. As a result, these organizations are marked by more complex and contradictory goals, less autonomy, less delegation of authority, more turnover, greater difficulty in linking individual performance with incentives, lower overall worker satisfaction and commitment, and greater variation in member characteristics and abilities. Drucker (1974) has proposed that the key difference between public and private organizations that influences their incentive to innovate is the "mode of payment." Public organizations are rewarded by budget increases, while private organizations are rewarded by satisfied customers and repeat business. Roessner (1979) attributes the lower number of innovations in public organizations to the fact that innovations in the private sector are stimulated by production efficiency while innovations in the public sector are motivated by bureaucratic self-interest (Yin, 1978). The trend towards "third-sector" organizations, for example, the U.S. Postal Service, reflects efforts by the federal government to make key public service organizations more responsive to market conditions.

The fact that analysts in the field do not totally agree on the constellation of organizational characteristics that enhance adaptability in turbulent and complex environments signals a strong need for further research in this area. While a number of empirical studies have tested various contingency theories of organizational design (Pennings, 1975; Dewar and Werbel, 1979), this line of research has been flawed by a lack of longitudinal data.' While studies of business failures typically examine the performance of a large subject pool over time, these studies generally rely exclusively on secondary data (Brough in Argenti, 1976; Altman, 1971). Consequently, their analyses tend not to be very rich or insightful. It is true that these studies are nicely complemented by several published case studies of the collapse of notable business enterprises (Smith, 1963; Birchfield, 1972; Daughen and Binzen, 1971), but there remains a substantial need for more systematic research on the organizational characteristics that foster adaptability. Populations of organizations that vary according to the salient organizational characteristics identified by Hedberg, Nystrom, and Starbuck (1976), Argenti (1976), and others should be identified and studied over time to determine whether these characteristics indeed predict organizational performance. The alternative societal conditions predicted for the future could be identified on a small scale today, and a study of the survival rates of various organizational configurations under these conditions could be conducted. Another possibility for this type of research is to simulate various types of environmental conditions in a laboratory setting and thus to build on the work of Miles (Chapter Three) and McCaskey (1974).

A second research question focusing on populations of organizations is, "What effect does decline in one organization have on other members of a population?" While this is not an ecological question, it is related to populations. This question is prompted by the work of Aiken and Hage (1968), who proposed that organizations respond to scarcity by establishing joint programs to distribute the costs of innovation. In their model, staff members propose more innovations than an organization can fund. To make up the difference, other organizations are invited to cosponsor new ventures. It is logical to assume that when resources shrink this process will increase. One of the consequences of joint programs is that they increase the couplings among members of a population; if only a few members of a population have to retrench, the entire network becomes richly joined. As a result, the network becomes less stable, less flexible, and, hence, less adaptable (Weick, 1976; Aldrich, 1979). A study is currently underway to test whether this deductive model can be verified in populations that contain declining organizations (Whetten, 1979a).

Organizational Level

Organizational decline has, to some extent, been examined at the population level, but most of the literature has used the organization as the unit of analysis. While the intent of population ecology studies is to identify gross organizational characteristics that predict survival, the research focus at the organizational level is on internal processes. The research question shifts from "Which members of the organizational population present at Time 1 were also present at Time 2?" to "What is happening in these organizations as they experience and react to the changing conditions between Time 1 and Time 2?" While the first question is analogous to a biologist's study of changes in a gene pool over generations, the second question has no analogue in biology since it focuses on the purposive actions unique to social systems. The first examines structural configurations, the second examines the structure-generating processes. The first is conducted by a diagnostician who, on the basis of surface conditions, makes inferences about what is inside; the second is conducted by an anatomist who examines internal conditions directly.

The theoretical perspective most commonly used in this type of organizational research is the resource dependence model (Yuchtman and Seashore, 1967; Pfeffer and Salancik, 1978; Aldrich and Pfeffer, 1976), which is closely related to the political economy model (Wamsley and Zald, 1973; Benson, 1975). These models assume that managers make strategic decisions based on their assessment of the political and economic conditions in their environment or, more specifically, that managers take actions to maintain adequate supplies of political legitimacy and economic resources.

Writers in this area tend to emphasize that organizations are either passive reactors or aggressive initiators in their dealings with the environment. This ideological split carries over to the study of decline. Some writers profess an organizational life cycle theory that includes an "inexorable and irreversible movement toward the equilibrium of death. Individual, family, firm, nation, and civilization all follow the same grim law, and the history of any organism is strikingly reminiscent of the rise and fall of populations on the road to extinction" (Boulding, 1950, p. 38). (See also Downs, 1967.) The "success breeds failure" and "failure stimulates further failure" organizational decline models that will be discussed later reflect this fatalistic philosophy (Starbuck, Greve, and Hedberg, 1978; Argenti, 1976).

A more optimistic view of decline is reflected in the work of Ansoff (1970) and Cyert and March (1963). These authors present a homeostatic model in which a decline in profits (or slack resources) triggers corrective actions to increase profits. While we are far from being able to make a definitive statement about the utility of these two models, the field is gradually accumulating enough case studies of decline to make possible a description of the contextual conditions under which each is likely to predominate. These studies tend to emphasize (1) the source of decline, (2) an organization's response to decline, or (3) the effects of decline on other organizational activities. Works addressing these three topics will be discussed in turn.

Sources of Decline

The kinds of crises that, if responded to improperly, precipitate organizational decline can originate within an organization (Greiner, 1972) or, more frequently, within the environment (Scott, 1976). Some authors have discussed the sources of crises as though they were objective phenomenon (Balderston, 1972), while others have argued that the real source of a crisis is in the misperceptions of organizational members (Starbuck, Greve, and Hedberg, 1978). A useful typology must therefore accommodate both orientations. A typology proposed by Levine (1978) meets this requirement since it examines both internal and external causes of crises. His four sources of decline are organizational atrophy, political vulnerability, problem depletion, and environmental entropy. These labels must be modified to extend this typology beyond the public sector for which it was developed. A modified model appropriate for business organizations as well contains organizational atrophy, vulnerability, loss of legitimacy, and environmental entropy. Such a typology includes a much wider range of causes than those previously proposed in the business literature. For instance, Miller (1977) and Argenti (1976) identify such causes as impulsive decisions that overextend the organization's assets, not responding to change, an executive who is either too powerful or poorly informed (absentee owner), and taking unnecessary risks. A discussion of the literature related to the modified model's four causes of decline follows.

Organizational Atrophy. The consequences that result when organizations lose muscle tone are a recurring theme in the literature. A recent formulation of this argument has appeared in the work of Hedberg, Starbuck, Nystrom, and their associates as the "success breeds failure" syndrome. Following the logic of Cyert and March (1963), they argue that organizations formulate heuristic programs for dealing with recurring problems. Unfortunately, "because situations appear equivalent as long as they can be handled by the same programs, programs remain in use after the situations they fit have faded away" (Starbuck and Hedberg, 1977, p. 250). The result is the often maligned phenomena of organizational inertia (Behn, 1977; Cyert, 1978). Organizations that habitually use programs based on their previous utility tend to become desensitized to environmental changes. As a result, organizations that were the most successful in the past become the most vulnerable to failure in the future.

While a decrease in responsiveness is generally associated with senility, this does not always hold true in organizations. The debilitating effects of success can occur at any age. Tornedon and Boddewyn (1974) in their study of divestiture found a common pattern: young, aggressive companies would generate high profits that then prompted the acquisition of overseas subsidiaries—often before the establishment of a policy for long-term overseas growth. Because of this topsy-turvy growth pattern produced by mercurial success, it would later become necessary for these companies to divest themselves of many of their acquisitions as changing business conditions made it apparent that the organizations had overextended themselves. This sawtooth cycle of rapid growth followed by drastic retrenchment is common, and it documents the fact that for organizations, as for human beings, the incidence of death is not perfectly correlated with poor health or old age. For example, Altman (1971) reports that in 1970 over 279 million-dollar firms went broke. Further, in terms of age, he reports that one third of bankrupt businesses were less than three years old, 53 percent were younger than five, and 23 percent were over ten. (Surprisingly, only 2 percent of the failures were less than one year old.)

Argenti (1976) has identified three patterns of organizational decline. These are shown in Figure 1. The second and third patterns illustrate the different varieties of the "success breeds failure" syndrome that we have discussed. An organization that follows the third pattern has established an excellent performance record. It is a major producer in its industry and is highly regarded as a solid ongoing business concern—examples would be Penn Central and Rolls-Royce. At the point of initial decline the company has lost touch "with [its] market or [its] customers or [its] employees. [Hence,] although a major change has occurred, no adequate response has been made. Perhaps two competitors have merged but the chief executive has decided 'it won't affect us.' Or the company has had its first strike, which the board dismisses as being 'one of those things' when in fact it is a sign that [it has] lost touch with the shop floor" (Argenti, 1976, p. 162). This pattern reflects the classic case of a large, old organization deluded by the myth of invulnerability. Such an organization confuses the achievement of age with immortality, that is, being immune to the travails of this life. As Argenti notes, this smugness precipitates a slow but very painful death.

The second trajectory of decline illustrates the risk of mercurial success. In this case, rapid growth is followed by a precipitous decline because managers, intoxicated with success, become careless. Typically this type of organization is formed by a charismatic entrepreneur afflicted with the Midas touch. Unfortunately, counsel to level off the organization onto a steady-state plateau is dismissed. This illustrates the extreme case of a growth-oriented business ideology, as reflected in the refrain, "Beyond the clouds lie the stars. Beyond the stars lies the Great Absurd" (Argenti, 1976, p.

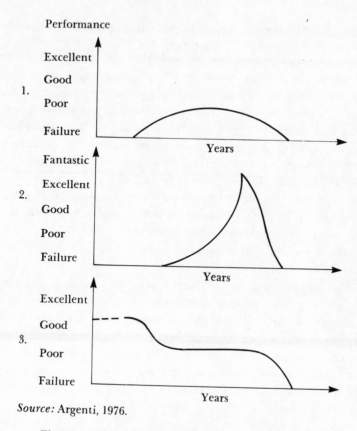

Source: Argenti, 1976.

Figure 1. Three Patterns of Organizational Decline

159). This problem appears to be age-old. It is reflected in Jethro's counsel to Moses in the Book of Exodus and was discussed by Weber (1947) as the need to routinize charisma. In his study of an English public school, Pettigrew (1979) found that the most critical phase in the organization's life cycle was at the peak of its early growth curve. At this point it was necessary for the entrepreneur-founder to resign and appoint a "manager" who could solidify his gains and initiate the mundane rules and coordination mechanisms required for continued development. Pettigrew reports (personal correspondence) that if the entrepreneur had not been replaced at this point in the organization's development, precipitous decline would have followed.

Neither slow-growing nor fast-growing organizations are

immune to decline, although the two types of organizations face different problems. The fast-growing organization is experienced in handling crises (Kotter and Sathe, 1978), so it has already established elaborate problem-solving routines. This organization's vulnerability to decline lies in its failure to identify sagging performance as a problem rather than in inadequate problem response. Having had little experience with this type of problem, the organization is likely to discount symptoms of impending decline. In contrast, slow-growing organizations tend to be very sensitive to changes in their vital signs. Hence, their vulnerability to decline is not in problem recognition but in problem response. These organizations have so little slack that they may not be able to survive long enough to respond to the problem.

Vulnerability. The second source of organizational decline is vulnerability. In his classic work on life cycles, Stinchcombe (1965) noted that organizations are particularly vulnerable in their infancy. During this time they must overcome the "liabilities of newness," some of which are temporary inefficiency due to inexperience, frequent interpersonal conflicts resulting from distrust, and the lack of a stable set of ties to customers, suppliers, and regulators. The difficulty that young organizations have clearing these initial hurdles is reflected in the death-rate statistics for businesses reported earlier. From these it appears that "infant mortality is more common than senility" (Argenti, 1976, p. 7). The first decline trajectory in Figure 1 highlights the vulnerability of young organizations. The problems caused by the inexperience of youth illustrate the "failure breeds further failure" form of decline. Argenti notes that business organizations that just never seem to get moving are typically formed by a person with a technical orientation, for example, an engineer, architect, or accountant.

In the public sector, political vulnerability is reflected in an agency's inability to resist budget decrements. Levine (1978) discusses some of the factors that contribute to vulnerability: "Small size, internal conflict, and changes in leadership, for example, seem less telling than the lack of a base of expertise or the absence of a positive self-image and history of excellence. However, an organization's age may be the most accurate predictor of bureaucratic vulnerability. Contrary to biological reasoning, aged organizations are more flexible than young organizations and therefore rarely die or even shrink very much" (p. 319). The postulated negative correlation between age and vulnerability is supported by Kaufman's (1976) study of turnover in federal agencies. He found that newly established agencies had the highest death rate of all federal agencies during the period from 1923 to 1973.

The fragility of a public institution's base of political support has been discussed by Mitnick (1978) and Shefter (1977). Shefter outlines a three-stage model of municipal government fiscal crisis. First, a social group (such as the unions in New York City) gains considerable power and demands a larger share of the public benefits. Second, the government agrees to the demands either because the group is too powerful to fight or because it is a natural ally. Third, the government finds itself too weak to finance these new claims by cutting benefits to other groups or by raising taxes. This disparity between promise and reality then triggers a political crisis that typically results in new government leadership.

Loss of Legitimacy. Benson (1975) has stressed the importance of legitimacy as an organizational resource and noted the propensity in some organizations to overemphasize the acquisition of economic resources and to overlook the value of cultivating political acceptance. This legitimacy is especially salient in the public sector. Rothman (1972) has linked the rise and fall of various criminal justice programs with shifts in societal ideology. As the prevailing views shifted from incarceration to rehabilitation of criminals, for example, an organization gained or lost public funding support, depending on which value it embodied.

Levine (1978) has noted that problem depletion is a major cause of loss of legitimacy. Once the problem for which an agency was organized has been resolved, that agency should presumably be terminated. However, Behn (1977) provides several interesting examples of the unrealistic optimism of this conclusion. For instance, the Temporary Commission of Investigation of the state of New York has recently issued its sixteenth annual report. The Federal Metal and Non-Metallic Mine Safety Board of Review was abolished only after its executive secretary confessed in a front-page interview that he had no work to perform. The ability of an agency or program to establish a powerful constituency that allows it to function independently of its enabling constitution makes it extremely difficult to terminate what appear to be anachronous organizations. This fact is reflected in the poor track record of American presidents who have attempted to overhaul the executive branch, despite the sage counsel of astute political and administrative advisers (Brown, 1977). Reflecting on this problem, Bardach (1976) and Biller (1976) lament that in general founders of new public programs do their job of institution building too well. As a result, it is most difficult to dismantle ineffective agencies. Behn (1976) argues that supporters of an existing organization have the upper hand in a debate over the fate of a facility because their examples of specific problems that would result from a termination order ("ten clients would have to travel 200 miles to receive comparable life-sustaining treatments") are more compelling than the opponents' vague complaints about inefficiency or ineffectiveness. Hence, while loss of legitimacy is a potential source of decline and termination, it is one of the environmental threats that many organizations are remarkably capable of deflecting.

   Environmental Entropy. The fourth source of decline stems from the reduced capacity of the environment to support an organization. Cyert (1978) has proposed that organizations in this situation have basically two options: (1) they can find another ecological niche, or (2) they can scale down their operation. In the literature, the first (proactive) alternative has been emphasized by business authors, while the second (reactive) alternative has been discussed primarily in the public and educational administration fields. The second group views the management of a declining organization as the unfortunate victim of circumstances, while the first group regards a crisis-ridden management as having neither the vision nor the will to initiate the innovations necessary to reverse the downward spiral of decline. Exemplifying the business orientation, Starbuck and Hedberg (1977), Ross and Kami (1973), and Barmash (1973) all argue that an organization's presence in a stagnating environment says more about the organization's management than about the capacity or potential of the environment. Barmash (1973) concludes his study of fifteen corporate disasters with a clear statement of this orientation: "Corporations are managed by men; and men, never forget, manage corporations to suit themselves. Thus corporate calamities are calamities created by men" (p. 299). Hall's (1976) analysis of the demise of the *Saturday Evening Post* supports this position inasmuch as he noted that the egos of top administrators clouded their judgment at critical points in the magazine's life cycle.

In contrast, work done in municipal public finance (Muller, 1975; Clark and others, 1976) and university administration (Green, 1974; Furniss, 1974; Trow, 1975) tends to emphasize the passive retrenchment option. This literature assumes that public organizations are captives of their environments—tethered to declining enrollments and eroding tax bases. This orientation is reflected in Biller's (1976) recommendation that public organizations adopt a matrix design so that expendable programs can be cut back easily when retrenchment becomes necessary.

While this dichotomy between the public- and private-sector literatures certainly reflects the fact that businesses have considerably more flexibility than public organizations in changing their goals, product lines, and so on, it also appears to reflect a different orientation regarding organization-environment relations in public and private organizations. Glassberg (1978), Boulding (1975), Cyert (1978), Millett (1977), and Molotch (1976) have all argued that one of the greatest needs in the public sector is for a new cadre of leaders who will aggressively respond to declining resources. This suggests a promising topic for research. The need to construct explanations for events in one's immediate environment has been discussed by Weick (1969, 1977a) and Pondy (1977), but little research has been conducted on this topic. Recently Bougon, Weick, and Binkjorst (1977) have used a methodology called *causal mapping* to trace this "sense making" process. Organizational members' beliefs regarding the sources of crises provide a rich setting for extending this pioneering work. Since the definition of a problem influences the solutions considered, it would be interesting to explore the possibility of institutional paradigms (that is, views in education, penology, city government, business, and so forth) that influence members in different types of organizations to construct highly predictable, but institutionally different, causal explanations for decline. The work reviewed here suggests that these paradigm-grounded causal maps do exist, but few attempts have been made to systematically study this phenomenon within a comparative perspective.

A related research topic involves the practice of denying that a crisis exists. Why do some administrators respond quickly to the first signs of decline while others explain them away? In his study of school districts with declining enrollments, Rodekohr (1974) found that several superintendents refused to accept the validity of data showing a decline in enrollment. In some cases this response was the result of the brief tenure of the administrator, but in other instances the superintendent was apparently simply not acknowledging this threatening information. "Creative accounting" is a related defense mechanism identified in several case studies of business failures (Argenti, 1976). In some cases business managers deliberately hide negative financial data so as to not alarm stockholders and bankers. In other cases, however, managers simply will not accept the implications of the negative information conveyed by doomsayers, and they juggle the accounting record until it gives what they are sure is a more accurate (and considerably more optimistic) reflection of the organization's health.

Responses to Decline

After managers have acknowledged that a crisis situation exists and have constructed a causal map for making sense out of it, a response is formulated. The literature on management responses to decline can be best organized around the central issue of attitude toward change. Figure 2 shows a continuum from "change positively valued" to "change negatively valued." The categories "generating," "responding," "defending," and "preventing" highlight important benchmarks along this dimension. Unlike the usual typology for organization-environment relations, this one does not range from reactive to proactive (Thompson, 1967). Instead, the two extreme categories are proactive strategies, while the center two are reactive responses. (This typology is similar to a model of managerial response to stress developed by Burgoyne (1975). His categories are avoidance, defense mechanisms, and learning. It is also similar to one proposed by Miles, Snow, and Pfeffer (1974):

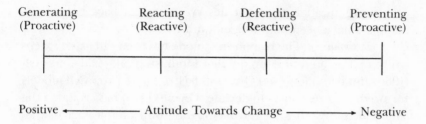

Figure 2. **Management's Responses to Environmentally Induced Change**

domain defenders, reluctant reactors, anxious analyzers, enthusiastic prospectors.)

Defending. The defensive response to impending decline is typically found in highly bureaucratic settings or in ideologically based institutions. Merton's (1957) classic work on the bureaucratic mentality proposed that members of large (usually governmental) organizations tend to undergo a psychological means-end shift over time; that is, adhering to the organization's rules and procedures becomes more important to them than fulfilling the objectives for which the rules were originally created. Thus, members will likely respond to a proposed budget cut by defending the efficiency of the organization and the diligence of its members (Whetten, 1979b; Pfeffer and Salancik, 1978). In an ideologically based organization, such as a mental health facility, members are geared to defend the integrity of the institution. Hence, they will likely react to a proposed budget cut by arguing that the government "ought" to maintain its commitment to the social values embodied in the mission of the threatened organization (Hirschman, 1970). This is illustrated in the case of a drug rehabilitation center in New York City that had a recidivism rate of 100 percent. When city officials attempted to close the facility, political supporters accused the city of dropping its commitment to drug rehabilitation. As a result the officials felt compelled to continue funding the program even though it was not fulfilling its intended purpose (Roessner, 1979). Thus, while the ideologist defends his or her organization by pointing out the symbolic political and social implications of a cutback, the bureaucrat uses facts and figures to demonstrate that his or her organization does not deserve to be cut back because its members have been both diligent and frugal.

Responding. The responding mode has been discussed extensively in the literature on public administration. Zald and Ash (1966) and Brouillette and Quarantilli (1971) have proposed models for predicting responses to decline. Levine (1978) has critiqued the common approaches to retrenchment, for example, across-the-board cuts, cuts based on performance, layoffs based on seniority. Mitnick (1978) outlined five steps for an agency responding to threatened termination. Furniss (1974), Smart and Vertinsky (1977), and Starbuck, Greve, and Hedberg (1978) propose that a special decision-making task force be formed to address issues of decline. They recommend that this "crisis corps" rely primarily on informal power and informal communication channels. This group would determine the severity of the crisis, present alternative courses of action, and in general prepare the organization to "weather out the storm." Boulding (1975) has called for the establishment of an "invisible college" for administrative officials in educational institutions to facilitate the exchange of lessons learned in responding to declining revenues and enrollments. To complement this informal network, a cadre of consultants who specialize in the management of declining organizations would be extremely useful. These people would be called into organizations in shock much as Red Adair is called into oil fields on fire.

Outside observers are particularly helpful in times of stress since they can help management avoid the common mistakes of solving the wrong problem and attaching the wrong solution to the right problem (Cohen, March, and Olsen, 1972). The first error is exemplified by the tendency to solve symptoms rather than underlying problems. Under crisis conditions managers prefer quick responses. An agreeable solution, even for the wrong problem, relieves tension and gives management the satisfaction of achieving success in the face of failure. Unfortunately, the true problem may continue to grow and surface later as a calamity. A classic example of this management fallacy was depicted in the recent film *China Syndrome*. After a malfunction at a nuclear power generator, management thought that it had found the cause but overlooked evidence of more fundamental problems that nearly resulted in an ecological catastrophe.

The common error of attaching the wrong solution to the right problem in managing municipal financial crises and university decline has been noted by Glassberg (1978), Cyert (1978), Wildavsky (1964), and Cyert and March (1963). Their concern is based on theoretical work in the area of decision making. Wildavsky (1964) argues that decision makers tend to make incremental responses because "men cannot rationally choose between alternatives drastically different from present reality" (Dahl and Lindbloom, 1953, p. 83). Cyert and March (1963) describe a similar tendency called "problemistic search"; that is, people tend to search for solutions in the area closest to the problem. It appears that this tendency increases as a function of stress (Smart and Vertinsky, 1977; Bozeman and Slusher, 1978). Glassberg (1978) argues that one of the most common mistakes in handling municipal fiscal crises is that public officials propose incremental solutions for quantum problems. In his study of the decline of the *Saturday Evening Post*, Hall (1976) found that problemistic search was one of the factors that precipitated that magazine's decline spiral. Between 1944 and 1946 the number of subscribers to the *Post* increased substantially. This in turn greatly increased production costs, and these led to a decline in the profit margin. Management's response was to increase the cost of a subscription, but this decision, which had the effect of drastically cutting back the number of subscribers, initiated a period of stagnation and eventual decline.

The defensive and responsive reactions described in this section have been discussed as though they were mutually exclusive decisions. In practice they are often linked together to form a more complex response pattern. In his analysis of the decline of civilizations, Toynbee (1947) noted that the initial response of a society to the threat of an invader is to retrench to traditional values. However, if the threat intensifies, then the victim tends to capitulate and embrace wholeheartedly the culture of the aggressors. This willingness to accept the bad aspects of the invaders' culture along with the good, eventually leads to the degeneration of the host society. The same pattern of retrenchment and eventual capitulation can be found in threatened organizations.

Preventing. A great deal has been written about organizations' deliberate efforts to manipulate their environments to increase their competitive advantages and to remove potential threats

(Hedberg, Nystrom, and Starbuck, 1976; Perrow, 1979; Penrose, 1952; Post, 1978; Galbraith, 1971). Tactics used include price fixing and other illegal practices (Staw and Szwajkowski, 1975), acquisitions (Pfeffer, 1972; Markham, 1973), buying political influence (Perrow, 1972), changing public opinion and influencing consumer preferences (Post, 1978), and shaping economic and social policy (Sethi, 1977; Post, 1978). The logic invoked in describing these practices is that since organizations must act to avoid uncertainty, administrators must act to prevent the need for responsive change (as opposed to self-initiated change). The skill with which managers can use these tactics came out in an interview with one of John D. Rockefeller's sons. Asked if his father had ever broken any laws in building his immense oil empire, the son responded that he could not think of any laws broken by his father but that he could name several that were enacted because of him. The extent to which businesses should be restrained (either by self-regulation or by outside regulation) from engaging in practices that reduce the need for responsive change, while producing harmful side effects for others, is at the heart of the current debate over corporate social responsibility (Marris, 1974; Preston and Post, 1975; Walton, 1977).

Generating. The opposite attitude toward change is expressed by writers in the generating category. While the literature in the previous three categories was based on descriptions of current business practices, the writers in this category tend to be academics who encourage businessmen to turn about and embrace the enemy, that is, to make a virtue of responsive change. Relying on case studies of organizations that suffered substantial losses because they were too slow to respond, these authors argue in favor of "self-designing organizations." These organizations are characterized by experimentation, informal communication lines, slack resources, loose criteria for performance evaluation, tolerance for occasional failure, ad hoc jobs, frequent movement of personnel within and between organizations, and, most of all, a high incidence of innovation (Hedberg, Nystrom, and Starbuck, 1976, 1977; Starbuck, Greve, and Hedberg, 1978; Weick, 1977b; Staw, 1977; Bennis and Slater, 1968; Toffler, 1970; Landau, 1973). Further, Hedberg, Nystrom, and Starbuck (1976) argue that these organizations should look more like collapsible tents than like stone palaces; that is, they should be characterized by minimal consensus, minimal contentment, minimal affluence, minimal faith, minimal consistency, and minimal rationality.

In reflecting on this literature, one is struck by the telling differences between the descriptive and prescriptive work. On the one hand, writers describe managers as being skilled at rigging the environment to prevent the need for change, slow in responding to unpredicted changes, inclined to select well-used solutions to problems, and disposed to think of innovation only in terms of incremental changes in current practices. On the other hand, the other writers warn managers that these practices will not be positively selected by the environments of tomorrow. This discrepancy reinforces the need for more ecological studies of organizations attempting to survive under different environmental conditions.

There is also a need for further theoretical development of the self-design orientation. The logical adequacy of this approach has been questioned by Wildavsky (1972) and Bozeman and Slusher (1978). In addition to responding to these criticisms, proponents need to give more consideration to the organizational and societal implications that widespread adoption of their self-design model would have. The prospect of managers, stockholders, workers, government regulators, and supporting social institutions all positively reinforcing frequent and significant innovations in production organizations suggests the possibility of a runaway innovation cycle that would have highly deleterious effects. There must be some negative loops built into the model to serve as a homeostatic mechanism, but thus far insufficient attention has been focused on this need. It is also questionable whether organizations have the capacity to become self-designing. This model suggests a level of rationality that organizations may simply not be capable of achieving, *especially during times of crisis when the need to self-design is greatest.* The work of March and Simon (1958), Cyert and March (1963), Cohen, March, and Olsen (1972), Rubin (1977), Benveniste (1977), and Smart and Vertinsky (1977) suggest that this is indeed the case. Forrester's (1971) "Counterintuitive Behavior of Social Systems" gives weight to this conclusion:

> Our first insights into complex social systems came from our corporate work. Time after time we have gone into a corporation which is having severe and well-known difficulties. The difficulties can be major and obvious, such

as a falling market share, low profitability, or instability of employment. . . . Generally speaking we find that people perceive correctly their immediate environment. . . . In a troubled company, people are usually trying in good conscience and to the best of their abilities to solve the major difficulties. Policies are being followed at the various points in the organization on the presumption that they will alleviate the difficulties. One can combine these policies into a computer model to show the consequences of how the policies interact with one another. In many instances it then emerges that the known policies describe a system which actually causes the troubles. In other words, the known and intended practices of the organization are fully sufficient to create the difficulty, regardless of what happens outside the company or in the marketplace. In fact, a downward spiral develops in which the presumed solution makes the difficulty worse and thereby causes redoubling of the presumed solution [p. 55].

This observation underscores the need for the self-design proponents to reconcile the incongruity between their prescriptions and the natural tendency for administrators under stress to reflexively select responses contrary to the prescribed responses. The fact that this incongruity exists is not by itself problematic, but the fact that it is hardly mentioned in the self-design literature is troubling. If managers under stress need to behave contrary to their reflexive patterns, considerable thought and research will be required to discover methods for countering these natural tendencies. Hence, the self-design literature needs to move beyond its prescriptive mode and come to grips with the knotty issues of implementation, especially during periods of stress-inducing decline.

Effects of Decline

A declining resource base has widespread effects. It affects the state of mind and career patterns of the staff and the manner in which business is conducted in the organization. At the level of the individual organizational member, the most profound effect of decline is increased stress. As slack resources dwindle, the margin for error in an organization decreases. While the stakes for making good decisions increase, the penalties for making bad ones also increase. As the tension and pressure mount, morale tends to sag (Behn, 1978) and high turnover follows (Levine, 1979). To check turnover in declining organizations, Levine (1979) suggests new forms of compensation that make exit very costly (for example, deferred payment schedules for fringe benefits like profit sharing and retirement).

A related consequence is increased interpersonal conflict. In declining organizations more people find that they are losing more often with little prospect for making up current resource losses in future allocations (Levine, 1978; Starbuck, Greve, and Hedberg, 1978). To alleviate these negative consequences, Cyert (1978) proposes establishing new goals and evaluation criteria early in the decline process as a means of reducing uncertainty and increasing integration. Yetten (1975) has argued for new leadership models adjusted to the stress factor in crisis situations. In this vein, Glassberg (1978) has examined the leadership styles of mayors that are most effective during fiscal crises, and Yetten (1975) and Levine (1979) both note that, in order to avoid conflict, managers in decline conditions rely less on participative decision making than they normally would.

This literature points out the need for research on the ability of conventional theories about leadership, conflict resolution, decision making, and communication to explain behavior during the crisis of retrenchment. Since they were typically developed and verified by means of observations from expanding organizations, there are scarcely any organizational models or theories that do not require recalibration for conditions of decline.

One of the more disturbing effects of decline is that it tends to penalize most those who can least afford it—and in some cases least deserve it. This occurs both at the individual and organizational levels. Generally, the first to be dismissed during a period of retrenchment are the low-skilled, low-income, minority (including women), young, or very old staff members. These are the people who will have the most difficulty absorbing the loss of wages and finding new jobs (Levine, 1978). The organizational effect of this action is to decrease the internal pool of variability within the organization and increase the average age of the labor pool (Levine, 1979). When these effects of involuntary discharges are coupled with the fact that those who choose to leave the organization are those best qualified to formulate creative responses, the overall result of decline on personnel turnover is to produce a "regression to the mean" in labor pool qualifications.

A similar phenomenon occurs at the departmental level. The most common form of retrenchment is to distribute the cuts more or less evenly across all units. This option is politically more feasible than cutting off an entire program or department because it is less likely to be sharply contested. The consequence of this approach is that a cutback hurts those that deserve it the least, that is, the most efficient. A highly efficient unit has the greatest difficulty implementing a retrenchment order since it had operated with less fat in the past (Levine, 1979).

Another effect of decline is on the rate of organizational innovation. While the literature suggests a strong relationship between decline and innovation, the sign (plus or minus) of the correlation is disputed. On the one hand, some authors have argued that decline will hamper innovation. For example, Smart and Vertinsky (1977) and Bozeman and Slusher (1978) have proposed that during crises managers are paralyzed by a fear of failure. Hence, they become more conservative rather than more innovative. In the public sector this takes the form of trimming the fat from existing programs rather than exploring radically new service delivery alternatives (Whetten, 1979b). On the other hand, Wilson (1972) has argued that organizations are not likely to adopt significant innovations until they experience a major crisis. The regenerative benefits of crises have also been stressed by Lindblom (1968) and Glassberg (1978).

This lack of consensus regarding the effect of decline on innovation highlights again the incongruity between prescriptions for and descriptions of the management of stressful situations and underscores the pressing need for more research on decision making under conditions of stress. One hypothesis that warrants examination is that organizations follow the response pattern of threatened nations, as this pattern was described by Toynbee (1947). A small amount of stress may cause members to "clutch," that is, to have their creative faculties impaired by fear. However, as the threat increases in intensity, a threshold may be reached that triggers a desperate effort to generate creative alternatives. This proposition is consistent with Miller's "general theory for the behavioral sciences." Miller (1955) argues that all "living systems respond to continuously increasing stress first by a lag in response, then by an overcompensatory response, and finally by catastrophic collapse of the system" (p. 27). Miller's three-stage response model highlights a paradox of innovation. If we first assume that the overcompensatory response of an organization facing decline-induced-stress is to initiate multiple innovations as an act of desperation, then we can conclude that under certain conditions innovation actually contributes to a system's collapse. Of course, not all innovations have this dysfunctional consequence, but when they are initiated under conditions of stress, it appears highly probable that this unintended consequence will result.

This conclusion points out the need for more research into the effect of innovation on decline. While it is implied in the self-design literature that a high level of innovation is associated with high organizational performance, others have argued that the relationship is curvilinear and that either too little or too much innovation leads to low performance (Smith, 1963; Argenti, 1976). This proposition is consistent with research on the effect of stress on individual performance that has shown performance to be highest at an optimal level of stress, that is, the highest point on an inverted U curve (Schuler, 1979).

The ultimate effect of decline is death—whether this is the outcome of a deliberate effort to terminate an ineffective public program or the consequence of poor management in a small business. While research on organizational death is beginning to emerge in the literature (Kaufman, 1976; Hall, 1976; Aldrich and Reiss, 1976; Behn, 1976), it is hampered by a lack of consensus on what organizational death represents. Does it occur when there is a change in the name of an organization? When all its members are replaced? When the facility is moved? Does it make a difference if these events are the result of a merger, as compared with a business failure? One of the most difficult situations to classify is the case in which a legal corporation ceases to exist but its organizational operation continues to function. In the business literature an organization is divided into three tiers. The enterprise controls the economic assets, the managerial level controls human resources, and the firm directs the production activity. In many mergers (and divestitures) there is no change at the firm or managerial levels— only the legal name of the enterprise is changed. Similarly, in a study of federal agencies, Kaufman (1976) found that the functions performed by a terminated agency are often transferred to another agency.

Some clarity can be achieved by distinguishing between the death and the failure of organizations. A study of death examines whether an organization still exists, a study of failure focuses on the causes of death. Organizational failure connotes total ineffectiveness due to managerial incompetence, political vulnerability, or environmental entropy (Pfeffer and Salancik, 1978). Hence, a failure would be considered a fatality in an organizational decline study even if its staff and programs (or products) are transferred to other organizations. In the business sector, organizational death due to failure is qualitatively very different from organizational death due to transformation, as in the case of a merger. An organization that is acquired must by definition have some marketable assets. The fact that it is purchased indicates that it is currently successful or has the potential to become successful. While both types of organizational death present interesting research issues, death due to failure is more closely related to our interest in the organizational consequences of the emerging era of scarcity.

Conclusion

The objectives of this chapter were to bring together a diverse body of literature relating to organizational decline and to identify some important research topics in the process. We have discussed the concept of decline and examined the conceptual and empirical work related to this topic at the population and organizational levels of analysis. At the organizational level we examined the causes, responses to, and effects of decline.

This review has identified two major disjunctions in the literature. First, authors addressing decline in the public sector tend to have a different orientation from those writing about crises in business organizations. In the business sector, organizational death is viewed as suicide, while in the public sector it is treated as homicide. In the private sector, declining profits are regarded as evidence of stagnating management rather than of environmental scarcity. Conversely, in the public sector, decline tends to be viewed as a characteristic of the environment rather than of the organization. Therefore, authors in this area speak of cutback management as though that were the only option. In the private sector this response is regarded as a last recourse—appropriate only after all proactive strategies have failed. This discrepant orientation reflects a difference in the level of autonomy in the two sectors. Public administrators generally have less freedom than private ones to relocate their organization to a new ecological niche. However, several authors have noted that this restriction is often more apparent than real; that is, public administrators may have more degrees of freedom than they choose to consider. Hence, the need for a more aggressive breed of public administrators has been stressed. To facilitate this process, the need for more dialogue between business and public administrators and for mechanisms for disseminating information about innovative options selected by public administrators have been noted.

Second, there is a significant discrepancy between descriptions of how managers actually react to decline-induced crises, and prescriptions for how they should react. Under pressure, managers tend to become more conservative rather than more innovative, more autocratic rather than more participative. Advocates of a self-design approach to organizational administration prescribe the opposite responses: in a crisis situation, managers should examine a wide range of alternatives, discredit past responses, and solicit extensive inputs from others. The fact that there is a discrepancy between ideal and actual behavior does not warrant concern. However, the fact that self-design proponents generally do not examine the feasibility of implementing their prescriptions does. Consequently, there is substantial need for research on organizational operations under crisis conditions to discover how innovative alternatives can be substituted for reflex reactions. Further, to avoid the dysfunctional consequences of innovation suggested by Miller's (1955) three-stage model of response to stress, we need more information on how managers can use innovation as a strategy based on calculation rather than on desperation. In the former case it is analogous to a rifle shot aimed at a specific target; in the latter case it is like a shotgun blast searching for a target. In general, there is a significant need for more interdisciplinary research on responses to stress. Research previously conducted at the physiological level (Selye, 1976; Cooper and Marshall, 1976; Gal and Lazarus, 1975), psychological level (McGrath, 1970; Levi, 1967), and organizational level (Sales, 1969; Colligan, Smith, and Jurrell, 1977; House, 1974; Smart and Vertinsky, 1977) needs to be integrated and applied to decline as a special case of stress.

To complement this research on stress there is a considerable need for case studies of organizational responses to decline. Especially critical is information about the choice between alternative responses. It is obvious that different organizations choose different options, but we have little data on the factors influencing this process of choice. Information on this topic can be collected from historical records of organizations that have undergone retrenchment, as well as from longitudinal participant observations. Accounts of how single organizations and entire industries have managed these situations provide a rich data base for the development of inductive models (Rubin, 1977; Smith, 1963).

Interdisciplinary research is especially important in assessing the effects of decline. The decline of an organization can affect its members' emotional health and morale, family stability, interdepartmental relations, decision-making procedures, community labor market dynamics, and interorganizational relations. Research on the likely effects of widespread decline in an era of scarcity might produce radical reformulations of our theories of job design, employee compensation, organizational design, career development, and leadership. In addition, it might produce arguments for new forms of government, commerce, and society. These and other challenging research frontiers lie ahead.

11

Organizational Disintegration: Roots, Processes, and Types

Amittai Niv

Communes are among the more extreme forms of social innovation. The Essenes, two thousand years ago, were the first to translate utopian ideals into a viable organization. Since then, the communal idea has never lost its vitality. Neither have communes changed their fundamental values, goals, methods of organization, or even their physical setups. But despite their underlying humanistic values and their founders' devotion, the history of communal ventures is a story of failure and disappointment. There is something about extreme innovation of this kind that usually prevents it from succeeding.

This chapter suggests a framework for analyzing the failure, or disintegration, of communes and compares that framework with other explanations suggested by the rich body of communal literature. The fates of two contemporary communes, one in the United States and the other in Israel, are then examined. This comparison enables us not only to explain failure but also to define processes that lead to survival and success. The last section of this' chapter is devoted to a discussion of the implications of our framework for the more general case of planned efforts to establish new social realities.

Communes can be distinguished from other forms of social organization along several dimensions. First, underlying all communes is a comprehensive ideology that is based on assumptions about human nature and the desired social order. The mission derived from these assumptions is to establish a social entity that will enable its individual members to grow and develop to their full potential. Ideology not only defines the shape and the content of the commune itself but, more important, defines its mission toward the external world. Second, communes are "total" institutions. Individual members perform all their roles and satisfy all their needs within the commune. Third, communes, regardless of their size, are complex systems. They have to perform a variety of functions, such as production, consumption, and education. Communes also require a complex matching network of single roles and tasks. Fourth, communes maintain clear boundaries with their external environment. Physical location of the commune, selective and careful recruitment and socialization of new members, and various means to control tangible exchanges with the rest of the world are among the devices that every commune establishes to set clear boundaries. Fifth, egalitarianism and equality, as values and as operational norms, form the one single most important dimension of every commune. Among the characteristics derived from it are common ownership of the means of production, central distribution of goods and services according to egalitarian principles, and equal access to education. Variations among communes, in this respect, range from a mechanistic approach to equality to the establishment of equal opportunity for everyone. Sixth, coming together to live in harmony is a characteristic shared by all communes. The primary, familylike, quality of interpersonal relations is both a goal in itself and a means to enable the commune to achieve its other goals. Finally, communes develop decision-making processes and management systems that, on the one hand, enable them to engage in effective decision making and, on the other hand, enable them to increase members' identification with and commitment to the commune and the cause it is serving. Many communes have been based on strong charismatic leaders. Others have developed systems of direct or indirect democracy.

Contemporary North American experiments and the Chinese communes are the two end points of a wide spectrum of communal forms. These forms differ from each other in terms of members' motivation to join (did they join voluntarily or were they coerced) and the kind of commitment required (that is, short-term or lifelong). Dilemmas associated with survival are mostly relevant for communes based on voluntary and lifelong membership. This type of commune is the subject of our analysis.

Stagnation and Assimilation

The Shakers were among the largest and longest-existing communal organizations in the United States. Established in the seventeenth century, they had, a hundred years later, 20,000 members spread over twenty-two colonies. Two main principles shaped this sect's history: autarky and a ban on family life. The first principle required the colony to fill all of its own physical needs. The second made the commune dependent on the recruitment of new members from the external world. Lacking needed equipment and know-how, the Shaker colonies gradually lost their ability to maintain a reasonable level of efficiency in their production operations. A decreasing standard of living was among the factors that made the recruitment of new members more and more difficult. The last Shaker colony was discontinued in the late 1930s.

The Society of True Inspiration, or Amana, was among the most successful communal organizations in nineteenth-century North America. A religious mission combined with a drive for economic success resulted in an expanding network of prosperous communes. At its peak, Amana incorporated seven communal villages. But in 1932, at a long meeting of all its members, the Amana communal organization decided to split into a church and a business enterprise. The latter became a large and successful corporation. But by giving up the basic principles of egalitarianism, totality, clear boundaries, and the primary, familylike quality of interpersonal relations, the Amana villages ceased to be communal organizations.

Disintegration of a commune as a result of lack of resources, as in the case of the Shakers, is here defined as stagnation. Usually it takes the form of physical abandonment of the commune. Assimilation is another and different form of communal disintegration. It occurs when a commune's main characteristics are transformed into noncommunal ones, as in the case of Amana. Historical evidence strongly indicates the tendency of communes to fail. The same conclusion can be reached by considering the logical processes underlying the communal phenomenon. The description and analysis of the latter will be done by using two ideal types of communal disintegration.

Model and Pioneer Communes

The key concept in our analysis of communal failure is the so-called ideal type. Before proceeding, it is important to clarify the meaning of this concept. We refer here to Weber's (1947) formulation:

> For the purpose of a typological scientific analysis, it is convenient to treat all irrational, affectually determined elements of behavior as factors of deviation from a conceptually pure type of rational action . . . it is convenient to determine in the first place what would have been a rational course, given the ends of the participants and adequate knowledge of all the circumstances. Only in this way is it possible to assess the causal significance of irrational factors as accounting for the deviations from this type. The construction of a purely rational course of action in such cases serves the sociologist as a type ("ideal type") which has the merit of clear understandability and lack of ambiguity. By comparison with this it is possible to understand the ways in which actual action is influenced by irrational factors of all sorts, such as affects and errors, in that they account for the deviation from the line of conduct which would be expected on the hypothesis that the action were purely rational [p. 92].

Our ideal types contain some of the basic assumptions that result in the comprehensive ideologies, typical characteristics, basic processes, and structural arrangements of communes. As here defined, these assumptions serve as the foundation of complete and purely rational structures. The assumptions are drawn from real categories of communes, which are here referred to as the Model ideal type and the Pioneer ideal type.

Underlying the communal ideology are assumptions about humanity and the social context of which human beings are a part. The Model commune assumes that human nature is "negative." The social order not only reflects the character of its individuals but also accelerates their "negativeness." This set of underlying assumptions was especially adopted by Christian sects. According to these assumptions humanity *is not* industrious, creative, frank, affective, collaborative, open, warm, trustworthy, committed to ideals, and an organic part of nature.

In contrast, the Pioneer commune assumes that human nature is "positive." Human beings are basically good, but the current social context is badly designed and, therefore, negatively influences the behavior of individuals. Some of the nineteenth-century North American communes, most contemporary communes in the United States, and all communes based on socialistic values share this view of the relationship between the positive nature of humanity and the negative aspects of the social order. When referring to human nature and society, the Pioneer ideal type assumes that change and improvement are possible and even desirable. The Model ideal type does not.

Differing assumptions lead to different value systems and hence to different structural arrangements. For instance, the Model commune, as an outcome of its negative view of human nature and pessimistic perspective on society, develops a communal system based on mechanical equality, asceticism as a way of life, primary, familylike interpersonal relations, and a quite mechanical view of the individual's growth and development. In the Pioneer commune the same values are given a different interpretation. Equality is defined as the equal right of members to their individual and different needs, asceticism is seen as only a temporary requirement, interpersonal relations tend to be more instrumental, and there is a strong belief in individualistic growth and development. The goals of the two types of communes, derived from their basic assumptions and central values, are quite different. The Model utopia hopes to isolate individuals from the existing social order. The Pioneer, in contrast, intends to change that same order.

Different assumptions, values, and goals are likely to lead to different characteristics. On the one hand, the Model commune will attract individuals who wish to withdraw from a corrupt society. It will require from its members total compliance with its values and norms. Its physical location will be in a remote and deserted area. Finally, the Model commune will usually develop into a relatively small communal organization. Growth, for this kind of commune, is not a strategic goal. The Pioneer commune, on the other hand, aspires to interact with the external world — to influence and change it. Members' commitment to the commune will be made in very broad and general terms, and the commune itself will be located in populated areas and will tend to grow and develop into a relatively large organization. Growth, for the Pioneer commune, *is* a strategic goal.

The two ideal types of commune will also differ in most internal processes. For instance, members of the Model commune will constitute a rather homogeneous population. There will be an ongoing effort to prevent internal differentiation of any kind. Exchange of information with the external world will be limited. Power and decision-making processes will be based on principles of direct democracy. Control systems will operate through the common background and shared norms of members. The Pioneer commune not only will attract heterogeneous membership but will stimulate a process of further internal differentiation. Communication channels with the external world will be wide open. Power will be applied quite differentially, and self-government will be based on representative democracy. Formal procedures will develop to make an effective control system possible.

The production subsystem of the Model commune will include only a small number of functional units. The technology applied will be simple, and the process will be labor-intensive. Most of its output will be consumed by the commune itself. Simple farming or crafts seem to best fit this description. Accounting for the nature of the Model commune's production subsystem are several factors. Simple structure and technology are related to resistance to division of labor and specialization and to avoidance of coordination through professional management. Limited financial resources add to the tendency to rely on the labor of members rather than on capital investments in expensive equipment. All these factors also fit the autarkic nature of the Model commune. Efficiency is not a factor to be considered, and neither is exchange with the external world. As a retreat from a corrupt world, the Model commune has to strive to develop a production subsystém that will make an autonomous existence possible. Self-sufficiency, or an autarkic production system, best fits this purpose.

The Pioneer commune will develop a production subsystem consisting of a large number of units. It will be capital-intensive and apply advanced technologies. Its output will be for markets external to the commune. It will have a complex structure and advanced technologies to allow its members to develop and specialize in various areas and directions. In addition to technical specialization, various opportunities in areas of management and coordination will exist. Available financial resources and principles of efficiency will encourage introduction of modern and market-oriented farming or industry into Pioneer communes.

The structural dimensions of the two ideal types of communes are summarized in Table 1. Thus far, we have discussed these two types of communes as stable entities. In other words, we have given a snapshot of two social systems. But both stagnation and assimilation result from continuing processes. The nature of these processes needs to be better understood.

Dynamics of Communes

External sources of changes within our ideal types are processes that take place in a commune's environment. Structural changes in the national economy, the introduction of new technologies, rapid developments in the political arena, changes in standard of living or life-style—these are among the many possible sources of external influence. Two aspects of such processes deserve further exploration: their interrelatedness and their clear pressure toward communal disintegration.

**Table 1. Main Features of Subsystems of
the Two Ideal Types of Communes**

	Model Commune	Pioneer Commune
Consumption		
Number of units	Few	Many
Expertise	Low	High
Technology	Simple	Advanced
Capital investment	Low	High
Amount of goods and services	Small	Large
Methods of distribution	Mechanical	Flexible
Strategic goal	To satisfy and reinforce similar needs	To satisfy and reinforce differential needs
Education and Socialization		
Number of units	Few	Many
Expertise	Low	High
Methods	Simple	Advanced
Capital investment	Low	High
Content	Conservative	Modern
Strategic goal	Indoctrination	General education
Leadership and Decision Making		
Number of functions	Few	Many
Expertise	Low	High
Methods	Direct democracy	Professional management
Content	Faith and devotion	Efficiency
Strategic goal	Identification with the cause	Prosperity of the commune
Control		
Number of units	Few	Many
Expertise	Low	High
Methods	Simple	Advanced
Content	Organizational Integrity	Organizational performance
Strategic goal	Social control	Appropriate operations

Communes are complex forms of social organization. Complexity, in this case, does not result from growing size but rather from the intensity of interconnectedness among internal elements. If an institution is both relatively small and "total," it will produce an enormous number of interconnections among its single elements. All the roles an individual plays, for example, are performed within the same system. Furthermore, the same individual has to satisfy all his or her needs within the same system. Thus, the first step in our analysis is to identify the most relevant connections among a commune's single elements. The concept of ideal types offers a framework for such an analysis.

Model and Pioneer communes not only differ from each other in their basic characteristics, but they also develop different disintegration processes. In the Model commune this process will take the form of an ongoing effort to minimize change. For example, socialization mechanisms are designed to maintain a membership that is as homogeneous as possible. Homogeneity is reinforced by keeping all subsystems (that is, production, consumption, education, decision making and control, interface mediation) relatively undeveloped. When this is successfully done, division of labor and specialization are minimized. At this point personnel interchangeability is almost complete. This minimization of change strategy is even more obvious in relation to the Model commune's external environment. Communes of this type, for instance, minimize the application of modern technologies, prefer an independent education subsystem, and sever almost all communication links with external sources. Ironically, if successfully applied, this strategy ultimately leads to stagnation.

The Pioneer commune represents a contrasting form of disintegration. Single elements within the commune tend to change and develop. The Pioneer commune, for example, will develop a rather loose set of criteria for absorbing new members. Its socialization processes will lead to a heterogeneous population. Various subsystems will tend to grow, diversify, and become complex. This will result in a growing amount of division of labor and specialization; hence, personnel will not be interchangeable. The socialization process will be strongly oriented toward general education and knowledge. Communication channels to and from the external world will be kept open. Again ironically, when successfully applied, this strategy will ultimately result in the commune's losing some, perhaps all, of its communal characteristics. We refer to this process of disintegration as assimilation.

Stagnation is a threat that all kinds of social organizations have to cope with. Business firms do so by maintaining positive balances; voluntary organizations work hard to recruit and motivate devoted members; and educational institutions do their best to continue to attract the right students, faculty, and financial resources. But assimilation is a problem faced only by deviant systems, that is, by systems that attempt to be different from the world with which they interact. Our analysis suggests that stagnation will characterize disintegration in communes of the Model ideal type, whereas assimilation will occur in Pioneer-like communes.

Out of more than a hundred communal organizations established during the nineteenth century in the United States, only a dozen lasted fifteen years or more. None of these exists today (Kanter, 1972, p. 63). Rates of disintegration among contemporary communes in the United States and in Western Europe are, if anything, higher. There are, however, a few impressive exceptions. But before these exceptions are examined, the form of analysis developed here will be compared with typical explanations of the survival problem, as presented in the rich literature on communes.

Images from the Literature

In 1841 George Ripley, followed by a group of Transcendentalist intellectuals, established a commune at Brook Farm near Boston, Massachusetts. This small group, enamored by the new social ideals, was never able to support itself physically or to set the foundations for a viable social organization. In 1846 a fire brought this short experiment to its end. The first report about Brook Farm was published in a book by Swift (1890). Codman (1894) added an account of his own personal experiences there, and Sears (1912) dedicated a book to his friends in that experiment. Orvis used letters written by members of the commune during its last four years in a book published in 1928. Haraszyi made another study of the same letters in 1937, and Burton (1939) repeated the effort two years later. Sams (1958) summarized the available data on Brook Farm and Curtis (1961) recently published another version of the Brook Farm story.

Despite their small size, high rate of failure, and relatively small impact on the surrounding world, communes draw a lot of attention. The coverage of a small and short-lived commune like

Brook Farm is typical in this sense. Although few of these studies explicitly discuss the dilemmas that communes encounter in their relations with the external world, the problem of survival is implicitly addressed by many of them. Studies that use a historical approach usually describe events and phases in the development of a given commune in great detail. Typical examples are the histories of the early Shakers (Neal, 1947; Chase, 1936), of nineteenth-century American communes such as Harmony, New Harmony, Oneida, and Zoar (Holloway, 1951; Houriet, 1971; Kateb, 1968), of the Hutterite movement (Hostetler, 1975) and of the kibbutz movement (Spiro, 1970).

The description usually starts with an account of the historical forces that led to the formation of the commune under study. Religious discrimination or the emergence of social movements that preached equality and justice in nineteenth-century Europe spawned many communes in the United States during that period. Other communes are seen as having their roots in the "Mayflower spirit." Contemporary communes in the United States are described as a reaction to alienation, dissatisfaction with middle-class culture, and the increasing generation gap within society. The kibbutz is presented against the evolution of a Jewish nationalistic trend in Eastern Europe at the end of the nineteenth century and the spread of socialistic ideologies in these countries. The second section of most historical studies deals with the 'coming together': organizing the founding group, crossing the ocean to the New World, purchasing the needed land, and starting to build the farm. Besides discussing establishment of the economic enterprise, these studies describe the time and energy that went into shaping social institutions. The studies generally end with descriptions of the commune's final crisis and the broader context within which the specific drama took place. Three main ingredients for establishing a commune are usually mentioned: a favorable historical background, the formulation of a comprehensive and meaningful ideology, and the emergence of a charismatic leader. Disintegration is explained by the decline in one or more of these three. Members' losing faith (crisis of ideology) and/or death of the charismatic leader are the factors most frequently cited to account for failure.

Two main weaknesses characterize this mode of explanation.

First, the 'why' questions are often not asked: Why, at a specific moment, did the members of Amana lose their faith in the communal mission? Or, why did the Shakers go through a leadership succession crisis more than a hundred years after their establishment? Second, this kind of analysis does not explain the few cases of success. Why have the Hutterites been able to maintain their faith for more than 400 years? How has the Bruderhof been able to pass successfully three times through a charismatic leadership succession? Analysis of the processes contributing to disintegration or survival is thus omitted in these accounts of communes.

An alternative to the historical approach is the atomistic approach in which specific aspects of a given commune are examined or the same aspect is compared in different communes. Most work of this type has been carried out in kibbutzim, the Israeli communes. Studies done in the areas of education and work illustrate the nature of the atomistic approach. Socialization of the young generation is a crucial matter for all future-oriented communes and the education system in the kibbutz is a powerful socialization agent. Shapira and Madsen (1974) assessed the impact of kibbutz education on competitive behavior. They compared, in a laboratory experiment, two groups of children—kibbutz and nonkibbutz—to examine competitive modes of behavior under various controlled situations. Their findings indicate "that kibbutz children are more cooperative within groups than are their urban counterparts. It is also clear that kibbutz children are competitively motivated, but that this motivation is channeled to between-group competition to a greater extent than to between-individual competition" (p. 145).

Bettelheim's (1969) controversial study of kibbutz education suggests that kibbutz socialization leads to an oppressed personality. Jay and Birney (1973) tested this hypothesis by using a battery of six personality tests with two groups of rural adolescents—kibbutz and nonkibbutz. Their main conclusion was that "contrary to the description given by Bettelheim, perhaps the nonkibbutz adolescent experiences a greater pressure from his environment than does the kibbutz adolescent" (p. 354). Amir (1969) evaluated the results of kibbutz education using behavioral, rather than experimental, test data. The performance of kibbutz-born soldiers in the army was used as a measure of the quality of education. Performance was evaluated by processing records of all recruits to the Israeli Defense Forces during the years 1961 to 1964 and analyzing them in terms of three behavioral criteria: volunteering for special fighting units, assessed suitability for command, and success in officers' school. Compared with the total soldier population at the same period, kibbutz-born soldiers scored three times higher in volunteering, two times higher in suitability for command positions, and twenty percent better in success in officers' school.

Values of equality and egalitarianism may be in conflict with organizational efficiency and effectiveness. The production subsystem and various aspects of work life are, therefore, of special interest in the kibbutz context. Among the numerous studies done in this field, those dealing with motivation are of special interest. Macarov (1972) applied Herzberg's theory and methodology to the kibbutz context and found that the Two-Factor Theory of work motivation well supported by the data and that the absence of salary as a consideration did not upset the theory. Eden (1975) reached similar conclusions by stating hypotheses derived from expectancy theory and confirming them with data that were collected by using detailed questionnaires in various kibbutzim.

Yuchtman (1972) explored the question of "why the expected positive relationship between the hierarchial position of the work role and its attractiveness is not obtained in the kibbutz" (p. 582) and found that "equity and equality norms coexist in the kibbutz. Specifically, the kibbutz maintains the egalitarian principle in the material sphere, and the equity principle in the nonmaterial sphere" (p. 592).

Education and work are only two out of many "single elements" of the kibbutz. Power distribution, internal differentiation and stratification, the paradox of ruling elites within an egalitarian society, specialization, and democratic decision making are some of the political aspects of the kibbutz that have been explored. On the interpersonal level, the conflict between the "community" and the "core family," the existence of pockets of anomie within the kibbutz, the absorption of the second generation, and processes associated with aging have been studied. Although the atomistic approach provides important insights into the complexities of communal life, it contributes little to a better understanding of the problem of survival or disintegration.

Several studies published in recent years do, however, directly address issues and problems associated with the survival of communes. Kanter (1972) defines the problem as "how people arrange to do the work that the community needs to survive as a group, and how the group in turn manages to satisfy and involve its members over a long period of time" (p. 64). The key factor in this mutual relationship is the individual's commitment to the cause that the commune stands for, to the commune as a social system, and to its other members. Going through documents left by nineteenth-century American communes, Kanter was able to identify 120 "mechanisms" that generate and maintain the commitment of individuals to their commune. Looking for the existence of such mechanisms within a sample of more than 110 communal organizations of that time, Kanter (1972) was able to reach the following conclusion: "Successful nineteenth-century communities built strong commitment through the sacrifices and investments of members on behalf of the community; through renunciation, which discouraged extra-group ties and built a strong family feeling within the community; through mortification, which offered identity changes for members; and through transcendence, which gave meaning and direction to the community by means of ideological systems and authority structures" (126).

Kanter thus moves from a simple description to an explanatory framework within which the survival problem of these communes can be explored. Nevertheless, taking "commitment" as the sole factor accounting for success or failure seems unnecessarily limited. While Kanter's indication for success is "survival over time," Katz and Golomb (1974) took as their main criterion "net growth." Their study referred to 240 Israeli kibbutzim and addressed three areas: system integration, economic effectiveness, and creative adaptation. These three areas define three levels of the commune: the individual, the social system (the single kibbutz), and the supra system (the Israeli society). The matrix of areas defined by these levels opens the way for a detailed analysis of single elements and their interrelationships within the system. For instance, when dealing with integration on the individual level, Katz and Golomb (1974) looked for "mechanisms" that link the individual to the community through symbols reflecting a common way of life, a common history, and common fate" (p. 287). Such mechanisms are physical separation from the surrounding society, ceremonials and festivals, common decision making, socialization processes for the second generation, and organizing production within cohesive teams.

In the same way, other integrating mechanisms are identified on the social system or commune level and the supra-system level (relationships with the broader society). The second area, economic effectiveness, is relatively easy to measure, it is "the degree to which a system mobilizes and utilizes internal and external resources to achieve its objectives" (1974, p. 301). The third area, creative adaptation, refers to required changes in values and norms. It requires the replacement of some of the basic values, the maintenance of others as they are, and the creative modification of still a third group of values and norms.

Mechanisms in each cell of the areas and levels matrix can be quantified and measured for each kibbutz and, later, compared against the performance of that kibbutz. Katz and Golomb applied this method to three groups of kibbutzim: the failing ones (negative growth), the survivors (nongrowth), and the successful ones (positive growth). The most important factor explaining performance turned out to be creative adaptation. It is "expected to be a causal factor with respect to both integration and effectiveness and moderate positive correlations with integration" (1974, pp. 405–6). Creative adaptation of values, according to Katz and Golomb, is one of three possibilities open for a system within a changing environment. The others are erosion and rigidity. Erosion will cause the system to lose its uniqueness, while rigidity will lead to maladaptation to the environment. Not only is creative adaptation a necessity for the kibbutz, but, according to the researchers, it can be successfully accomplished. In terms of the conceptual framework developed in this chapter, erosion and rigidity sound very much like assimilation and stagnation.

A few differences between Kanter's study and the work of Katz and Golomb are worth mentioning. The "dependent" variable or the "end-product" in Kanter's study is survival: for how long is a commune able to operate as a viable social system. Katz and Golomb, however, define their "dependent" variable as growth rate. Kanter assumes a passive posture by the commune towards its environment. Katz and Golomb assume a very active one. Kanter refers to the commitment of individuals to the system as the sole explanatory factor for a commune's success. But Katz and Golomb see adaptation of the commune to its external environment as a more important factor. The first approach represents a closed system view while the second reflects an open system one.

A possible explanation for the different views can be found in the fact that the two studies address two different types of communes. Most of the communes included in Kanter's sample are very close to the Model ideal commune, but the kibbutzim studied by Katz and Golomb are clearly associated with the Pioneer ideal commune. The system approach to the study of communal survival thus becomes a special case within the broader framework based on our ideal types.

Is Disintegration Inevitable?

Ideal types are pure rational constructs. Reality, in most cases, differs from what is prescribed by these constructs. Our analysis suggests that to the extent that communes conform to the ideal typical models that we have developed, they sow the seeds of their own destruction. However, communes that depart in certain ways from the ideal type may avoid disintegration. These departures may, in fact, represent a set of survival mechanisms. By closely examining cases where disintegration has been avoided, we may learn something about the requirements for survival.

Dove Cote

Dove Cote—as it will be called here—is a successful commune located in the northeastern part of the United States. The organization with which it is affiliated has four communes with a total membership of one thousand and was established in Germany after the First World War. Its ideology is derived from the principles of Anabaptism. Its "operational" formula has been summarized in the following way: "The faith given to its members by God makes it possible for them to discard everything in their previous lives that clashed with it. They now want to live till their dying day for this new task. . . . They believe in the unconditional reality of God the Father, the Son, and Holy Spirit. To them God is neither a fine ideal sprung out of wishful thinking, nor a vague, indefinite Something" (Arnold and Arnold, 1974, p. 8).

Dove Cote does not intend to change the world. Instead, it wants to enable its members to withdraw and isolate themselves in an effective way from the corrupted world. Since it closely corresponds to the Model ideal type of commune, we would predict its disintegration through stagnation. But at some crucial points, particularly in its product and education subsystems, Dove Cote clearly departs from the ideal type. One would expect a Model commune to have a self-sufficient and autarkic production system, since such a subsystem is vital for maintaining a commune's independence from the world. In fact, Dove Cote owns and operates an effective market-oriented industry (high-quality toys and furniture). This industry accounts for almost 90 percent of Dove Cote's income. One would also expect a commune such as Dove Cote to develop a completely independent educational subsystem, with the young being carefully socialized from their first day until their complete absorption as full-fledged members. Yet, in fact, all of Dove Cote's children attend a noncommunal high school. Moreover, all the commune's youngsters are given the opportunity to pursue higher education in liberal arts or vocational colleges external to the commune.

These two departures from the rational Model ideal type of commune seem in particular to protect Dove Cote from stagnation. Running a modern and profitable production subsystem not only satisfies immediate physical needs but also creates an opportunity for differential development and satisfaction of its members in their economic activities. Exposing the younger generation to the external world has its merits. First, it forces each youngster to make a choice regarding membership in the commune as his or her own way of life. Second, and no less important, by exposing these youngsters to the external world, the commune turns them into internal change agents. Agents of this kind are vital for successful adaptation to the changes that take place in the external environment.

Careful selection and activation of the right "survival mechanisms" are necessary for the success of those departures that prevent the commune from disintegrating and, at the same time, enable it to maintain its basic characteristics. Dove Cote's industry is market oriented. But Dove Cote has little direct contact with customers or suppliers. All sales, for instance, are made through a well-developed mail order system. Also, within its specific market niche, Dove Cote does not experience real competition. This favorable situation is possible because of the control the commune has over most production factors, such as design and quality. The technology is craft rather than mass production; this ensures high quality and, no less important, the avoidance of many of the negative social consequences associated with industrialization.

Moreover, Dove Cote's educators have a strong say in the curriculum and teaching methods used in the regional high school that their children attend. The patterns of higher education mesh, to a great extent, with Dove Cote's character. Teachers' colleges and vocational schools are the institutions that most of its youngsters prefer to attend. They enroll in small groups at the same institution, stay off campus, and keep a car that enables them to spend at least a few evenings every month back at their home commune. Finally, parents of students who live outside the commune are aware of the pressures exerted by the two poles—the commune and the academic setting. Parents, especially mothers, play an important role in reducing the impact of these pressures. Formal arrangements, like minimizing the other duties of parents, stimulate such a support system. These departures, however, have to be managed in a way that enables the commune to stay close to its ideal type and thus maintain its identity as a unique social system. To be effective, departures have to be introduced in a systemic way. For instance, by giving high priority to vocational training, the commune can enjoy the advantages of higher education while minimizing the latter's negative consequences. But this will turn out to be a creative solution only after the commune develops a production subsystem advanced enough to absorb the graduates of such training programs.

Stony Hill

Stony Hill (also a fictitious name) is a prosperous kibbutz in Israel. Its ideology and actual setup both identify Stony Hill as a Pioneer type of commune. Underlying its ideology are assumptions about the positive nature of humanity. Existing social orders, according to this ideology, prevent individuals from actualizing their positive potentials. Stony Hill, like other kibbutzim, is thus a leader in the struggle to change and improve the current society. Such a mission requires a rather high level of exchange with the world external to the commune. The "give and take" process between Stony Hill and its environment is apparent in all aspects of daily life. However, this high exchange rate, combined with the effects of the commune's relative smallness, exposes Stony Hill to the threat of assimilation.

Survival mechanisms in this case involve departures from the Pioneer type of commune in an effort to reduce or eliminate exchange with the external world. As in the case of Dove Cote, such departures not only must have their own internal logic but must be consistent with various elements within the system. Risk avoidance and an artificial environment are the main survival mechanisms used in Stony Hill's production subsystem. Compared with other kibbutzim of the same age and size, Stony Hill was, and still is, extremely cautious in developing its production units—for example, its more specialized farm operations. A conservative approach also characterized its introduction of industry as a central economic venture. When the final decision about industrialization was taken, Stony Hill opted for a low-risk and low-profit business. This conservative approach minimizes the possibility of an economic disaster that could endanger Stony Hill's well-being and autonomy, requires less interaction with factors external to the commune, and is closely associated with conflict avoidance in other parts of the system. A business venture such as Stony Hill's slows the rate of internal specialization, reduces the pressure toward maximization of profits, and does not require a highly diversified and differential managerial elite. Conservatism, as here described, is not only an exchange-regulating device but also an internal stabilizing mechanism. Like other kibbutzim, most of Stony Hill's exchanges with the external world are through an intermediate environment. In the production subsystem, this intermediate environment is organized in the form of regional and nationwide purchasing, raw material handling, final processing of products, and marketing operations. Intermediate enterprises of this kind are owned and operated by several kibbutzim in a cooperative form. In addition to economies of scale, this kind of organization minimizes direct exposure to the external environment.

Economies of scale are also achieved in Stony Hill's educational subsystem. Its high school is a joint venture with several kibbutzim located within the same geographical region. Stony Hill's teenagers refer to the education system within which they are raised as a "greenhouse." The child is protected in this subsystem not only against external stimuli but also from undesirable influences within the commune. The children's subsystem thus both provides an ideal model of a communal society and, through the formal socialization agents, makes control of the educational process possible. Reducing and regulating contacts between children and parents by locating the high school in an isolated setting is a radical expression of control of basic processes. Another example of departure from the ideal type is the curriculum in Stony Hill's school, since it is in line with the curriculum designed by the national authorities. But it nevertheless contains enough elements to ensure an educational framework adapted to a social system that "deviates" from the society within which it is embedded.

In conclusion, departures are crucial to prevent disintegration of a commune. But the purposes and cause for which the commune stands must be maintained. The delicate balance between departure and integrity is, in essence, the secret of communal long-range survival.

12

A Framework for Understanding Organizational Failure

William G. Ouchi

I was recently called upon by an agency of the federal government to provide expert counsel in a sex discrimination suit against a major industrial firm. My expert advice was limited to a narrow subquestion in the case: What is an organization? The law in this case states quite clearly that the statute in question applies only to a single establishment. The government sought to prove that the entire corporation, which consisted of many plants and offices in various geographical locations, comprised a single "establishment," while the defendent corportion sought to show that each physical

Reprinted with permission from *Administrative Science Quarterly,* 1980, *25*.

building constituted a separate "establishment." Questions of law aside, the role into which I was thrust gave me cause for embarrassment: surely any organizational theorist must be able to clearly determine what constitutes an organization. Just as surely, I realized that we have no theoretical basis on which to make such a determination.

What is an organization? Why do organizations exist? These are questions that we ignore because we have no answer to them. Indeed, our research paradigms would be crippled if we did not ignore these questions and proceed as though the answers to them were too obvious to deserve notice. If asked what an organization is, however, many of us would refer to Barnard's ([1938] 1968) technological imperative, which argues that formal organizations will arise when technological conditions demand physical power, speed, endurance, mechanical adaptation, or continuity that are beyond the capacity of a single individual (pp. 27–28). Yet on closer scrutiny, we can observe that when the stone is too large or the production facility too complex for a single person to master, what is called for is cooperation, and cooperation need not take the form of a formal organization. Grain farmers who have need of a large grain elevator do not form corporations that take over the individual farms, turning the farmers into employees; instead, the individual farmers band together into a cooperative to own and operate the elevator, leaving all other functions divided just as they were formerly.

Others would refer to March and Simon (1958), who argue that an organization will exist as long as it can offer to its members inducements that exceed the contributions that it asks of them. While this position serves us well in explaining the conditions under which an organization will continue to exist, it does not explain how an organization is capable of achieving this alchemy, that is, of creating a whole that is so much greater than the sum of its parts that it can give to each part more than that part contributed.

Most of us, however, would refer to Blau and Scott (1962), who define a formal organization as a purposive aggregation of individuals who exert concerted effort toward a common and explicitly recognized goal. Yet we can hardly accept this definition whole, suspecting along with Simon (1945) that individuals within organizations rarely have anything like goal congruence or even common understanding of goals and that they behave in a far less rational manner than Blau and Scott's definition suggests.

One final point of view on the question of why organizations exist was sketched out in an inquiry by Coase (1937) and has recently been developed by Williamson (1975). In this view, a corporation exists when it is capable of mediating the economic transactions among its members at lower "transactions costs" than a market mechanism can provide. For example, when the production technology demands teamwork that leads to joint outputs that resist efforts to separate out the value of each person's contribution, then market mechanisms become inefficient compared to bureaucracies. The bureaucratic corporation achieves its superior mediating properties because it is capable of taking labor inputs from a number of workers, evaluating the performance of each through a hierarchical authority system, and offering rewards that induce each worker to bend to the goals of the firm, even though those corporate goals only partly intersect with the goals of the individual. In this transactions cost model, markets and bureaucracies are compared with respect to their efficiency in achieving mediation of economic transactions. Under certain conditions, markets are more efficient because they can achieve mediation without the administrative overhead of managers, accountants, or personnel departments. Under other conditions, however, a market mechanism becomes so cumbersome that it will be less efficient than a bureaucracy, despite the large administrative apparatus of every bureaucratic organization. It is this transactions cost approach that lies behind the analysis to be pursued here.

This chapter expresses the view that the nature of organizations can be understood from the standpoint of efficiency. That is not to say that power or authority cannot also serve as basic points of departure for such an inquiry. Indeed, it is precisely because power and authority have been the basis for most of organizational theory that there may be much to be gained by more systematically applying an efficiency view to our understanding of organizations.

The Efficiency Criterion in Organizational Theory

Before we embark on a discussion of markets, bureau-cracies, and clans, we must raise two additional issues. What, first of all, is the role of an efficiency criterion in organizational research? The transactions cost approach explicitly regards efficiency as the fundamental cause that determines the development of organiza-tional forms. This emphasis makes our approach somewhat un-usual compared to other organizational theories. Second is the issue of the Weberian theory of bureaucratic organization, which has both explicitly and implicitly shaped almost all contemporary approaches to organizational theory, sometimes with the result that inappropriate and misleading points of view have developed. To fully appreciate the implications of the transactions cost approach, we must first place it in a broader frame of reference than the Weberian theory provides.

One objective of organizational theory is to develop a pre-scriptive science, that is, one that is capable of accurately predict-ing, under certain conditions, which organizational forms will succeed and one that can also provide a basis for policy recommen-dations to the practitioner. Where economic organizations are concerned, one fundamental basis for such predictions has been the relative efficiency of one or another form. Where the unit of analysis has been an industry or an entire economy, economists have had considerable success in demonstrating that certain or-ganizational forms, such as cartelization or extreme concentration, produce less efficient outcomes than do those forms that conform more nearly to a competitive model. In such cases, the efficiency of the exchange network can be assessed through measures such as the price (interest rate) paid by issuers of municipal bonds when there are only three buyers versus the more competitive condition that obtains when there are more buyers. Having a relatively clear measure of efficiency, the researcher can then compare more ver-sus less concentrated markets and arrive at a prescriptive model.

When the unit of analysis is a single organization, however, the question becomes whether a corporation of type A is more efficient than a corporation of type B. The efficiency of the organi-zational form is difficult to assess because there is no criterion with which to make the comparison; that is, a measure of the overall profitability of the firm will include effects not only of organizational form but also of competitive conditions, regulations, general economic conditions, and a host of other factors. It is ordinarily impossible to separate out the effects of organizational form alone, although some notable progress has recently been made (Rumelt, 1974).

Organizational theorists, however, have always felt the need for an efficiency criterion in their theories. Certainly any of them would include among the major contributions to the field the work of Weber ([1947] 1968), Barnard ([1938] 1968), Thompson (1967), and Lawrence and Lorsch (1967). Each of these studies was based on a deep concern with the efficiency of organizational forms; yet while each has made a great theoretical contribution, none has fulfilled its promise in empirical research and in the development of a prescriptive science of organizations. Each of these studies has produced a rich stream of research, but we are still without an answer to the most fundamental question—"Why do economic organizations exist?"—because the answer to this question must rest on an efficiency point of view.

The problem here is not to develop techniques for an empirical study of the efficiency of organizational forms, but rather to develop the theoretical basis from which such techniques may flow. At present, we are limited to the gross measures of corporate profitability or the questionnaire measures of perceived effectiveness employed by Lawrence and Lorsch and many others. What does it mean to conceptualize the efficiency of an organizational form? Are we limited to the concept of survival over a very long run, as employed in the ecological models (Hannan and Freeman, 1977)?

What we find in Williamson (1975) and will discuss here is that the concept of transactions cost has the property of being an efficiency point of view that, conceptually, is amenable to the microanalysis of an organization. Systematic development of this concept will make it possible to lay the groundwork for a prescriptive science that can provide hypotheses to predict the conditions under which markets, bureaucracies, or clans will be more efficient. In addition, it will in the future also be possible to specify in more detail the conditions under which a functional, divisional, or matrix form will be more efficient and to do this in a manner that is subject to empirical test. Our goal will be to identify those organizational properties that give rise to the costs of mediating transactions between individuals and to identify the variety of organizational forms that can efficiently provide this mediation' under certain conditions.

The problem of organizational efficiency is one that Weber explored in great depth, and his resolution of the problem has influenced the development of organizational theory in ways that are both subtle and far reaching. In his discussion of the "sociological categories of economic action," particularly in the sections concerning "calculations in kind" and "types of economic division of labor," Weber ([1947] 1968) discusses the question of efficiency in detail. In brief, he subscribes to the view that when competitive market conditions can be met, a market is superior to a bureaucracy as a mediation device. However, Weber does not explicitly adopt a market versus bureaucracy approach but rather begins from the position that large organizations (or systems of legitimate domination) exist and then asks how they can be made most efficient. He argues forcefully that attempts to simulate market or price mechanisms within organizations will fail and that only arbitrary and thus misleading attributions of performance can be arrived at where interdependent work is concerned. He goes on to describe a set of conditions that, in his view, clearly make bureaucracy the solution of choice: "Experience tends universally to show that the purely bureaucratic type of administration . . . is, from a purely technical point of view, capable of attaining the highest degree of efficiency and is in this sense formally the most rational known means of exercising authority over human beings. It is superior to any other form in precision, in stability, in the stringency of its discipline, and in its reliablity. . . . The choice is only between bureaucracy and dilettantism in the field of administration" (p. 223).

Our objective here is not to engage in Weberian interpretation but to point out that, first, Weber was deeply concerned with the question of efficiency in administration and, second, that he arrived firmly at the conclusion that the bureaucratic type was the

most efficient form of administration possible. Had Weber foreseen the tremendous developments in the field of accounting or
had he focused on a comparison between markets and bureaucracies as efficient modes of mediation rather than focusing on
the relative efficiency of traditional, charismatic, and rational-legal
forms of legitimate domination, he might have come to a different conclusion. But he was interested primarily in the relative
economic efficiency of different forms of legitimate power, and he
concluded that the bureaucratic form based on rational-legal authority was to be preferred above all others.

Those of us who study industrial organizations, however,
have no reason to confine ourselves to questions of domination,
and we therefore have no reason to be bound by the Weberian
argument. Our objective ought to be to discover those industrial
organizational forms that are most efficient and then separately relate these questions of efficiency to questions of power in society.
The perils of combining the two issues emerge quite clearly in a
recent book by Lindblom (1977). Lindblom attempts to deal simultaneously with questions of efficiency and with questions of the
distribution of power in society, and he ends up by dividing all
relationships into exchange, authority, and preceptoral ones. While
the questions that he addresses are much broader than those addressed here, we can see that his concern with both efficiency and
power produces a confusion for the organizational theorist similar
to that found in Weber. For example, because Lindblom views only
market-mediated relationships within an exchange framework, he
applies questions of efficiency only to that category. Therefore, he
is incapable of assessing preceptorial or persuasive relationships as
having efficiency properties, and he views them instead as power
relations of a subtle kind. A transactions cost approach, however,
might view all three of his categories as alternative mechanisms for
mediating transactions and compare them systematically from an
efficiency point of view. Their implications for the distribution of
power in society could then be separately assessed. While such an
approach is not global, it is at least within the reach of present
theoretical frameworks.

The problem that Weber has left us with is that we are incapable of thinking about organizations except as bureaucracies. Vir-

tually every organizational theorist bases his work, either explicitly or implicitly, on the Weberian model. Few of us can think of large organizations without referring to the Weberian categories. Even humanistic scholars have set forth their visions of ideal organizations by describing their nonbureaucratic features (Bennis, 1966). The tremendous power of this unconscious acceptance of the Weberian model has recently led to some interesting developments that bear mention.

Most organizational theorists take for granted that the basic variables that describe the structure of an organization include size, complexity, specialization, formalization, administrative ratio, and centralization. Many seem to have forgotten that these variables came into use not very long ago, during a period when scholars were experimenting with them as possible operational representations of the conceptual Weberian dimensions of bureaucracy (see Udy, 1962; Blau, 1963; Hall, 1963). These variables have come into such common use that they are now often used to represent all organizations, without thought to whether the sample under study can reasonably be said to fit the Weberian bureaucratic type. Consequently, the terms *bureaucracy, complex organization,* and *formal organization* have become interchangeable. If one perceives the choice of administrative forms as Weber did, that is, as being between bureaucracy and dilettantism, then this approach is reasonable. But if one takes the view that bureaucracy is but one form of mediation of economic exchange, then the use of these variables becomes problematic. Let us consider some examples of this confusion.

Although sociologists have long regarded professionalized bureaucracies such as schools and hospitals as not being true bureaucracies, they have nonetheless proceeded as though these organizations can be adequately represented by those structural variables that are derived from the bureaucratic model. It is then with some surprise that they report that hospitals (Becker and Gordon, 1966) and school systems (Meyer and Rowan, 1977) are quite anomalous when viewed as bureaucracies. Other sociologists have theorized that professionalized bureaucracies are "organized anarchies" (Cohen, March, and Olsen, 1972) or have referred to them as "loosely coupled organizations" (Weick, 1976). These new models have gained quick acceptance in some circles and have been criticized in others as constituting the "cute school of organization theory."

Both the praise and the criticism are instructive. On the one hand, we are inclined to accept these models because all of us feel that there are many organizations that are not adequately described by bureaucratic dimensions and we feel constrained by the dominance of the Weberian point of view. On the other hand, the epithet "cute" implies an attractiveness that is without substance, and these models are indeed without substance in the sense that they only point out the inadequacy of bureaucratic theory without supplying their own alternative explanation for the existence of these nonbureaucratic organizations. Most importantly, however, these recent developments have crystallized the inadequacy of bureaucratic theory and have demonstrated our need for a way to think about the efficiency of organizations more broadly than an approach based on structural-bureaucratic variables allows.

The nature of industrial organizations is fundamentally economic. Hence, while an efficiency point of view will not satisfy all avenues of organizational inquiry, it must certainly be a central part of our understanding of organizations. Contemporary organization theory owes a greater intellectual debt to sociology than to economics; as a result, it has much to gain by integrating more economic concerns. As the sociologist is fundamentally concerned with questions of power in society and has passed that tradition on to organization theory, the economist is fundamentally concerned with questions of the efficiency of exchange in society and has at least as much to contribute to us.

Markets, Bureaucracies, and Clans

Questions such as "Why do organizations exist?" and "What is an organization?" are usually beyond the scope of any one point of view. A complete answer, one that will be satisfying to scholars of all persuasions, will not be found here. Yet it may be possible to supply an answer that will provide some insight into these questions.

The task is to describe the forms of cooperation in the realm of economic activity. To do this, we can first present the problem of cooperation as defined for this analysis and then present the alternative solutions that flow from that particular definition of the problem. The problem of cooperation is here viewed from the perspective provided by Mayo (1945) and by Barnard ([1938] 1968). In this view, the fundamental problem of cooperation stems from the fact that individuals have only partially overlapping goals and, left to their own devices, will pursue incongruent objectives and act in uncoordinated ways. The problem of any collectivity that has an economic goal is to find a means for efficiently controlling these diverse individuals.

From this definition of the problem of cooperation have flowed many helpful ideas. Some writers (for example, Etzioni, 1965; Weick, 1969) have emphasized the tension between individual autonomy and collective interests that must attend cooperative action, while others (for example, Simon, 1945) have emphasized the impossibility of achieving completely cooperative effort among diverse individuals. The specific problem of interest here focuses on the efficiency with which transactions are carried out between individuals who are engaged in cooperative action. Cooperative action, in the sense used here, necessarily involves interdependence between individuals. This interdependence calls for transactions or exchanges between individuals in which each gives something of value (for example, his or her labor) and each receives something of value (for example, money) in return. In a market relationship, the transaction is directly between the two parties and is mediated by a price mechanism in which the existence of a competitive market reassures both parties that the terms of exchange are equitable. In a bureaucratic relationship, each party contributes labor to a corporate body that mediates the relationship by placing a value on the contribution of each person and then compensating that person fairly. The perception of equity in this case depends upon a social agreement that the bureaucratic hierarchy has the legitimate authority to provide this mediation. It is critical that all the individuals involved regard the transaction as an equitable one that meets the standards of reciprocity, which Gouldner (1961) has described as a universal requirement for collective life.

It is this demand for equity that brings on transactions costs. If it is a requirement that a norm of reciprocity be supported, then it is necessary that each party to a transaction be satisfied that an equitable exchange of contributions and payments has occurred. Economists have considered this problem in detail ever since Coase (1937) offered the observation that firms and markets are two alternative mechanisms for achieving the same objective, namely the mediation of transactions between individuals. More to the point, perhaps, Alchian and Demsetz (1972) have pointed out that where "teamwork" is involved, the determination of who has contributed just how much value to the joint product is a difficult undertaking. Individuals who suspect the possibility of dishonest claims of performance from other individuals will demand explicit, verifiable measures of performance. Such measures can be obtained only at some nontrivial cost (for example, an army of accountants) and are considered here to be a cost of maintaining that transaction. It is thus both the underlying suspicion of the motives of other parties and the extent of technological interdependence that bring about transactions costs.

Given individuals with at least partially incongruent objectives, therefore, the problem of cooperation is often solved by the measurement of the contribution of each individual, followed by an equitable distribution of rewards (we will assume that an equitable distribution is one that corresponds to the value provided by each individual, although other forms of distribution could also be viewed as equitable). We have identified two principal mechanisms for effecting this mediation of transactions, namely, a market and a bureaucracy. These are the alternatives that have received the greatest attention from organization theorists (Barnard, [1938] 1968; Weber, [1947] 1968) and from economists (Coase, 1937; Arrow, 1974). But the paradigm suggests the possibility of a third mechanism; that is, if the objectives of individuals are mostly congruent (not mutually exclusive), then the conditions of reciprocity and of equity can be met quite differently.

Both Barnard and Mayo pointed out that organizations are difficult to operate because their individual members do not share a selfless devotion to the same objectives. Mayo (1945) argues that organizations operated more efficiently in preindustrial times, when new members typically entered through an apprenticeship during which they were socialized into accepting all the objectives of the craft or organization. They would then automatically seek to do that which served the organization. Barnard ([1938] 1968) poses the problem thus: "A formal system of cooperation requires an objective, a purpose, an aim. . . . It is important to note the complete distinction between the aim of a cooperative effort and that of an individual. Even in the case where a man enlists the aid of other men to do something which he cannot do alone, such as moving a stone, the objective ceases to be personal" (pp. 42–43).

While Barnard, like Arrow, poses markets and bureaucracies as the basic mechanisms for achieving the continued cooperation of individuals, he allows also for the possibility of reducing the goal incongruence in a manner consistent with Mayo's view of the preindustrial organization. Barnard observes that "efficiency or equilibrium can be secured either by changing motives in individuals . . . or by its *productive* results which can be distributed to individuals" (p. 57). He notes further that the "form of persuasion that is most important is the inculcation of motives. In its formal aspects this is a process of deliberate education of the young and propaganda for adults" (p. 152). His conclusion is that an "organization can secure the efforts necessary to its existence, then, either by the objective inducement it provides or by changing states of mind. It seems to me improbable that any organization can exist as a practical matter which does not employ both methods in combination" (p. 141).

The idea that internalization of values can in part substitute for external means of control is not limited to Barnard. In discussing the use of coercive, utilitarian, and identitive modes of control, Etzioni (1965) provides a quite similar framework. Stinchcombe (1959) has illustrated the substitution of bureaucratic for craft (socialized) means of administration, and Lipset, Trow, and Coleman (1956) have illustrated the socializing effects of apprenticeship in an industrial union. Yet none of these models permits us to offer predictions concerning the conditions under which one or another method of control will be used. Perhaps that is because these models do not take up questions of efficiency in administration and therefore offer no systematic position from which to compare the efficiency of various modes of intermediation of transactions. The objective in this chapter is not so much to explain forms of domination or of authority as to concentrate on the efficiency of mechanisms of social control and thus to maintain that focus thought by Barnard to be essential to an understanding of economic organizations.

If the socialization of individuals into an organization is complete, then the basis of reciprocity can be changed. For example, it has been well documented (Abegglen, 1958; Nakane, 1973; Dore, 1973) that Japanese firms prefer to hire only inexperienced new workers, socializing them quite completely to accept the company's goals as their own and compensating them purely according to length of service, number of dependents, and other nonperformance criteria. In this case, it is not necessary for the organization to obtain clear measures of performance for the purpose of controlling or directing the effort of employees, since their natural (socialized) inclination is to do what is best for the firm. It is also unnecessary to arrive at explicit, verifiable measures of value added for the purpose of achieving an equitable distribution of rewards, since equity in this instance is achieved through nonperformance-related criteria that, as it happens, are relatively inexpensive to determine (length of service and number of dependents can be ascertained at relatively low cost). Thus, we see that industrial organizations can, in some instances, rely to a great extent on socialization as the principal mechanism of mediation or control, and we can see that this "clan" form (the term *clan* as used here conforms to Durkheim's ([1893] 1933) meaning of an organic association that resembles a kin network but does not necessarily include blood relations, p. 175) is capable of great efficiencies in the mediation of transactions between interdependent individuals.

Markets, bureaucracies, and clans may therefore be distinguished as three distinct mechanisms present in any real organization, but we may also expect to find certain forms dominant in some cases and other forms dominant elsewhere. The next objective, of course, is to begin to specify the conditions under which the requirements of each form are most efficiently satisfied. It is appropriate to note at this point that we have by now altered our earlier understanding of the terms *organization* and *formal organization*. In the broader language necessary to encompass both economics and organization theory, an organization may be thought of as any stable pattern of transactions. In this definition, a market is every bit as much an organization as is a bureaucracy or a clan. A particular firm or hospital or school may contain elements of market, of bureaucracy, and of clan, or it may be predominantly one or the other. The only requirement for this discussion is that we maintain a clear distinction between "bureaucracy" and "organization." As used here, the term *bureaucracy* refers specifically to the Weberian model, while the term *organization* refers to any stable pattern of transactions between individuals or aggregation of individuals.

Market Failures Framework

How can we specify in a general way the conditions under which a market, a bureaucracy, or a clan will provide the most efficient mediation of transactions, that is, will minimize transactions costs? We can most effectively approach this question by examining more closely the approach to markets and hierarchies provided by Williamson (1975)—an approach that builds on earlier statements of the problem by Coase (1937) and others (for a more detailed description of the functioning of each mechanism, see Ouchi, in press).

In order to comprehend the paradigm, it is helpful to conceive of market transactions, or exchanges, as consisting of contractual relations. Each exchange is governed by one of three types of contractual relations, all of which have the property of being completely specified. That is, in a contractual relationship, nothing is left to the imagination: because each party is bound to deliver only that which is specified, the contract must specify everything about the exchange, including who must deliver what under every possible future state of nature. The simplest form of contract is the "spot" or "sales" contract. This kind of contract comes into play when you walk up to the candy counter, ask for a candy bar, and pay your twenty-five cents. In such a transaction, all obligations are fulfilled on the spot; money is exchanged for candy, and there are no future ramifications of the exchange. Spot contracts are simple, and all exchange could occur through this medium without burdensome costs. However, the spot contract is, by definition, incapable of dealing with future transactions, and the fact that most exchange relationships involve such long-term obligations rules out the possibility of transacting all exchange through this device.

A common device for dealing with the future is the "contingent claims contract," a document that specifies, again completely, the obligations of each party to an exchange, contingent upon all possible future states of nature. Now, if we could write contingent claims contracts that covered all eventualities, then all exchange could take place through this medium. However, it is easy to demonstrate that, given a future that is either complex or uncertain, the task of completely specifying such a contract becomes infeasible due to the bounded rationality of individuals. To leave such a contract incompletely specified is an alternative but one that will succeed only if each party can trust the other to interpret the uncertain future in a manner that is acceptable to him. Thus, given uncertainty, bounded rationality, and opportunism, contingent claims contracting will fail.

Now, it would seem unnecessary to deal with the future by trying to anticipate it in a giant, once-and-for-all contract. Why not instead employ a series of contracts, each one written for a short period of time within which future events can confidently be foreseen? This would overcome the obstacles of uncertainty and opportunism and would permit "sequential spot contracting," another complete form. The problem is that in many exchange relationships, the goods or services exchanged are unique (in the case of commodities, such as newsprint, lead pipe, or transistors, they are not unique), and the supplier requires somewhat specialized knowledge of how best and most efficiently to supply the customer. Under these conditions, the supplier learns over time to be more efficient, and this specialized knowledge gives him a "first-mover" advantage. This advantage enables him to bid more effectively on subsequent contracts than can any potential competitors. Knowing this, competitors will not waste their time bidding; thus, a situation of "small-numbers bargaining," or bilateral monopoly, in which there is only one buyer and only one seller is produced. Under this condition, the competitive pressures that result in fair prices are absent, and each party will make opportunistic claims on the other, dishonestly claiming higher costs or poor quality, whichever is in his selfish interest. In order to maintain such an exchange, each party will have to go to considerable expense to provide adequate audits of the true expenses or performance of the other. Here the market relationship fails because of the confluence of opportunism with small-numbers bargaining, even though the limitations of uncertainty and bounded rationality have been overcome.

Thus, under some conditions no form of market relationship, that is, of complete contracting, is feasible. Figure 1 summarizes the conditions that lead to market failure. According to the paradigm, no one of the four conditions alone is sufficient to produce market failure, but almost any pairing of them will do so (the main pairings are linked with arrows). It is Williamson's (1975) contention that the use of bureaucratic organization ("hierarchy" or "internal organization," in his language) will overcome the shortcomings of market exchange, although he also devotes some attention to the shortcomings of bureaucratic organizations. The translation from microeconomics to organization theory is complicated because most microeconomists, including Williamson, do not distinguish among the terms *formal organization, organizations,* and *bureaucracy.*

The bureaucratic organization has two principle advantages over the market relationship that enable it to function effectively despite conditions of bounded rationality, uncertainty and complexity, opportunism, and small-numbers bargaining. First, the bureaucratic organization makes use of the employment relation, which is an incomplete contract. Although Williamson does not make this argument, we can see that the employment relation is critical to the bureaucratic organization. In accepting an employment relation, a worker agrees to receive wages in exchange for submitting to the legitimate right of the organization to appoint superior officers who can (1) direct the work activities of the employee from day to day (within some domain or "zone of indifference"), thus overcoming the problem of dealing with the future

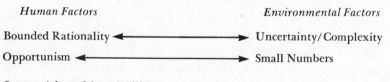

Source: Adapted from Williamson, 1975.

Figure 1: The Market Failures Framework

all at once; and (2) closely monitor the performance of the employee, thus minimizing the problem of opportunism, even though the job may be unique and thus subject to the difficulties created by small-numbers bargaining. An organizational superior can monitor the performance of a subordinate much more closely and effortlessly than a customer can audit a supplier in a market relationship.

The second advantage of the formal organization is that it can create trust among employees much more readily than the parties to a market can create trust among themselves. Because members of an organization have cause to assume some commonality of purpose and because they learn that long-term relationships will reward good performance and punish poor performance, they develop trusting attitudes (or goal congruence) that reduce opportunistic tendencies and thus also reduce the need for monitoring of performance.

In summary, the market failures framework argues that markets fail when the costs of completing transactions become unbearable. At that point, the inefficiencies of bureaucratic organization will be preferred to the relatively greater costs of market organization, and exchange relationships will move from the one domain into the other. Although we do not have space to fully consider his position here, Williamson (1975) argues that the transactional efficiency of bureaucratic organization is its only reason for existence. He contends quite convincingly that previous arguments to the effect that technological indivisibilities or efficiencies require corporate forms are incorrect, as we have also pointed out.

Clans and the Market Failures Framework

Transactions costs can be said to arise entirely from the need to establish equity, as we have argued above. In the case of market relations, opportunism is assumed, and thus equity is provided through contractual protections accompanied by clear auditing of performance. Williamson moves directly to bureaucratic hierarchies as the principal alternative to markets, but let us take a different tack.

If we adopt the view that transactions costs arise from equity considerations, then our interpretation of Figure 1 will be different from Williamson's. In Figure 1 we have a summary of the conditions that complicate the demonstration that an equitable balance has taken place. From our point of view, Figure 1 contains some redundancy, which we can see more clearly by reference to Simon's work (1957) on the employment relation. Simon emphasizes that under an employment contract the employer pays a worker a premium over what would be the "spot" price for a given piece of work. This premium is, from the point of view of the worker, a "risk premium" that compensates him for the likelihood that he will be asked to perform duties that are significantly more distasteful to him than those within his zone of indifference, which is the range of tasks implied in the employment contract. It is the uncertainty surrounding the likelihood of such tasks that determines the size of the risk premium. In other words, if the employee completely agreed with all objectives of the employer, which is equivalent to completely trusting the employer never to request a distasteful task, then the risk premium would be zero.

The employment relation is relatively efficient when ambiguity concerning the measurement of performance is high and ambiguity or uncertainty regarding the goals of the employer is low. In an employment relation, each individual employee depends upon the employer to effect an equitable distribution of rewards, and thus each employee must place high confidence in the trustworthiness of the employer. Otherwise, employees will demand contractual protections such as union representation, and transactions costs will rise.

We thus see that the critical element in the efficiency of market versus employment relations involves (1) the ambiguity over the measurement of individual performance and (2) the trustworthiness or goal congruence (also known as lack of opportunism) between the employee and employer. We can now reformulate the transactions cost problem as follows: in order to efficiently mediate transactions, any organizational form must either reduce the ambiguity over performance, or else it must reduce goal incongruence between parties. Put this way, we can see that market relations achieve efficiency when ambiguity over performance is low and that they can thus tolerate relatively (but not unlimited) high levels of opportunism or goal incongruence.

Now, the obvious next question is: What is that alternative form of mediation that succeeds by minimizing goal incongruence and should be able to tolerate high levels of ambiguity over performance? Clearly, it will be a form that embodies a strong employment relation, that is, a relation in which the risk premium is minimized. The answer, of course, is what we have referred to as the clan, which is, in a way, the obverse of the market relation, since it achieves efficiency under conditions of high performance ambiguity and low opportunism. In the sense used here, any occupational group that has organic solidarity can be thought of as a clan. Thus a profession, a labor union, or a corporation may each be a clan. The professionalized bureaucracy may be understood as a response to the need for efficient transactions within professions (clan) and between professions (bureaucracy).

Perhaps the clearest exposition of the clan form of mediation appears in what Durkheim ([1893] 1933) refers to as the case of organic solidarity and its contrast with contractual relations:

> For organic solidarity to exist, it is not enough that there be a system of organs necessary to one another, which in a general way feel solidarity, but it is also necessary that the way in which they should come together, if not in every kind of meeting, at least in circumstances which most frequently occur, be predetermined. . . . Otherwise, at every moment new conflicts would have to be equilibrated. . . . These conflicts would incessantly crop out anew, and consequently, solidarity would be scarcely more than potential, if mutual obligations had to be fought over entirely anew in each particular instance. It will be said that there are contracts. But, first of all, social relations are not capable of assuming this juridical form. . . . A contract is not self-sufficient, but supposes a regulation which is as extensive and complicated as contractual life itself. . . . A contract is only a truce, and very precarious; it suspends hostilities only for a time [p. 365].

This solidarity to which Durkheim refers contemplates a union of objectives among individuals that stems from their necessary dependence upon one another (this dependence is itself a necessary accompaniment to the division of labor that attends all industrial societies). While Durkheim contemplated the development of industrial clans as a substitute for contractual (market) relations, he was also centrally concerned with the issue of autonomy under conditions of extreme interdependence: "But does not the division of labor by making each of us an incomplete being bring on a diminution of individual personality? That is a reproach which has often been leveled at it. . . . We take off from the principle that man ought to realize his nature as man. . . . But this nature does not remain constant throughout history; it is modified with societies. . . . in more advanced societies, his nature is, in large part, to be an organ of society, and his proper duty, consequently, is to play his role as an organ. . . . far from being trammeled by the progress of specialization, individual personality develops with the division of labor" (p. 403).

Goal congruity as a central mechanism of control in organizations also appears repeatedly in Barnard ([1938] 1968): "The inculcation of belief in the real existence of a common purpose is an essential executive function. It explains much educational and so-called morale work in political, industrial, and religious organizations that is so often otherwise inexplicable" (p. 87). He later notes that "the most intangible and subtle of incentives is that which I have called the condition of communion. . . . It is the feeling of personal comfort in social relations that is sometimes called solidarity, social integration. . . . The need for communion is a basis of informal organization that is essential to the operation of every formal organization" (p. 148).

Descriptions of organizations that display a high degree of goal congruence, typically through relatively complete socialization brought about by high inclusion (Etzioni, 1965), are also found in Lipset, Trow, and Coleman (1956), Argyris (1964), Selznick (1966), and Clark (1970). In each case, the authors describe the organization as one in which the determination of individual performance is difficult. However, such organizations are not "loosely coupled" nor are they "organized anarchies" simply because they lack market and bureaucratic mechanisms. A clan, as Durkheim points out, provides great regularity of relations and may in fact be more directive than are other, more explicit mechanisms.

That clans display a high degree of discipline is emphasized by Kanter (1972) in her study of utopian communities, some of which established successful businesses—for example, Oneida and Amana. Kanter points out that all successful utopian communities "had a somewhat fixed daily routine throughout their history" (p.

121). But Kanter also notes that this discipline was not achieved through contractualism or through surveillance (except self-surveillance) but through an extreme form of deindividuation. In successful utopian communities, there is the belief that individual interests are best served by a complete immersion of each individual in the interests of the whole: "In many cases it is felt that the good of the community transcends personal whim, for only if the community operates smoothly and harmoniously can the individual be fulfilled" (p. 41). These clans employ a great variety of social mechanisms that serve the principal purpose of eliminating differences in objectives, goals, and values among individuals: "Utopia is held together by commitment rather than coercion, for in utopia what people want to do is the same as what they have to do; the interests of the individuals are congruent with the interests of the groups" (p. 1).

Kanter observes that utopian communities of the sort that she studied are smaller than are modern corporations, but she notes the possibility that they could serve as models for industrial organizations in language that echoes both Durkheim and Mayo: "Utopian communities are important not only as social ventures in and of themselves but also as challenges to the assumptions on which current institutions are organized. The work organization of nineteenth-century groups, for example, with its job rotation, communal work efforts, mutual criticism, shared ownership, equality of compensation, participatory decision making, infusion with spiritual values, and integration with domestic life, may provide alternative models for contemporary work organizations" (p. 236).

More recently, Ouchi and Jaeger (1978) and Ouchi and Johnson (1978) have reported on modern industrial organizations that closely resemble the clan form. In these organizations, a variety of social mechanisms work to reduce differences between individual and organizational goals and produce a strong sense of community (see also Van Maanen, 1975; Katz, 1978). Where individual and organizational interests overlap to this extent, opportunism is unlikely to occur, and equity in rewards can be achieved at relatively low transactions costs. Moreover, these organizations are typically ones that are in high-technology or closely integrated industries, where teamwork is common, technologies change often, and ambiguity over the performance of individuals is therefore high. Under these conditions, transactions between individuals are most efficiently mediated through a form of employment relation that minimizes the need for clear, verifiable measures of performance.

Bureaucracies and the Market Failures Framework

Transactions costs can be minimized through one of two extreme means: driving the measurability of performance up when goal congruence is low or driving goal congruence up when measurability of performance is low. These two methods or "pure types" we have identified as markets and clans. Yet it is rarely the case that, in an industrial setting, transactions can be arranged so that performance can be evaluated clearly enough to arrive at prices and to operate a market; it is also rare that goals can be made so compatible that a clan can operate. Whereas a market cannot tolerate even moderately high levels of performance ambiguity and a clan cannot tolerate even moderate levels of goal incongruence, a bureaucracy can operate in exactly those regions of ambiguity and incongruence.

We have noted that a bureaucratic organization succeeds because it replaces complete forms of contracting with a single incomplete contract, which is the employment contract. However, the bureaucratic organization specifically does not rely upon the complete integration of goals that characterizes the clan. Instead, it settles for a partial agreement that develops over time, and it combines this moderate level of goal agreement with extensive auditing practices. Weber ([1947] 1968) goes to great lengths to point out that, whereas market transactions are formally the most rational form of exchange, they require a clarity of measurement that is rarely attainable. Although it is possible to arrive at arbitrary measures that could be used as "prices," these would lead to inefficiency in administration. Weber also rejects the possibility that "communal" relationships could serve as the basis for organizing economic activity, since they are fundamentally affectual or traditional rather than having the rational properties of bureaucratic relations.

While he may have underestimated markets and clans, Weber sees that the conditions of industrialization rarely suit the needs of markets or clans and that therefore what is called for is a mixed form, one that rests on a normative acceptance of legitimate authority combined with a rational attempt at performance auditing. Thus, the bureaucratic organization specifies both rules of procedure and rules of output with which actual performance can be compared. But because these rules do not perfectly capture all the desired elements of performance, they are combined with an emphasis on technical expertise that provides some skill training and some socialization into craft or professional standards in an attempt to reduce opportunism. Having thus created professionals within a bureaucratic setting, whose primary affiliation is to a professional body rather than to the employer, Weber then calls for a career orientation, which increases the sense of affiliation or solidarity with the employer and further reduces goal incongruence.

This complex of characteristics represents a mix of market and clan mechanisms that can succeed even when performance ambiguity and goal incongruence are both moderately high. It is thus adapted to the middle range of conditions—the range that may characterize the majority of transactions in an industrial setting. It is hardly surprising, then, that the majority of organizations in an industrial setting should be primarily of the bureaucratic type, since under these conditions a bureaucracy is frequently the form that minimizes transactions costs. Again, the bureaucratic form minimizes transactions costs because it most efficiently assures employees of an equitable distribution of rewards when both performance ambiguity and goal incongruence are moderately high.

Despite these desirable properties of the bureaucratic type, it has continually been under attack and under revision. As Williamson points out, the move from U-form (functional) to M-form (divisional) organization among many large firms has been motivated by a desire to simulate a capital market within a bureaucratic framework because of the superior efficiency properties of markets over bureaucracies. By regrouping the parts of the organization, it is possible to create subentities, each of which is sufficiently autonomous from the others to permit precise measurement and the determination of an effective price mechanism through which division general managers may be controlled. Although each division may still internally operate as a bureaucracy, the efficiencies that accrue from this partial market solution are often large, offsetting the diseconomies of functional redundancy that many times accompany divisionalization.

Perhaps because it is not a pure type in the sense that a market or a clan is, a bureaucracy always exhibits its failings quite clearly. Despite many attempts to do away with or to supercede bureaucratic forms, however, they remain the dominant type in industrial settings.

Having distinguished three mechanisms of intermediation, we can now summarize them and attempt to set out the general conditions under which each form will most efficiently mediate transactions between individuals.

In Table 1, we can discriminate among markets, bureaucracies, and clans along two dimensions: their underlying normative and informational prerequisites. Let us consider each in turn.

Normative requirements here refer to the basic social agreements that all members of the transactional network must share if it is to function efficiently, that is, without undue costs for performance auditing or monitoring. If these minimum social agreements are not present, the mechanism will not be efficient. A norm of reciprocity, according to Gouldner (1961), is one of only two social agreements that have been found to be universal among societies across time and cultures (the other is the incest taboo). A norm of reciprocity, protected by the foreknowledge that violations

Table 1. An Organizational Failures Framework

Mode of Control	Normative Requirements	Informational Requirements
Market	Norm of reciprocity	Prices
Bureaucracy	Norm of reciprocity	Rules
	Legitimate authority	
Clan	Norm of reciprocity	Traditions
	Legitimate authority	
	Common values and beliefs	

will be subject to severe punishment, provides the minimum protection against opportunism without which exchange is impossible. If there were no such widely shared norm, then a potential trader of, say, fish for boats would have to consume so much energy in setting in advance the contractual terms of exchange and in afterwards auditing the performance of the other party that the costs of the potential transaction would become unbearable. Under such conditions, a division of labor is unthinkable and social existence impossible. It is not surprising therefore, that a norm of reciprocity underlies all exchange mechanisms.

A norm of legitimate authority, as discussed above, is critical for two reasons. In the first place, it permits the assignment of organizational superiors who can, on an ad hoc basis, specify the work assignments of subordinates, thus obviating the need for a contingent claims employment contract that would be either so complex as to be infeasible to write, so confining as to seriously hamper the effectiveness of the organization, or else so incomplete as to lead to many disagreements. In the second place, legitimate authority permits organizational superiors to closely audit the performance of subordinates in a way that is impossible within a market relationship. In a bureaucracy, legitimate authority will commonly take the rational-legal form, whereas in a clan it may more commonly take traditional forms (see Blau and Scott, 1962). Legitimate authority is not ordinarily created within the organization but is maintained by other institutions such as the church and the educational system (Weber, [1947] 1968; Blau and Scott, 1962; Barnard, [1938] 1968). While the legitimacy of a particular organization may be greater or smaller as a result of its managerial practices, authority is fundamentally maintained within society as a whole. (Inkeles and Smith, 1974, describe this as a property of "modern" societies.)

It is important to note that Weber regarded efficiency in administration as being equivalent to use of the rational-legal form of authority or legitimate domination. He may have been correct in asserting that the rational-legal form is better suited to industrial society than are either the traditional or charismatic forms of authority. However, he confounded authority with efficiency, while we have argued that the use of legitimate authority is efficient only under some conditions, not universally.

Common values and beliefs provide the harmony of interests that erase the possibility of opportunistic behavior. (In Williamson, opportunism is a universal tendency of individuals to further their self-interest, even through the devices of lying, cheating, and stealing. Here, opportunism is treated as equivalent to incongruence of goals between individuals. It seems reasonable to assert that the two definitions are compatible, because an interaction between two people of incompatible goals will often be perceived by each as evidence of the untrustworthiness of the other.) If all members of the organization have been exposed to a long apprenticeship or other socialization period, then they will share basic, underlying personal goals that are compatible with the goals of the organization. In this condition, auditing of performance is unnecessary except for educational purposes, since no one will purposely attempt to depart from organizational goals.

It is possible to assert that a norm of reciprocity is universal, that legitimate authority is accepted in most formal organizations, and that common values and beliefs are relatively rare in formal organizations. Thus the normative prerequisite for a market mechanism is present in every society. The idea of legitimate rational-legal authority is present in most "modern" societies but can vary widely among organizations in its degree of acceptance. Humanists have often contended that authoritarian management will weaken the legitimacy ascribed to an organization's authority and therefore narrow the zone of indifference within which tasks can be reordered. Commonality of values and of beliefs about how to maximize those values appears to be relatively uncommon in industrial organizations. Etzioni (1965) has described this form of control as being common only to "total" organizations such as the military and mental hospitals. Light (1972) describes its role in ethnically bound exchange relationships. However, we have also noted that a partially complete form of socialization may be effective (accompanied by market or bureaucratic mechanisms) across a wider range of organizations than "total" ones. Mayo (1945) contended that instability of employment, which upsets the long socialization period necessary, is the chief enemy of the development of this form of control.

As for the informational prerequisites of each form of control, we can note the differences among prices, rules, and traditions. Prices are a highly sophisticated form of information; they provide sufficient information for decision making in all cases. However, correct prices are difficult to arrive at, particularly when technological interdependence, novelty, or other forms of ambiguity are present to obscure the boundary between tasks or between individuals. Rules, by comparison, are relatively crude informational devices. A rule is specific to a problem, and therefore a large number of rules are necessary to control organizational responses. A decision maker must know the structure of the rules in order to be assured of applying the correct one in any given situation; the difficulty of acquiring this kind of knowledge will lead to errors in decision making. Moreover, an organization can never specify a complete set of rules to cover all possible contingencies. Instead, it specifies a much smaller set of rules to cover the most routine decisions. Exceptions are referred up the hierarchy where policy makers can invent rules as needed. As Galbraith (1973) has pointed out, under conditions of uncertainty or complexity, the number of exceptions will become so great that the hierarchy becomes overloaded and the quality of decision making suffers.

Traditions may be viewed as either more refined than prices and rules or as less refined. Traditions are the implicit rules that govern behavior. Because traditions are not written down in an organized fashion, they are not easily accessible to neophytes, and a new member of an organization will not be able to function effectively until he or she has spent a number of years learning the traditions (Van Maanen and Schein, 1978). In terms of the precision of performance evaluation that they permit, traditions may be cruder than either prices or rules. A tradition is ordinarily stated in a general way that must be interpreted in order to apply to a particular situation. Nevertheless, the collective set of traditions in a formal organization may produce a unified, although implicit, philosophy or point of view. If such a unified view exists, then it may be functionally equivalent to a theory about how that organization should work. Clearly, a member who grasps such an essential theory can then deduce from it an appropriate rule to govern any possible decision, and this produces a very elegant and complete form of control. Equally clearly, a disruption of the socialization process will inhibit the passing on of traditions and will result in organizational inefficiency.

Humanistic View of Organizational Failure

Williamson (1975) has described his formulation as a "failures" framework in order to express the idea that while market forms of mediation are generally to be preferred, they will fail in the sense of becoming less efficient than bureaucratic forms and thus, under some conditions, will be replaced by bureaucratic forms. Bureaucratic forms can also be said to experience a similar kind of failure under other conditions—for example, when they repress individual autonomy. From an efficiency point of view, we ought to expect bureaucratic forms to fail when they raise opportunism to a high level through overly close surveillance, but it is rare that such an organization actually closes its doors and goes out of business. What accounts for this apparent weakness in our efficiency point of view?

Humanistic social psychologists have long argued that bureaucratic organizations will fail under a variety of circumstances: when workers are placed in a dependent state that denies them the possibility of psychological success (Argyris, 1964), when lack of trust among employees distorts cooperation and communication (Likert, 1967), when jobs are specialized to the point of dehumanization (Mayo, 1945), and when control is based exclusively on following a set of rules (Bennis, 1966).

Organizations will succeed to the extent that they are able to motivate their employees and thereby release their potential energy and creativity (Maslow, 1954). In order to do so, they must create working conditions under which people are able to pursue internally generated objectives and experience independence (Argyris, 1964). In order for a superior to give subordinates this much freedom, he must adopt a trusting attitude towards them, and he must hold fundamental beliefs about human nature that predispose him to give his subordinates psychological independence from his direction and control (McGregor, 1960). A critical element of trust, however, is the firm belief that, left to specify their own objectives, subordinates will choose to pursue objectives that are harmonious with the efficiency objectives of the firm. However, the interests of individuals are necessarily different from the goals of the firm, with the result that such trust is unwarranted and will not develop (Udy, 1962). Under some conditions, the adoption of a trusting attitude by management may engender more compliant attitudes and willing cooperation by subordinates, but this is rare (Mayo, 1945).

More commonly, a modern organization adopts the attitude that workers are not to be trusted and that their objectives are fundamentally incompatible with those of the organization. Thus the organization employs a variety of devices that have the sole objectives of closely monitoring not only output but also work behavior, of controlling every action, and of rewarding desired performance and punishing undesired performance. To further this end, jobs are specialized and simplified to the point that each job can be quickly learned and easily monitored. This reductive process destroys the uniqueness and thus the bargaining power of each jobholder while increasing the auditing capabilities of the organization. However, these changes also have the effect of creating psychologically unsatisfying jobs. Workers, denied the possibility of psychological growth in their work, become emotionally disabled, manifesting lower levels of motivation and of energy not only in their work but in many other areas of life (Argyris, 1964). The organization, denied the willing cooperation of its employees, becomes a battleground and has diminished powers of coordination.

This unhappy condition is a direct result of the industrialization of our civilization over a relatively short period of time (Durkheim [1893] 1933). In traditional societies, it was indeed true that individual interests meshed with the interests of the firm, and explicit monitoring and external control were not necessary. In those traditional settings, new employees were typically taken into a firm through an apprenticeship that not only taught them the technical skills of their craft but also imbued them with the underlying values and beliefs that characterized the group they were entering. A work relationship typically extended over a lifetime and even across generations, thus allowing for very complete merging of individual and organizational interests (Mayo, 1945).

Opportunism is nothing more or less than incompatibility of objectives between employee and employer. When socialization is complete, an employee who behaves selfishly is nevertheless contributing to achievement of the objectives of the organization and thus will have no incentive to lie, cheat, or steal. When socialization is incomplete, the employee's goals will frequently be incompatible with organizational goals, and the employee will then be tempted to lie, cheat, and steal in order to accomplish his personal objectives. If modern industrialization does in fact lead to such instability of employment that socialization is rarely complete (industrialization does not always have that result; see Ouchi and Johnson, 1978), then we can expect opportunism to be characteristic of most employees.

Now, if we have not done too much violence to the subtleties of the humanistic social psychologists, we can observe that their organizational failures framework not only corresponds to but also illuminates Williamson's market failures framework. The humanists have argued, just as Williamson has, that formal organizations can employ one of two essential mechanisms of control: either they can build up interpersonal trust and thereby reduce the danger of opportunism or they can closely monitor performance and thereby suppress opportunism. However, we see in the work of the humanists that these two styles of managing are directly opposed, a point that is not well developed in the market failures framework. If we follow Mayo, we would furthermore come to doubt that the fundamental conditions necessary for the creation of a unity of objectives and values among the members of a firm can be achieved. The best that he hopes for is the creation of cohesive subgroups within the organization, a device that may bring about psychological protection but that we can expect to lead to greater needs for control and auditing, since each group will defend its members when they seek to pursue common group ojectives, which may differ from the firm's objectives. (Likert's (1967) link-pin design is one mechanism for coordinating these differential groups.)

A great weakness of the humanistic school has been that it cannot point to an empirical example of organizational failure in the manner that an economist can point to many examples of market failure; that is, organizations may indeed fail psychologically but that does not necessarily lead to their going out of business. An organization that fails to build trust can, according to the humanists as well as the economists, continue to do business effectively by relying upon close monitoring of performance. Put in this form, however, the argument suggests an explanation for the economic success of firms that have failed psychologically: the costs of psychological failure are not borne entirely by the firm but rather are passed on to society in general. Employees who reach the point of emotional disability and therefore become unsatisfactory workers are the first to be laid off during depressions or, in extreme cases, are fired. The firm that has "used up" people emotionally does not have to face the cost of restoring them. In much the same manner that firms were able until recently to pollute the air and water without paying the costs of using up these resources, they continue to be able to pollute our mental health with impunity.

If we accept this notion of psychological health as an externality, we then have a consistent view of organizational failure derived from the humanistic point of view: an organization will govern exchange relationships more effectively than will a market only if it fosters interpersonal trust. Trust will bring about psychological energy and maximum motivation and productivity, and it will moderate the effects of opportunism. Therefore, the organization will be capable of complex transactions without incurring the high costs of monitoring these transactions. Moreover, a climate of trust will enlarge the zone of indifference within which each employee allows his or her activities to be specified and will thus further improve the firm's ability to adapt to an uncertain future without prespecifying obligations in a complete fashion.

Under conditions of industrial instability, however, the commonality of interests that is essential to trust will fail to develop. Organizations lose most of their advantages over markets under such conditions, and many organizations could be expected to fail. But organizations in our society are capable of resorting to close monitoring, punishment, and specialization in order to survive, provided that they do not have to pay the costs of the psychological damage that they create under this mode of control. Ultimately, however, we can expect that a society that has conferred legitimate power upon work organizations will withdraw at least some of that power if abuses are perceived to be both widespread and severe (Parsons and Shils, 1951). It can be argued that just such a development has been occurring in Western Europe since 1952, when German industry adopted "codetermination," in which workers' councils make some policy decisions with management. In Sweden, Norway, West Germany, Italy, and France, the former authority of management to hire, fire, supervise, and promote has been greatly abridged through legal and political action (Roberts, Okamoto, and Lodge, 1978).

It is not inevitable for bureaucratic organizations to lose their capacity for interpersonal trust. Just as the market failures framework specifies the conditions under which markets cannot operate efficiently, however, this humanistic organizational failures framework specifies the conditions under which bureaucratic organizations cannot operate efficiently and demonstrates how a market imperfection (the inability to price mental health) permits the continued existence of inefficient organizations.

Organizational Instability

We have observed that under conditions of extreme uncertainty and opportunism, transactions costs may rise generally. Indeed, Denison (1978) has observed that, during the period 1965–1975, net productivity in the United States declined due to changes in "the industrial and human environment within which business must operate" (p. 21). Output per unit of input has declined for two reasons: 78 percent of the decline is due to increased costs of air, water, and safety on the job, and the remaining 22 percent is attributable to increased needs for surveillance of potentially dishonest employees, customers, and contractors, as well as of garden-variety thieves.

The resources put into improvements in air, water, and safety are not a net loss to society, although they may reduce corporate profitability, and they are not our major concern. The increased need for surveillance in business, however, may represent the fact that the cost of monitoring transactions has risen. Mayo (1945) might have predicted this change as one inevitable result of the instability that accompanies industrialization. In our framework, we could advance the following explanation: exchange relationships, in general, are subject to so much informational ambiguity that they can never be governed completely by markets. Thus, they have been supplemented through cultural and clan mechanisms in each organization and in the economy generally. As instability, heterogeneity, and mobility have increased in the United States, however, the effectiveness of these cultural mechanisms has been vitiated. The result has been an increase in bureaucratic mechanisms of surveillance and control. Although the use of bureaucratic surveillance may be the optimal strategy under present social conditions, it is nonetheless true that we as a nation are devoting more of our resources to transactional matters than we did ten years ago, and that represents a net decline in our welfare.

It is probably true that, to a greater or lesser degree, all organizations are in a state of at least partial failure. It may be that the degree of uncertainty and opportunism that characterize American society is such that no mechanisms of control ever function very well. We have already observed that the conditions necessary for a pure market, bureaucracy, or clan are rarely if ever met in reality. Even a combination of these control mechanisms may be inefficient in many cases, however. In new technologies and in public-sector organizations, the rate of change, the instability of employment, or the ambiguity of performance evaluation simply overwhelm all attempts at rational control.

In these cases, exchange in an organizational form becomes institutionalized. It is the central thesis of Meyer and Rowan (1977) that school systems are, by their nature, incompatible with any form of rational control. They have no effective price mechanism, they have no effective bureaucratic control, and they do not have internally consistent cultures (see also Meyer and others, 1978). As a result, school systems (as distinguished from education, which need not involve large organizations) continue to grow and to survive because the objectives that they supposedly pursue have been accepted as necessary by the members of society. Thus, as long as a school system or other institutionalized organization continues to symbolically pursue the accepted objectives, it will be supported by society. Since rational control is not feasible within the school, no one knows whether it is actually pursuing these goals, but it is the property of an institutionalized organization (the church is another example) that it need not give evidence of performance (see also Ouchi, 1977).

To some extent, all work organizations are institutionalized. The fundamental purposes of all viable organizations must be at least somewhat acceptable with respect to broad social values (Parsons and Shils, 1951). If employees, customers, and the public-at-large all grant legitimacy to the basic activities of a company, then they will continue to support it even when they have no evidence that their support will result in desired outcomes. It is the institutionalization of organizations that permits them to survive even under conditions that severely limit their capacity for rational control. Because no organization can consistently apply effective mechanisms of internal control, all organizations remain intimately dependent upon their legitimacy in the society. Ultimately, organizational failure will occur only when the society deems the basic objectives of the organization to be unworthy of continued support.

This chapter has undoubtedly raised many more questions than it has answered. My objective, indeed, has been to see what new kinds of questions we can ask about organizations by applying a novel theoretical framework to them. I have glossed over a number of topics that deserve much closer scrutiny. The exercise, however, suggests that we can take the old ideas of uncertainty, of legitimate authority, of socialization, and of bureaucracy and that, by looking at them through the transactions cost perspective and by using Williamson's market failures framework, we can discover new connections between apparently disparate concerns within organizational theory.

With respect to the sex discrimination suit mentioned at the beginning of this chapter and the question of what constitutes an "establishment," we now have at least a partial answer. We cannot provide a general definition of an organization that will suit the varying purposes of the many legal traditions that underlie, for example, sex descrimination and antitrust suits, but neither are we at a complete loss. Applying our efficiency criterion, we can assert that it is reasonable to define as an organization any set of individuals who carry out a stable pattern of transactions. More precisely, we can determine whether the organization is primarily of the market, bureaucratic, or clan type. If it is of the bureaucratic type, we can include all those individuals who submit to a common set of rules and procedures, as well as to a system of legitimate authority, within one organization. If it is of the clan type, we can include all those who have undergone a socialization procedure and who can reasonably be expected to hold similar values and objectives within some economic domain. If it is of the market variety, then for the purposes of this particular suit no organization exists: the purpose of the suit was to protect women against opportunistic behavior on the part of the firm. But if market conditions obtain, then opportunism is rendered ineffectual and does not call for a remedy. If, as is more likely, the defendent corporation is of the U-form (functional) type, then we would point out that market transactions are impractical between functions and that, therefore, opportunism must indeed be minimized in order for equity to obtain within the corporation as a whole. Although our standard is not as clear-cut as we would like, we at least have a systematic criterion by which to evaluate each department or plant in question in order to determine the extent to which it is part of the larger corporation.

What is an organization? An organization, in our sense, exists when there is stable pattern of transactions among individuals or aggregations of individuals. Our framework thus can be applied to the analysis of relationships among individuals or among subunits within a corporation, or it can be applied to the transactions among firms in an economy. Why do organizations exist? We see clearly now the need for greater precision in our language in order to answer this question. In our sense, all patterned transactions are organized, and thus all stable exchanges in a society are organized. When we ask, "Why do organizations exist," we usually really mean to ask, "Why do bureaucratic organizations exist," and the answer is quite clear. Bureaucratic organizations exist because, under certain specifiable conditions, they are the most efficient means for an equitable mediation of transactions between parties. In a similar manner, we can observe that market organizations exist and clan organizations exist because each of them, under certain conditions, offers the lowest transactions cost.

13

Findings and Implications of Organizational Life Cycle Research: A Commencement

Robert H. Miles

The creative use of both imperfect metaphors and nonconventional approaches to understanding have surfaced in this book a number of new issues and implications for organization theory and research. The most fundamental conclusion is that developmental perspectives, largely ignored until now, can contribute greatly to our understanding of organizational behavior and effectiveness.

Sampling a wide variety of settings, focusing on different episodes of life within them, and conducted at different levels of analysis, the chapters contained in this book reveal that organizations cannot be fully understood apart from their histories, and they suggest some alternative pathways for organizational theory and research. The authors came to these conclusions independently at roughly the same time in the history of organizational theory and research, and, at the very least, it is likely that the perspectives represented here are a harbinger of change for the field.

Findings and questions of the nature generated by these essays have important implications for both the method and substance of research on organizations. In this final chapter, I will review some of the substantive issues raised by the authors about the creation, transformation and decline of organizations and populations of organizations. Because many more ideas have been generated than I can discuss even fleetingly in this closing chapter, I will concentrate on those that seemed most important to me in working with each author on the creation, transformation, and finalization of his chapter. Although I use the format of the book to organize my summaries and interpretations, it should be obvious by now that the boundaries between periods of organizational history cannot be drawn definitively. This ordering only provides a way to begin to discuss the development of organizations.

Organizational Creation and Early Development

Organizational creation is perhaps the most important epoch in the life of an organization. It is during this stage that an idea takes substance and begins to move toward realization. The chapters in this part of the book demonstrate that the choices made at the time of creation—choices about ideology and meaning, planning, organizing and learning, recruitment and socialization of members, and external relations with constituents and rivals—powerfully shape the direction and character of organizational development. Kimberly demonstrates the importance of entrepreneurs in generating meaning and energy for a new venture. Miles and Randolph stress the role of initial organizing attempts in shaping the character of organizational learning and the belief systems and outcomes that emerge as a result. Van de Ven demonstrates the effects of different planning processes on the subsequent initiation, development, and performance of new organizations. And Pennings outlines the characteristics of the urban context and the population of existing organizations within an urban area that facilitate or constrain the creation of new business ventures. As a result, the findings generated by these exploratory studies contribute to areas of real deficiency in our knowledge of organizations. But the differences among these approaches and findings also raise a number of issues that require further investigation.

Organizational Creation. The first issue concerns the boundaries around the concept of organizational creation. None of the authors confine the concept of organizational creation by the narrow analogue of human birth; instead, all view the birth of organizations as starting with an idea, continuing through conception and incubation, and terminating sometime after the equivalent of human birth. For example, Van de Ven defines organizational creation as a process that begins with the inception of an idea, enters a planning phase, proceeds to implementation, and culminates with the institutionalization of organizational structures and processes. Though not explicit on this issue, both Kimberly and Randolph and I refer to the first three of these phases as organizational creation and to the episode linking implementation to institutionalization as "early development."

The conceptual difficulties with boundaries around organizational creation also extend backwards. At what point do we make a distinction between prehistory, or what Sarason (1972) refers to as "confronting history," and organizational creation? Indeed, the history that founders bring with them from earlier settings tends to shape the ones they conceive and develop. Thus, it seems unwise to draw these boundaries too firmly; in fact, one might argue that we should look backward in time for connections that contained the seeds of the present venture. Such an argument challenges us not to draw boundaries but to identify linkages that help to define the process and outcomes of organizational creation.

Individuals, Organizations, and Environments. The authors also differ in emphasis on the roles of individuals, structures and processes, and environments in shaping the creation and early development of organizations. Kimberly and Randolph and I emphasize the role of charismatic *leadership*, while Pennings employs the concepts of urban *context* and organizational population *ecology* to explain the creation of new business ventures. Van de Ven, in contrast, emphasizes the role of the planning *process* in shaping the birth and early development of public agencies, though the nature of the planning process he found to be most effective was one in which the planners became the doers and the process itself accommodated the interests of strategic constituencies located in the community environment. This confluence of forces—key individuals, initial organizing choices, and environmental forces—undoubtedly is at work in the creation and early development of virtually all new organizations, but under what circumstances will each one occupy center stage?

Pennings would point to the central role of the host environment in conditioning both the choice of whether to initiate a new enterprise and the likely outcomes of that choice. Kimberly would argue that, although the environment often creates the niche, a "man of vision" is required to capitalize on that opportunity by creating meaning and symbols for it, generating resources to support its activities, and recruiting others from existing organizations to join in the new venture. Observing that structuralists are apt to argue that individuals do not contribute very much to organizational effectiveness, Kimberly insists upon another interpretation; that is, he argues that most theorists and researchers have focused on chronologically mature organizations in which structures, processes, and norms have become institutionalized to the point that the person at the top becomes less important in explaining how organizations turn out. Thus, the individual may be far more important in the creation of organizations and, particularly, during the start-up of innovative settings than is generally thought. If so, structuralists will have to adjust their frames if they hope to comprehend and help others effectively manage the process of organizational creation.

One way to look at the influence on organizations of individuals is to examine the effects of turnover of key personnel at various stages in an organization's development. For example, the loss of the founder or members of the core group may be disastrous if it occurs during the time a new, and particularly an innovative, venture is attempting to get off the ground. But this kind of turnover may be fortuitous if the entrepreneurial focus or inno-

vative orientation of these individuals inhibits the process of institutionalization at later stages of organizational development. Indeed, Pfeffer and Salancik (1978) have argued that executive succession is one important factor in the process of organizational
adaptation. It provides a window for the expression of new ideas
that may be translated into appropriate strategic directions for an
enterprise that is no longer in tune with the contingencies it faces.

Different or Just New? The chapters on organizational creation make a distinction between organizations that are new and
different and organizations that are simply new. The arguments
and evidence generated in this collection suggest that to the "liability of newness" (Stinchcombe, 1965) we must add the "liability of
uniqueness" when considering the creation of innovative organizations. Although accomplished competitors and other rivals for resources are an important part of the external environment of a new
but conventional organization, much of the knowledge required to
get the organization off the ground is in existence—all that the
founders have to do is locate and tap it. In these settings new roles
and relationships must be learned but not invented. Relations with
existing organizations must be developed, but much of their form
and content will not be unique. The meaning of the new but conventional setting will be understood more readily, not only by its
own members but by other organizations upon which the setting is
dependent.

As Kimberly suggests, the creation of truly innovative organizations in many respects exacerbates the difficulties in getting a
conventional organization off the ground. Or, as Lodahl and
Mitchell put it, the birthing of an innovative organization is an exercise in "the creation and maintenance of meaning." Experimentation and invention take primacy over technical efficiency in the
start-up of an innovative organization, and the amount of slack
acquired by founders to permit these activities to go forward can be
expected to covary with their venture's relative effectiveness as an
innovation. Thus, "institutional" and "charismatic" skills are a very
important part of the entrepreneur's toolbag. The first must be
relied upon to establish legitimacy for the innovation among its
uncertain constituents; the latter must be used to create the meanings and symbols needed to attract new members and motivate

coordinated effort among them. Indeed, the innovative organization, especially during start-up, resembles Ouchi's clan, whose common values, beliefs, and goals take the place of the kind of authority that is feasible only where cause and effect are measurable and their relationship is well mapped.

Organizational Growth Versus Aging. Another aspect of the early development of organizations that requires more theoretical development and research is the relative influence on organizations of growth in membership versus organizational aging or maturation. Virtually all previous research has confounded these processes. Lodahl and Mitchell, for instance, point to the increasing size of staffs, as well as to the depleted energy of the founder, or "founder burnout," as sources of ideological drift within their innovative universities. Growth in size creates greater distance, both physical and psychological, among members of the organization, and this tendency is reinforced, in most cases, by the process of organizational subdivision. Thus, organizational growth, by itself, can have very powerful effects on both the various internal structures and processes that emerge within the organization and on the relative influence of those structures and processes versus the influence of the founder and core group.

Although the effects of rapid growth on organization and management have been demonstrated, the validity of these demonstrations is suspect because of their failure to account for the effects of organizational aging or maturation. As new organizations get off the ground, they learn many things from their early performance, some of which become institutionalized in the form of relatively enduring values, norms, structures, and processes. Moreover, their members change in ways that have implications for the health and efficiency of their organizations. Eager young founders and core group members may find their responsibilities and priorities divided as they acquire spouses, children, and vested property interests enroute to middle age. Members drawn to a new setting because of the uniqueness and challenge it offered may sour and leave when they find that successful early experimental tasks have devolved into routine jobs; when they see their close, personal relationships break down into formal, impersonal ones; and when they witness a noticeable "drift" away from the founding ideology toward steady-state efficiency. Although we have not presented a study that separates these effects, the fact that significant changes took place over the early development sequences in both my simulated organizations and Walton's Topeka work system, despite the absence of growth in organizational size, demonstrates that the aging or maturation process itself has important consequences for the development and outcomes of infant organizations and their members.

Organizational Transformations

Beyond the extremes of organizational existence lies a sometimes brief, sometimes lengthy "mid-life" in which transformations may be expected to occur. The studies in this section highlight the dialectical quality of organizational development. They suggest that organizational transformation is an ongoing fact of life, particularly for organizations that begin as innovations, and they reveal some of the internal cultural, political, and technical dynamics that are the sources of this transformation process.

Organizational Drift. The studies of the new medical school, the British universities, the high-commitment manufacturing plants, and the Martin Luther King Health Center all describe tensions that emerged between the establishment and maintenance of meaning, on the one hand, and the pressure toward rationalization and efficiency, on the other, during the creation and early development of these innovative organizations. In each case, these organizations had to develop new forms of work processes to be able to operationalize their unique ideology. However, their ideological uniqueness, together with their experimental work systems, made them deviants among the other organizations upon which they depended, at least in part, for their existence. Because of their innovative nature, a pattern emerged in the early development of all four settings. In each, the initial emphasis was on the establishment of meaning, followed by the development, largely through enactment of the organization itself, of accommodative work systems and of external relations to protect the core ideology and to secure needed resources. But both internal and external forces eventually created tensions between the maintenance of meaning and the need for operational efficiency.

Within these organizations, learning through enactment caused the experimental technology to become beaten down, thereby eliminating some of the intrinsic rewards that were required to sustain the innovative ideological character of the enterprise. Organizational growth began to translate itself into structural differentiation along vertical and horizontal axes within the medical school and the British universities, causing a breakdown in personal interactions and a loss of contact between newcomers and the founding group and between the core group and its leader.

During the same period, changes were also occurring among the members. For example, Walton observed that within his high-commitment work systems human skills increased while the technology was becoming less and less capable of engaging them. The aging or maturation process within individuals also worked against the maintenance of the organization's innovative character. Members once eager to devote all their energy to the enterprise grew weary and founders suffered "burnout." All these factors contributed to the drift within these innovative enterprises toward conventionality.

External forces also play a part in organizational drift. Other organizations linked with an innovative one may put pressures on it to conform. Parent corporations may urge innovative divisions, as in the case of Walton's plants, to conform to company-wide policies and procedures and may exact performance demands that are out of rhythm with developments occurring within the innovative work systems. Reference group norms may encourage old members to behave in ways that protect their careers, as in the case of Kimberly's medical school faculty, and newcomers may be inadequately socialized into a system that has become large and differentiated.

Thus there are many reasons why the history of social innovations is one of failure. Moreover, the prospect of organizational drift appears to be characteristic, to varying degrees, of social innovations in general. But if this early transformation seems inevitable, our authors disagree as to its implications. Kimberly, for example, argues that the system of work and style of leadership required during the infant stage of an innovative organization may limit its future development. Noting that early success is paradoxical in nature, Kimberly takes the position that innovative organizations must transform themselves if they are to endure and prosper, and this same theme appears in my discussion of simulated organizations. Lodahl and Mitchell, by contrast, lament the prospect of drift, which they view as "deadly" for an innovative organization, and suggest ways by which the leadership may prevent or minimize it. They emphasize the development of institutional, as opposed to technical, managements skills. Such pioneers of innovative organizations, according to Lodahl and Mitchell, must create a new methodology that will "support or subvert the intended innovation." They see as part of this institutional function of management the need to create a "cycle of vigilance," that is, an ongoing process for assessing the state of congruence between the ideals of the innovative organization and its reality and for determining the possibilities for corrective action if needed.

Finally, Walton argues that the evolution of an innovative work system is not only inevitable but functional as well. He observes that one of the causes of the decline in member commitment within the Topeka work system was that "the plant community had lost its sense that the work system would need to evolve continually. . . . Rather, within the work force there was a widely shared and deeply felt responsibility to protect and preserve the work system launched [several years earlier]."

Thus, although our authors disagree on the value of organizational drift, they all noted the emergence of this phenomenon in their very different but innovative organizations, and they were in general agreement as to its causes. Whether this phenomenon is generalizable is unclear, but it appears to be a major and inevitable early transformation in innovative organizations.

The Dialectical Quality of Mid-Life. Although Tichy found a form of organizational drift in the early development of the Martin Luther King Center, where again we find the tension between ideology and efficiency, he pushes us further to consider those ongoing organizational transformations that are fueled by the mutually causal interactions among cultural, political, and technical cycles within organizations. In his view, the problems posed by these cycles are never resolved; instead, they represent continuing dilemmas.

Organizations, according to Tichy, vary over time in the amount of energy they invest in making adjustments in each of these cycles, and, at any given time, one cycle or some combination of cycles may be in need of adjustment. These adjustments lead to transformations of organizations because focusing attention on one cycle creates problems in the others. Tichy's analysis highlights the need to build into management an awareness of these organizational cycles, as well as the skills for regulating them.

In closing this review of the organizational transformation studies, I am reminded of Sarason's (1972) advice to the creators of new settings. He encourages them to recognize that the building of organizations is never complete and that "there will always be problems" (p. 284). Yet he also notes that "the necessity for anticipating problems and consequences [is] an activity or process notably absent or found in only diminished degree in the creation of most settings" (p. 17). It is my hope that the broad approaches of the present studies will stimulate further research and result in a greater understanding of how to anticipate and manage the internal dialectics of organizations and the transformations they create.

Organizational Decline and Termination

Very few contemporary studies of organizational development focus on the decline and termination of organizations. The concentration instead has been on the problems posed by rapid organizational growth—concentration made inevitable by the rapidly expanding economies of most industrialized nations in the period after the Second World War. Under such conditions the management of organizational decline and termination is a humiliating experience and one that subject organizations and their managers are loathe to have studied or publicized. Moreover, people in general, and especially the young scholars in the nascent field of organizational behavior, are prone to push the reality of death from their day-to-day consciousness. Throughout history societies have shown virtually no concern for the inevitable prospect of death or for preparing individuals for the occasion of dying. Only recently has the concept of the hospice, a place where terminal patients reside while they prepare for certain death, become a reality.

The conditions of our common existence, however, are showing signs of transition. Many segments of society are now facing the prospect of scarce rather than abundant resources, and as a result a need for knowledge about how to manage organizational decline and termination has begun to emerge. The final set of chapters in this volume provides a basis for developing this area of organizational theory and research. Each author provides new perspectives on the backside of the organization life cycle— perspectives that should stimulate much needed research. Moreover, because the authors look at these processes through different lenses, their chapters taken together raise a number of theoretical issues.

Dimensions of Organizational Failure. First, it seems important to distinguish among different dimensions of organizational failure. For instance, organizations may fail on one or more of several grounds: (1) *technical* failure, or the inability to achieve and maintain economic efficiency in required transactions; (2) *political* failure, or the inability to achieve and maintain legitimacy among strategic constituencies; and (3) *cultural* failure, or the inability to achieve and maintain ideological bases. But failure in one of these aspects of organizational life may not lead necessarily to termination of the organization as a whole; instead, it is likely that the form of organization under consideration will have a bearing on which dimension of failure is most likely to lead to termination. For example, since people join a kibbutz in large measure because of the ideological community it provides, cultural failure may be more of a factor in organizational termination in a kibbutz than either technical or political failure. In contrast, ideological failure should not be expected to have nearly as much influence as technical failure on the ultimate termination of a conventional production system. Finally, these dimensions of failure may be quite loosely coupled in some organizations and quite tightly connected in others. Walton's high-commitment work systems are an example of the latter: the technical systems were designed unconventionally to accommodate high-commitment value systems. A breakdown in ideology within these uniquely designed work systems would, therefore, have almost immediate consequences in terms of production efficiency.

Referents of Organizational Failure. Just as it is possible to distinguish the dimensions of organizational failure, we can think of failure with respect to a number of referents: (1) the organization's *form*, (2) the organization's *goals*, and (3) the organization's external *environment*. As examples of the first category, markets may devolve into bureaucracies, bureaucracies into clans, and innovative organizations into conventional ones. Each of these transformations indicates the failure of a particular form of organization, but none forecloses the possibility that both the original parties and the activities linking them may persist, only within another organizational form.

Second, failure may be judged in terms of the goals set for the organization by its founders or by those presently in control of it. Indeed, organizations may be judged failures not in terms of their *relative* effectiveness but more concretely in terms of their achievement of goals they have chosen for themselves. Thus, initial goal choices may have an important bearing on the speed with which organizations fail. Comparisons of the goals of three widely known public organizations may be used to illustrate this point.

The now-defunct Office of Economic Opportunity (OEO) initially set a goal of the "elimination of poverty in America" but could not demonstrate much progress toward this lofty objective and was terminated a few years after its start. In contrast, the Environmental Protection Agency (EPA) set its initial goal more modestly as "pollution abatement," making it relatively easy for the agency to demonstrate that it was making progress. Moreover, this kind of goal statement left plenty of room for organizational maneuvering and virtually assured the EPA that it would always have something to do. Finally, the National Aeronautics and Space Administration (NASA) set its initial goal as one of "reaching the moon within ten years." As a result of different goal choices, all made during the creation of these public organizations, OEO has ceased to exist, EPA continues to grow and prosper, and NASA, for several years after achieving touchdown on the moon, languished near death for want of resources. The point I wish to make is that goal choices made very early in the life of an organization can have an important influence on both the quality and duration of its life.

Finally, failure often has an environmental referent, and this fact has become more important given the multidivision, multidomain character of many contemporary organizations. Take, for example, member firms of the American tobacco industry confronted for the last quarter-century with the threat to their market posed by the controversy over smoking and health (Miles and Cameron, 1977). Philip Morris began the 1950s with one of the smallest shares of the cigarette market in the industry; yet through skillful use of market segmentation and overseas expansion, supported by product innovation, advertising, and lobbying, this firm had become an industry leader by 1975. In contrast, Liggett and Myers, capitalizing on its distinctive competence in consumer marketing, opened up entirely new domains of activity by acquiring nontobacco companies, changed its name to the Liggett Group, and effectively exited the threatened tobacco industry. Which firm has been more successful? Philip Morris, because it captured the lion's share of an uncertain cigarette market? Or Liggett, because it "failed" to compete effectively in that market and created new domains to support its continued existence?

Illustrations of the environmental referents of organizational failure abound in other industries as well. Thus, during the recent "electronics revolution" in the United States watchmaking industry, traditional industry leaders became threatened with extinction because developments in the semiconductor industry had made it possible to produce a lower-cost, more accurate electronic timepiece—the digital watch—than the centuries-old mechanical device. As digital watches became accepted in the U.S. market, many marginal producers of mechanical timepieces were forced out of business. The traditional industry leaders fared little better during this shake-out.

However, one leading firm in the traditional watchmaking industry, Hamilton Watch Company, did not acquiesce to the electronic threat (Barney and Miles, 1978). Instead Hamilton acquired its own digital manufacturing capability, changed its name to HMW, Inc., and sold its mechanical watch company to the Swiss! As a result, HMW is alive and well today even though it had been temporarily exposed to what Whetten refers to as environmental entropy in its primary market. These examples drawn from two different industries make it clear that failure almost always has an environmental referent and that failure in one domain of operation may be quite functional for the survival of the enterprise as a whole. They also demonstrate that the process of organizational choice of forms, goals, and domains of operation can shape in nontrivial ways the development and decline of social and economic systems.

Termination as Success. One form of organizational termination not given explicit consideration so far is *success* in goal attainment; that is, organizations may cease to exist because they have accomplished their purposes or missions. Project organizations terminate after they have developed the new product or process for which they were created. Military commands and political campaign organizations disband after they have won a contest. On a more general level, the Civil Rights Movement of the 1960s also falls into this category of termination. Although organizational success as termination may not strike readers as a problem worthy of investigation, the persistence of organizations beyond the achievement of their purpose has ominous implications.

Moreover, organizational persistence in the face of success may be more widespread than usually thought. For example, in his book *Are Government Organizations Immortal?*, Kaufman (1976) reports that although the population of public organizations in the United States has grown exponentially over the fifty years between 1923 and 1973, very few have ceased to exist. In addition, of the 175 such organizations in existence in 1923, eighty-five percent were still alive fifty years later. Moreover, in most of the cases of organizational death, the activities were not terminated but were reassigned to or taken up by other public organizations.

Kaufman's analysis revealed a number of plausible explanations for organizational persistence in the public sector. They included the job preservation motive of employees and the support received from outside friends, associations, and interest groups; the legislative and statutory bases that gave birth to agencies; the federal govenment's incremental, as opposed to zero-based, budgeting system that blunts attempts to question the fundamental legitimacy of agencies; and the degree of insulation agencies have from executive supervision.

But the prospect of dysfunctional persistence is not limited to the public sector. Scientists and engineers in research and development project offices have been found to push for their organization's continuation long after the project for which it was created has been completed (Miles, 1980). For example, Miller and Rice (1967) have observed that "the individual scientist tends to commit himself primarily to his project team. This probably facilitates the work of the group on the project; but unless the organization also provides the team member with a higher-order group with which to identify himself, the task of the project team may be redefined and its life prolonged to the detriment of the overall task of the research enterprise" (pp. 225–26). Persistence in the face of goal achievement, therefore, constitutes another form of organizational failure that often goes unnoticed when we think about the end of organizations.

Organizational Aftermath. Just as prehistory has important consequences for the kind of organization that is created and the developmental course it follows, the termination of an organization has its aftermath, and this aftermath may become an important part of the prehistory of future organizational creations. Members take what their experience has taught them to the organizations they subsequently join or create. Outsiders also form beliefs about failing organizations, and this accumulated knowledge among founders, members, and constituents of both new and existing organizations shapes the range of possibilities they may be willing to consider. For these reasons, it is important that research go forward on individual adjustments and consequences under conditions of organizational decline and termination.

Fortunately, the role of the organizational pathologist can be much more positive and rewarding than that of its counterpart in society-at-large. In most instances, the termination of an organization does not coincide with the death of its members, who depart the sinking ship for more stable berths in other organizations. Research into the experiences and beliefs of these victims, therefore, would be of value not only in helping others to avoid premature organizational termination but also in assisting survivors to make this transition and to understand the kinds of influences they are likely to have on the organizations they later create or join.

Life Cycles of Organizational Populations

I have postponed until now discussion of the population or ecological level of analysis. But just as it is important to identify the issues surrounding the creation, development, and termination of individual organizations, it is also helpful to understand why and how *populations* of organizations emerge, transform, and decline. Pennings' work on the influence of the urban context in the creation of small firms and Brittain and Freeman's study of population dynamics within an industry setting help provide this kind of understanding.

Urban Ecology and Organizational Population Dynamics. First, Pennings argues that the rate of creation in independent business ventures can be explained to an important degree by the characteristics of both the embedding urban context and the population of existing firms within a particular urban area. He treats the birthrates of new firms as part of the succession and replacement that occurs within a growing, stagnating, or declining urban population of organizations. Instead of focusing on *how* organizations get started and develop—the subject of chapters pursuing analysis on the organizational level of analysis—Pennings attempts to explain *why* they are encouraged to do so and *why* their attempts are likely to succeed or fail. By limiting this explanation to small, freestanding business ventures, Pennings is able to confine his analysis to the immediate urban context.

The "entrepreneurial conductiveness" of an urban area is, in Pennings' view, a function of its rate of growth and level of differentiation, as well as of the existence of marginal individuals (entrepreneurs) and a reinforcing entrepreneurial culture in an urban setting. Added to these urban features are characteristics of the existing urban population of organizations. Entrepreneurial conduciveness, for instance, is increased to the extent that the organizational population is not highly concentrated and is abundant in economic and social resources. Although Pennings does not support his conceptual framework with empirical evidence, the typology of urban contexts he develops should stimulate research on the concept of entrepreneurial conduciveness.

Industry Ecology and Organizational Population Transformation. Freeman and Brittain shift the focus of analysis to transformations within populations of organizations, focusing attention on the characteristics of an industry that give rise to the creation, proliferation, and failure of the different types of firms that make up the industry's population. For example, they argue that firms competing on the basis of "first-mover" advantages rather than on the basis of efficiency will tend to proliferate more rapidly into niches opened up within high-technology industries undergoing rapid change, but they add that the former will also fail more rapidly as efficiency strategists move into the niches pioneered by the first movers.

The variation-proliferation-selection principle used to explain these population transformations has its antecedents in the characteristics of the industry, of the member firms within it, and of the individuals within member firms. At the industry level, a number of factors influence the rate of population transformation, including the industry's age, its rate of technological and social change, its learning economies, its growth rate, and its entry barriers. At the level of member firms, first-mover specialist firms emerge and proliferate in new industry niches until their success encourages generalist firms, pursuing efficiency strategies, to move in to capitalize on niche maturity. The underlying assumption, of course, is that firms are largely saddled with their founding strategy and lack the motivation or ability to transform themselves into forms more compatible with the changing character of the niche they occupy. Because of the assumption of strategic inertia at the firm level, transformations of the industry population as a whole are more likely to occur, according to Brittain and Freeman, through the formation of new firms than through the transformation of individual firms, and this brings us to the individual level of analysis.

Since firms are assumed to cling to their strategies, innovations will tend to be stifled in the generalist firms that seek to avoid the high risks associated with first-mover strategies; these firms will prefer instead to compete on the basis of efficiency in mature industry markets. Yet these firms are the ones that can devote the most resources to research and development. Consequently, as Brittain and Freeman observe, new technologies often are developed in established generalist firms but because of inertia are not immediately implemented. One reason is that if innovations were taken to market, they would compete against existing products for which generalists enjoy established distribution channels and predictable cash flows.

It is Brittain and Freeman's contention, therefore, that new specialist firms are established by former employees of generalist firms to pioneer new industry niches. This process, they believe, is especially prevalent in rapid-growth industries in which member firms develop somewhat unusual demographic characteristics, including compressed age distributions within their hierarchies. The result is a dampening effect in terms of the perceived career opportunities of aggressive and proficient members who know where new niches are opening and, consequently, are likely to leave generalist firms, taking neglected technological innovations with them.

Although Brittain and Freeman develop their model from an archival analysis of a single, high-technology industry, the characteristics they isolate to explain population dynamics and interfirm behaviors may be used, as in Pennings' case, to form the basis of a typology of industries. And this preliminary typology may be used to extend their research into other industries with the objective of developing a new framework for understanding industrial development and behavior.

Inertia and Captivity. The population-level perspective on organizational development and transformation makes two important assumptions. The first is that organizations are characterized more by inertia than by adaptability and that, as a consequence, their developmental course is shaped largely by the dictates of environmental determinism rather than by strategic choice. Second, both the urban and industry models developed in this volume assume, at least implicitly, that the populations of organizations under investigation are captured by their immediate contexts (that is, by a particular industry or urban context).

Although this deterministic perspective may apply to small ventures with few slack resources and little imagination on the part of executive leadership, one need only scan the *Wall Street Journal*

to discover the limitations of its assumptions about closed environmental systems and organizational inertia. Corporations, relying on
the strategic choice process, may be found moving into and out of
product lines, markets, industries, and even continents (Miles,
1980; Miles and Cameron, 1977) to balance their investment
portfolios and minimize their exposure to risk. In so doing, these
multidivision, multiindustry organizations are certain to tax the
limits of the population ecology perspective. Moreover, the process
of organizational adaptation does not appear to be limited to the
giant private corporation, as analyses of the adaptive transformations within the Tennessee Valley Authority (Selznick, 1949) and
the YMCA (Zald, 1970) in the public and nonprofit sectors have
demonstrated.

The utility of the population ecology perspective, therefore,
lies in its ability to sketch the contingencies posed by different
organizational contexts. In addition, one may discover that, as
Deeks (1976) and Pennings have suggested, environmental selection accounts for a considerable portion of the biographies of small,
new, independent firms that do not have the slack resources, the
experience, and the legitimacy to engage in major adaptive transformations and environmental maneuverings. At the same time, it
seems clear that research into strategic processes, focusing on the
sources and applications of organizational volition and adaptation,
will be needed to fully understand the rise and fall of large, complex organizations and their urban and industry populations.

Prospects

The ideas generated and the issues raised in this book
should provide the basis for new directions in organizational theory
and research. But I must confess to a gnawing concern about the
possibility of overintellectualization of this new perspective. Embedded in the chapters I have reviewed are some very immediate
and practical problems that affect people and their societies in
important ways. The personal and social costs of ill-advised or improperly managed organizational creations, transformations, and
terminations, or, in some cases, the absence of these dynamics in
individual organizations and populations of organizations, can be

extremely high. The failure to comprehend, anticipate, and manage these dynamics risks individual savings and investment capital, threatens security and well-being, and tugs at the fabric of social progress. Therefore, my hope is that researchers will begin to develop theories and select research agenda that are high in relevance to these social and economic problems.

One way to crystallize this concern is to describe two areas with the potential for addressing in an immediate way some of the practical problems surfaced by our developmental perspective. Take, for instance, the occasion of a new business creation. We presently know little about the kinds of advice entrepreneurs have at their disposal as they contemplate the creation of a new enterprise. To be sure, lawyers, bankers, and certified public accountants are likely to be involved. But what kinds of advice are they likely to offer? One has the impression that many of the issues raised in this volume would not be part of the early discussions among the founder and these professionals. Yet these issues are very real, and awareness of them might assist potential founders in anticipating and preparing for the social, as well as the economic and technical, requirements of organizational creation.

Similarly, research on the other end of the organization life cycle might distill information from members, advisers, and constituents of declining or terminating organizations that could be of assistance in managing or coping with these processes. Information of this kind might guide public policy as it bears on the creation and termination of organizations. Thus, in addition to advancing some new perspectives for understanding organizations in general, the preliminary findings and issues generated in this volume argue for practice-focused research into the management of and public policy toward some of the most extreme and critical, though so far neglected, phases in the lives of organizations and their members.

Publication of this book represents, in one sense, the end of a project whose purpose has been to explore the potential of some developmental perspectives for organizational theory and research. In the process, the project enabled a core group of professionals to sketch the broad outlines of a beginning framework, to introduce some important concepts and issues, and to identify likely avenues and obstacles for the work that we hope will follow.

But we are still far away from a general theory and an inclusive set of propositions for this developmental perspective; therefore, just as each new venture is influenced by the conditions of its own prehistory, the end of this exploratory project, we hope, will become the prehistory for a new wave of organizational theory and research.

References

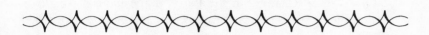

Abegglen, J. C. *The Japanese Factory: Aspects of Its Social Organization.* New York: Free Press, 1958.

Abrahamson, M., and Dubick, M. "Problems of Urban Dominance: The U.S. in 1890." *American Sociological Review,* 1977, *42,* 756–768.

Ackoff, R. L. *Redesigning the Future: A Systems Approach to Societal Problems.* New York: Wiley, 1974.

Aiken, M., and Hage, J. "Organizational Interdependence and Intraorganizational Structure." *American Sociological Review,* 1968, *33,* 912–930.

Alchian, A. A., and Demsetz, H. "Production, Information Costs, and Economic Organization." *American Economic Review,* 1972, *62,* 777–795.

Aldrich, H. E. "Centralization Versus Decentralization in the Design of Human Service Delivery Systems: A Response to Gouldner's Lament." In R. C. Sarri and Y. Hasenfeld (Eds.), *The Management of Human Services.* New York: Columbia University Press, 1978a.

Aldrich, H. E. "Social Structure and the Creation of New Organizations." Working Paper No. 28, New York State School of Industrial and Labor Relations, Cornell University, 1978b.

Aldrich, H. E. *Organizations and Environments*. Englewood Cliffs, N.J.: Prentice-Hall, 1979.

Aldrich, H. E., and Pfeffer, J. "Environments of Organizations." *Annual Review of Sociology*, 1976, *2*, 79–105.

Aldrich, H. E., and Reiss, A. "Continuities in the Study of Ecological Succession: Changes in the Race Composition of Neighborhoods and Their Businesses." *American Journal of Sociology*, 1976, *81*, 846–866.

Alonso, W. "Location Theory." In J. Freeman and W. Alonso (Eds.), *Regional Policy*. Cambridge, Mass.: M.I.T. Press, 1975.

Altman, E. I. *Corporate Bankruptcy in America*. Lexington, Mass.: Heath, 1971.

Amir, Y. "The Effectiveness of the Kibbutz-Born Soldiers in the Israeli Defense Forces." *Human Relations*, 1969, *22*, 333–334.

Ansoff, I. H. "The Firm of the Future." *Harvard Business Review*, 1965, *43*, 162–178.

Ansoff, I. H. "Toward a Strategic Theory of the Firm." In I. H. Ansoff (Ed.), *Business Strategy*. New York: Penguin Books, 1970.

Argenti, J. *Corporate Collapse*. New York: Halstead Press, 1976.

Argyris, C. *Integrating the Individual and the Organization*. New York: Wiley, 1964.

Argyris, C. *Intervention Theory and Method*. Reading, Mass.: Addison-Wesley, 1970.

Argyris, C., and Schön, D. A. *Organizational Learning: A Theory of Action Perspective*. Reading, Mass.: Addison-Wesley, 1978.

Aris, S. *The Jews in Business*. London: Jonathan Cape, 1970.

Arnold, H., and Arnold, A. *Living in Community*. Rifton, N.Y.: Plough Publishing House, 1974.

Arrow, K. J. *The Limits of Organization*. New York: Norton, 1974.

Ashby, W. R. *An Introduction to Cybernetics*. New York: Wiley, 1956.

Balderston, F. E. "Varieties of Financial Crises." Ford Foundation Program for Research in University Administration, University of California, Berkeley, 1972.

Bales, R. F., and Strodtbeck, F. L. "Phases in Group Problem Solving." *Journal of Abnormal and Social Psychology*, 1951, *46*, 485–495.

Bardach, E. "Policy Termination as a Political Process." *Policy Sci-*

ences, 1976, *7,* 123–131.

Barmash, I. *Great Business Disasters.* New York: Ballantine Books, 1973.

Barnard, C. I. *The Functions of the Executive.* Cambridge, Mass.: Harvard University Press, 1938.

Barney, J., and Miles, R. H. "The Electronic Revolution in the Watch Industry: A Decade of Environmental Changes and Corporate Strategies." Working Paper, Harvard Business School, 1977.

Bass, B. "When Planning for Others." *Journal of Applied Behavioral Science,* 1970, *6,* 151–172.

Beckard, R., and Harris, R. *Organizational Transitions: Managing Complex Change.* Reading, Mass.: Addison-Wesley, 1977.

Becker, S. W., and Gordon, G. "An Entrepreneurial Theory of Formal Organizations, Part I." *Administration Science Quarterly,* 1966, *11,* 315–344.

Behn, R. D. "Closing the Massachusetts Public Training Schools." *Policy Sciences,* 1976, *7,* 151–172.

Behn, R. D. "Policy Termination: A Survey of the Current Literature and an Agenda for Future Research." Washington, D.C.: Ford Foundation, 1977.

Behn, R. D. "Closing a Government Facility." *Public Administration Review,* 1978, *38,* 332–338.

Ben Refael, E. "The Utopia and Its Conflicts: Theoretical Aspects of Stratification Process in the Kibbutz." *Megamoth,* 1974, *20,* 211–223 (in Hebrew).

Bennis, W. G. *Changing Organizations.* New York: McGraw-Hill, 1966.

Bennis, W. G., Benne, K. D., and Chin, R. (Eds.). *The Planning of Change.* New York: Holt, Rinehart and Winston, 1961.

Bennis, W. G., and Slater, P. E. *The Temporary Society.* New York: Harper & Row, 1968.

Benson, J. K. "The Interorganizational Network as a Political Economy." *Administrative Science Quarterly,* 1975, *20,* 229–249.

Benson, J. K. "Innovation and Crisis in Organizational Analysis." *Sociological Quarterly,* 1977, *18,* 5–18.

Benveniste, G. B. *Bureaucracy.* San Francisco: Boyd and Fraser, 1977.

Berger, P. L. *Pyramids of Sacrifice.* New York: Basic Books, 1974.

Berger, P. L., and Neuhaus, R. J. *To Empower People.* Washington,

D.C.: American Enterprise Institute for Public Policy Research, 1977.

Berry, B. J. L., and Kasarda, J. D. (Eds.). *Contemporary Urban Ecology.* New York: Macmillan, 1977.

Bettelheim, B. *The Children of the Dream.* London: Macmillan, 1969.

Beyer, J., and Lodahl, T. "A Comparative Study of Patterns of Influence in United States and English Universities." *Administrative Science Quarterly,* 1976, *21,* 104–129.

Biller, R. P. "On Tolerating Policy and Organizational Termination: Some Design Considerations." *Policy Sciences,* 1976, *7,* 133–149.

Birchfield, R. *The Rise and Fall of JBL.* (NBR Books, 1972)

Blau, P. M. "Critical Remarks on Weber's Theory of Authority." *American Political Science Review,* 1963, *57,* 305–316.

Blau, P. M. *Exchange and Power in Social Life.* New York: Wiley, 1964.

Blau, P. M. "The Hierarchy of Authority in Organizations." *American Journal of Sociology,* 1968, *73,* 453–467.

Blau, P. M. "A Formal Theory of Differentiation in Organizations." *American Sociological Review,* 1970, *35,* 2101–2118.

Blau, P. M., and Schoenherr, R. A. *The Structure of Organizations.* New York: Basic Books, 1971.

Blau, P. M., and Scott, W. R. *Formal Organizations.* San Francisco: Chandler, 1962.

Bloomfield, D. K., and others. "A Role for Practicing Physicians in Basic Medical Education." *Journal of the American Medical Association,* 1972, *213,* 187–188.

Bogue, E. G. "Alternatives to the Growth-Progress Syndrome." *Educational Forum,* 1972, *37,* 35–43.

Bolton Committee. *Report of the Committee of Inquiry on Small Firms.* London: Her Majesty's Stationery Office, 1971.

Bonacich, E. "A Theory of Middleman Minorities." *American Sociological Review,* 1973, *38,* 583–594.

Boswell, J. *The Rise and Decline of Small Firms.* London: Allen & Unwin, 1973.

Bougon, M., Weick, K., and Binkjorst, D. "Cognition in Organizations: An Analysis of the Utrecht Jazz Orchestra." *Administrative Science Quarterly,* 1977, *22,* 606–639.

Boulding, K. E. *A Reconstruction of Economics.* New York: Wiley, 1950.

Boulding, K. E. "The Economics of the Coming Spaceship Earth." In H. E. Daly (Ed.), *Toward A Steady-State Economy.* San Francisco: W. H. Freeman, 1973.

Boulding, K. E. "The Management of Decline." Address to the Regents' Convocation of the State University of New York, Albany, September 20, 1974.

Boulding, K. E. "The Management of Decline." *Change,* 1975, *64,* 8–9.

Bozeman, B., and Slusher, E. A. "Scarcity and Environmental Stress in Public Organizations: A Conjectural Essay." Working Paper, Maxwell School, Syracuse University, 1979.

Braun, E., and MacDonald, S. *Revolution in Miniature: The History and Impact of Semiconductor Electronics.* Cambridge, England: Cambridge University Press, 1978.

Brouillette, J., and Quarantilli, E. L. "Types of Patterned Variation in Bureaucratic Adaptations to Organizational Stress." *Sociological Inquiry,* 1971, *41,* 39–45.

Brown, D. S. "Reforming the Bureaucracy: Some Suggestions for the New President." *Public Administration Review,* 1977, *37,* 163–170.

Burgoyne, J. G. "Stress Motivation and Learning." In D. Gowler and K. Legge (Eds.), *Managerial Stress.* New York: Wiley, 1976.

Burns, T., and Stalker, G. M. *The Management of Innovation.* London: Tavistock, 1961.

Burton, K. *Paradise Planters: The Story of Brook Farm.* London: Longmans, 1939.

Bylinsky, G. "How Intel Won Its Bet on Memory Chips." *Fortune,* 1973, *94,* 142–147.

Campbell, D. T. "Variation and Selective Retention in Sociocultural Evolution." *General Systems,* 1969, *16,* 69–85.

Campbell, D. T., and Stanley, J. C. *Experimental and Quasi-Experimental Designs for Research.* Chicago: Rand McNally, 1963.

Cangelosi, V. E., and Dill, W. R. "Organizational Learning: Observations Toward a Theory." *Administrative Science Quarterly,* 1965, *10,* 175–203.

Carlton, D. W. "Models of New Business Location." Working Paper No. 7756, Department of Economics, University of Chicago, 1978.

Cartter, A. M. "After Effects of Blind Eye to Telescope." *Educational Record*, 1970, *51*, 333–338.

Chadwick, G. F. "The Limits of the Plannable: Stability and Complexity in Planning and Planned Systems." *Environment and Planning*, 1977, *9*, 1189–1192.

Chamberlin, E. H. *The Theory of Monopolistic Competition*. Cambridge, Mass.: Harvard University Press, 1933.

Chapman, S. J., and Ashton, T. S. "The Sizes of Businesses, Mainly in the Textile Industry." *Journal of the Royal Statistical Society*, 1914, *77*, 510–522.

Chase, D. "The Early Shakers: An Experiment in Religious Communism." Unpublished doctoral dissertation, University of Chicago, 1936.

Child, J. "Organization Structure, Environment, and Performance: The Role of Strategic Choice." *Sociology*, 1972, *6*, 1–22.

Christaller, W. *Central Places in Southern Germany*. Englewood Cliffs, N.J.: Prentice-Hall, 1966.

Clark, B. R. "Interorganizational Patterns in Education." *Administrative Science Quarterly*, 1965, *10*, 224–237.

Clark, B. R. *The Distinctive College: Antioch, Reed, and Swarthmore*. Chicago: Aldine, 1970.

Clark, T. N. "Community Structure, Decision Making, Budget Expenditures, and Urban Renewal in 51 American Communities." *American Sociological Review*, 1968, *33*, 546–593.

Clark, T. N., and others. "How Many New Yorks? The New York Fiscal Crisis in Comparative Perspective." Report No. 72 of *Comparative Study of Community Decision Making*, University of Chicago, April 1976.

Coase, R. H. "The Nature of the Firm." *Economica*, 1937, *4* (new series), 386–405.

Codman, J. T. *Brook Farm, Historic and Personal Memoirs*. Boston, Mass.: Arena (Copley Square), 1894.

Cohen, A. M., Bennis, W. G., and Wolkon, G. H. "The Effects of Changes in Communication Networks on the Behaviors of Problem-Solving Groups." *Sociometry*, 1962, *25*, 351–367.

Cohen, M. D., March, J. G., and Olsen, J. P. "A Garbage Can Model of Organizational Choice." *Administrative Science Quarterly*, 1972, *17*, 1–25.

Cohen, M. D., and March, J. G. *Leadership and Ambiguity*. New York: McGraw-Hill, 1974.

Colligan, M. H., Smith, M. J., and Jurrell, J. J. "Occupational Incidence Rates of Mental Health." *Journal of Human Stress*, 1977, *4*, 34–39.

Collins, O. F., and Moore, D. G. *The Organization Makers*. New York: Meredith Corporation, 1970.

Collins, R. "Cuises and Deeling of Educational Systems." Unpublished manuscript, University of Virginia, Charlottesville, 1979.

Commoner, B. *The Poverty of Power: Energy and the Economic Crisis*. New York: Knopf, 1976.

Cooper, A. C. "Incubator Organizations and Technical Entrepreneurship." In *Technical Entrepreneurship: A Symposium*. Milwaukee: Center for Venture Management, 1972.

Cooper, C. L., and Marshall, J. "Occupational Sources of Stress: A Review of the Literature Relating to Coronary Heart Disease and Mental Ill Health." *Journal of Occupational Psychology*, 1976, *49*, 11–28.

Counte, M. A., and Kimberly, J. R. "Organizational Innovation in a Professionally Dominated System: Responses of Physicians to a New Program in Medical Education." *Journal of Health and Social Behavior*, 1974, *15*, 188–198.

Cummings, L. L. "Emergence of the Instrumental Organization." In P. S. Goodman, J. M. Pennings, and Associates (Eds.), *New Perspectives on Organizational Effectiveness*. San Francisco: Jossey-Bass, 1977.

Curtis, E. R. *A Season in Utopia: The Story of Brook Farm*. New York: Thomas Nelson, 1961.

Cyert, R. M. "The Management of Universities of Constant or Decreasing Size." *Public Administration Review*, 1978, *38*, 344–349.

Cyert, R. M., and March, J. G. *A Behavioral Theory of the Firm*. Englewood Cliffs, N.J.: Prentice-Hall, 1963.

Dahl, R., and Lindblom, C. *Politics, Economics, and Welfare*. New York: Harper & Row, 1953.

Daiches, D. *The Idea of a New University*. Cambridge, Mass.: M.I.T. Press, 1970.

Dalton, G. W., Lawrence, P. R., and Greiner, L. E. *Organizational Change and Development.* Homewood, Ill.: Irwin, 1970.

Daly, H. E. "Introduction." In H. E. Daly (Ed.), *Toward a Steady-State Economy.* San Francisco: W. H. Freeman, 1973.

Daly, H. E. *Steady-State Economics.* San Francisco: W. H. Freeman, 1977.

Daughen, J. R., and Binzen, P. *The Wreck of the Penn Central.* Boston: Little, Brown, 1971.

Deeks, J. *The Small Firm Owner-Manager: Entrepreneurial Behavior and the Practice of Management.* New York: Praeger, 1976.

Delbecq, A. L., and Van de Ven, A. H. "A Group Process Model for Problem Identification and Program Planning." *Journal of Applied Behavioral Science,* 1971, 7, 466–492.

Denison, E. F. "Effects of Selected Changes in the Institutional and Human Environment upon Output per Unit of Input." General Series Reprint No. 335. Washington, D.C.: Brookings Institution, 1978.

Dewar, R., and Werbel, J. "Morale and Conflict: Universalistic Versus Contingency Predictions." Paper presented at Academy of Management meetings in Atlanta, Ga., 1979.

Dore, R. *British Factory-Japanese Factory.* Berkeley: University of California Press, 1973.

Dornbusch, S. M., and Scott, W. R. *Evaluation and the Exercise of Authority: A Theory of Control Applied to Diverse Organizations.* San Francisco: Jossey-Bass, 1975.

Downs, A. *Inside Bureaucracy.* Boston: Little, Brown, 1967.

Drucker, P. *Management: Tasks, Responsibilities, and Practices.* New York: Harper & Row, 1974.

Duncan, R. B. "Modifications in Decision Structure in Adapting to the Environment: Some Implications for Organizational Learning." *Decision Sciences,* 1974, 5, 705–725.

Durkheim, E. *The Division of Labor in Society.* (G. Simpson, Trans.) New York: Free Press, 1933. (Originally published in 1893.)

Durkheim, E. *Suicide.* (J. A. Spaulding and G. Simpson, Trans.) New York: Free Press, 1951. (Originally published in 1897.)

Dvorin, E. P., and Simmons, R. L. *From Amoral to Humane Bureaucracy.* San Francisco: Harper & Row, 1972.

Edelman, M. *Politics as Symbolic Action.* New York: Academic Press, 1971.

Eden, D. "Intrinsic and Extrinsic Rewards Both Have Motivation and Demoting Effects." Unpublished paper, Department of Labor Studies, Tel Aviv University, 1975.

Electronic Industries Association. *Electronic Market Data Book.* Washington, D.C.: Electronic Industries Association, 1976.

Etzioni, A. *A Comparative Analysis of Complex Organizations.* New York: Free Press, 1961.

Etzioni, A. "Organizational Control Structure." In J. G. March (Ed.), *Handbook of Organizations.* Chicago: Rand McNally, 1965.

Evan, W. M. "An Organizational Set Model of Interorganizational Relations." In M. Tuite, M. Radnor, and R. Chisolm (Eds.), *Interorganizational Decision Making.* Chicago: Aldine, 1972.

Fenno, R. *Power of the Purse.* Boston: Little, Brown, 1966.

Filley, A. C., House, R. J., and Kerr, S. *Managerial Process and Organizational Behavior.* (2nd ed.) Glenview, Ill.: Scott, Foresman, 1976.

Fisher, C. S. "Toward a Subcultural Theory of Urbanism." *American Journal of Sociology,* 1975, *80,* 1319–1341.

Forrester, J. W. "Counterintuitive Behavior of Social Systems." *Technological Review,* 1971, *8,* 53–68.

Fox, D. M. *The Discovery of Abundance.* Ithaca, N.Y.: Cornell University Press, 1967.

Freeman, J., and Hannan, M. T. "Growth and Decline Processes in Organizations." *American Sociological Review,* 1975, *40,* 215–228.

Friedmann, J. *Retracking America: A Theory of Transactive Planning.* New York: Doubleday, 1973.

Furniss, T. "Retrenchment, Layoff, and Termination." *Educational Record,* 1974, *55,* 159–170.

Gal, R., and Lazarus, R. S. "The Role of Activity in Anticipating and Confronting Stressful Situations." *Journal of Human Stress,* 1975, *2,* 4–20.

Galbraith, J. K. *The Industrial State.* Boston: Houghton Mifflin, 1971.

Galbraith, J. R. *Designing Complex Organizations.* Reading, Mass.: Addison-Wesley, 1973.

Galbraith, J. R. *Organization Design.* Reading, Mass.: Addison-Wesley, 1977.

Gamson, W. A., and Scotch, N. "Scapegoating in Baseball." *American Journal of Sociology,* 1964, *70,* 69–76.

Gans, H. J. *The Urban Villagers.* New York: Free Press, 1962.

Geertz, C. *The Interpretation of Cultures.* New York: Basic Books, 1974.

Glassberg, A. "Organizational Responses to Municipal Budget Decreases." *Public Administration Review,* 1978, *38,* 325–332.

Glassman, R. "Persistence and Loose Coupling." *Behavioral Science,* 1973, *18,* 83–94.

Goodman, P. S., and Bazerman, M. "Institutionalization of Planned Organizational Change." In B. M. Staw and L. L. Cummings (Eds.), *Research in Organizational Behavior.* Vol. II. Greenwich, Conn.: Jai Press, 1979.

Goodman, P. S., Pennings, J. M., and Associates. *New Perspectives on Organizational Effectiveness.* San Francisco: Jossey-Bass, 1977.

Gould, L. C. "Juvenile Entrepreneurs." *American Journal of Sociology,* 1969, *74,* 710–719.

Gouldner, A. W. "The Norm of Reciprocity." *American Sociological Review,* 1961, *25,* 161–179.

Green, A. C. "Planning for Declining Environments." *School Review,* 1974, *82,* 595–600.

Greiner, L. E. "Patterns of Organizational Change." In G. Dalton, P. R. Lawrence, and L. E. Greiner (Eds.), *Organizational Change and Development.* Homewood, Ill.: Irwin, 1970.

Greiner, L. E. "Evolution and Revolution as Organizations Grow." *Harvard Business Review,* 1972, *50,* 37–46.

Gross, N., Giaquinta, J., and Bernstein, M. *Implementing Organization Innovations.* New York: Basic Books, 1971.

Hage, J., and Aiken, M. "Program Change and Organizational Properties." *American Journal of Sociology,* 1967, *72,* 503–519.

Hage, J., and Aiken, M. *Social Change in Complex Organizations.* New York: Random House, 1970.

Hall, R. H. "The Concept of Bureaucracy: An Empirical Assessment." *American Journal of Sociology,* 1963, *69,* 32–40.

Hall, R. H. "Professionalization and Bureaucracy." *American Sociological Review,* 1968, *33,* 92–104.

Hall, R. H. *Organizations: Structure and Process.* (2nd ed.) Englewood Cliffs, N.J.: Prentice-Hall, 1977.

Hall, R. I. "A System Pathology of an Organization: The Rise and Fall of the Old *Saturday Evening Post.*" *Administrative Science Quarterly,* 1976, *21,* 185–211.

Hannan, M. T., and Freeman, J. H. "Environment and the Structure of Organizations." Paper presented at annual meeting of American Sociological Association, Montreal, September 1974.

Hannan, M. T., and Freeman, J. H. "The Population Ecology of Organizations." In M. W. Meyer and Associates (Eds.), *Environments and Organizations: Theoretical and Empirical Perspectives.* San Francisco: Jossey-Bass, 1978a.

Hannan, M. T., and Freeman, J. H. "Internal Politics of Growth and Decline." In M. W. Meyer and Associates (Eds.), *Environments and Organizations: Theoretical and Empirical Perspectives.* San Francisco: Jossey-Bass, 1978b.

Hannan, M. T., Freeman, J. H., and Tuma, N. B. "Organizational Ecology." Mimeographed report, Stanford University, 1978.

Haraszvi, Z. *The Idyll of Brook Farm, as Revealed by Unpublished Letters in the Boston Public Library.* Boston: Trustees of the Public Library, 1937.

Havelock, R. G. *Planning for Innovation Through Dissemination and Utilization of Knowledge.* Ann Arbor: Institute for Social Research, University of Michigan, 1973.

Hawley, A. *Human Ecology.* New York: Ronald Press, 1950.

Hawley, A. *The Urban Society.* New York: Ronald Press, 1971.

Hawley, W. E., and Rogers, D. *Improving the Quality of Urban Management.* Beverly Hills, Calif.: Sage, 1974.

Hedberg, B. L. T., Nystrom, P. C., and Starbuck, W. H. "Camping on Seesaws: Prescriptions for a Self-Designing Organization." *Administrative Science Quarterly,* 1976, *21,* 41–65.

Hedberg, B. L. T., Nystrom, P. C., and Starbuck, W. H. "Designing Organizations to March Tomorrow." In P. C. Nystrom and W. H. Starbuck (Eds.), *Prescriptive Models of Organizations.* North-Holland/TIMS Studies in the Management Sciences, Vol. 5. Amsterdam: North-Holland Publishing, 1977.

Heilbroner, R. L. *Business Civilization in Decline.* New York: Norton, 1976.

Hill, N. *Think and Grow Rich.* New York: Hawthorn Books, 1967.

Hirschman, A. O. *Exit, Voice, and Loyalty.* Cambridge, Mass.: Harvard University Press, 1970.

Hirschman, A. O., and Lindblom, C. E. "Economic Development, Research and Development, Policy Making: Some Converging Views." *Behavioral Science,* 1962, *8,* 211–222.

Hoefler, D. C. "Semiconductor Family Tree." *Electronic News,* 1968, p. 5.

Hoefler, D. C. "Silicon Valley Genealogy." Chart prepared by Semiconductor Equipment & Materials Institute, Mountain View, Calif., 1976.

Holloway, M. *Heavens on Earth: Utopian Communities in America, 1680–1880.* London: Turnstile Press, 1951.

Hostetler, J. A. *Hutterite Society.* Baltimore: Johns Hopkins University Press, 1975.

Hourlet, R. *Getting Back Together.* New York: Coward, McCann and Geoghegan, 1971.

House, J. S. "Occupational Stress and Coronary Heart Disease: A Review and Theoretical Integration." *Journal of Health and Social Behavior,* 1974, *15,* 12–27.

Howell, R. P. "Comparative Profiles—Entrepreneurs Versus the Hired Executive: San Francisco Peninsula Semiconductor Industry." Technical Entrepreneurship: A Symposium. Milwaukee: Center for Venture Management, 1972.

Hrebiniak, L. G. *Complex Organizations.* St. Paul, Minn.: West Publishing, 1978.

Indik, B. P. "The Relationship Between Organization Size and Supervision Ratio." *Administrative Science Quarterly,* 1964, *9,* 301–312.

Inkeles, A., and Smith, D. *Becoming Modern.* Cambridge, Mass.: Harvard University Press, 1974.

Iversen, W. R. "Electronics Review." *Electronics,* July 1979.

Jackson, J. H., and Morgan, C. P. *Organization Theory: A Macro Perspective for Management.* Englewood Cliffs, N.J.: Prentice-Hall, 1978.

James, F., and Struyk, R. *Intrametropolitan Industrial Location: The Pattern and Process of Change.* Lexington, Mass.: Lexington Books, 1975.

Jay, J., and Birney, R. C. "Research Findings on the Kibbutz Adolescent: A Response to Bettleheim." *American Journal of Orthopsychiatry,* 1973, *4,* 347–354.

Johnson, J. M. "Dimensions of Small Business Investment Corporations and Venture Capital Financing." *American Journal of Small Business,* 1978, *2,* 16–22.

Kanter, R. M. *Commitment and Community.* Cambridge, Mass.: Harvard University Press, 1972.

Kateb, G. "Utopias and Utopianism." *International Encyclopedia of the Social Sciences,* 1968, *16,* 267.

Katz, D., and Golomb, N. "Integration, Effectiveness, and Adaptation in Social Systems: A Comparative Analysis of Kibbutzim Communities." *Administration and Society,* 1974, *6,* 283–315.

Katz, D., and Kahn, R. *The Social Psychology of Organizations.* New York: Wiley, 1966.

Katz, R. "Job Longevity as a Situational Factor in Job Satisfaction." *Administrative Science Quarterly,* 1978, *23,* 204–223.

Kaufman, H. "The Direction of Organizational Evolution." *Public Administration Review,* 1973, *33,* 300–307.

Kaufman, H. "The Natural History of Human Organizations." *Administration and Society,* 1975, *7,* 131–149.

Kaufman, J. *Are Government Organizations Immortal?* Washington, D.C.: Brookings Institution, 1976.

Kimberly, J. R. "Environmental Constraints and Organizational Structure: A Comparative Analysis of Rehabilitation Organizations." *Administrative Science Quarterly,* 1975, *20,* 1–9.

Kimberly, J. R. "Issues in the Design of Longitudinal Organizational Research." *Sociological Methods & Research,* 1976a, *4,* 321–347.

Kimberly, J. R. "Organizational Size and the Structuralist Perspective: A Review, Critique, and Proposal." *Administrative Science Quarterly,* 1976b, *21,* 571–597.

Kimberly, J. R. "Issues in the Creation of Organizations: Initiation, Innovation, and Institutionalization." *Academy of Management Journal,* 1979, *22,* 437–457.

Kimberly, J. R. "Managerial Innovation." In P. C. Nystrom and W. H. Starbuck (Eds.), *Handbook of Organizational Design.* New York: Oxford University Press, 1980.

Kimberly, J. R. "Data Aggregation in Organizational Research: The Temporal Dimension." *Organization Studies,* in press.

Kimberly, J. R., Counte, M. A., and Dickinson, R. O. "Design for Process Research on Change in Medical Education." Proceedings of the 11th Annual Conference on Research in Medical Education, American Association of Medical Colleges, 1972, pp. 26–31.

Kimberly, J. R., and Nielsen, W. R. "Assessing Organizational Change Strategies." In P. C. Nystrom and W. H. Starbuck (Eds.), *Prescriptive Models of Organizations.* North-Holland/TIMS Studies in the Management Sciences, Vol. 5. Amsterdam: North-Holland Publishing, 1977.

Kolarska, L., and Aldrich, H. "Exit, Voice, and Silence: Consumers' and Managers' Responses to Organizational Decline." Working Paper, School of Industrial and Labor Relations, Cornell University, 1978.

Kotter, J., and Sathe, V. "Problems of Human Resource Management in Rapidly Growing Companies." *California Management Review,* 1978, *21,* 29–36.

Landau, M. "On the Concept of a Self-Correcting Organization." *Public Administration Review,* 1973, *33,* 533–542.

Lawler, E. E., III, Jenkins, G. D., Jr., and Herline, G. E. "Initial Data Feedback to General Foods—Topeka Pet Foods Plants—Selected Survey Items." Unpublished paper, Institute for Social Research, University of Michigan, July 1974.

Lawrence, P. R., and Lorsch, J. W. *Organization and Environment: Managing Differentiation and Integration.* Homewood, Ill.: Irwin, 1969.

Leontief, W. *Input-Output Economics.* New York: Oxford University Press, 1966.

Levi, T. *Stress: Sources, Management, and Prevention.* New York: Liveright, 1967.

Levine, C. H. "Organizational Decline and Cutback Management." *Public Administration Review,* 1978, *38,* 316–325.

Levine, C. H. "More on Cutback Management: Hard Questions for Hard Times." *Public Administration Review,* 1979, *39,* 179–183.

Levins, R. *Evolution in Changing Environments.* Princeton, N.J.: Princeton University Press, 1968.

Lewin, K. "Frontiers in Group Dynamics." *Human Relations,* 1947, *1,* 5–41.

Light, I. H. *Ethnic Enterprise in America.* Berkeley: University of California Press, 1972.

Likert, R. *The Human Organization: Its Management and Value.* New York: McGraw-Hill, 1967.

Lincoln, J. R. "Community Structure and Industrial Conflict." *American Sociological Review,* 1978, *43,* 199–219.

Lindblom, C. E. *The Policy-Making Process.* Englewood Cliffs, N.J.: Prentice-Hall, 1968.

Lindblom, C. E. *Politics and Markets.* New York: Basic Books, 1977.

Lippitt, R., Watson, J., and Westley, B. *The Dynamics of Planned Change.* New York: Harcourt Brace Jovanovich, 1958.

Lipset, S. M., Trow, M. A., and Coleman, J. S. *Union Democracy.* New York: Free Press, 1956.

Litzinger, W. D. "The Motel Entrepreneurs and the Motel Manager." *Academy of Management Journal,* 1965, *8,* 268–281.

Liu, B. C. *Quality of Life Indicators in U.S. Metropolitan Areas: A Statistical Analysis.* New York: Praeger, 1976.

Lodahl, T. "Structure Versus Process in the Study of Organizations." Address given at American Sociological Association meetings, Montreal, 1974.

Lotka, A. J. *Elements of Physical Biology.* Baltimore: Williams and Wilkins, 1925.

Macarov, D. "Work Patterns and Satisfactions in an Israeli Kibbutz: A Test of the Hertzberg Hypothesis." *Personal Psychology,* 1972, *25,* 483–493.

MacArthur, R. H., and Wilson, E. O. *The Theory of Island Biogeography.* Princeton: Princeton University Press, 1967.

McCaskey, M. B. "Tolerance for Ambiguity and the Perception of Environmental Uncertainty in Organizational Design." Paper presented at the Management of Organization Design Conference, Pittsburgh, October 1974.

McClelland, D. S. "Need Achievement and Entrepreneurship—A Longitudinal Study." *Journal of Personality and Social Psychology,* 1965, *1,* 389–392.

McDonald, J. "The Men Who Made T. I." *Fortune,* 1961, *62,* 116–123.

McGrath, J. E. *Social and Psychological Factors in Stress.* New York: Holt, Rinehart and Winston, 1970.

McGregor, D. *The Human Side of Enterprise.* New York: McGraw-Hill, 1960.

McKelvey, B. "Comment on the Biological Analogue in Organizational Science." *Administrative Science Quarterly,* 1979, *24,* 488–493.

McKenney, J. L. "A Field Research Study of Organizational Learning." Working Paper No. 78-23, Harvard Business School, 1978.

Mackintosh, I. M. "Large-Scale Integration: Intercontinental Aspects." *IEEE Spectrum,* June 1978, pp. 51–56.

Mahoney, T. A., and Weitzel, W. "Managerial Models of Organizational Effectiveness." *Administrative Science Quarterly,* 1969, *14,* 357–365.

Maier, N. R. F., and Hoffman, L. R. "Quality of First and Second Solution in Group Problem Solving." *Journal of Applied Psychology,* 1960, *44,* 278–283.

Maier, N. R. F., and Solem, A. R. "The Contribution of the Discussion Leader to the Quality of Group Thinking." *Human Relations,* 1952, *3,* 155–174.

Mansfield, E. *The Economics of Technological Change.* New York: Norton, 1968.

March, J. G., and Simon, H. A. *Organizations.* New York: Wiley, 1958.

Markham, J. W. *Conglomerate Enterprise and Public Policy.* Boston: Graduate School of Business Administration, Harvard University, 1973.

Marris, R. *The Corporate Society.* New York: Macmillan, 1974.

Maslow, A. H. *Motivation and Personality.* New York: Harper & Row, 1954.

Mayo, E. *The Social Problems of an Industrial Civilization.* Boston: Division of Research, Graduate School of Business Administration, Harvard University, 1945.

Meadows, D. H., and others. *The Limits to Growth.* New York: Universe Books, 1972.

Merton, R. K. *Social Theory and Social Structure.* (rev. ed.) New York: Free Press, 1957.

Merton, R. K. *Social Theory and Social Structure.* New York: Free Press, 1968.

Meyer, J. W., and Rowan, B. "Institutionalized Organizations: Formal Structure as Myth and Ceremony." *American Journal of Sociology,* 1977, *83,* 340–363.

Meyer, J. W., and others. "Instructional Dissensus and Institutional Consensus in Schools." In M. W. Meyer and Associates (Eds.), *Environments and Organizations: Theoretical and Empirical Perspectives.* San Francisco: Jossey-Bass, 1978.

Meyer, M. W., and Associates. *Environments and Organizations: Theoretical and Empirical Perspectives.* San Francisco: Jossey-Bass, 1978.

Miles, R. E., Snow, C. C., and Pfeffer, J. "Organization-Environment: Concepts and Issues." *Industrial Relations,* 1974, *13,* 244–264.

Miles, R. E., Jr. *Awakening from the American Dream.* New York: Universe Books, 1976.

Miles, R. H. *Macro Organizational Behavior.* Santa Monica, Calif.: Goodyear Publishing, 1980.

Miles, R. H., and Cameron, K. S. "Coffin Nails and Corporate Strategies: A Quarter-Century View of Organizational Adaptation to Environment in the U.S. Tobacco Industry." Working Paper No. 3, Research Program on Government Business Relations, School of Organization and Management, Yale University, 1977.

Miles, R. H., and Randolph, W. A. "Slices from the Early Life of Organizations: An Exploratory Study of Organizational Learning and Development." Paper presented at 39th annual meeting of Academy of Management, Atlanta, Ga, 1979a.

Miles, R. H., and Randolph, W. A. *The Organization Game: A Simulation in Organizational Behavior, Design, Change, and Development.* Santa Monica, Calif.: Goodyear Publishing, 1979b.

Miller, D. "Common Syndromes of Business Failure." *Business Horizons,* 1977, *20,* 43–53.

Miller, D., and Mintzberg, H. "Strategy Formulation in Context: Some Tentative Models." Working Paper, McGill University, 1974.

Miller, E. J., and Rice, A. K. *Systems of Organization*. London: Tavistock, 1967.

Miller, J. G. "Toward a General Theory for the Behavioral Sciences." *American Psychologist*, 1955, *10*, 513–531.

Millett, J. D. "The Changed Climate of Planning." In J. D. Millett (Ed.), *New Directions for Higher Education: Managing Turbulence and Change*, no. 19. San Francisco: Jossey-Bass, 1977.

Mintzberg, H., Raisinghani, D., and Theoret, A. "The Structure of 'Unstructured' Decision Processes." *Administrative Science Quarterly*, 1976, *21*, 246–275.

Mitnick, B. "Deregulation as a Process of Organizational Reduction." *Public Administration Review*, 1978, *38*, 350–357.

Molotch, H. "The City as a Growth Machine: Toward a Political Economy of Place." *American Journal of Sociology*, 1976, *82*, 309–332.

Moore, G. "VSLI: Some Fundamental Challenges." *IEEE Spectrum*, April 1979, pp. 30–47.

Muller, T. *Growing and Declining Urban Areas: A Fiscal Comparison*. Washington, D.C.: Urban Institute, 1975.

Nakane, C. *Japanese Society*. (rev. ed.) Middlesex, England: Penguin Books, 1973.

Neal, J. *By Their Fruits: The Story of Shakerism in South Union Kentucky*. Chapel Hill: University of North Carolina Press, 1947.

"New Leaders in Semiconductors." *Business Week*, March 1, 1976, pp. 40–46.

Nielsen, F., and Hannan, M. T. "The Expansion of National Education Systems: Tests of a Population Ecology Model." *American Sociological Review*, 1977, *42*, 479–490.

Orvis, M. D. *Letters from Brook Farm, 1844–1847*. Poughkeepsie, N.Y.: Vassar College, 1928.

Ouchi, W. G. "The Relationship Between Organizational Structure and Organizational Control." *Administrative Science Quarterly*, 1977, *22*, 95–113.

Ouchi, W. G. "A Conceptual Framework for the Design of Organizational Control Mechanisms." *Management Science*, in press.

Ouchi, W. G., and Jaeger, A. M. "Type Z Organization: Stability in the Midst of Mobility." *Academy of Management Review*, 1978, *3*, 305–314.

Ouchi, W. G., and Johnson, J. B. "Types of Organizational Control and Their Relationship to Emotional Well-Being." *Administrative Science Quarterly*, 1978, *23*, 292–317.

Ozbekan, J. "Planning and Human Action." In P. A. Weiss (Ed.), *Hierarchically Organized Systems in Theory and Practice*. New York: Macmillan, 1971.

Parsons, T., and Shils, E. A. "Values, Motives, and Systems of Action." In T. Parsons and E. A. Shils (Eds.), *Toward A General Theory of Action*. Cambridge, Mass.: Harvard University Press, 1951.

Peale, N. V. *The Power of Positive Thinking*. Englewood Cliffs, N.J.: Prentice-Hall, 1952.

Pennings, J. M. "The Relevance of the Structural-Contingency Model for Organizational Effectiveness." *Administrative Science Quarterly*, 1975, *20*, 393–410.

Pennings, J. M. "Strategically Interdependent Organizations." In P. C. Nystrom and W. H. Starbuck (Eds.), *Handbook of Organizational Design*. New York: Oxford University Press, 1980.

Pennings, J. M., and Goodman, P. S. "Toward a Workable Framework." In P. S. Goodman, J. M. Pennings, and Associates (Eds.), *New Perspectives on Organizational Effectiveness*. San Francisco: Jossey-Bass, 1977.

Penrose, E. T. "Biological Analogies in the Theory of the Firm." *American Economic Review*, 1952, *42*, 804–819.

Perrow, C. *Organizational Analysis: A Sociological View*. Belmont, Calif.: Wadsworth, 1970.

Perrow, C. *The Radical Attack on Business: A Critical Analysis*. New York: Harcourt Brace Jovanovich, 1972.

Perrow, C. *Complex Organizations: A Critical Essay*. (2nd ed.) Glenview, Ill.: Scott, Foresman, 1979.

Peterson, R. A. *Small Business: Building a Balanced Economy*. Erin, Ontario: Porcepic, 1977.

Peterson, R. A. "Entrepreneurship in Organizations." In P. C. Nystrom and W. H. Starbuck (Eds.), *Handbook of Organizational Design*. New York: Oxford University Press, 1980.

Peterson, R. A., and Berger, D. G. "Entrepreneurship in Organizations: Evidence from the Popular Music Industry." *Administrative Science Quarterly*, 1971, *16*, 97–106.

Pettigrew, A. M. "On Studying Organizational Cultures." *Administrative Science Quarterly,* 1979, *24,* 570–581.

Pfeffer, J. "Merger as a Response to Organizational Interdependence." *Administrative Science Quarterly,* 1972, *17,* 382–394.

Pfeffer, J. "Power and Resource Allocation in Organizations." In B. Staw and G. Salancik (Eds.), *New Directions in Organizational Behavior.* Chicago: St. Clair Press, 1977a.

Pfeffer, J. "Usefulness of the Concept." In P. S. Goodman, J. M. Pennings, and Associates (Eds.), *New Perspectives on Organizational Effectiveness.* San Francisco: Jossey-Bass, 1977b.

Pfeffer, J. "Some Consequences of Organizational Demography: Potential Impacts of an Aging Work Force on Formal Organizations." Paper presented before Committee on Aging, National Research Council, National Academy of Sciences, 1979.

Pfeffer, J., and Salancik, G. R. *The External Control of Organizations: A Resource Dependence Perspective.* New York: Harper & Row, 1978.

Pianka, E. R. "On R and K Selection." *American Naturalist,* 1970, *104,* 592–597.

Pianka, E. R. *Evolutionary Ecology.* New York: Harper & Row, 1978.

Pondy, L. R. "Effects of Size, Complexity, and Ownership on Administrative Intensity." *Administrative Science Quarterly,* 1969, *14,* 47–61.

Pondy, L. R. "The Other Hand Clapping: An Information-Processing Approach to Organizational Power." In T. H. Hammer and S. B. Bacharach (Eds.), *Reward System and Power Distribution in Organizations: Search for Solutions.* Ithaca: New York State School of Industrial and Labor Relations, 1977.

Porter, D. O., and Olsen, E. A. "Some Critical Issues in Government Centralization and Decentralization." *Public Administration Review,* 1976, *36,* 72–84.

Post, J. E. *Corporate Behavior and Social Change.* Reston, Va.: Reston Press, 1978.

Pred, A. *The Spatial Dimensions of U.S. Urban-Institutional Growth.* Cambridge, Mass.: M.I.T. Press, 1966.

Pressman, J. L., and Wildavsky, A. B. *Implementation.* Berkeley: University of California Press, 1973.

Preston, L. E., and Post, J. E. *Private Management and Public Policy.* Englewood Cliffs, N.J.: Prentice-Hall, 1975.

Price, J. L. *Organizational Effectiveness: An Inventory of Propositions.* Homewood, Ill.: Irwin, 1968.

Pugh, D., Hickson, D. J., and Hinings, C. R. "An Empirical Taxonomy of Structure of Work Organizations." *Administrative Science Quarterly,* 1969, *14,* 115–126.

Rabinovitz, F. F. *City Politics and Planning.* Chicago: Aldine, 1969.

Rainey, H. G., Backoff, R. W., and Levine, C. H. "Comparing Public and Private Organizations." *Public Administration Review,* 1976, *36,* 223–234.

Randolph, W. A., and Miles, R. H. "The Organization Game: A Behaviorally Played Simulation." *Exchange: The Organizational Behavior Teaching Journal,* Spring 1979, pp. 31–35.

Roberts, B. C., Okamoto, H., and Lodge, G. C. "Continuity and Change in the Industrial Relations Systems in Western Europe, North America, and Japan." Draft report of the Trilateral Task Force on Industrial Relations to the Trilateral Commission, May 1978.

Robinson, J. *The Economics of Imperfect Competition.* London: Macmillan, 1933.

Rodekohr, M. "Adjustments of Colorado School Districts to Declining Enrollments." Unpublished doctoral dissertation, University of Colorado, Boulder, 1974.

Roessner, J. D. "Public Agencies' Capacity to Innovate." Paper presented at Coventuring in Public Issues Conference sponsored by the Charles F. Kettering Foundation, Montauk Point, N.Y., 1979.

Rogers, E. M., and Shoemaker, F. *The Communication of Innovation.* (2nd ed.) New York: Free Press, 1971.

Ross, J. E., and Kami, M. J. *Corporate Management in Crisis.* Englewood Cliffs, N.J.: Prentice-Hall, 1973.

Ross, M. G. *Community Organization: Theory and Principles.* New York: Harper & Row, 1955.

Rothman, D. J. "Of Prisons, Asylums, and Other Decaying Institutions." *The Public Interest,* 1972, no. 26., 3–17.

Rotter, G., and Portugal, S. "Group and Individual Effects in Problem Solving." *Journal of Applied Psychology,* 1969, *53,* 338–341.

Rubin, I. "Universities in Stress: Decision Making Under Conditions of Reduced Resources." *Social Science Quarterly,* 1977, *58,* 242–254.

Rubin, I. "Loose Structure, Retrenchment, and Adaptability in the University." Paper presented at Midwest Sociological Society meetings, April 1979.

Rumelt, R. P. *Strategy, Structure, and Economic Performance.* Boston: Division of Research, Harvard Business School, 1974.

Rushing, W. A. "The Effects of Industry Size and Division of Labor on Administration." *Administrative Science Quarterly,* 1967, *12,* 267–295.

Sales, S. M. "Organizational Roles as a Risk Factor in Coronary Heart Disease." *Administrative Science Quarterly,* 1969, *14,* 325–336.

Sams, H. W. (Ed.). *Autobiography of Brook Farm.* Englewood Cliffs, N.J.: Prentice-Hall, 1958.

Sarason, S. B. *The Creation of Settings and the Future Societies.* San Francisco: Jossey-Bass, 1972.

Schein, E. *Process Consultation.* Reading, Mass.: Addison-Wesley, 1969.

Scherer, F. M. "Research and Development Resource Allocation Under Rivalry." *Quarterly Journal of Economics,* 1967, *81,* 359–394.

Scherer, F. M. *Industrial Market Structure and Economic Performance.* Chicago: Rand McNally, 1970.

Schön, D. A. *Beyond the Stable State.* New York: Norton, 1971.

Schuler, R. S. "Definition and Conceptualization of Stress in Organizations." *Organizational Behavior and Human Performance,* in press.

Schumacher, E. F. *Small Is Beautiful.* New York: Harper & Row, 1973.

Schumpeter, J. A. *The Theory of Economic Development.* Cambridge, Mass.: Harvard University Press, 1934.

Scott, W. G. "Organization Theory: A Reassessment." *Academy of Management Journal,* 1974, *17,* 242–254.

Scott, W. G. "The Management of Decline." *Conference Board Record,* 1976, *8* (6), 56–59.

Sears, J. V. *My Friends at Brook Farm.* New York: Desmond Fitzgerald, 1912.

Selye, H. *The Stress of Life.* (rev. ed.) New York: McGraw-Hill, 1976.

Selznick, P. *TVA and the Grass Roots.* Berkeley: University of California Press, 1949.

Selznick, P. *Leadership in Administration.* New York: Harper & Row, 1957.

Selznick, P. *TVA and the Grass Roots.* New York: Harper & Row, 1966.

Semiconductor Industry Association. 1979 Yearbook and Directory. Cupertino, Calif.: Semiconductor Industry Association, 1979.

Sethi, S. P. *Up Against the Corporate Wall: Modern Corporations and Social Issues of the Seventies.* Englewood Cliffs, N.J.: Prentice-Hall, 1977.

Shapero, A. R. "The Displaced, Uncomfortable Entrepreneur." *Psychology Today,* 1975, November, pp. 83–88.

Shapira, A., and Madsen, M. C. "Between and Within Group Cooperation and Competition Among Kibbutz and Nonkibbutz Children." *Developmental Psychology,* 1974, *10,* 347–354.

Shefter, M. "New York City's Fiscal Crisis: The Politics of Inflation and Retrenchment." *The Public Interest,* 1977, *48,* 98–127.

Sills, D. L. *The Volunteers.* New York: Free Press, 1957.

Silverman, D. *The Theory of Organizations.* New York: Basic Books, 1971.

Simon, H. A. *Administrative Behavior.* New York: Free Press, 1945.

Simon, H. A. *Models of Man.* New York: Wiley, 1957.

Simon, H. A. "The Architecture of Complexity." Proceedings of the American Philosophical Society, 1962, *106,* 467–482.

Simon, H. A. "Birth of an Organization: The Economic Cooperation Administration." *Public Administration Review,* 1963, *13,* 227–236.

Skinner, B. F. *Science and Human Behavior.* New York: Free Press, 1953.

Skinner, G. W., and Winckler, E. A. "Compliance Succession in Rural Communist China: A Cyclical Theory." In A. Etzioni (Ed.), *A Sociological Reader on Complex Organizations.* (2nd ed.) New York: Holt, Rinehart and Winston, 1969.

Smart, C., and Vertinsky, I. "Designs for Crisis Decision Units." *Administrative Science Quarterly,* 1977, *22,* 640–657.

Smith, B. L. R., and Hague, D. C. (Eds.). *The Dilemna of Accountability in Modern Government.* New York: St. Martin's, 1971.

Smith, R. A. *Corporations in Crisis.* New York: Doubleday, 1963.

Sorlie, W., and others. "An Innovative One-Year Basic Science Program in Medical Education." *Illinois Medicine,* 1971, *40,* 206–209.

Spilerman, S. "Structural Characteristics of Cities and the Severity of Racial Disorders." *American Sociological Review,* 1976, *41,* 771–793.

Spiro, M. *Kibbutz: Venture in Utopia.* New York: Schocken Books, 1970.

Starbuck, W. H. "Organizational Growth and Development." In J. G. March (Ed.), *Handbook of Organizations.* Chicago: Rand McNally, 1965.

Starbuck, W. H. *Organizational Growth and Development.* New York: Penguin Books, 1971.

Starbuck, W. H. "Organizations and Their Environments." In M. D. Dunnette (Ed.), *Handbook of Industrial and Organizational Psychology.* Chicago: Rand McNally, 1976.

Starbuck, W. H., and Hedberg, B. "Saving an Organization from a Stagnating Environment." In H. Thorelli (Ed.), *Strategy + Structure = Performance.* Bloomington: Indiana University Press, 1977.

Starbuck, W. H., Greve, A., and Hedberg, B. L. T. "Responding to Crises." *Journal of Business Administration,* 1978, *9,* 111–137.

Statistical Abstract of the United States. U.S. Department of Commerce, Bureau of the Census, 1976.

Staw, B. M. "The Experimenting Organization." *Organizational Dynamics,* 1977, *6* (1), 2–18.

Staw, B. M., and Szwajkowski, E. "The Scarcity-Munificence Component of Organizational Environments and the Commission of Illegal Acts." *Administrative Science Quarterly,* 1975, *20,* 345–354.

Stebbins, G. L. "Pitfalls and Guideposts in Comparing Organic and Social Evolution." *Pacific Sociological Review,* 1965, *6,* 3–10.

Steers, R. "Problems in the Measurement of Organizational Effectiveness." *Administrative Science Quarterly,* 1975, *20,* 546–558.

Stinchcombe, A. L. "Bureaucratic and Craft Administration of Production: A Comparative Study." *Administrative Science Quarterly,* 1959, *4,* 168–187.

Stinchcombe, A. L. "Social Structure and Organizations." In J. G.

March (Ed.), *Handbook of Organizations.* Chicago: Rand McNally, 1965.

Sutton, F. X., and others. *The American Business Creed.* Cambridge, Mass.: Harvard University Press, 1956.

Swift, L. *Brook Farm: Its Numbers, Scholars, and Visitors.* New York: Macmillan, 1890.

"Texas Instruments: Big Opportunities in Small Packages." *Forbes,* March 1, 1969, pp. 32–37.

Thompson, J. D. *Organizations in Action.* New York: McGraw-Hill, 1967.

Thompson, W. *A Preface to Urban Economics.* Baltimore: Johns Hopkins University Press, 1966.

Tichy, N. *Organization Design for Primary Health Care.* New York: Praeger, 1977.

Tichy, N. *Strategic Change Management.* St. Paul, Minn.: West, forthcoming.

Tilton, J. E. *International Diffusion of Technology: The Case of Semiconductors.* Washington, D.C.: Brookings Institution, 1971.

Toffler, A. *Future Shock.* New York: Random House, 1970.

Tornedon, R. J., and Boddewyn, J. J. "Foreign Divestments: Too Many Mistakes." *Columbia Journal of World Business,* 1974, *9* (3), 87–94.

Toynbee, A. J. *A Study of History.* Vols. 1–4 (abridged by D. C. Somervell). New York: Oxford University Press, 1947.

Trist, E. "Action Research and Adaptive Planning." In A. W. Clark (Ed.), *Experimenting with Organizational Life.* New York: Plenum Press, 1976, 223–236.

Trow, M. "Notes on American Higher Education: Planning for Universal Access in the Context of Uncertainty." *Higher Education,* 1975, *4,* 1–11.

Tushman, M., and Nadler, D. "Information Processing as an Integrating Concept in Organizational Design." *Academy of Management Review,* 1978, *3,* 613–624.

Udy, S. H., Jr. "Administrative Rationality, Social Setting, and Organization Development." *American Journal of Sociology,* 1962, *68,* 299–308.

Utterback, J. "The Process of Technological Innovation Within the Firm." *Academy of Management Journal,* 1971, *14,* 75–88.

Vacca, R. *The Coming Dark Age.* New York: Doubleday, 1973.

Van de Ven, A. H. *Group Decision Making and Effectiveness.* Kent, Ohio: Kent State University Press, 1974.

Van de Ven, A. H. "Book Review of H. E. Aldrich, Organizations and Environments." *Administrative Science Quarterly,* 1979, *24,* 320–326.

Van de Ven, A. H. "Community Program Planning and Innovation: Test of the Program Planning Model." *Human Relations,* in press.

Van de Ven, A. H., and Koenig, R., Jr. "A Process Model for Program Planning and Evaluation." *Journal of Economics and Business,* 1976, *28,* 161–170.

Van Maanen, J. "Police Socialization: A Longitudinal Examination of Job Attitudes in an Urban Police Department." *Administrative Science Quarterly,* 1975, *20,* 207–228.

Van Maanen, J., and Schein, E. H. "Toward a Theory of Organizational Socialization." Manuscript, Sloan School of Industrial Administration, Massachusetts Institute of Technology, 1978.

Volterra, V. *Leçons sur la théorie mathématique de la lutte pour la vie* [*Lessons about the Mathematical Theory of the Struggle for Life*]. Paris: Gauthiers-Villars, 1931.

Walton, C. *The Ethics of Corporate Conduct.* Englewood Cliffs, N.J.: Prentice-Hall, 1977.

Walton, R. E. "How to Counter Alienation in the Plant." *Harvard Business Review,* 1972.

Walton, R. E. "Teaching an Old Dog Food New Tricks." *Wharton Magazine,* 1978, *2* (2), 38–48.

Wamsley, G., and Zald, M. N. *The Political Economy of Public Organizations.* Lexington, Mass.: Heath, 1973.

Warner, W. K., and Havens, A. E. "Goal Displacement and the Intangibility of Organizational Goals." *Administrative Science Quarterly,* 1968, *12,* 539–555.

Warren, R. L. *Truth, Love, and Social Change.* Chicago: Rand McNally, 1971.

Webbink, D. W. "The Semiconductor Industry: A Survey of Structure, Conduct, and Performance." Washington, D.C.: Federal Trade Commission, 1977.

Weber, M. *The Theory of Social and Economic Organization.* (A. M. Henderson and T. Parsons, Trans.) New York: Oxford University Press, 1947.

Weber, M. *Economy and Society*. (G. Roth and C. Wittich, Eds., E. Fischoff and others, Trans.) 3 vols. (4th ed.) New York: Bedminster Press, 1968. (Originally published 1947.)

Weick, K. E. *The Social Psychology of Organizing*. Reading, Mass.: Addison-Wesley, 1969.

Weick, K. E. "Educational Organizations as Loosely Coupled Systems." *Administrative Science Quarterly*, 1976, *21*, 1–19.

Weick, K. E. "Enactment Processes in Organizations." In B. M. Staw and G. R. Salancik (Eds.), *New Directions in Organizational Behavior*. Chicago: St. Clair Press, 1977a.

Weick, K. E. "Organization Design: Organizations as Self-Designing Systems." *Organizational Dynamics*, 1977b, *6* (2), 30–46.

Weiner, C. "How the Transistor Emerged." *IEEE Spectrum*, January, 1973, pp. 24–33.

Whetten, D. A. "Organizational Interdependence and Innovation." Presented at Coventuring in Public Issues Conference sponsored by Charles Kettering Foundation, Montauk Point, N.Y., 1979a.

Whetten, D. A. "Organizational Responses to Scarcity: Difficult Choices for Difficult Times." Working Paper, College of Commerce and Business Administration, University of Illinois, 1979b.

Whetten, D. A. "Organizational Decline: A Neglected Topic in Organizational Behavior." Working Paper, College of Commerce and Business Administration, University of Illinois, 1979c.

Wildavsky, A. *Politics of the Budgetary Process*. Boston: Little, Brown, 1964.

Wildavsky, A. "The Self-Evaluating Organization." *Public Administration Review*, 1972, *32*, 509–520.

Williamson, O. E. *Markets and Hierarchies: Analysis and Antitrust Implications*. New York: Free Press, 1975.

Wilson, J. Q. "Innovation in Organization: Notes Toward a Theory." In J. Thomas and W. Bennis (Eds.), *The Management of Change and Conflict*. New York: Penguin Books, 1972.

Wirth, L. "Urbanism as a Way of Life." *American Journal of Sociology*, 1938, *44*, 3–24.

Yarmolinsky, A. "Institutional Paralysis." *Daedalus*, 1975, *104* (1), 61–67.

Yetten, P. W. "Leadership Style in Stressful and Nonstressful Situations." In D. Gowler and K. Legge (Eds.), *Managerial Stress*. New York: Wiley, 1975.

Yin, R. K. *Changing Urban Bureaucracies: How New Practices Become Routinized*. Santa Monica, Calif.: Rand Corporation, 1978.

Yuchtman, E. "Reward Distribution and Work-Role Attractiveness in the Kibbutz: Reflections on Equity Theory." *American Sociological Review*, 1972, *37*, 581–595.

Yuchtman, E., and Seashore, S. E. "A System Resource Approach to Organizational Effectiveness." *American Sociological Review*, 1967, *32*, 891–903.

Zaks, R. *Microprocessors: From Chips to Systems*. Berkeley, Calif.: Sybex, Inc., 1977.

Zald, M. N. "Urban Differentiation, Characteristics of Boards of Directors, and Organizational Effectiveness." *American Journal of Sociology*, 1967, *73*, 261–272.

Zald, M. N. *Organizational Change: The Political Economy of the YMCA*. Chicago: University of Chicago Press, 1970.

Zald, M. N., and Ash, R. "Social Movement Organizations: Growth, Decay, and Changes." *Social Forces*, 1966, *44*, 327–341.

Zaltman, G., Duncan, R. B., and Holbek, J. *Innovations and Organizations*. New York: Wiley, 1973.

Name Index

Subject Index